D1598084

Amphibians in Captivity

Marc Staniszewski

Color art by the author, assisted by J. R. Quinn, unless otherwise noted.

Title page photo: **The Mexican Burrowing Toad, *Rhinophrynus dorsalis*. Photo: K. Lucas.**

Distributed in the UNITED STATES to the Pet Trade by T.F.H. Publications, Inc., One T.F.H. Plaza, Neptune City, NJ 07753; distributed in the UNITED STATES to the Bookstore and Library Trade by National Book Network, Inc. 4720 Boston Way, Lanham MD 20706; in CANADA to the Pet Trade by H & L Pet Supplies Inc., 27 Kingston Crescent, Kitchener, Ontario N2B 2T6; Rolf C. Hagen Ltd., 3225 Sartelon Street, Montreal 382 Quebec; in CANADA to the Book Trade by Vanwell Publishing Ltd., 1 Northrup Crescent, St. Catharines, Ontario L2M 6P5 ; in ENGLAND by T.F.H. Publications, PO Box 15, Waterlooville PO7 6BQ; in AUSTRALIA AND THE SOUTH PACIFIC by T.F.H. (Australia), Pty. Ltd., Box 149, Brookvale 2100 N.S.W., Australia; in NEW ZEALAND by Brooklands Aquarium Ltd. 5 McGiven Drive, New Plymouth, RD1 New Zealand; in Japan by T.F.H. Publications, Japan—Jiro Tsuda, 10-12-3 Ohjidai, Sakura, Chiba 285, Japan; in SOUTH AFRICA by Lopis (Pty) Ltd., P.O. Box 39127, Booysens, 2016, Johannesburg, South Africa. Published by T.F.H. Publications, Inc.

MANUFACTURED IN THE UNITED STATES OF AMERICA
BY T.F.H. PUBLICATIONS, INC.

Contents

Acknowledgments

If it were not for my father Stefan, I would almost certainly not have taken such an interest in this engrossing hobby. It was he who introduced me to the wonderful world of reptiles and amphibians when he presented me with a garter snake when I was just six years old in 1973. All my experience gained since that day is the result of an ongoing alliance, and I deeply appreciate all of his advice and understanding. I would like to extend my thanks to the following people without whose help this book may not have been possible: Jonathan Davies of the Camera Shop in Kidderminster for all his support and knowledge of photographic aspects; Scott Jones of Bristol University for his vast experience and knowledge of herpetology; Dr. Andrew Portman for advice on the veterinary procedures and medication of amphibians; and last but not least my mother Janet and sister Lisa, who have had to tolerate almost 20 years of the ear-deafening croaking of frogs, snakes appearing from the back of the TV, and many hundreds of other "creepy crawlies" that found their way into our home.

Ascaphus truei, the Tailed Frog of the Pacific Northwest, is a true "missing link" in frog evolution, but not because of the tail. Its bone and muscle structure relates it to the most primitive living and fossil frogs. The tail actually is a type of penis found only in the male—admittedly unique among frogs but not a relict from remote ancestors. Photo: Dr. D. Green.

A pair of New Zealand Frogs, *Leiopelma hochstetteri*, in amplexus. These rather dull but fascinating little frogs represent some of the paradoxes found in the classification of frogs. Supposedly the closest relative of *Leiopelma* among living frogs is *Ascaphus* from North America, half a planet away. Some taxonomists put these two frogs in a single family, others separate them on the basis of common sense and a few minor characters. Photo: Dr. D. Green.

Introduction

Amphibians always have enjoyed a better relationship with man than their close relatives the reptiles. Whereas snakes and lizards are often looked upon as dangerous and evil, frogs and toads have been characterized as intelligent or comical creatures in cartoons, fairy tales, and fantasy. Newts and salamanders, however, have not been able to escape their mythological portrayal as magical beasts. In fact, when we discover some of the species that make up the class Amphibia we begin to learn why these creatures often are associated with fictional imagery. In terms of shape and coloration amphibians include some of the most beautiful, bizarre, and fascinating of all living creatures, yet when compared to higher animal classes our overall understanding of their evolution and behavior still remains unclear.

Today herpetology—the study of reptiles and amphibians—is a growing interest throughout the world and one that gives many people from all walks of life a great deal of pleasure and satisfaction. Although snake keeping predominates in the hobby due to an almost complete understanding of captive requirements and breeding techniques of many species, the current trends suggest that more and more people are taking a specific interest in amphibians. It is easy to see why, for they generally are inexpensive to maintain, require relatively small living quarters, demand little attention, and (when captive conditions are adequate although not necessarily perfect) they may reward their keeper by breeding regularly.

The human population explosion in the latter part of the twentieth century has put extreme pressure on amphibians. With afforestation and urban encroachment all too common features of today's world, natural living space becomes a premium and competition for territory, food, and mates intensifies. Unfortunately amphibians have been unable to adapt as they are small, relatively defenseless, and sensitive to the slightest climatic changes. Pollution of the life-giving water that is so important to many species has a similarly drastic effect on wild populations. Further exploitation through the collection of millions of amphibians for restaurant cuisine and the pet trade has placed additional pressure on these creatures so that today it is up to us, the hobbyists, to ensure that we provide the best conditions possible and encourage our specimens to breed.

The following chapters have been written not only with this in mind but also to discuss recently described techniques for the successful captive maintenance and breeding of many species. It is aimed at no single class of people, being ideal for both new hobbyists who have just obtained their first newt or frog, and advanced hobbyists.

% of Amphibians Compared
to Other Vertebrates

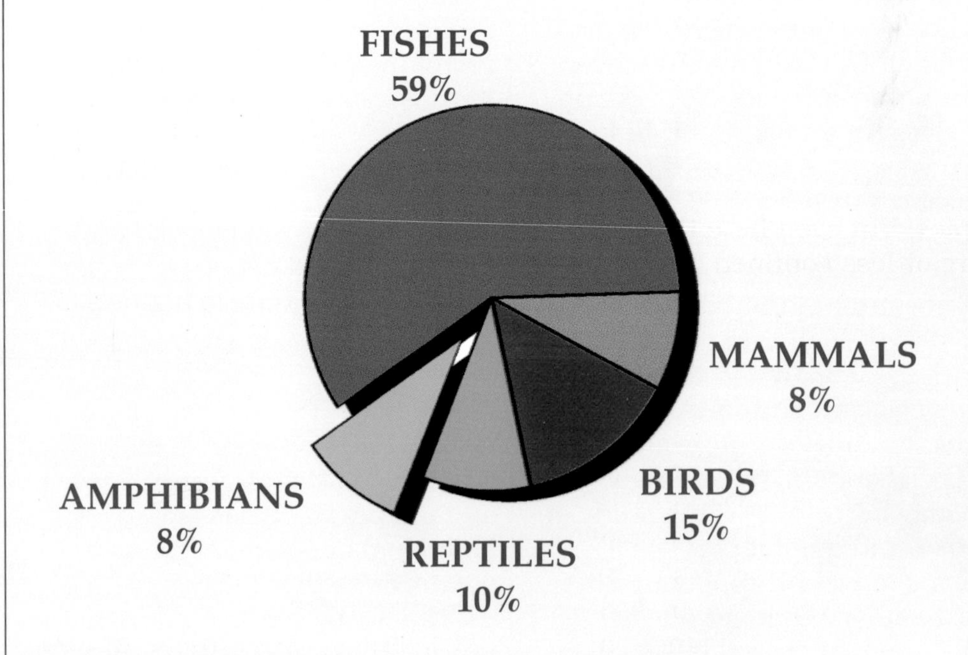

Amphibians comprise only a small part of the total number of described vertebrate species, though many new species are described each year.

About Amphibians

The three living orders of the class Amphibia constitute around 4520 species, some 0.3 percent of all described living animal species. Anura (frogs) is by far the most successful order, with at least 3970 species distributed throughout the world apart from the poles and a few islands. The highest percentage of these occurs in the humid tropics.

Caudata (salamanders) is a mainly northern temperate order comprising over 390 species. Several genera are found in the Central American, South American, and Southeast Asian tropics, but even here they are more or less confined to specialized cool microhabitats such as high altitudes, protected niches high in the trees, and caves.

The final order, Apoda (caecilians), is a warm temperate/tropical group with around 160 known species living from Mexico to northern Argentina, southern and southeastern Asia including some Indian Ocean islands, and parts of Africa. Once they were thought to be rare, but recent study proves that they are quite common, with possibly another 200 or 300 species as yet undescribed.

EVOLUTIONARY HISTORY

In the latter half of the Devonian period around 380 million years ago, the shifting continental land masses and changing climates of the Earth often caused swampy lakes and rivers to dry up. With increasing numbers of fishes competing for less space and food, over a period of millions of years certain groups of fishes similar to *Dipterus* (ancestors of the modern lungfishes) and crossopterygians (lobe-finned fishes) were forced to develop primitive lungs in the form of modified swim bladders. This enabled them to either survive extended periods of drought or travel across dry land to seek water unsuitable for more typical fishes. Initially such movement was clumsy as proper limbs had not yet evolved, but toward the end of the Devonian 350 million years ago a group of carnivorous crossopterygians called Rhipidistia, and in particular a genus called *Eusthenopteron*, made the complete transition from water to land and gave rise to two lines of amphibian development: Labyrinthodontia and Lepospondyli.

The order Labyrinthodontia progressively unfolded seven true amphibian groups: Ichthyostegalia, Embolomeri, Rhachitomi, Trematosauria, Stereospondyli, Proanura, and Anura. The group Ichthyostegalia contained the earliest known true amphibian, a squat, 3-foot creature with a skull composed of many bones, a jaw containing labyrinthine ("maze-like") teeth, and a dorsally-finned tail, all attributes of its crossopterygian ancestors. It differed from fishes in having the first true external ears, eyes presumably equipped for vision out of water, proper limbs, and a skeleton modified for a terrestrial existence through a stronger backbone and vertebral column supported by pectoral and pelvic girdles. Even though ichthyostegids were the first amphibians to conquer dry land, overall dominance initially was restricted by the dry weather that prevailed during that period. Their thin skin made them liable to desiccate quickly and they required water in which to deposit their eggs, suggesting that they never ventured very far from lakes and rivers, a trait carried forward to many modern amphibians. (Of course no soft parts are preserved, so anything said about the soft anatomy and behavior of fossil amphibians is largely speculation based on living amphibians.)

The Carboniferous period started 20 million years later, and amphibians dominated for 60 million years. Their primitive lungs were perfected, their skeletal structures were made stronger and more flexible, and thicker skin was equipped with moisturizing glands. Other groups began to emerge from the labyrinthodont evolutionary line, each better prepared for land-dwelling than its ancestor. The most important evolutionary group was the Embolomeri because it contained the genus *Seymouria*, whose members revealed attributes of both amphibians and reptiles and eventually gave rise to the first true reptiles.

With the climate gradually becoming warmer and inland water rapidly drying up, the reptiles that had first appeared on the scene at the end of the Carboniferous period now began to take over. Amphibians slowly dwindled between the Permian and Triassic periods, too slow to adapt and easy prey for the carnivorous dinosaurs and other large reptiles. The advent of the Jurassic period 175 million years ago saw a return by many amphibians, including the enormous amphibians from the order Stereospondyli, to a semi-aquatic existence in the few lakes available.

Near the end of the Cretaceous period 70 million years ago, modern mammals and the first flowering plants evolved. The Earth's climate became progressively cooler and, for poorly understood reasons, many of the labyrinthodont amphibians and the great dinosaurs suddenly became extinct.

One group of labyrinthodonts, the Anura, along with members of the order Lepospondyli that had been evolving separately from those first land-dwelling crossopterygian fishes, managed to survive whatever catastrophe had befallen their relatives. These eventually gave rise to the three amphibian orders living today. (Actually, this scenario is not accepted by all paleontologists. Many workers believe that all the living amphibians share a common ancestor and that

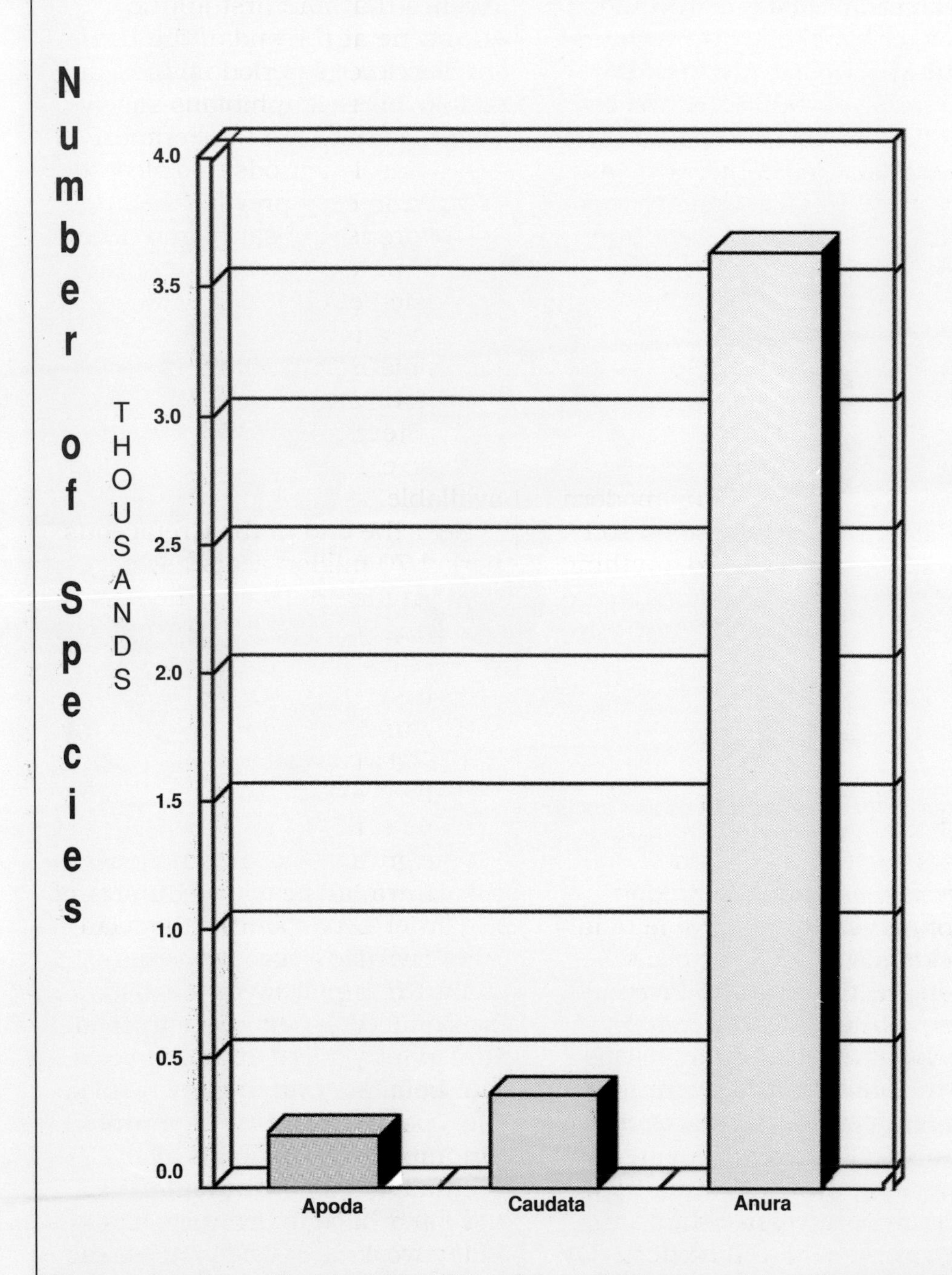

Frogs and toads greatly outnumber all the other amphibians now living. Since more new species of frogs are described each year than are new salamanders and caecilians, this ratio is likely to continue.

salamanders are no more closely related to caecilians than they are to frogs. They would put all the living amphibians in a single group, a superorder or subclass, the Lissamphibia.)

ANURANS: FROGS AND TOADS

Fossils show that the earliest known ancestor of frog and toads appeared around 230 million years ago in the Triassic period of what is now Madagascar. Belonging to the group Proanura ("before frogs"), it was called *Triadobatrachus*, and its fossils are the only definite proanuran remnants ever to be discovered. Anatomically this 10–cm creature comprised attributes from both the crossopterygian fishes (labyrinth teeth) and modern day anurans (long hind limbs, relatively short body, and wide, flat skull, plus shortened backbone).

A period of 60 million years divides the fossilized remains of *Triadobatrachus* from the first fossils of members of the true Anura. We can surmise that those species of frogs evident in the middle Jurassic period (so-called "ancient frogs") were very similar to certain Australasian and Eurasian species of today. The next group, called "middle frogs," evolved around 100 million years ago in the Cretaceous period; a surprising number of modern anuran groups date from this evolutionary period. The most recent group of anurans (the "new frogs") contains all of today's remaining anuran families and dates back to the Eocene, 50 million years ago, when ancestors of today's mammals ruled the earth.

Overall distribution of the frogs and toads.

A SUMMARY OF ANURAN CLASSIFICATION

Suborder Amphicoela

Ascaphidae: Tailed Frogs. Only genus: *Ascaphus*. Distribution: Northwestern North America. Species: 1.

Leiopelmatidae: New Zealand Frogs. Only genus: *Leiopelma*. Distribution: New Zealand. Species: 3.

Suborder Aglossa

Pipidae: Tongueless Frogs. Three to five genera recognized, including *Pipa, Hymenochirus, Xenopus*. Distribution: Africa and South America. Species: 28.

***Leiopelma hochstetteri*, family Leiopelmatidae. Photo: Dr. D. Green.**

A male *Ascaphus truei*, family Ascaphidae. Photo: Dr. D. Green.

Suborder Opisthocoela

Discoglossidae: Disc-tongued Frogs. Four genera, *Alytes, Barbourula, Bombina, Discoglossus*. Distribution: Europe and northern Africa through southern Asia to Philippines and Borneo. Species: 16.

Rhinophrynidae: Proboscis Frogs. Only genus: *Rhinophrynus*. Distribution: Southern Texas into Central America. Species: 1.

Suborder Anomocoela

Pelobatidae: Spadefoot Toads. Eight or nine genera, including *Leptobrachium, Megophrys, Scutiger, Pelobates, Scaphiopus*. Distribution: North

A mating pair of *Rhinophrynus dorsalis*, family Rhinophrynidae. Photo: R. T. Zappalorti.

America, Europe, and Asia. Species: Over 90.

Pelodytidae: Parsley Frogs. Only genus: *Pelodytes*. Distribution: Europe and western Asia. Species: 2.

SUBORDER DISPLASIOCOELA

Brachycephalidae: Armored Toads. Two genera: *Brachycephalus, Psyllophryne*. Distribution: Brazil. Species: 3.

Dendrobatidae: Poison and Rocket Frogs. Six to 10 genera recognized, including: *Colostethus, Dendrobates, Epipedobates, Minyobates, Phyllobates*. Distribution: Central and South America. Species: Over 150.

Hyperoliidae: Reed Frogs. About 20 genera, including *Afrixalus, Hyperolius, Kassina, Leptopelis*. Distribution: Africa and outlying islands. Species: Over 225.

Microhylidae: Narrow-mouthed Toads. About 65 genera in some nine subfamilies, including: Asterophryninae: *Asterophrys*;

Phyllobates lugubris, family Dendrobatidae. Photo: K. Lucas.

***Dendrobates ventrimaculatus*, family Dendrobatidae. Photo: A. v. d. Nieuwenhuizen.**

Brevicipinae: *Breviceps*; Cophylinae: *Cophyla*; Dyscophinae: *Dyscophus*; Genyophryninae: *Cophixalus, Oreophryne*; Melanobatrachinae: *Hoplophryne*; Microhylinae: *Dermatonotus, Gastrophryne, Hypopachus, Kaloula, Microhyla*; Otophryninae: *Otophryne*; Scaphiophryninae: *Scaphiophryne, Pseudohemisus*. Distribution: Most of globe.

***Leptopelis brevirostris*, family Hyperoliidae. Photo: P. Freed.**

Species: Over 300.

Phrynomeridae: Rubber Frogs. Only genus: *Phrynomerus*. Distribution: Southern Africa. Species: 5. Note: Placed in Microhylidae by some workers.

Ranidae: True Frogs. Between 50 and 80 genera, depending on how *Rana* and some other large

***Breviceps mossambicus*, family Microhylidae. Photo: K. H. Switak.**

genera are broken up, in at least four subfamilies (often given full family rank), including: Arthroleptinae: *Arthroleptis, Cardioglossa, Astylosternus*; Hemisotinae: *Hemisus*; Mantellinae: *Mantella, Mantidactylus*; Raninae: *Ceratobatrachus, Conraua, Occidozyga, Platymantis, Phrynobatrachus, Ptychadena, Pyxicephalus, Paa, Rana, Staurois, Tomopterna*. Distribution: Most of globe (except Australasia and most of South America). Species: About 670, over 200 in *Rana*.

Rhacophoridae: Flying Frogs, Old World Treefrogs. About nine genera, including: *Boophis, Chirixalus, Chiromantis, Philautus,*

***Rana galamensis*, family Ranidae. Photo: K. H. Switak.**

Polypedates, Rhacophorus. Distribution: Africa and Asia. Species: At least 200.

Sooglossidae: Seychelles Frogs. Two genera: *Nesomantis, Sooglossus.* Distribution: Western Indian Ocean islands. Species: 3.

SUBORDER PROCOELA

Bufonidae: True Toads. About 30 genera recognized, including: *Ansonia, Atelopus, Bufo, Capensibufo, Dendrophryniscus, Melanophryniscus, Nectophryne, Nectophrynoides, Pedostibes, Peltophryne, Pseudobufo, Schismaderma, Wolterstorffina.* Distribution: Most of globe (except Australasia). Species: At least 365, including over 200 in *Bufo.*

Centrolenidae: Glass Frogs. Two or three genera: *Centrolene, Cochranella, Hyalinobatrachium* (genera subject to various interpretations). Distribution: Tropical America. Species: About 100.

Heleophrynidae: Ghost Frogs. Only genus: *Heleophryne.* Distribution: South Africa. Species: 5.

Hylidae: Treefrogs. About 40 genera, including: *Flectonotus, Gastrotheca, Hemiphractus, Acris, Anotheca, Hyla, Osteocephalus, Pseudacris, Scinax, Smilisca, Trachycephalus, Litoria, Cyclorana, Agalychnis, Pachymedusa, Phyllomedusa.*

***Heleophryne natalensis*, family Heleophrynidae. Photo: J. Visser.**

***Cochranella fleishmanni*, family Centrolenidae. Photo: P. Freed.**

***Hyla cipoensis*, family Hylidae. Photo: Dr. I. Sazima.**

Distribution: Most of globe (except most of Africa and Asia). Species: About 720, including almost 300 in *Hyla* and over 100 in *Litoria*.

Leptodactylidae: Rainfrogs. 50 or more genera, including: *Ceratophrys, Chacophrys, Lepidobatrachus, Hylodes, Leptodactylus, Physalaemus, Alsodes, Caudiverbera, Eleutherodactylus, Hylactophryne, Odontophrynus, Proceratophrys, Syrrhophus, Telmatobius*. Distribution: Southern North America and all of Central and South America plus Australasia. Species: Nearly 950, with over 500 in the genus *Eleutherodactylus*.

Myobatrachidae: Australian Frogs. About 20 genera, including: *Limnodynastes, Notaden, Rheobatrachus, Crinia, Pseudophryne, Uperoleia*. Distribution: Australia and New Guinea. Species: 110 or so. Note: This family often is not recognized by herpetologists.

Pseudidae: Shrinking Frogs. Two genera: *Lysapsus, Pseudis*. Distribution: South America. Species: 3.

Rhinodermatidae: Mouthbrooding Frogs. Only genus: *Rhinoderma*. Distribution: Chile. Species: 2.

***Left: Uperoleia rugosa*, family Myobatrachidae. Photo: J. Coborn. *Right: Limnodynastes salmini*, family Myobatrachidae. Photo: R. D. Bartlett.**

Above: Pseudophryne australis, family Myobatrachidae. Photo: R. D. Bartlett.
Below: Pseudis paradoxa, family Pseudidae. Photo: R. T. Zappalorti.

CAUDATA: SALAMANDERS, NEWTS, AND SIRENS

The earliest point at which Lepospondyli (presumed by some to be the ancestors of the salamanders and caecilians) can be traced is remains of foot-long snake-like species of the order Aistopoda found in rocks from the Carboniferous period 250 million years ago. Within the same period two other orders evolved, with one (Nectridia) containing eel-like creatures reminiscent of today's amphiumas. Nectridians probably lived an entirely aquatic existence, and it is possible that the modern caudate amphibians evolved from such creatures. The other order (Microsauria) was wrongly thought to be the ancestor of the dinosaurs (its name means "little lizard"), but that has since been rejected. Its members were snake-like in appearance.

Modern salamanders probably date back to the Lower Cretaceous period some 100 million years ago, although this is difficult to pinpoint because hardly any fossilized remains have been discovered. Today's caudates have retained many of the primitive traits not only of aistopodids and nectridids (elongated bodies, small limbs, and highly aquatic existence) but also of the fishes (sensory lateral line systems for detecting water-borne vibrations when in a larval form or aquatic breeding state).

Overall distribution of the salamanders and newts.

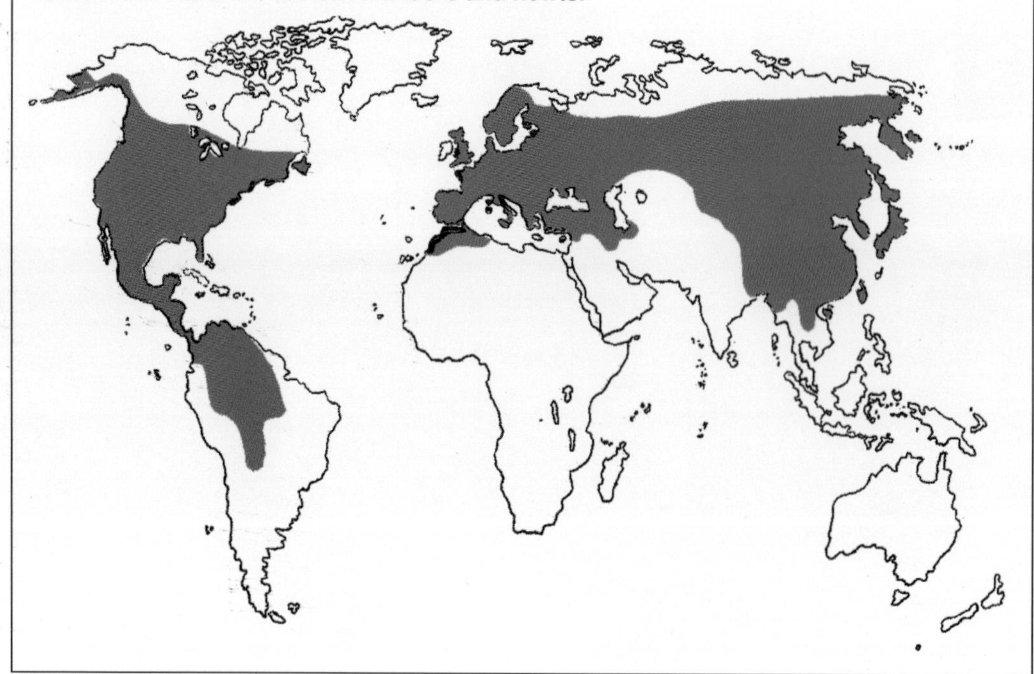

A SUMMARY OF CAUDATE CLASSIFICATION

SUBORDER CRYPTOBRANCHOIDEA

Cryptobranchidae: Giant Salamanders. Two genera: *Andrias, Cryptobranchus.* Distribution: Eastern North America and western Asia. Species: 3.

Hynobiidae: Primitive Salamanders. About seven genera, including: *Batrachuperus, Hynobius, Onychodactylus, Ranodon, Salamandrella.* Distribution: Eastern Europe and cooler Asia. Species: About 36.

SUBORDER PROTEOIDEA

Proteidae: Waterdogs and Olms. Two genera: *Necturus, Proteus.* Distribution: Eastern North America and southeastern Europe. Species: 6. Note: Often recognized as two full families, Proteidae and Necturidae.

SUBORDER AMPHIUMOIDEA

Amphiumidae: Amphiumas. Only genus: *Amphiuma.* Distribution: Southeastern North America. Species: 3. Note: Often considered to be closely related to Salamandridae.

SUBORDER AMBYSTOMATOIDEA

Ambystomatidae: Mole Salamanders. Two genera: *Ambystoma, Rhyacosiredon.* Distribution: North America and Mexico. Species: 32.

Dicamptodontidae: Cope's Salamanders. Only genus: *Dicamptodon.* Distribution: Western North America. Species: 2 or 3.

Rhyacotritonidae: Torrent Salamanders. Only genus: *Rhyacotriton.* Distribution: Western North America. Species: 4.

SUBORDER PLETHODONTOIDEA

Plethodontidae: Lungless Salamanders. 28 genera in two subfamilies, including: Desmognathinae:

The Olm, *Proteus anguinus*, a unique European representative of the family Proteidae. Art: J. R. Quinn.

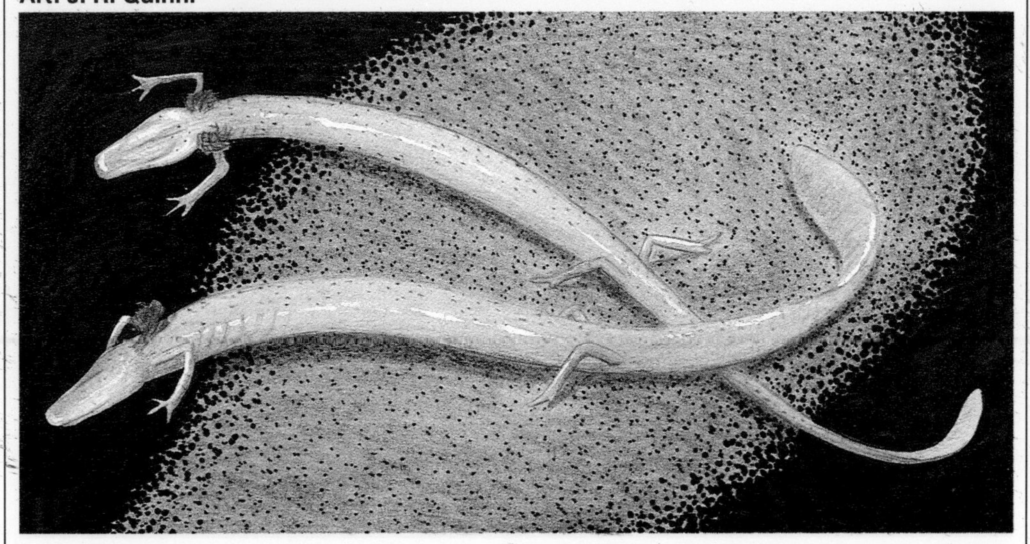

Above: **A torrent salamander, *Rhyacotriton variegatus*, family Rhyacotritonidae. Art: J. R. Quinn.**

Above: ***Typhlomolge rathbuni*, the Texas Blind Salamander, a close relative of *Eurycea* in the family Plethodontidae. Art: J. R. Quinn. *Below:* A Mount Lyell Salamander, *Hydromantes platycephalus*, of the family Plethodontidae. This genus is found in California and the northern Mediterranean area. Art: J. R. Quinn.**

Desmognathus, Leurognathus, Phaeognathus; Plethodontinae: *Aneides, Batrachoseps, Bolitoglossa, Ensatina, Eurycea, Gyrinophilus, Hydromantes, Oedipina, Plethodon, Pseudoeurycea, Pseudotriton, Typhlomolge*. Distribution: North, Central, and South America, plus northern Mediterranean. Species: Almost 250, with over 65 in *Bolitoglossa* and more than 40 in *Plethodon*.

SUBORDER SALAMANDROIDEA

Salamandridae: Newts. 15 genera, including: *Chioglossa, Cynops, Euproctus, Neurergus, Notophthalmus, Paramesotriton, Pleurodeles, Salamandra, Taricha, Triturus, Tylototriton*. Distribution: North America, North Africa, Eurasia. Species: About 55.

Sirenidae: Sirens. Two genera: *Pseudobranchus, Siren*. Distribution: Southeastern North America. Species: 3 or 4.

The land or eft stage of the Eastern Newt, *Notophthalmus viridescens*, family Salamandridae.

Overall distribution of the caecilians or apodans.

APODA: CAECILIANS

Apodans (now more properly called gymnophionans, order Gymnophiona) are legless burrowing amphibians of which fossilized remains (with traces of legs, incidentally) only recently have been discovered. First described as a snake by Seba in 1735, even today scientists are unsure when they evolved, but various anatomical studies of modern species suggest they may have been with us for millions of years. Anatomically apodans are considered retrogrades because limbs and (not in all species) eyes have disappeared. The skull and the degenerate scales of the skin also are very primitive, resembling those of the first amphibians. However, some species have eliminated the need for an aquatic larval state by laying eggs in moist subterranean chambers, with some species protecting their own eggs and young. Some give live birth.

A SUMMARY OF APODAN CLASSIFICATION

Caeciliaidae (formerly Caeciliidae): Common Caecilians. Over 20 genera, including: *Caecilia, Dermophis, Hypogeophis, Siphonops.* Distribution: Central and South America, central Africa, Seychelles, India. Species: About 90.

Ichthyophiidae: Slimy Caecilians. Two genera: *Caudacaecilia, Ichthyophis.* Distribution: Southern Asia. Species: 37.

Rhinatrematidae: American Caecilians. Two genera: *Epicrionops, Rhinatrema.*

Distribution: South America. Species: About 9.

Scolecomorphidae: African Caecilians. Two genera: *Crotaphatrema, Scolecomorphus.* Distribution: Africa. Species: 5.

Typhlonectidae: Aquatic Caecilians. Four genera, including: *Chthonerpeton, Typhlonectes.* Distribution: South America. Species: About 20.

Uraeotyphlidae: Indian Caecilians. Only genus: *Uraeotyphlus.* Distribution: India. Species: 4.

CLASSIFICATION

For someone who has just taken an interest in amphibians, being confronted by the system of scientific classification can be daunting to the extent of discouraging. Yet this doesn't have to be the case because there are no rules that state we have to describe species by their scientific names. Although it is very helpful to learn about classification when common names cause confusion, more important are the ways in which we keep our amphibians in the captive environment. Learning scientific names is a gradual process, and the more involved you get in the hobby the more you will want to learn.

Classification or taxonomy is the logical ordering or grouping of living organisms. It has caused confusion and controversy for many centuries and even today often is a matter for argument. In the middle 1700's it was the Swedish naturalist Linnaeus who established the foundations for modern classification when he developed the binomial system of scientific nomenclature to categorize all organisms. Using the morphology (form and structure) of the organism as the basis of his system, he assigned each species a scientific name comprised of a generic name, where it showed similarities with other species, and a unique specific name. For example, the scientific name of the European Marbled Newt is *Triturus marmoratus*, *Triturus* being the generic name and *marmoratus* the specific name.

A rule to follow when writing scientific names is that the generic name always begins with a capital letter whereas specific and subspecific names start with lower case letters. All three are usually italicized, bracketed, or underlined to distinguish them from common names.

During the late nineteenth century scientists attempted to express evolutionary relationships between living organisms. Gradually additional evidence such as paleontology, geographical distribution, genetics, and embryology began to form the basis for the systematic classification of today, although Linnaeus's morphological school of thought still played an important part.

Today a trinomial system of scientific nomenclature often is used because even within a single species there can be differences between geographical races that warrant recognition but not separation from the specific rank. Here a subspecific name is used to identify those slight differences. Where a species has a subspecific name identical to the specific name this indicates it is the nominate form, the first subspecies to be described. For example, the nominate form of the European Marbled Newt is *Triturus marmoratus marmoratus*, and there is another form that, although similar in coloration and habits, attains a distinctly smaller size and was named *Triturus marmoratus pygmaeus*.

The problems associated with the use of common, everyday names can still be seen today. For instance, the terms "frog" and "toad" originated in England specifically to be applied to two native species occurring there. The agile, slimy type was the European Common Frog (*Rana temporaria*) and the warty dry-skinned type was the European Common Toad (*Bufo bufo*). Unfortunately this was incorrectly carried over to other species on observation of their appearance alone. For instance, in the family Hylidae the members are called treefrogs because most have a smooth skin and the slender build of typical frogs of the genus *Rana*, but biologically they resemble toads of the genus *Bufo*. Common names have been around for so long they tend to maintain their popularity with both scientists and amateurs, but the scientific name helps to overcome language barriers (and even local dialect). For example, the salamander *Triturus vulgaris* is called the Common Newt in England, Teichmolch in Germany, and Watersalamander in Holland. Even in different parts of its native England this newt is described under a variety of names such as smooth newt, English newt, pond newt, garden newt, eft, and water lizard. (And don't forget that even the group names can be confusing—newts themselves are just a group of salamanders, not a group distinct from salamanders.)

BIOLOGY OF AMPHIBIANS

CAECILIANS

Largest: The terrestrial species Thompson's Caecilian (*Caecilia thompsoni*) of Colombia attains 4.7 feet (144 cm). Smallest: The Seychelles Caecilian (*Hypogeophis brevis*) rarely grows above 4.5 inches (11.4 cm).

On first impressions a caecilian resembles a giant earthworm, but once seen in motion it has a distinctly serpentine look, a characteristic that until 1879 led these amphibians to be classified as reptiles and categorized into their own order. Structurally, apodans are geared to a subterranean existence. The body is long and slender and all traces of limbs have vanished both internally and externally. Unlike other amphibians, primitive scales are present in the form of microscopic discs embedded just beneath the epidermal layer, though on most species these

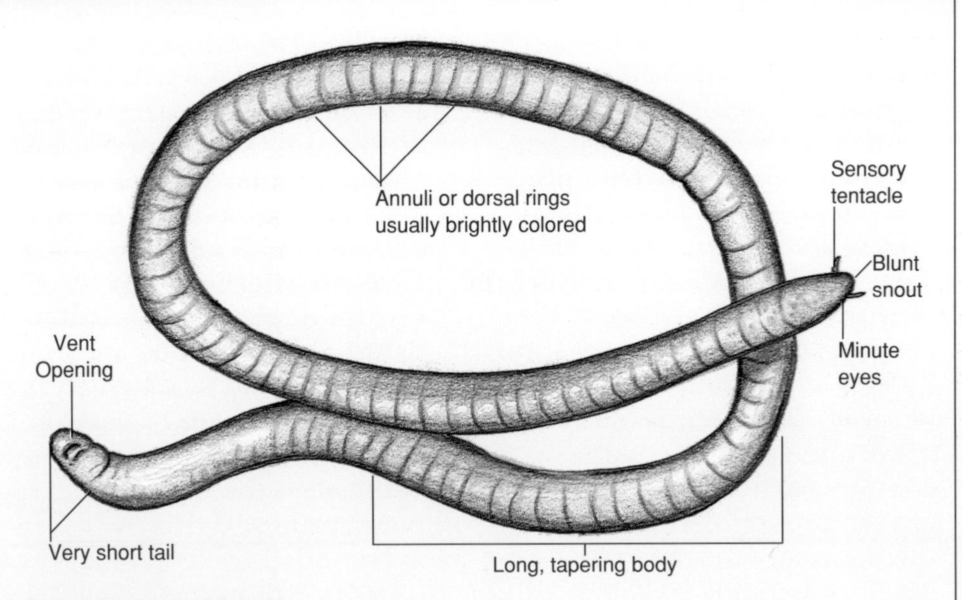

External structure of a caecilian.

occur only on the dorsal region (scales have yet to be noted in some species but probably are present). The body is superficially segmented by a series of circular depressions called rings or annuli that further enhance the wormlike appearance. The smooth, shiny outer epidermis is, in parallel with all other amphibians, profusely moistened by lubricating glands located beneath the skin. These aid movement through soils and the exchange of oxygen and waste gases through the skin surface.

The main burrowing tool is the head with its blunt, compact skull constructed of many thickened bones essential to combat the stresses of tunneling. The rather immobile jaws mean that caecilians are able to eat mostly smaller items of prey such as arthropods and worms, although the familiar Asian Sticky Caecilian (*Ichthyophis glutinosus*) is known to prey on small burrowing snakes. The upper jaw is equipped with a double row of backwardly curving, hooked teeth allowing it to hold on to slippery earthworms. The lower jaw has a single set of tiny pointed teeth that interlock between the upper double row when the mouth is closed.

Although caecilians have functional eyes at birth, these tend to become atrophied, degenerating in size and ability to function. They are also progressively covered by layers of skin and the surrounding bones thicken as the caecilian grows until it is effectively blind. Eyes can be seen as tiny black dots in younger specimens and in adults of a few species. Caecilians have no tympanum (membranous ear drum found in many amphibians) or outer ear, relying on sensing ground vibrations through the lower jaw much like a snake or most salamanders.

Like most subterranean animals, caecilians have other means by which to locate prey, danger, or a mate. Besides having a very keen sense of smell, positioned on either side of the apodan snout between the eye and the nostril is a pit that houses a retractile sensory tentacle. These tentacles contain nerve endings that collect odorous particles from the soil or air. On retracting they transmit the information to highly developed organs situated within the pits that relay the information to the brain. This organ is similar to the Jacobson's organ of snakes and lizards, the main difference being that reptiles use their tongues as detectors whereas caecilian tongues are small, rigid, and largely immobile.

The breathing apparatus of land-dwelling adult apodans is very similar to that of snakes; the right lung has become elongated and the left lung is reduced to the extent of being either barely functional or a useless vestige. In the aquatic genus *Typhlonectes* the lungs are virtually without function; the animals instead breath through their skin, which is loose and wrinkled, creating many pockets that trap and absorb dissolved oxygen. Waste gases are ejected via these pockets.

Most apodans are oviparous, producing a clutch of 6 to 50 eggs either in gelatinous strings or clumps that, depending on the species, are laid in humid burrows near a small stream or pool or just below the water surface. In smaller species a single egg may be no larger than 2 mm in diameter, while in larger species 5 to 8 mm is normal. Eggs are characterized by a central nucleus that usually is light brown or yellow in coloration and from which the embryo will begin to develop. The pole is held intact by an elastic skin called the vitelline membrane and this is surrounded by several layers of a translucent protective jelly. In terrestrial caecilians the female will coil around, incubate, and guard her eggs, during which time they absorb moisture from the surrounding soil and swell. The larvae develop feathery external gills inside the egg capsule but prior to hatching these are quickly absorbed and the larvae make their way to the source of water. On either side of the head are breathing pores that lead to internal gills connected to the throat as in fishes. Larvae remain aquatic for several months or more and develop large eyes, tailfins, and a distinctly newtlike appearance (minus legs and external gills). They congregate in shaded parts of the stream or pool or remain concealed in the muddy floor where they feed on crustaceans and aquatic worms. Sensory tentacles gradually appear and are used to hunt food in the latter stages of larval development. On metamorphosing the eyesight of

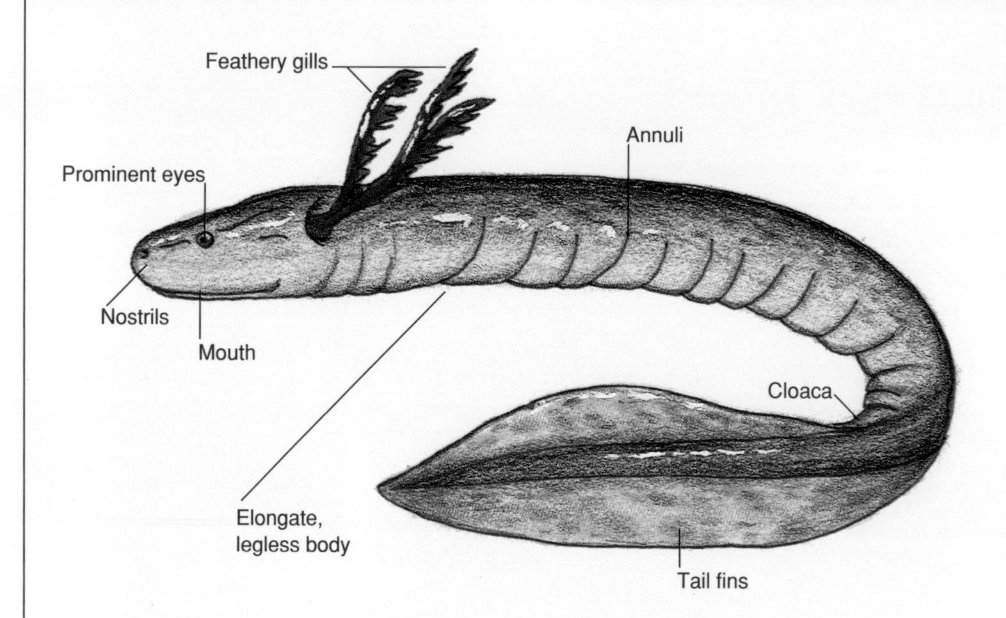

A caecilian larva. Sometimes this stage is passed in the egg.

the young terrestrial caecilians is already degenerating, the breathing pores have closed up to activate the lungs, and refuge is sought in a soft, moist soil. They may not reappear on the surface for another two or three years, when sexual maturity is reached.

Members of the genus *Typhlonectes* are viviparous (live-bearing) apodans, retaining eggs and hatchling larva within the body and giving birth to 5 to 15 fully developed miniature replicas of the mother.

SALAMANDERS

Largest: The aquatic Chinese Giant Salamander (*Andrias davidianus*) from the cool mountain streams of northeastern, central, and southern China holds the record of largest living amphibian. One huge specimen measured 71 in (180 cm) and weighed 143 pounds, although the normal for this species is 39 in (99 cm) and 24.25 pounds. Its close relative the Japanese Giant Salamander (*Andrias japonicus*) from southern Japan is recognized as the largest amphibian in terms of average length, with adults usually attaining 41 in (104 cm), although 63 in (160 cm) has been reported. The largest terrestrial caudate is the western North American Barred Tiger Salamander (*Ambystoma tigrinum mavortium*), which can attain 14 in (35.6 cm).

Smallest: The California Slender Salamander (*Batrachoseps attenuatus*) rarely grows to more than 2.75 in (7 cm), while adult male Italian Newts (*Triturus italicus*) of southern Italy have an average length of 2.5 in (6.4 cm). (Quoted lengths are snout to tip of tail.)

The term salamander comes

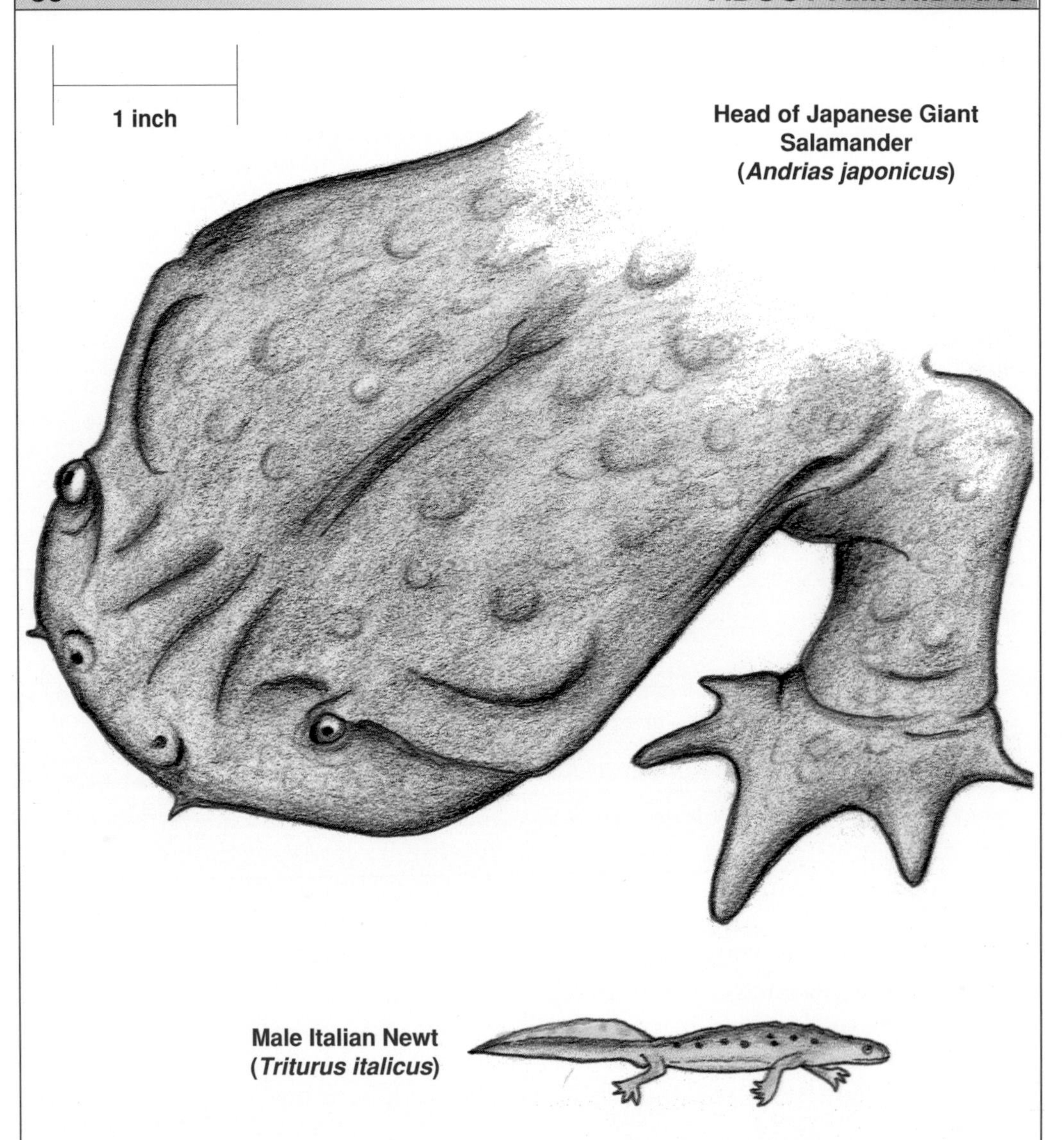

Size difference between the largest and one of the smallest salamanders.

from the Greek and means "fire animal." It was given to the European Fire Salamander (*Salamandra salamandra*), which used to emerge from the flames of firewood collected from forests. Although the belief that this amphibian was impervious to fire was totally untrue (it simply sought refuge in the moist atmosphere beneath the logs), this was just one of the mystical powers attributed to what is a secretive and timid creature. Another story was that these salamanders were born from rain clouds, probably attributable to the fact that in central Europe throughout much of the year salamanders were rarely seen, yet following a heavy rainstorm thousands suddenly appeared crawling around meadows and forests as if they had actually fallen from the sky. Another myth was that they were deadly poisonous, perhaps slightly closer to the truth. Certainly the toxins secreted by Fire Salamanders as well as Red Efts (*Notophthalmus viridescens*) and coastal newts (*Taricha*) can be lethal to small animals and cause considerable discomfort in man should the poison enter the eyes or bloodstream. In addition, many other newts and salamanders secrete distasteful skin secretions to deter predators.

Salamanders (caudates or, formerly, urodeles) represent some of the most colorful of all amphibians yet many species are so secretive they rarely have been observed. Predominantly a Northern Hemisphere order, a few genera occur south into central South America and southern Asia. Throughout their range, almost without exception they prefer rather cooler conditions than the two other amphibian orders. Even in the tropics they tend to inhabit cool, humid microhabitats such as deep,

External structure of a stylized salamander.

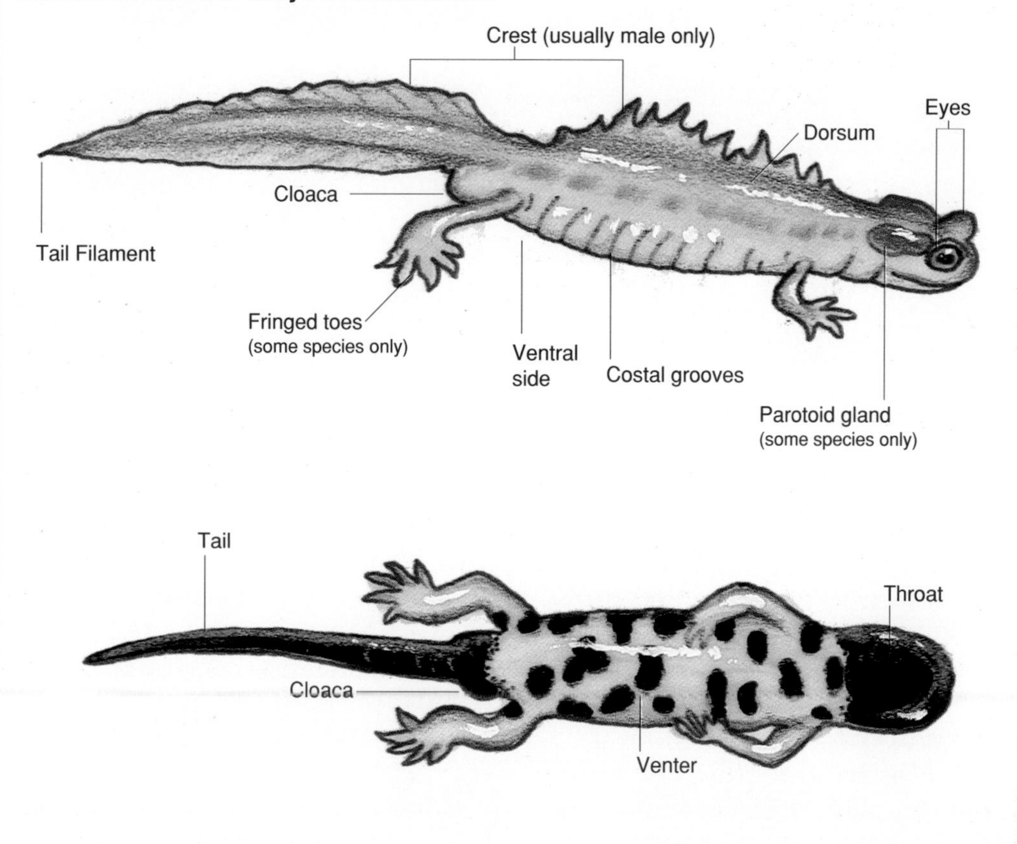

sunless valleys or montane regions.

The majority of salamanders rarely attain more than 8 inches and are characterized by a large, wide, flattened head attached to a long, slender, cylindrical body culminating in an even longer tail. Most species have four limbs with four digits on the front legs and five digits on the hind legs. Some species, such as the North American sirens (Sirenidae), amphiumas (*Amphiuma*), and slender salamanders (*Batrachoseps*) as well as the Central American worm salamanders (*Oedipina*) have evolved elongated bodies coupled with a reduction in limb size or even total loss of hind limbs. This equates to the evolutionary pattern of many lizards (notably skinks and anguids) and may suggest the path that salamanders have followed.

The tail varies in length and shape throughout genera, but its main functions are for balance, as an aquatic tool, for reproductive behavior, occasionally for holding on to branches, or a combination of some or all of these functions. Terrestrial newts and salamanders tend to walk in an awkward, undulating gait with the body and tail raised off the ground, yet for those species that spend some or all of their time in water, their movements are agile and graceful.

The skeleton tends to be fairly uniform, with well-developed and strong pelvic and pectoral girdles (pelvic girdles are absent in sirens) present while the skull and regions of the backbone are heavily interlaced with cartilage. In some species the body can be flattened, enabling the creature to climb into tight crevices.

Compared to apodans and anurans, caudate teeth do not show much specialization. They usually are small, needlelike projections and form a single row in each jaw, although primitive salamanders of the family Hynobiidae have a double row of caecilianlike teeth (vomerine teeth) on the upper jaw. Initially in the larval stage teeth may be completely absent, developing as the salamander grows. In later life the teeth become brittle or fall away easily and are constantly being replaced. The North American Hellbender (*Cryptobranchus alleganiensis*) is one of the few salamanders that can inflict a nasty bite on man with its long, sharp teeth.

Many newts and salamanders can regenerate missing parts of their body such as digits, limbs, or tails, although sometimes the regenerated part of the body may grow too short or too long or be oddly shaped. This process is known as regeneration and should not be confused with autotomy, which is the voluntary loss of the tail at a point where the vertebrae are weakened and the muscles and blood vessels have special constrictures. Autotomized tails often are regenerated.

Caudate eyes usually are large, prominent, and located near or on top of the head. Vision is not

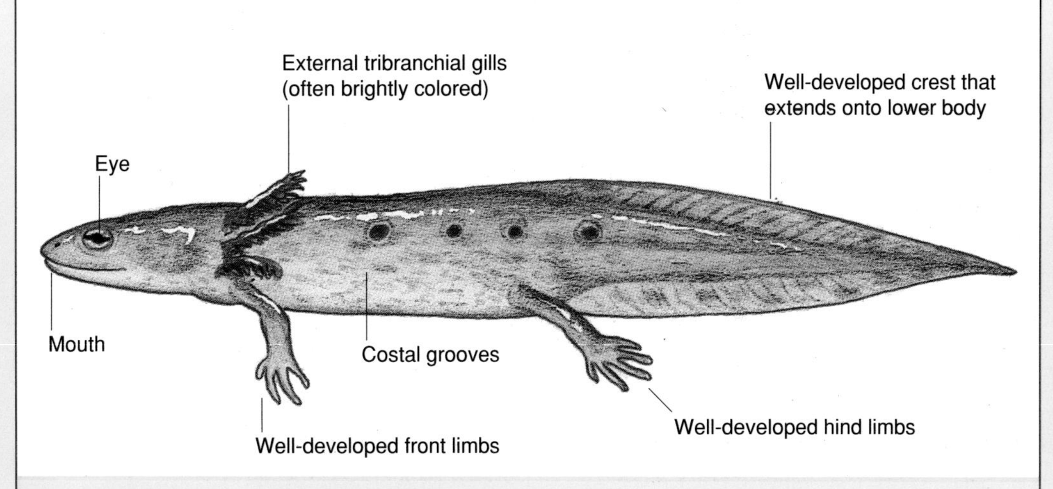

External structure of an aquatic salamander larva.

particularly acute, responding only to movement, and at long distances is thought to be blurred. Eyelids usually are present. The lower eyelid has several openings that continually exude moistening and cleansing secretions. Some cave-dwelling and subterranean salamanders have completely lost their eyes.

Like other amphibians, the salamander olfactory system forms the most acute sense and plays a very important part in their behavior. Air is drawn in through the external nostrils and passes through sensory nasal cavities that relay messages to the cavity of the mouth via ducts called the choanae or internal nostrils. Located in the oral cavity is a section of nasal epithelium that forms a complex Jacobson's organ and besides analyzing airborne odors also is used to determine food content in the mouth. It is the action of the hyoid apparatus in the lower jaw that draws air in through the nostrils; this can be seen clearly in the form of regular throat pulsing. In addition, there is an occasional "gulping" of air directly into the lung(s).

Reduction of one or both lungs is common among many salamanders, while members of the most successful caudate family, the Plethodontidae, have no lungs whatsoever and are commonly known as lungless salamanders. To compensate for lack of conventional breathing apparatus, the skin inside and around the mouth, beneath the arms, and often at the base of the feet contains dense networks of blood vessels and capillaries through which oxygen and waste gases diffuse. This almost certainly is a recent development because all primitive amphibians probably had lungs. Also contained within the skin are many dermal glands that exude a moistening secretion and often encompass either a distasteful or toxic fluid.

Mating rituals are well documented among aquatic salamanders, especially newts. Males often are flamboyantly adorned in crests and beautiful colors. After mating, most species deposit eggs either on land or in water in a safe place away from predators. Newts of the family Salamandridae usually bend the foliage of pond plants around individual eggs to hide and protect them, while other species attach them to the underside of large-leafed plants or rocks. Terrestrial egg-layers lay small clumps of eggs in moist burrows beneath rocks or rotting trees or may excavate nests in damp soil. The eggs of salamanders have a structure similar to that of the caecilians. Generally speaking, eggs laid on land contain a greater proportion of yolk than do eggs laid in water because the developing larvae may require nourishment for a much longer period before hatching.

Some salamanders, such as the Fire Salamander, have abandoned the egg-laying stage and are ovoviviparous, retaining the eggs and then the developing larvae inside the oviduct. Although larvae number fewer than those produced in a typical egg-layer's batch, the well-developed larvae that are deposited into shallow water stand a much greater chance of survival. Some other newts, namely the Alpine Salamander (*Salamandra atra*) and Turkish species of *Mertensiella*, have progressed even further in having a true gestation period and are viviparous amphibians. These species tend to inhabit barren places where most of the year is spent in hibernation or estivation and where water is very sparse. Usually only one to six larvae develop in the uterus, where they are nourished by a special uterine "milk." After lengthy gestation periods of up to two years the mother gives birth to fully developed young.

FROGS AND TOADS

Largest: The Goliath Frog (*Conraua goliath*) from the Cameroon and Equatorial Guinea rainforests is thought to be the largest frog, attaining 14 in (35.6 cm) and 6 pounds, although there are recent reports of an as yet undescribed species from the Djaya highlands of New Guinea that may be even larger. The largest toad in the world is the Colombian Blomberg's Toad (*Bufo blombergi*) at 9.8 in (24.9 cm), although the Cane Toad (*Bufo marinus*) is a close second at 9.5 in (24 cm).

Smallest: There have been many contenders for smallest anuran because new species are continually being discovered, especially in the equatorial regions. At present the record belongs to a Brazilian species, *Psyllophryne didactyla*, from the family Brachycephalidae. With an

Facing page: **A Four-toed Salamander, *Hemidactylium scutatum*, guarding its egg clutch. Photo: R. T. Zappalorti.**

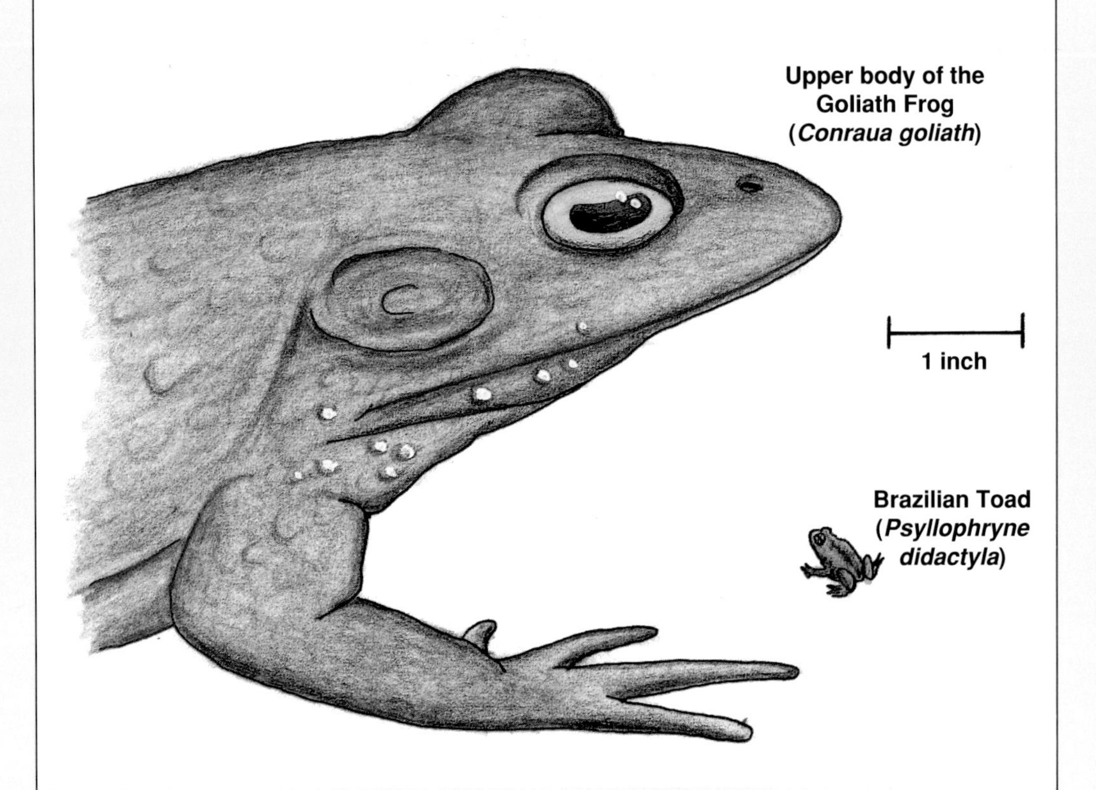

Size difference between the largest and the smallest frogs.

average snout-vent length of only 0.4 in (9.7 mm), it also is the smallest amphibian in the world. Many frogs of several families are well under an inch (25.4 mm) in body length when fully mature.

In terms of structure and behavior Anura is the most diverse amphibian order, and the range of habitats frogs have managed to adapt to is quite remarkable: high mountains where snow and ice are evident ten months of the year, arid deserts where rain may fall just once every three years, and even around and in the sea (though admittedly just in brackish ponds at the edge of the shore). In most anurans the skeletal structure is fundamentally simple and typified by long, powerful folded hind limbs, shorter fore limbs, a short backbone containing six to ten vertebrae, and an open, flat skull. The hind limbs are particularly well developed and contain four apparent external segments as opposed to three as in most land animals. This enables them to

Facing page: **The largest described frog, *Conraua goliath* from streams of western Africa. Photo: M. Panzella.**

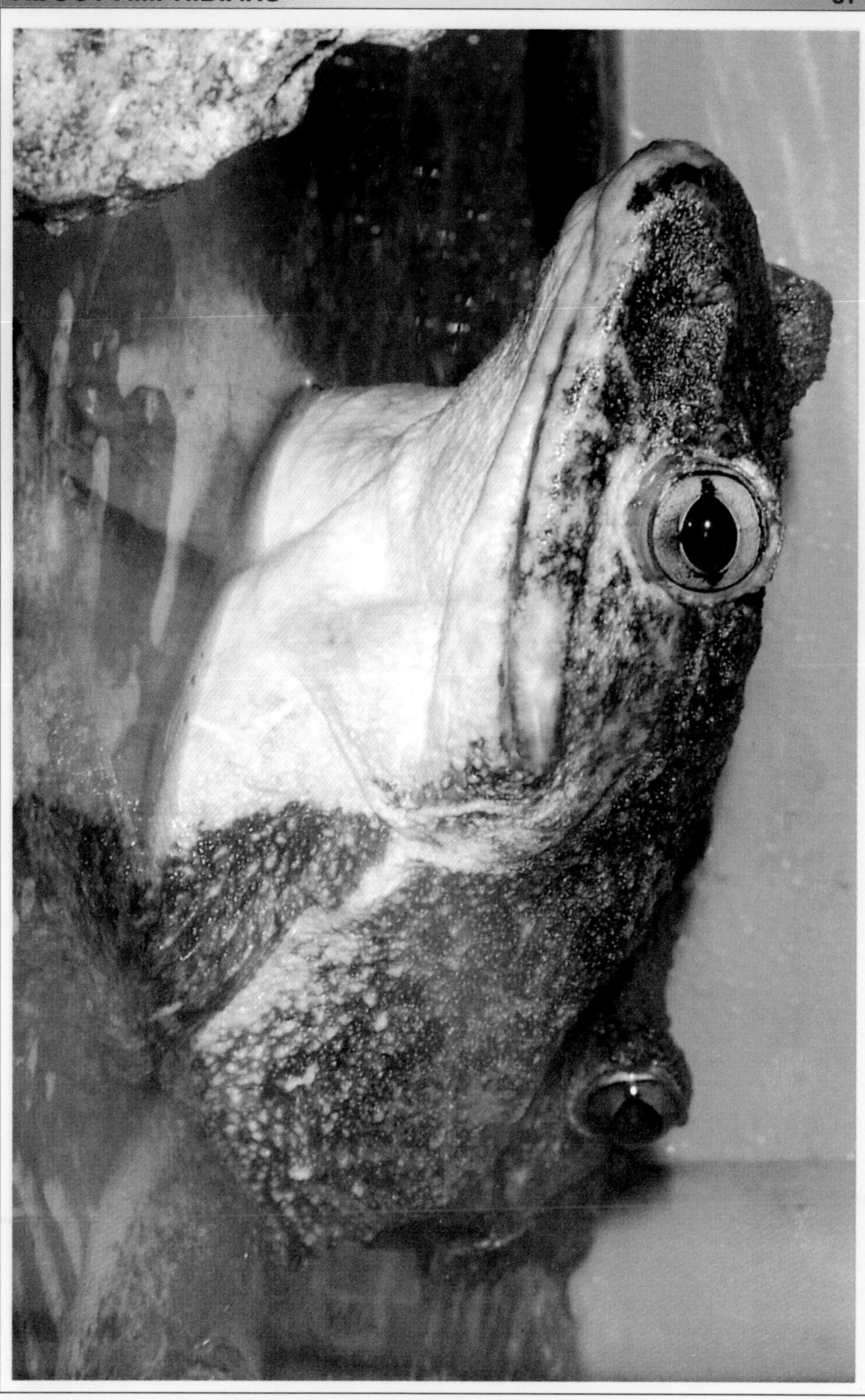

gain excellent leverage when leaping and swimming. Anurans also have huge modified girdles attached to the rear legs and in agile species such as treefrogs (Hylidae) and typical frogs (Ranidae) these are thin and quite flexible, allowing for more spring.

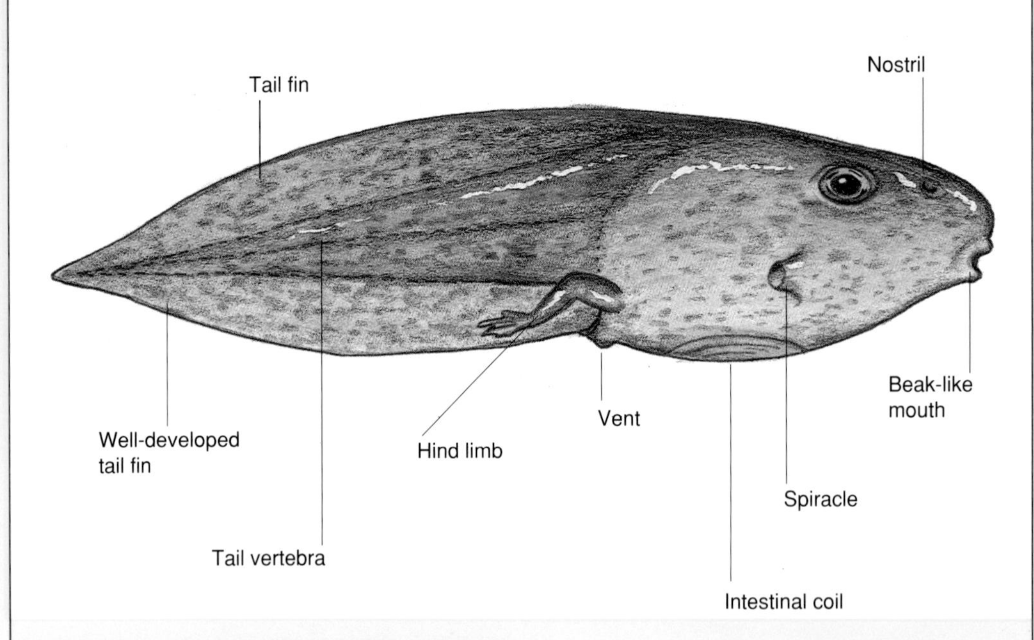

External Structure of a Typical Frog Tadpole

In contrast, some frogs and many toads are quite heavily built, their rear limbs quite short and their pelvic girdle thicker and more rigid. Such types as the South American horned frogs (*Ceratophrys*) and African Bullfrog (*Pyxicephalus adspersus*) are called "squatting" species because they remain in one place for long periods, while many bufonid toads tend to walk rather than hop.

Apart from a few families such as Pipidae (aquatic frogs) and Bufonidae, most frogs possess teeth on the upper (rarely also lower) jaw. These usually are in the form of a row of many tiny pinlike projections. In some species a second set of modified denticles is present in the palate, the vomerine teeth; these are thought to aid the frog in maintaining a secure grip on slippery prey such as worms and slugs. In genera such as *Ceratophrys* and *Megophrys* the teeth have become extremely long and sharp; along with the African Bullfrog, they have several sharp bony projections (odontodes) growing from the lower jaw. These frogs, by the way, can inflict very

EXTERNAL STRUCTURE OF A GENERALIZED FROG

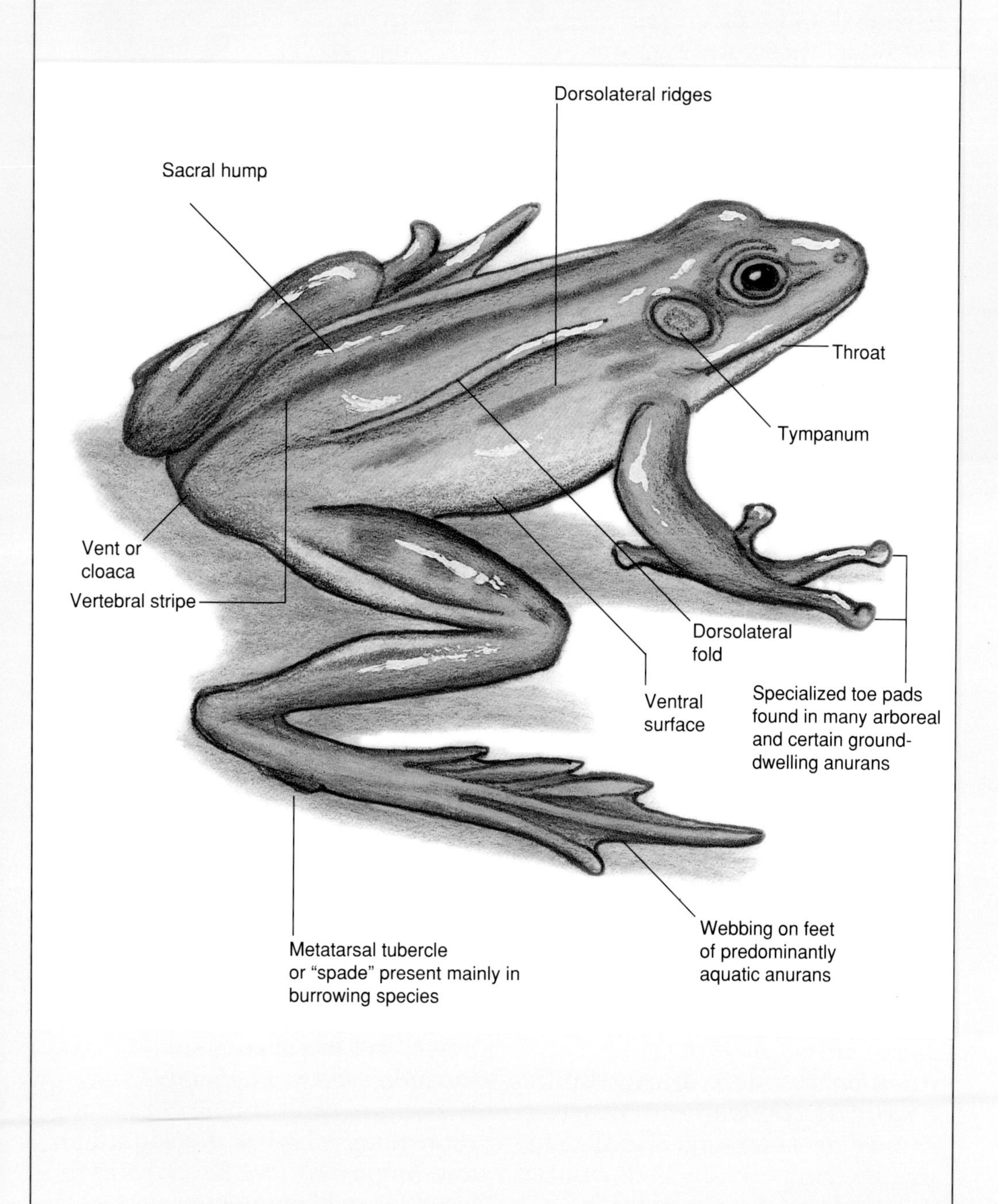

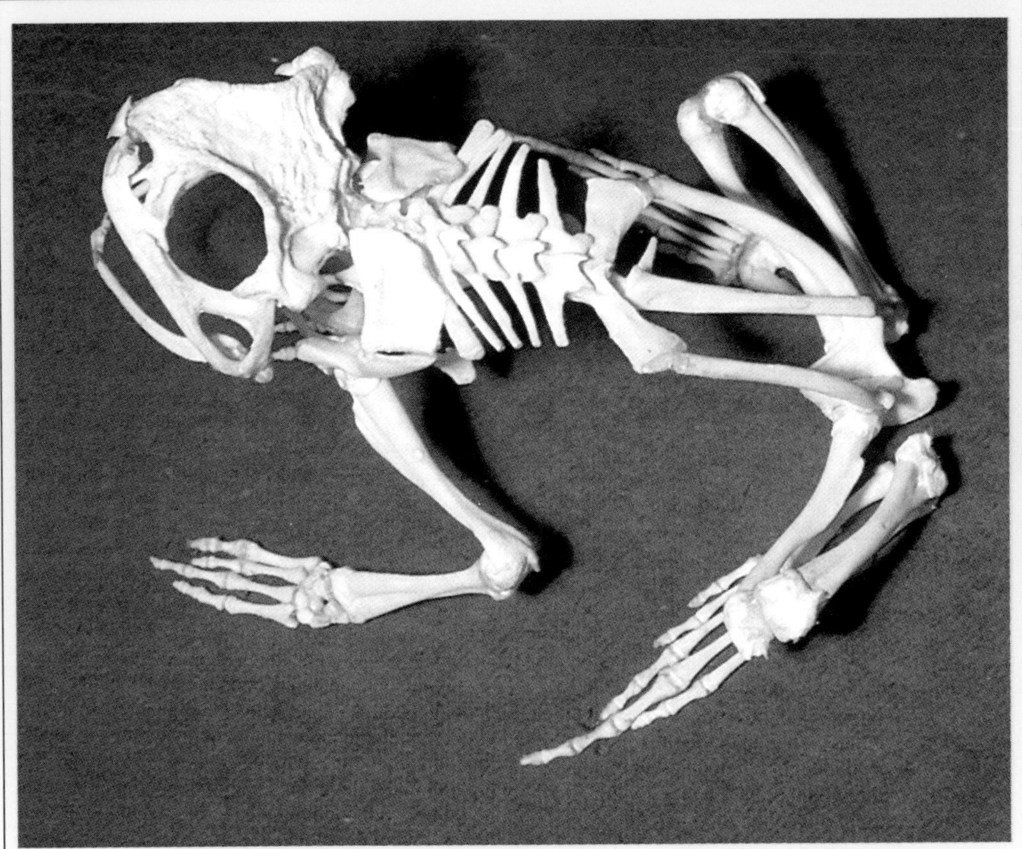

Cleaned, articulated skeleton of a Marine Toad, *Bufo marinus*. Notice especially the shortened backbone and greatly elongated pelvic girdle. Photo: R. T. Zappalorti.

painful bites and may draw blood. Only hylids, some ranids, and several discoglossids have teeth on both jaws.

The eyes of frogs are quite well-developed and are able to distinguish both color and patterns. Some of the treefrogs have the most acute vision of all amphibians. In most cases the shape of the pupil reveals whether the frog is diurnal or nocturnal. If it is round, heart-shaped, or triangular the species in question probably is diurnal; if it is horizontally or vertically elliptical the frog probably is crepuscular or nocturnal. As with salamanders, the eyes continually are washed with secretions from the lower eyelid, and most anurans will blink occasionally to give the eye surface a cleaning. Most rely on sight to detect prey, responding to its movement before attacking. Some species, notably the bufonids and the African Bullfrog, "learn" to eat non-living food items such as raw meat or dead mice in captivity.

The tongue of the frog represents a highly specialized and important tool in capturing food. Usually connected to the front of the lower mandible (jaw), the tongue is heavily coated with sticky mucus and can be flicked out by muscular action to snare prey. Discoglossids possess rigid tongues and thus have to lunge at their prey, clumsily stuffing it into their mouth with the aid of the forearms. Aquatic frogs such as *Pipa* and *Xenopus* do not have tongues and use their specialized forearms and hands to scoop prey into their mouths.

Male frogs are perhaps best known for their vocal attributes and perhaps were among the first animals on Earth to evolve a true voice. Although some salamanders can emit basic squeaks or grunts, each species of frog has its own unique call. Many species can alter their own voice very slightly either in frequency or noise level, and after extensive studies scientists have been able to determine the purpose of some of these differences: warning off rival males, staking claim to a territory, a show of excitement or fear, and most importantly to attract the attention of females. The way in which anurans vocalize is quite a simple mechanism. With the lungs full of air, the nostrils and mouth are closed, forcing the air forward past a sequence of vocal cords into an inflatable vocal sac located in the floor of the mouth. This may be single or a pair of pouches that may be visible externally at the corners or center of the throat. From here the air is forcibly returned back across the

A male Carpenter Frog, *Rana virgatipes*, courting a female. Notice the greatly inflated balloon-like vocal sacs. Photo: R. T. Zappalorti.

vocal cords to the lungs and so on, creating the ongoing chorus.

In frogs the ear is concealed beneath the skin just behind the eye and usually is marked by a circular area of thin stretched skin called the external eardrum or tympanum. Female frogs in particular have a well-developed sense of hearing, especially in areas occupied by high densities of different species. In order not to choose a male of the wrong species and risk an infertile pairing, she is able to recognize the call of her own species however slight the difference. In fact, the use of sound analysis equipment to produce "maps" of calls (sonograms) can not only allow a herpetologist to distinguish frog species just by call, it also has led to the discovery of many new forms that cannot be distinguished easily or at all by external structure and color.

Virtually all frogs still rely on the lungs for breathing, but because their lungs have no muscular action (there is no diaphragm), air is pumped in and out via the nostrils by raising and lowering the floor of the mouth, a feature they share with lunged salamanders.

It is in the external appearance such as coloration, body shape, and skin adornments that the most notable differences are seen among the almost 4000 species. The largest family, Leptodactylidae, is the most diverse in terms of size, shape, and coloration. In typical frogs (Ranidae) and typical toads (Bufonidae) shape and coloration are fairly uniform, yet in terms of size here we see the greatest divergence. In families such as poison frogs (Dendrobatidae) and narrow-mouthed toads (Microhylidae) the reverse is apparent, where size is mostly invariable but shape or coloration is very diverse.

Certain frogs have adopted distinctive habitats or habits and in doing so have evolved accordingly to adapt. For instance, members of the Dendrobatidae, Hylidae, Hyperoliidae, and Rhacophoridae (among others) have evolved specialized toe pads that enable them to live a truly arboreal (tree-dwelling) existence. Horned frogs and bullfrogs have huge mouths that allow the passage of enormous meals, essential in times of drought and food scarcity. Frogs that inhabit arid regions, such as spadefoots (Pelobatidae) and water-holding frogs (*Cyclorana*), have enlarged metatarsal tubercles called spades on their hind feet allowing them to burrow into damp soil.

Almost all known species of frogs are oviparous, depositing eggs singly, in tiny clumps, in gelatinous strings, or in huge masses of jelly known as spawn. The amazing fecundity of some species is well known, with the female Cane Toad (*Bufo marinus*), one of the world's most widely distributed amphibians, being able to deposit over 35,000 eggs. At the opposite end of the scale, the Cuban frog *Eleutherodactylus (Sminthillus) limbatus* is so small it is only able to deposit one egg

FEATURES ON THE HEAD OF A TYPICAL TOAD, FAMILY BUFONIDAE

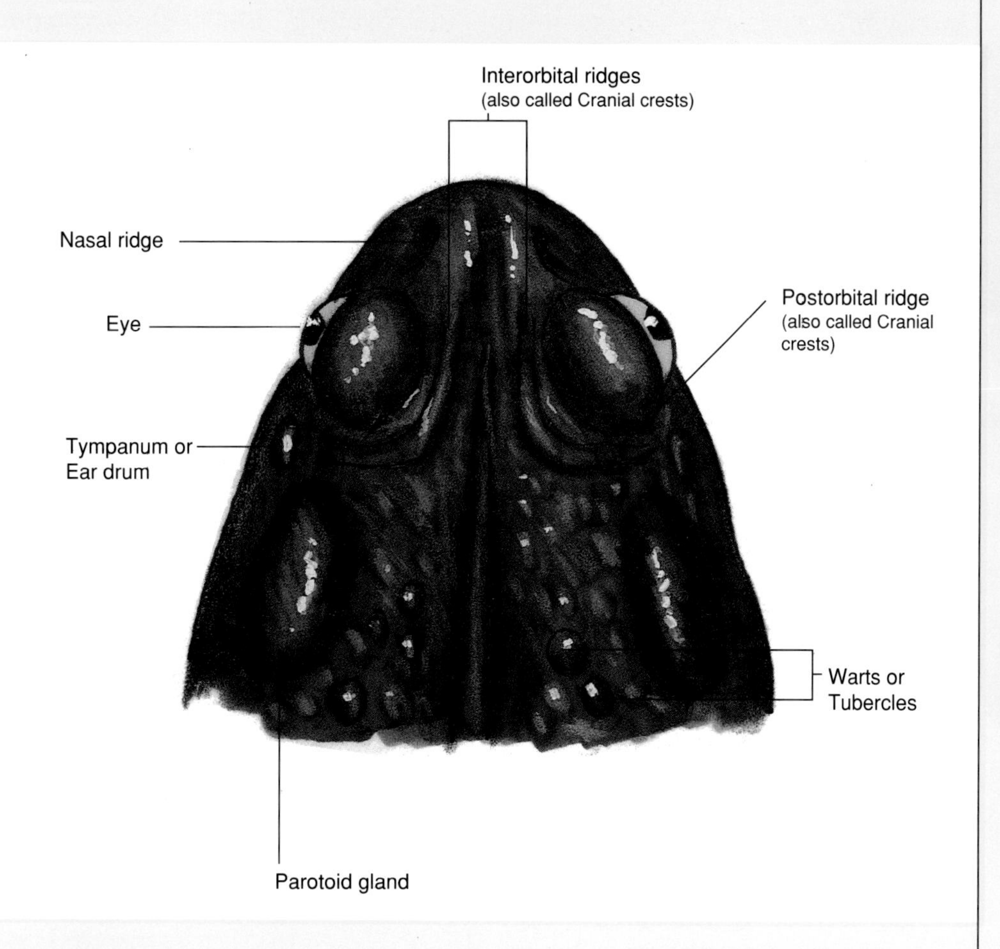

A water-holding frog, *Cyclorana* sp. Photo: M. Panzella.

after every mating. The reason why most anurans lay such large numbers of eggs is because of the vast array of creatures that devour eggs, tadpoles, and newly-metamorphosed froglets or toadlets. The adults themselves form part of the diet for a myriad of creatures.

In composition the anuran egg is very similar to that of caecilians and salamanders although it very often has a larger embryo and thicker layers of protective jelly. After the eggs hatch the resultant larvae, known of course as tadpoles, initially are inactive as they absorb the remainder of their yolk sac. In some species, such as the European Midwife Toad (*Alytes obstetricans*), the male carries the eggs for several months before dropping them in a pool. Here well-formed tadpoles break out and stand a better chance of survival. In extreme cases such as the Surinam Toad (*Pipa pipa*) the female maneuvers her eggs onto her back, where a chemical released by the eggs softens the female's skin, into which the eggs sink before the skin hardens again. Mouth-brooding, where the male picks up newly hatched tadpoles from eggs laid on land which then develop into froglets within a vocal pouch, occurs in the Chilean rhinodermid frogs. In the Australian species *Rheobatrachus silus* and *vitellinus* the female actually swallows her eggs, which then hatch and develop in her stomach for around eight weeks. During this time she is unable to eat; digestive juices would be fatal to her brood.

The adaptations of so many frogs and toads produce an endless source of discovery and interest, one that we can often observe for ourselves in captivity, but only if captive conditions are correct.

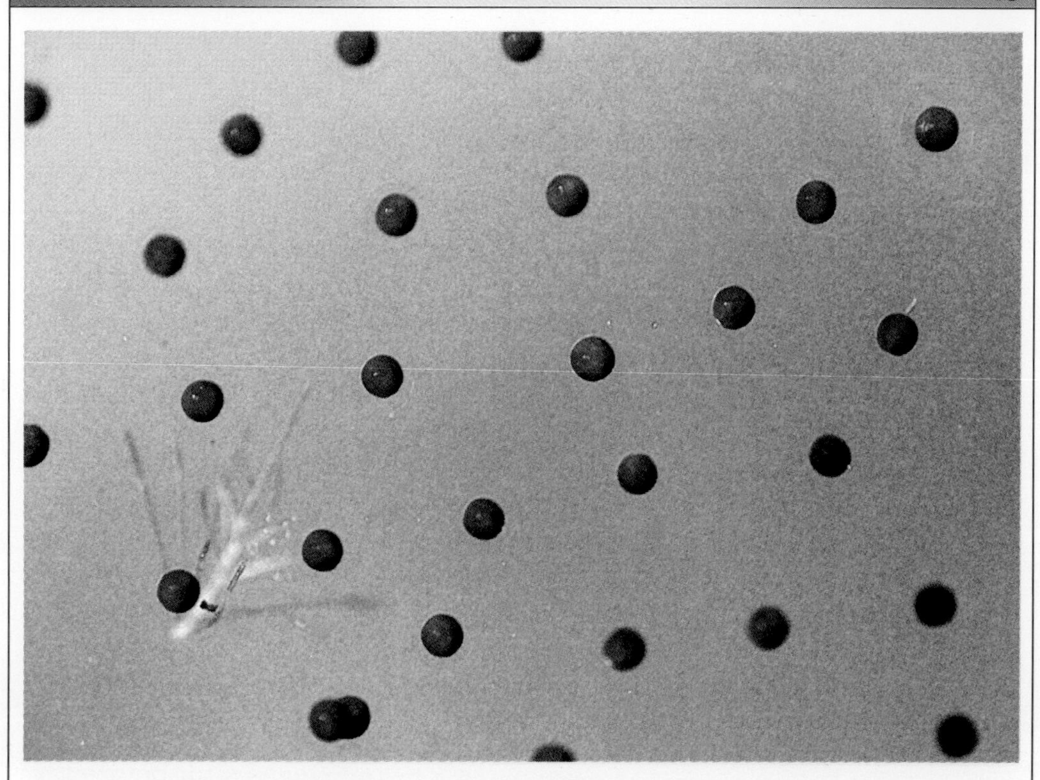

Life cycle of the Cuban Treefrog, *Osteopilus septentrionalis. Top:* Fertilized eggs. *Bottom:* Young tadpoles, some still with obvious external gills. Photos: R. D. Bartlett.

Life cycle of the Cuban Treefrog, *Osteopilus septentrionalis*. *Top:* Metamorphosing froglet with fully developed legs and tail. *Bottom:* Free-living froglet with tail mostly resorbed. Photos: R. D. Bartlett.

Initial Care

WORDS OF ADVICE

Before embarking into the hobby of amphibian keeping, it is advisable to accumulate as much information as possible on the subject and/or join a specialist society that may offer welcome and expert advice. The same can be said for hobbyists wanting to obtain a rare or desirable species for the first time. A good general book may only help in identifying the captive requirements (i.e., furnishings, heating, lighting, hygiene, and health care) of amphibians in general and should be backed up by specialist books, scientific papers, and herpetological journals that detail specific information on a particular species such as preferred habitat, climatic conditions, lighting levels, whether it is a secretive or fearless, peaceful or pugnacious, solitary or gregarious species, and also breeding behavior and techniques. The more selective a species is in its climatic and habitat preferences, the more information and often more experience are required to successfully maintain (and breed) it in captivity.

The Species Selection sections in the latter part of this book are intended to discriminate between the "easy," "intermediate," and "difficult" species of all three amphibian orders in terms of their captive adaptability. Beginners are advised to start with an "easy" species that will thrive in captivity and thus develop confidence to attempt a more difficult type. The secret is to build up experience gradually and never rush into acquiring an amphibian about which little is known. Remember that amphibians are not toys that can hold the owner's attention for a month or so before being forgotten or discarded; they are living creatures that sense fear and excitement and respond to pain and stress.

CONSIDERATIONS BEFORE ACQUIRING AN AMPHIBIAN

Size

Fortunately, most amphibians are relatively small in terms of length and bulk. Even the larger frogs and toads that grow over 8 inches tend to be "squat" by nature and so are quite content with a relatively small terrarium. More consideration must be made to the number of amphibians obtained. Overcrowding a terrarium is unhealthy and stressful to all of the occupants and is best avoided. Highly active and agile species also need a spacious container where they can leap or run around without colliding with the container walls too often. Many salamanders and territorial anurans, although relatively small, tend to be solitary, rarely tolerating other individuals within a certain area and warding them off with a painful nip.

Habits

• Activity. A large majority of amphibians are nocturnal, meaning that they rarely venture from their hiding places during the daylight hours. If a species is required that is active during the day, then it makes sense to find out this information beforehand. Certain amphibians are burrowers, spending most of their lives hidden and rarely if ever coming to the surface. Most species that come from naturally hot, dry terrains are fossorial (burrowers), sleeping in cool soils and only surfacing to feed and breed after the onset of cool or rainy weather. Fortunately, some fossorial amphibians such as horned frogs (*Ceratophrys*) will adapt to less natural setups in the captive environment.

• Feeding. Some species of amphibians are specialized feeders, preying on only one or

The endangered Houston Toad, *Bufo houstonensis*, of southeastern Texas has responded well to captive-breeding programs. Photo: P. Freed.

two particular types of food; an example is the many caecilians that eat only termites. Providing a constant source of such food could cause major difficulties. Other species, such as Fire Salamanders, have a preference for small white or gray slugs, and even these can be difficult to locate in areas that experience freezing winters or baking summers. Fortunately, most species can be coaxed onto other foods when preferred morsels are scarce.

Restricted to a single valley in California, *Bufo exsul*, the Black Toad, is a candidate for sudden extinction. Photo: K. Lucas.

Endangered Species and Laws

It is worth noting that an increasing number of species are now protected by international laws, and those listed in the IUCN Red Data Books are strictly protected. It is worthwhile contacting your national and regional environmental protection departments, which will be able to provide you with a list of those species both from your own and other countries that either require exemption licenses before they can be kept or are

A pair of Costa Rican Golden Toads, *Bufo periglenes*, in amplexus. Photo: P. Freed.

completely prohibited from keeping. This should prevent you from running the risk of a hefty fine or even imprisonment.

Appearance and Response

It helps to know what to look for in terms of health before purchasing any amphibian, although obviously it may be difficult to examine the amphibian internally. In particular, attention should be paid to the following:

- Physical Appearance:
  a) Bright and clear eyes;

The Golden Toad suddenly disappeared from favorable habitats in its small Costa Rican range and may be extinct. Photo: P. Freed.

b) Shiny, unblemished, and unbroken skin (especially around the tops of the limbs, jaws, eyes, and tympanic membrane);

c) Complete sets of mobile, sturdy limbs with untwisted joints and most of the digits present (although many caudates can regrow these);

d) A sound visible bone structure;

e) Sufficient body weight but not obesity;

f) Absolutely no signs of ill-treatment and disease.

• Response:

g) Active species should be alert to movement or attempt to escape from human hands;

h) Nocturnal species should respond to light.

ACQUIRING AMPHIBIANS

In recent years the number of places dealing in amphibians and other "exotic" pets has risen dramatically to cope with the demands of a growing number of people now interested in the hobby. Thus it can be difficult knowing exactly which outlet is the best in terms of stocking healthy specimens, a good selection of species, advice and help, and their cost. Amphibians generally can be obtained from three different sources: the wild; a local pet store, tropical fish shop, or other commercial seller of amphibians and supplies for their care; a herpetological club or society. Most amphibian keepers probably either purchase their specimens from a pet shop or collect them in the wild. Today there are so many regulations concerning the taking of amphibians that it probably is no longer safe to collect in many areas, so a good, clean pet shop with a broad selection of species—and willing to special order other species—may be your best bet.

• Collecting from the wild. One of the most argued issues of recent years and probably for many years to come is the conservation of our natural world. We have all heard about man's unrelenting encroachment into virgin forests, destroying every living thing in his path and then condemning it under a landscape of concrete. Yet areas still abound where amphibians are present in sufficient numbers for a few to be collected for captive propagation. Remember that in many countries national and local laws do exist that prohibit the collection of any wild amphibians, although licenses for taking small numbers sometimes are issued under special circumstances such as research and conservation projects. Another point is that many species of amphibians may not adapt well to captive conditions or may harbor diseases and parasites. It is good advice to always purchase captive-bred specimens WHENEVER POSSIBLE, although some species such as Marine Toads, Cuban Treefrogs, and African reed frogs are so common in the wild that captive breeding is just not economically viable. On the other hand, other desirable species may not be present in

Captive-breeding tends to increase the number of unusual colors or forms of an animal available to hobbyists. This albino American Bullfrog, *Rana catesbeiana*, represents a form that is bred commercially. Photo: R. D. Bartlett.

sufficient captive-bred quantities to satisfy demand. This is a sign that either a species is rare (and protected) or virtually impossible to keep.

By all means study and photograph amphibians in their natural habitat, and if you really do have to collect, then in the future, if you are able to breed them, release a good proportion of healthy, captive-bred specimens back into the same vicinity. If they don't breed release them anyway. (Note, however, that many herpetologists now worry about dangerous diseases being introduced into natural populations along with reintroduced animals; consult your veterinarian and local environmental department before returning any animals to the wild.)

TRANSPORTING AMPHIBIANS

The proper movement of amphibians is critical because most species are fairly delicate creatures and have a thin, fragile skin that tears easily. The container in which amphibians are moved should be sturdy, sufficiently ventilated, and loosely packed with a moistened material such as live sphagnum moss or pieces of soft sponge in which the creature can dig to prevent being knocked around. For aquatic species, a strong plastic bag filled with water and plenty of pond weed will reduce excessive harsh movement, while tropical amphibians may require some form of heat, especially in parcels that may be in transit several days in a cool storage area. This can be overcome by placing the container or plastic bag in a sturdy styrofoam box containing sealed thermal heat pads that react on exposure to air to produce sufficient warmth for up to 36 hours. Even so, transportation of most warm-temperate to tropical amphibians should be avoided when very cold weather is prevalent as such creatures can succumb from exposure to low temperatures within a short period.

HANDLING

Handling of most amphibians should be very restricted, in particular those species where the skin forms an important part in respiration such as lungless salamanders (Plethodontidae). The only situations were amphibians are likely to be handled on a regular basis are during transference from one container to another, i.e., during transportation, cleaning a terrarium, or when close inspection is required to determine healthiness and ailments.

Caecilians can be difficult to handle as they tend to squirm and thrash about and in the process cause themselves injury. Smaller species can be scooped up with a plastic cup, while larger types need to be grasped gently around the neck with one hand, the lower body resting in the other. In all such cases hands need to be wet.

Salamanders generally are slow-moving creatures that are easily caught but dislike handling because of the heat generated by humans. Most typical newts and plethodons are quite delicate and should be held resting on the outstretched moistened palm. Minimize handling by capturing them with a small fishing net or plastic cup. Ambystomatids and *Salamandra* species tend to be more robust, having somewhat drier skins, and can be gently grasped with the head and fore limbs resting over the index finger, the thumb gently pressing against the neck, and the abdomen held in the palm of the hand. Fully aquatic types should be caught in a fishing net before being transferred to another water–holding container so that handling is completely avoided.

Frogs can present problems where handling is concerned, as many will attempt to avoid capture by leaping frantically around. Once caught, the next problem is keeping hold of them due to the slimy skin. Smaller frogs can be held in a completely closed wet hand, while larger species can be grasped by the hind limbs. Handling of ranids, hylids, and other similar species should be kept to a minimum because the fragile skin is easily damaged. Conversely, anurans such as smaller African Bullfrogs and the majority of bufonid toads appear content resting on the palms of human hands because of the generated heat, often settling down and falling asleep!

In the case of amphibians that secrete poisons from skin glands, such as salamandrids, dendrobatids, some hylids, and many bufonids, it is preferable to wear thin plastic gloves, especially if nicks and cuts are present on the hands. Amphibians that are pugnacious by nature, including Ornate Horned Frogs and the Hellbender, can inflict a nasty bite with their sharp teeth and strong jaws. For these species it is advisable to wear wet, soft leather gloves or use a bucket or net to scoop them out of their container.

Always wash your hands after handling any amphibian, and never put it or your hands near your face. Almost all amphibians produce skin toxins that can sting if in contact with delicate tissue such as the lips, nose, and eyelids. Some amphibians, such as the California Newt, *Taricha torosa*, could theoretically cause severe poisoning if touched to the tongue. Never take your pets for granted. Photo: W. P. Mara.

Housing Amphibians

QUARANTINE

All amphibians carry pathogens (agents that can cause disease), but the concentration in which these occur depends on a specimen's current health and the source from which it was acquired. After acquiring any amphibian from any source, it should be isolated from all other specimens for a minimum period of four weeks. This action is called quarantine and allows both the specimen to settle down after the stress of moving and regular monitoring by the hobbyist to determine what is a specimen's state of health. It would be reckless to introduce a new arrival into a terrarium containing a thriving colony of the same amphibians, only to have the colony perish within a few weeks because the new specimen was infected with a deadly pathogen. Remember that many of the diseases described further on in this book are very difficult to detect until late stages.

A quarantine container should comfortably house one specimen, and a plastic shoe box, aquarium, or custom-built terrarium can all serve for this purpose depending on the size of the specimen. Basic requirements should include a basal substrate that retains a suitable degree of moisture (i.e., live sphagnum moss or a synthetic rubber foam material), a bowl of water for bathing, a few rocks or pieces of bark to hide under, and preferred temperature and humidity levels. If a species is semiaquatic or fully aquatic, arboreal, or fossorial, then suitable provisions should be made for such habits.

The objective of a quarantine container is to keep it fairly simple so that regular observations and occasional close inspections are possible. Obviously some of the more difficult species may demand near perfect environments, but these are an exception to the rule. Once a specimen is deemed in good condition, only then should it be introduced to an existing setup or a suitable and permanent terrarium for it be arranged.

HOUSING

Containers suitable for use as amphibian terraria and aquaria come in many shapes, sizes, and materials, some more suitable and more attractive than others. The four fundamental requirements of any container are that it be escapeproof, leakproof, adequately ventilated (although not so much that the terrarium becomes a wind tunnel), and spacious enough to house however many specimens are intended to be maintained.

Small Containers

Many pet shops sell a variety of small plastic terraria that are excellent for temporary housing of amphibians or even for permanent housing of smaller species. Additionally, plastic shoe boxes, lunch boxes, and food containers such as ice cream tubs and glass candy jars are just a few examples of everyday items that can be utilized for an ideal amphibian terrarium. Although these household products are not

Many hobbyists keep a few small plastic terraria on hand for emergencies and as temporary housing. Photo courtesy of Hagen.

as visibly attractive as an aquarium or custom-built terrarium, they can claim several distinct advantages. For hobbyists where space is at a premium, their size allows for more species to be kept in a smaller area, and the size factor also makes cleaning out very easy. They are particularly useful for maintaining smaller amphibia that would perhaps be lost in a large terrarium, and for individually rearing newly metamorphosed amphibians where closer checks on health and growth are possible and competition for food and space is nonexistent.

The enclosed nature of the containers gives desirable humidity levels for many amphibia, but whichever type of small container is utilized, be sure that it has a tight fitting lid into which are drilled enough small holes for adequate ventilation. Alternatively, cut one large hole, say a quarter of the lid area, and place over it a piece of pre-heated aluminum gauze (as used for car body repairs) that is slightly larger than the hole it is placed over. It will then fuse firmly into the plastic.

Other small containers that are useful include the plant terrariums and seed propagators available from horticultural centers. More expensive models have heating elements and humidifiers that can be externally controlled. These are especially worth looking at for tropical forest-dwelling amphibians.

The Aquarium

All-glass aquaria or tanks can be obtained from most tropical fish shops and pet stores and come in various shapes (rectangular, squares, hexagonal) and can be made to almost any size. Cheaper plastic versions can also be used but may scratch, eventually discolor, and become brittle. Aquaria are ideal for amphibians because they are leakproof, retain high humidity, and allow clear observation of the specimens. They can be used immediately for fully aquatic and terrestrial amphibians, but for semi-aquatic species such as newts that spend only part of the year in the water, some modification may be required such as partitioning or implementation of some sort of shelf.

For shy or secretive species the "openness" of four glass sides can be rather stressful. To overcome this simply use a paper or plastic background scene sheet, gluing it to the sides and back of the aquarium so that only a front view is possible.

Amphibians, especially salamanders, are masters of escape, so ensuring that the lid of the aquarium is tight-fitting is critical. Most aquaria are supplied with a hood for a tropical fish display which encompasses strip lighting and/

Any pet shop stocks a variety of sizes and shapes of all-glass aquaria that can serve as perfect homes for almost all amphibians. They are relatively cheap, easy to find, and fit an array of accessories. Photo courtesy of California Aquarium Supply.

Tight-fitting screen covers, preferably ones that lock into place, are necessary for many amphibians—even a small salamander can climb up vertical glass walls to escape. Photo courtesy of Four Paws.

or incandescent lamp fixtures. Such hoods often are loose-fitting and have gaps or ventilation openings through which many amphibia could escape. Such openings obviously must be securely covered with tape or plastic and all the corners must be secured to ensure a tight fit. If possible, try and obtain the flat lids that are made specifically for herptiles. These have a sliding door for swift entry into the aquarium, plugged openings for light fixtures and cables, plus good ventilation where the holes aren't too large.

Many pet shops carry a variety of terraria in several sizes and designs, including some specifically made for tree-dwelling frogs (tall, well-ventilated tanks). They also stock locking tank lids of several types that allow you to safely access the tank for feeding and cleaning without removing the lid and also to control the humidity of the container to some extent.

PLACEMENT OF THE TERRARIUM

You may have a room put aside to house all your aquaria and terraria, or you may prefer to have one or two attractive display cabinets situated in a living room. Custom-built terraria or aquaria that have been meticulously furnished to recreate a natural setting and placed within a book shelf, on top of a table, or constructed to fit neatly into an alcove in a wall or above a fireplace provide a focal point for any room.

Before putting the terrarium in place, considerations need to be made as to how much sunlight

Attractive background sheets both are easy on the eye of the hobbyist and help shy amphibians feel more at home in a darkened habitat. Photo courtesy of Creative Surprizes.

that position receives. Direct sunlight, especially in the summer season, can be a deathtrap for amphibians even if it only catches the terrarium for ten minutes. Where any uncertainty of the sunlight's strength exists in a room, using artificial lighting means an amphibian terrarium can be situated in the gloomiest corner or even in complete darkness.

External temperatures also play an important role. Rooms that are already heated restrict or prevent the need for internal terrarium heating, although it is always best to have a supplementary back-up with a thermostat just in case. Yet such warmth would not be suitable for many salamanders and cold-temperate frogs. Rooms that receive no heat most of the time can chill tropical species if their terrarium heaters are underpowered or no provision is made for low external temperatures. In such circumstances correctly powered heating units that are thermostatically regulated are essential.

ARRANGING THE TERRARIUM

The terrarium can be a miniature playground for the landscape architect. It can be molded and manipulated to form a highly attractive section of rainforest or cool temperate woodland bog. The possibilities are endless and limited only by space, personal taste, and the artistic ability of the hobbyist. Yet there is a question: is it necessary to go to all this trouble? Perhaps for a zoological reptile house or other public display the answer is yes, because such places need to attract people. You as a hobbyist may feel the need to recreate a slice of nature, especially if the terrarium is to be a focal point in a popular room. On the other hand, many of the amphibians available to hobbyists will live and breed quite happily in the most basic of setups, and only a small number will not. The way in which a terrarium is decorated also depends on other factors. The creation and upkeep of a detailed natural layout can be costly. The more detailed a terrarium is, the more time-consuming it is to construct and the more time is required afterward for general maintenance.

Many hobbyists like to cover at least part of the terrarium floor with safe wood chips. Photo courtesy of Four Paws.

Furnishings also can depend on the amphibian's habitat preference. For example, certain salamanders such as mountain salamanders (*Euproctus*) and red salamanders (*Pseudotriton*) prefer moving water to breed, so provisions for such an environment should be considered. Conversely, mole salamanders (*Ambystoma*) and anurans such as horned frogs (*Ceratophrys*) tend to spend much of their time buried in leaf litter or moss, meaning that over-elaboration is unnecessary. Remember that many amphibians lead a double life on land and in water. If space does not allow both of these habitats to be combined into one terrarium, then the same terrarium can be completely transformed to one or the other at the relevant time, suggesting that a detailed setup might be less favorable.

WATER

Before examining the different approaches for arranging a terrarium, the aspect of using water in an amphibian setup is a highly important yet often overlooked factor in successful maintenance. All amphibians absorb moisture through their skin, with many returning to water at some stage in their life to breed, bathe, or slough their skin. In terraria that have a water source either in the form of a bowl or the aquatic section of an aqua-terrarium, contact with water will be more

When used as part of a terrarium scene, ceramic and plastic decorations can fit in well and spice up the appearance of the terrarium. Photo courtesy of Blue Ribbon Pet Products.

frequent because of the enclosed space in which to explore. Therefore the use of clean water free of harmful toxins and excessive alkalinity or acidity is vital.

The most common source of water is from the tap, and in most cases this has been disinfected by a chlorination or fluoridation process. The amount of such disinfectant residuals that are still present depends on the exact way in which the water was treated, and it will do little to harm amphibians that enter water only occasionally, but for those species that spend long periods bathing, swimming, or are predominantly aquatic, allow the water to stand for 24 hours in a container with a broad surface area, during which chlorine evaporates into the atmosphere. Aquatic eggs and larvae of all amphibians should never be placed directly into tap water even if it has stood for 24 hours. First it should be mixed in equal proportions (50:50) with pre-boiled rain or matured pond water. If your local water source adds ammonia during processing (to produce the extremely toxic compound chloramine), you will have to add detoxifying agents available from your pet shop in order to be sure of the safety of the water.

Some waters also are hard (high in minerals, usually calcareous salts), which can cause blockages in larval respiratory systems or stunt growth. This can be improved by boiling then drawing off the top three-quarters of the water with a siphon and discarding the remainder. Avoid using water that has been treated with a household water softener, as this may contain residual chemical salts that are lethal to amphibians.

Most amphibians prefer a pH (a measure of the acidity or alkalinity) in the region of 5.8 to 7.8. Species that either fall outside this range or have a strict pH requirement will be mentioned in the species sections. The lower the pH the higher the acidity, 0 being the maximum acidity, 7 neutral, and 14 the maximum alkalinity. Test kits and electronic units are available for testing pH and may prove a worthwhile investment, especially if there is uncertainty about water quality. Similar kits for testing nitrate and ammonia levels resulting from decaying vegetation and amphibian defecation in aquatic setups are useful and are readily available at any pet shop.

THE SUBTERRANEAN TERRARIUM

Caecilians and some salamanders spend virtually their entire lives tunneling through soft soils or moving around disused rodent burrows, while other salamanders inhabit caves. For troglodytic (cave-dwelling) salamanders, consistently cool temperatures and high humidity are essential and, depending on where you live, specialized electronic equipment may be required to achieve these conditions.

In the case of burrowing amphibians, an equal parts mixture of sifted peat moss and chopped live sphagnum moss makes an excellent medium because it retains both moisture and its springiness. Plastic containers, aquaria, and deep glass trays within a wooden terrarium should be preferred to a

All amphibians need water, and most of them need water bowls. This Marbled Salamander, *Ambystoma opacum*, looks at home in a simple saucer of water. Photo: W. P. Mara.

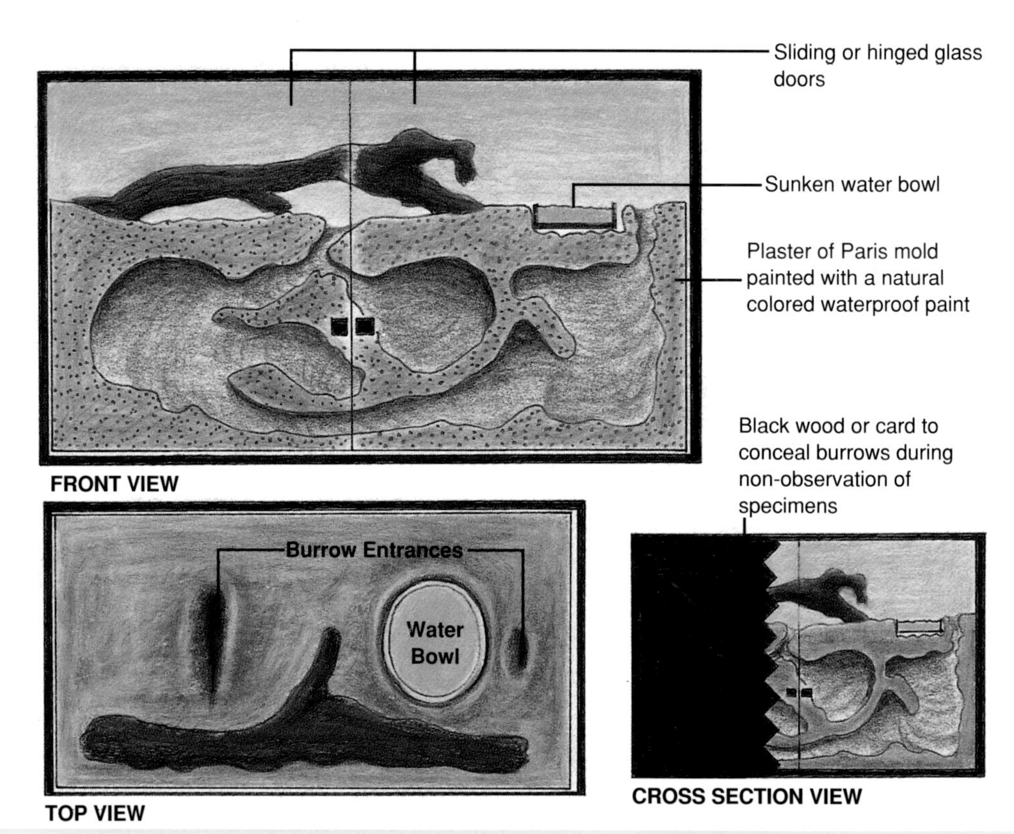

Diagrams for the construction of an artificial cave setup in a terrarium.

plain wooden terrarium only because the high humidity of this substrate will eventually seep in and warp the wood no matter how thoroughly the gaps have been sealed. After filling the container to three-quarters its depth, gently firm the substrate down before placing on the surface a few large decorative logs, pieces of cork bark, or slabs of lighter rocks such as tufa. Humidity levels will remain high beneath these even when the rest of the substrate begins to dry out, and they will be a favorite haunt of burrowers. A small water bowl should also be sunk into the substrate.

It is possible to view secretive amphibians such as cave salamanders (*Hydromantes*), certain plethodons, and American spadefoots (*Scaphiopus*) by constructing a plaster of Paris cast that slots neatly into a glass-fronted terrarium. In the plaster are set a network of tunnels that lead to a large underground hollow or "cave." The front part of the hollow should open out onto the glass door(s). To give the effect of darkness a wooden or black card "trap door" should be fixed to the outside of the glass with Velcro to block out the false hollow entrance. This is easily lifted when the salamanders need to be observed. To protect and give the plaster of Paris a natural finish it should be painted with a gray or brown waterproof paint. To maintain high humidity simply open the terrarium door and thoroughly mist the hollow with a hand sprayer several times a day. Where ambient air temperatures surrounding the aquarium are too warm (i.e., above 15°C, 59°F) for these salamanders to exist, then humidifying and cooling equipment located within the aquarium is essential.

THE TERRESTRIAL TERRARIUM

For predominantly terrestrial species this setup provides permanent housing, while for hobbyists who have limited space it can provide the land habitat of newts for part of the year before being completely transformed to an aqua-terrarium. The way in which this terrarium is furnished depends on the amphibian being kept. Remember that the more detailed the furnishing are, the more attention the setup requires for a healthy, disease-free environment.

Woodland and Forest

Ground-dwelling amphibians such as salamandrids and ranids spend much of their time concealed in and foraging through the damp, leafy, mossy undergrowth of woodlands. The base of the terrarium should have a 4– to 6-inch layer of small rocks that allow the amphibian access to hiding places in the gaps and crevices. This then is covered with a 1– to 2-inch layer of live sphagnum moss, a scattering of dead leaves (ideally large leaves of maples or beeches for temperate setups, large houseplant leaves for subtropical and tropical

A tropical woodland terrarium setup.

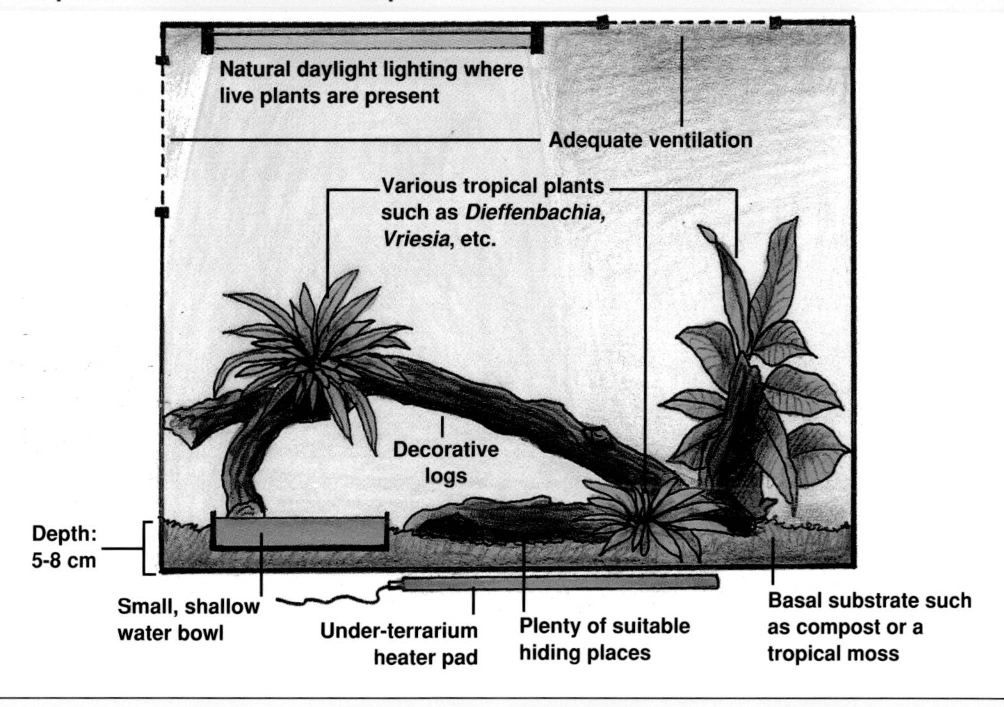

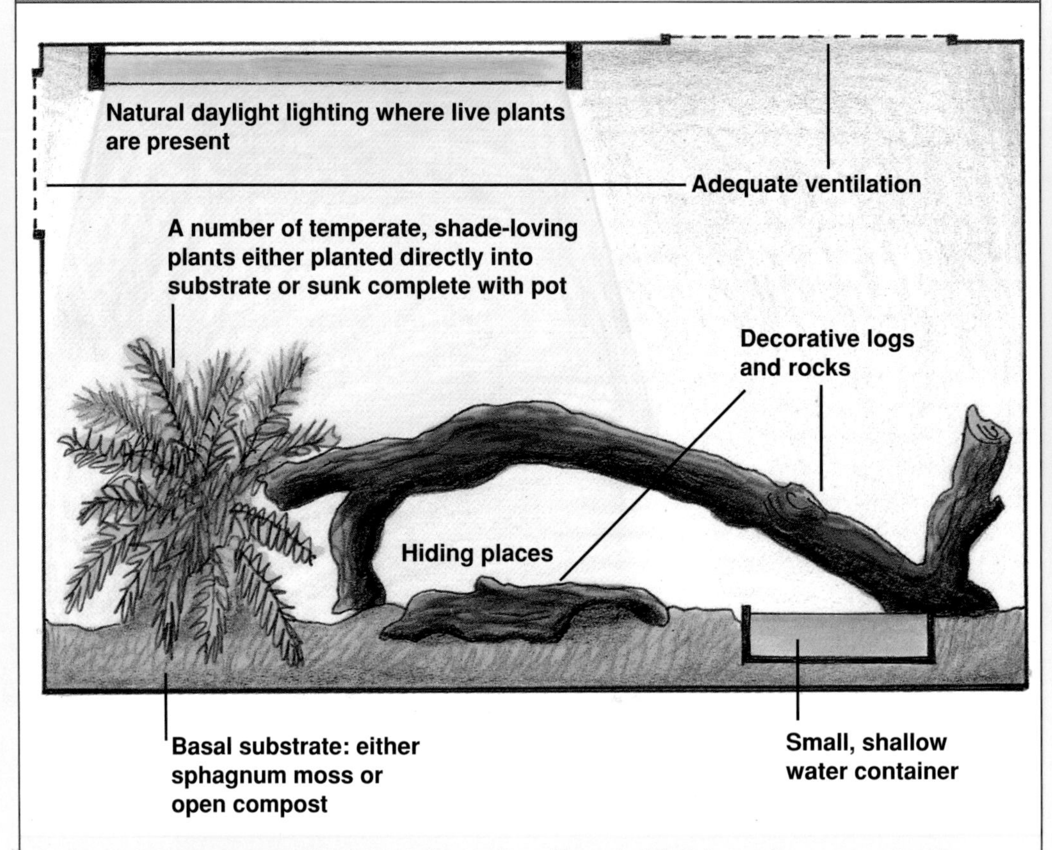

A simple temperate woodland terrarium setup. Many hobbyists prefer a very simple terrarium design that is easy to change and to keep clean.

setups), or a layer of chipped bark. Leaves and bark should first be sterilized in boiling water or over steam to destroy any potentially dangerous microorganisms. A water bowl should be placed toward one side of the terrarium, its size and depth dependent on the species's partiality to water. The remainder of the terrarium can be attractively furnished with robust logs, one or two rocks (granite, slate, or sandstone) and a selection of living plants.

Plants suitable for temperate setups that grow well indoors include ivies (*Hedera*), which can be trained to creep around logs, sedum, and arum lilies (*Zantedeschia aethiopica)* along with a variety of low-growing ferns. Suitable plants for the tropical terrarium include many popular house plants, with *Cryptanthus, Fittonia, Hedera helix, Maranta, Syngonium*, and the many miniature tropical ferns being particularly eye–pleasing. All plants should be grown in pots that are sunk into the substrate and provided with sufficient water and fertilizer as would be the case in the garden or home.

Grassland and Meadow

This habitat is mainly for cool-temperate and high altitude

By using processed sphagnum moss plugs it is possible to quickly establish plants in the terrarium. Photo courtesy of Aquarium Products.

amphibians such as the European and American typical frogs (*Rana*), newts, many true toads, Asian hynobiid salamanders, and some plethodons. Various subtropical anurans such as running frogs (*Kassina*) also occur in humid grasslands. An aquarium or terrarium incorporating a glass tray is most suitable because a moist basal substrate consisting of a peaty compost is required. In this can be planted low-growing or regularly trimmed grasses such as *Agrotis* and *Pennisetum* and small flowering plants including *Calceolaria* and *Primula*. Locate a shallow water bowl toward one side of the terrarium. Finally, put in a few pieces of bark, broken clay plant pots, and decorative rocks and logs for specimens to shelter beneath.

A grassland or meadow terrarium setup.

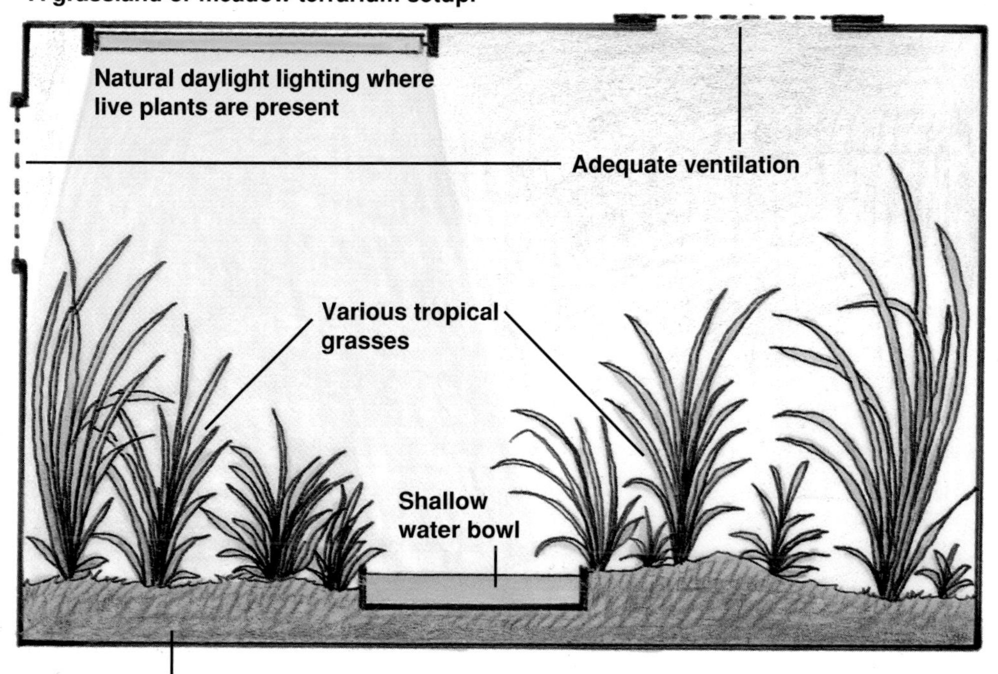

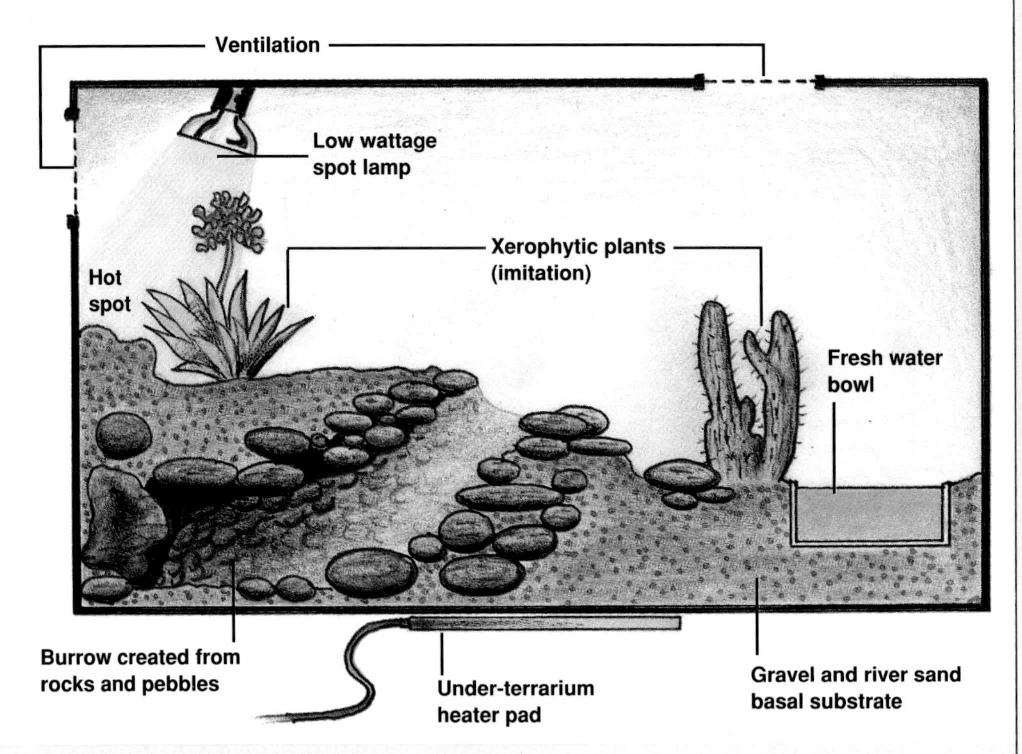

Schematic for a savannah or desert terrarium setup.

Savannah and Desert

Very few amphibians are true desert-dwellers because their permeable skins do not survive extended exposure to hot, dry environments. Surprisingly, some of the most popular anurans in captivity today, including the African Bullfrog and Ornate Horned Frog, are among those that have adapted to these harsh conditions. They manage this by being fossorial, burrowing deep into the soil and then covering themselves with a "cocoon" composed of several layers of sloughed epidermis, which reduces water loss. The basal substrate should consist of a gritty river sand that has been thoroughly washed to remove lime deposits that would otherwise cause sand to set like concrete. A few rocks placed on the surface will make the terrarium a little more appealing, but plants are irrelevant.

In truth, this specialist terrarium is only essential when breeding the mentioned species is to be attempted, for they also adapt to other setups. Australasian species such as the extremely popular non-fossorial White's Treefrog (*Litoria caerulea*), which inhabits arid areas and has a waxy skin that reduces water loss, and bufonids such as the Cane or Marine Toad (*Bufo marinus*) would make interesting inhabitants of this setup. Just remember to provide a small bowl of water in case they become too desiccated.

The Tall Planted Terrarium

The way a tall planted terrarium is furnished depends upon a species's habits, but the secret is to not include so many plants that the amphibians are always hidden from view. A basic requirement is a moist, soft basal substrate such as a compost that contains no insecticides, and into which several tall-growing plants and a few mosses are planted directly. Alternatively, plants can remain in pots that are then concealed with live sphagnum moss. Types of plants depend on the climatic conditions of the terrarium; *Dieffenbachia, Ficus, Philodendron, Sansevieria*, and *Scindapsus* are suitable for a tropical setup, while *Hosta, Hedera, Lilium*, miniature irises, and passion flowers are good temperate plants. An attractive piece or two of bogwood or driftwood can also be added, while the remainder of the setup depends on the species being kept, particularly its breeding behavior:

- Tropical anurans such as various dendrobatids and hylids (especially *Hyla bromeliacea*) have little or no need for a large water source in which to deposit eggs, instead utilizing water collected in the bracts of bromeliads and between leaves of plants. A shallow water dish no more than a few inches deep is sunk into the substrate, mainly for bathing. Holes drilled into branches can be packed with compost, providing a suitable anchor for epiphytic bromeliads, Spanish Moss (*Tillandsia usneoides*), and staghorn ferns (*Platycerium*).
- Climbing salamanders (*Aneides, Bolitoglossa*), certain arboreal *Eleutherodactylus* rainfrogs, and some microhylids require robust branches for their climbing activities, and in these are drilled large hollows for egg-laying sites. A small water bowl is required only for occasional bathing, with high humidity being much more important, especially when eggs are laid.
- Arboreal frogs such as the tropical rhacophorids require a shallow body of water in which to release tadpoles hatching from foam nests or sticky clumps of spawn that have been attached to vegetation, branches, or rocks that overhang the water source. Although furnishing this tank is similar to that of more typical tropical frogs, be sure that several plants, rock edges, or branches are directed over or actually enter the pool. The pool itself should be around 2 or 3 inches deep, with a gravel base and plenty of water plants such as dense-growing Willowmoss (*Fontinalis gracilis*) and Java Fern (*Ceratopteris thalictroides*), which grow well under artificial light.

Bear in mind that extremely high humidity levels are necessary for these frogs to

A tall planted terrarium setup that works well for dendrobatid and hylid frogs.

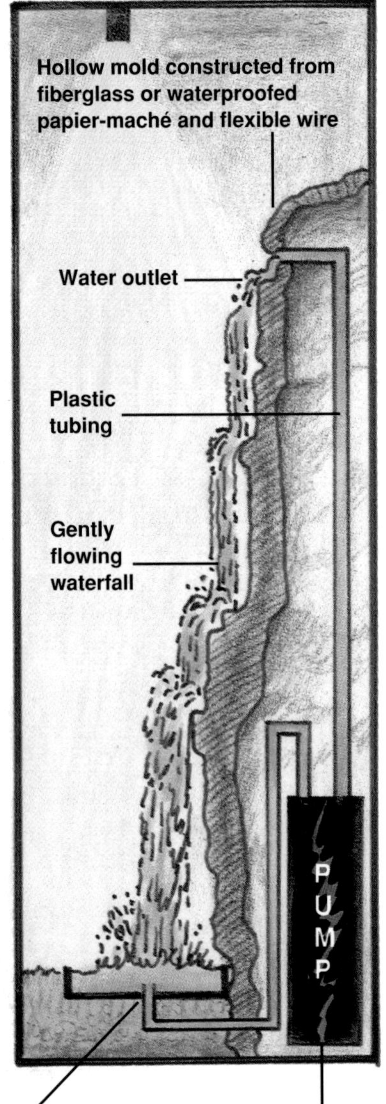

This simple tall planted terrarium works well for some climbing salamanders and frogs of the genus *Eleutherodactylus*.

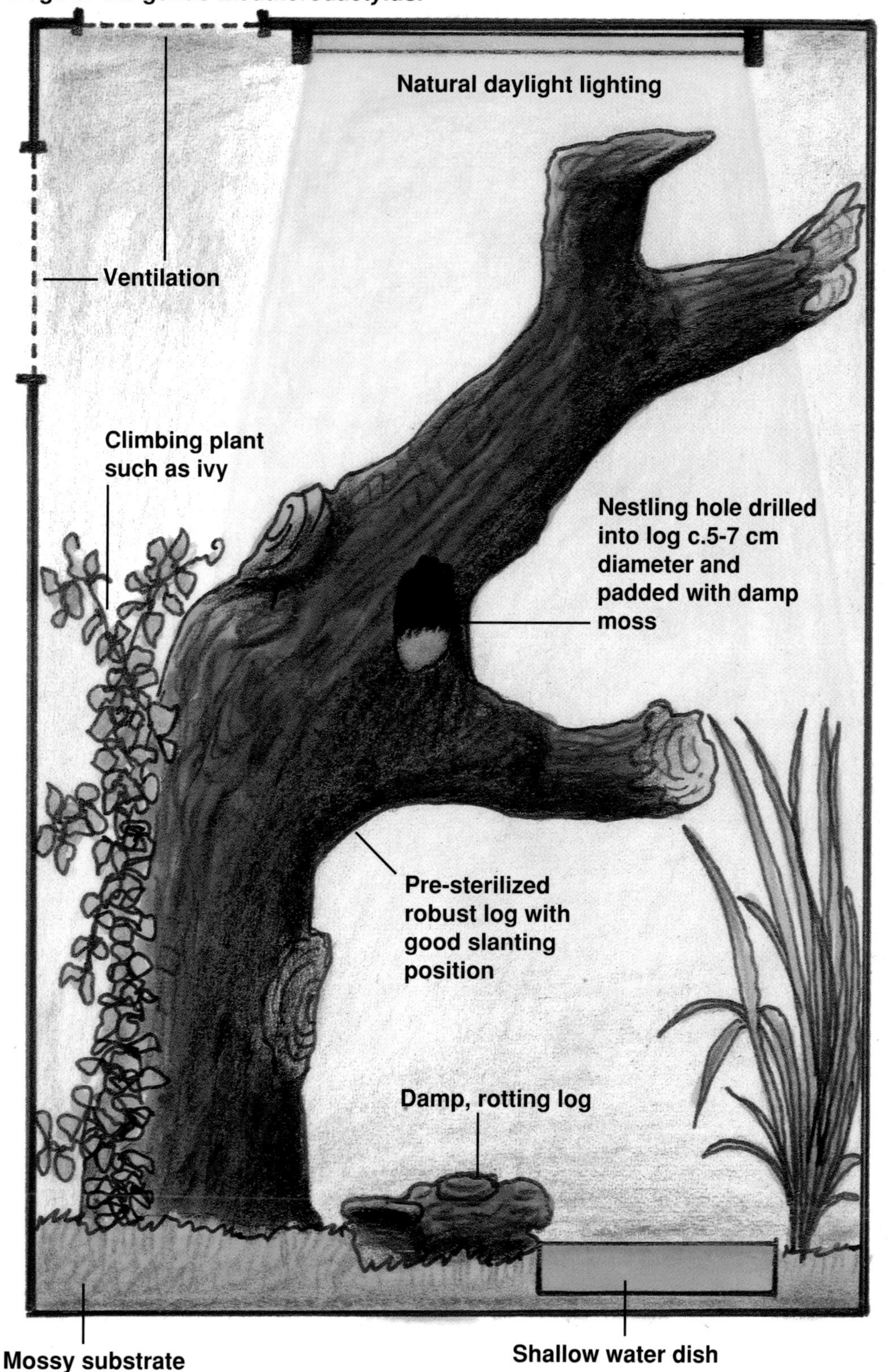

Foam nest treefrogs (Rhacophoridae) and other frogs that attach their eggs to objects overhanging water will appreciate this type of tall planted terrarium.

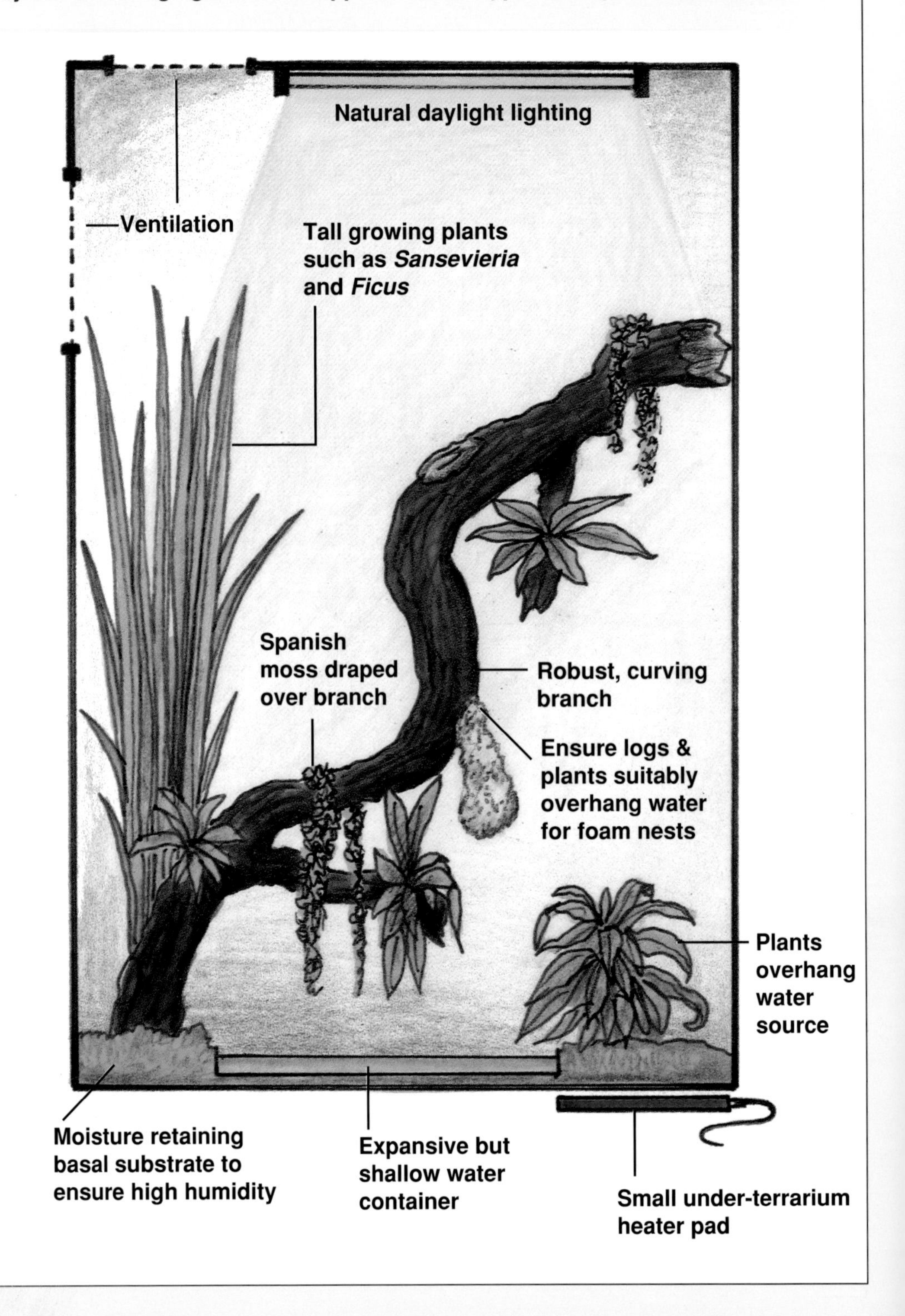

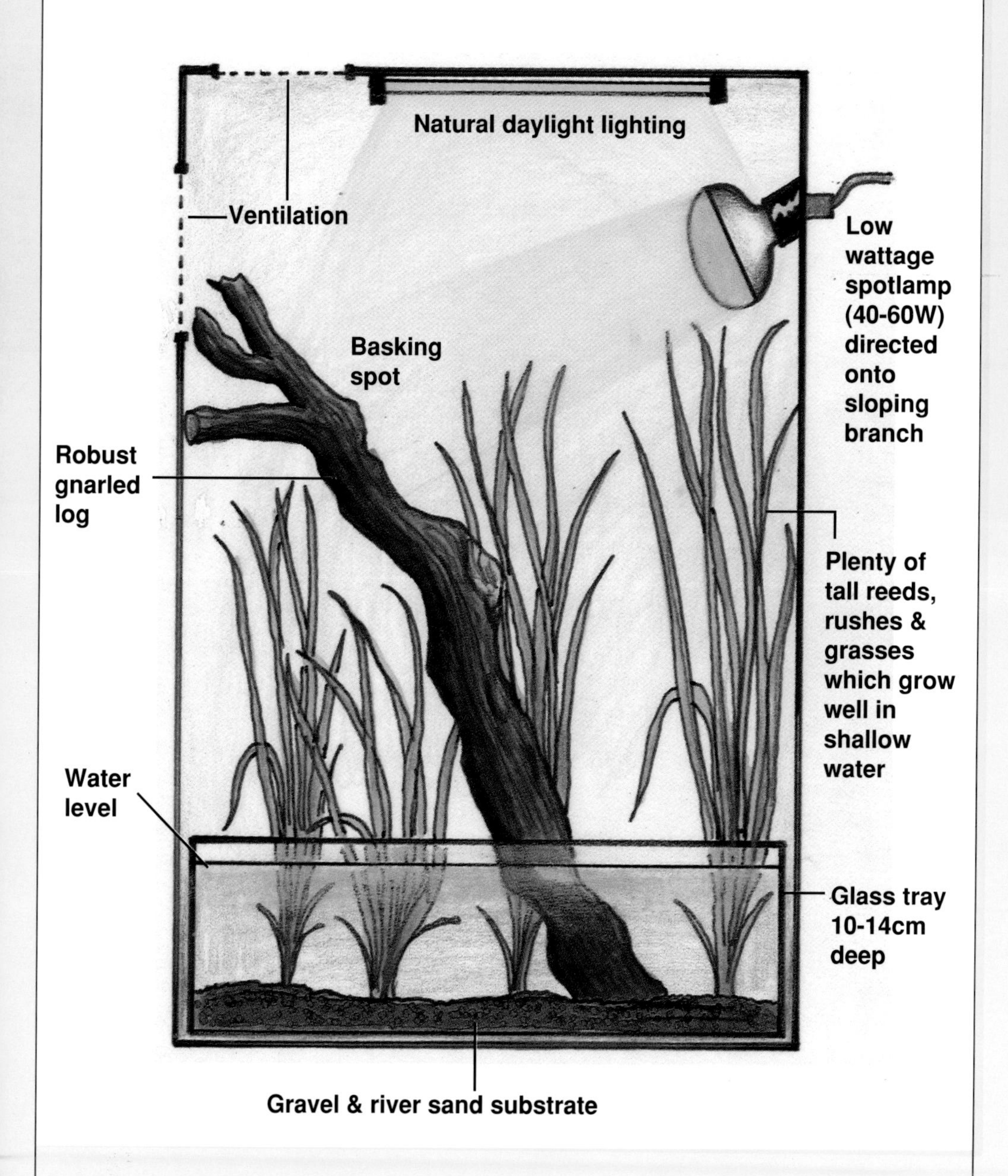

The relatively high standing water level works well for hyperoliids and some treefrogs in this tall planted terrarium design.

ensure that egg clumps or foam nests don't dry out. Incorporating a power-lift filter so water is lifted from the pool to an elevated position and then trickles back into the pool will create high humidity and keep water fresh. By using a suitably large rock or constructing a fiberglass frame that slots into a terrarium, an attractive small-scale waterfall could be created.

• Species such hyperoliids that inhabit reeds or other vegetation associated with the edges of ponds can be maintained in a terrarium in which the base consists of a water reservoir 1 to 6 inches deep in the form of either a large bowl or a glass tray. The bottom is filled with a layer of gravel or washed river sand and then with water. Water plants such as fanworts (*Cabomba*) and water trumpets (*Cryptocoryne*) are best for tropical setups, while *Elodea*, *Egeria densa*, and hornwort (*Ceratophyllum*) are ideal in cooler terraria. Floating plants, including *Nuphar* (spatterdock) species and Frog-bit (*Hydrocharis morsus-ranae*), will further enhance the terrarium. Rocks and robust driftwood branches should protrude from the water along with several pots containing tropical or temperate reeds, water rushes, and irises. If of sufficient depth, the water should include an undergravel filtration system to keep it in pristine condition.

Several types of bromeliads form most of the plantings in this beautiful terrarium. Notice the natural cork backing. Photo: R. Bechter.

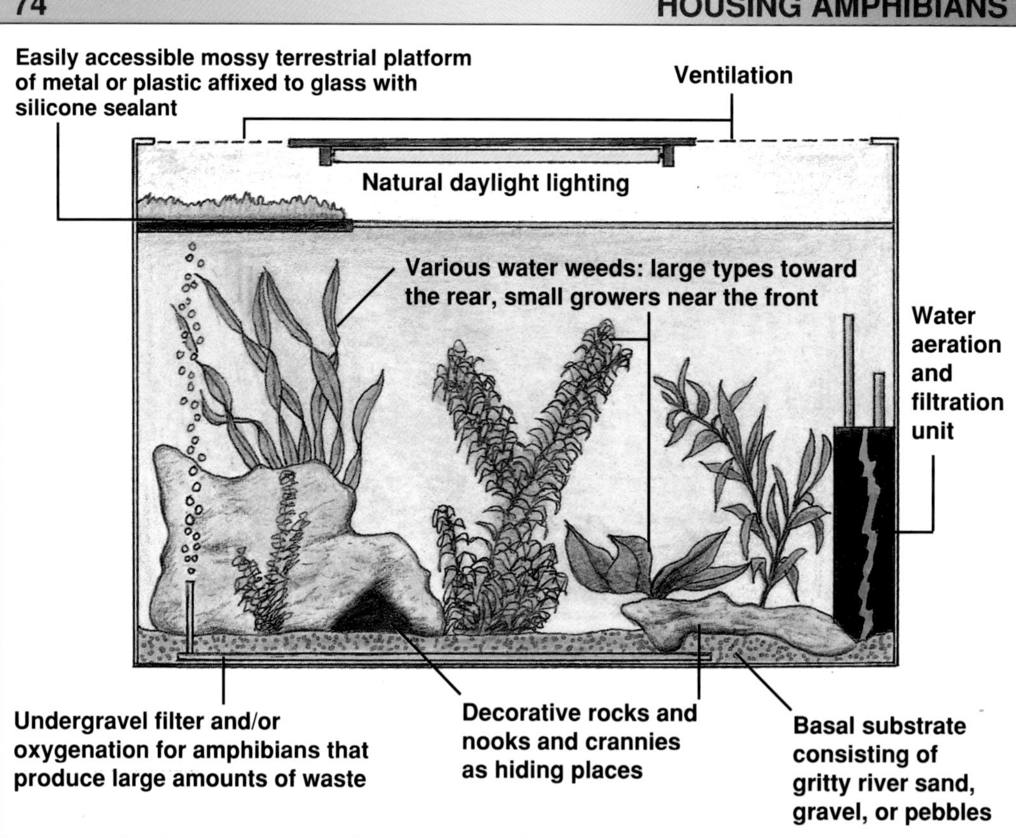

For fully aquatic newts and clawed frogs you need to set up an aquarium.

AQUATIC HABITATS

This type of display houses some of the most popular, interesting, and easily maintained amphibians such as Axolotls and various pipids. It also can provide temporary housing for amphibians such as newts that cyclically congregate in water to attract mates, perform courtship rituals, mate, and then lay eggs. The aquatic environment also is needed for the eggs and larvae produced by the majority of amphibians to progress through to metamorphosis stage.

A glass aquarium is really the only choice for this setup, but if you wish it can be set into a wooden cabinet to reduce the "openness" that can cause stress in some amphibians. The substrate can be one of three materials; river sand, smooth gravel, or large pebbles (particularly useful for robust or destructive types such as Axolotls). Set into the substrate a few rocks that aren't so big that they give an unnatural impression of depth. All of the water plants named in the arboreal and aqua-terrarium setups are useful for less robust species. Many species of newts (*Triturus*) prefer broad-leafed water plants that they wrap around their eggs. *Hygrophilia polysperma*, Eel Grass (*Vallisneria spiralis*), and even lily pads (*Nuphar* and *Nymphaea*) are particular favorites. For robust and destructive amphibians only

Don't be afraid to use high quality artificial plants in your terraria and aquaria. They look good and require minimal care compared to living plants. Photo courtesy of Hagen.

water plants with strong rootstocks and stems may survive. *Anubias*, water lace (*Aponogeton*), *Cryptocoryne*, and Amazon swordplants (*Echinodorus*) are good examples. Bunches of smaller plants should be fixed together with lead strips and placed toward the front, with larger plants located at the rear of the aquarium. Do not include so many plants that your specimens cannot be observed. Prune existing plants regularly.

As a precautionary measure, a small shelf of land should always be made available onto which even the most aquatic amphibians can climb. This can be in the form of a rigid plastic shelf fixed to one corner with silicone sealant or a slab of rock that protrudes from the water.

THE AQUATERRARIUM

This setup integrates both land and water and is suitable for those species that spend much of their time around the edges of ponds, streams, and rivers (e.g., fire-bellied toads, *Bombina*), those that congregate in water only part of the year to mate and spawn (e.g., typical newts, *Triturus*), and for salamanders that deposit their well-developed larvae into water (e.g., Fire Salamander, *S. salamandra*). There are several methods of achieving a land and water combination.

• Partitioning: Glass can be used to partition the aquarium into two halves by fixing it in place with aquarium silicone sealant. One part is filled with water, the other with a basal substrate such as sphagnum moss or peaty soil along with some decorative plants, rocks, and logs.
• Shelf: For species that enjoy basking and rarely burrow, a piece of rigid plastic can be used to create a shelf. This is sealed horizontally, but at a slight angle, to the aquarium side to give a gentle slope into the water. On this shelf are placed moss, logs, and plants before the aquarium is filled with water until it slightly overlaps the lower lip of the plastic.
• Logs and Rocks: A robust log can be used as a partition for a more natural effect, although water will leak through into the land area. Here use washed gravel to place the moss, logs, rocks, etc., on top. Alternatively, large rocks or slabs that have fairly flat tops can emerge from the water

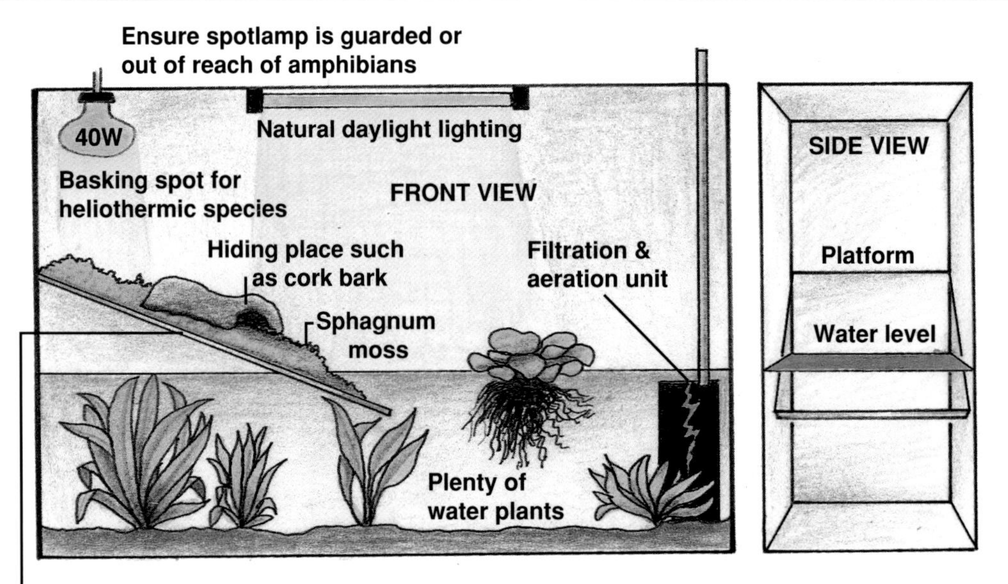

Diagram of an aquaterrarium for fire-bellied toads and adult newts, animals that need limited access to land.

This aquaterrarium is designed for amphibians that need a bit more access to land, including many types of newts and other salamanders as well as ranid frogs.

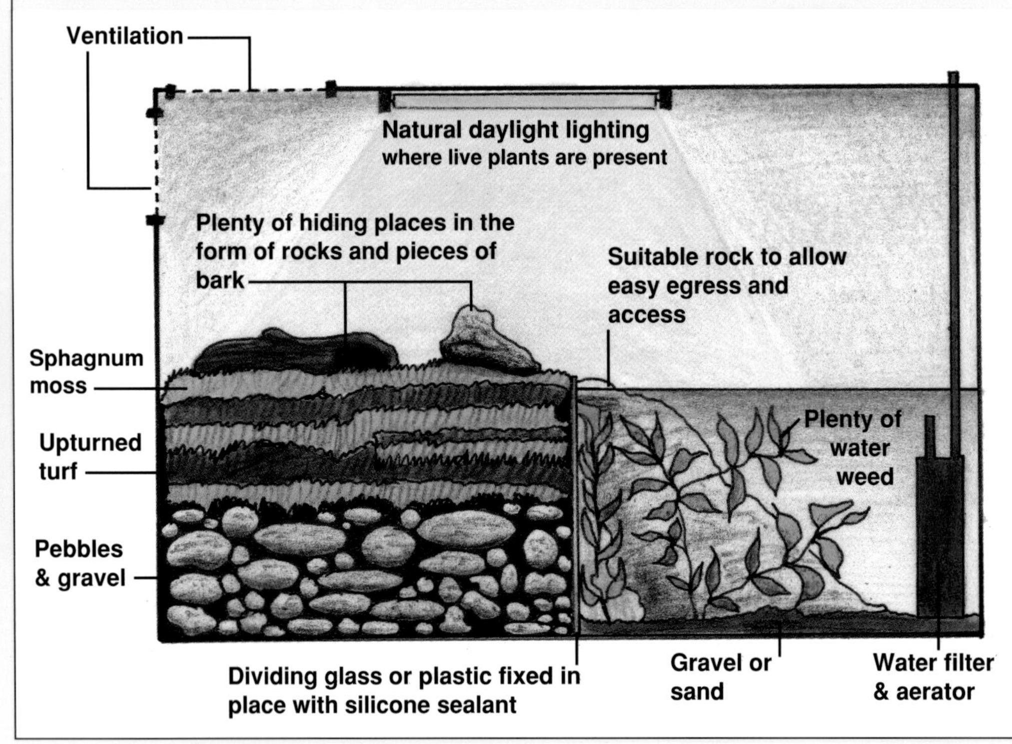

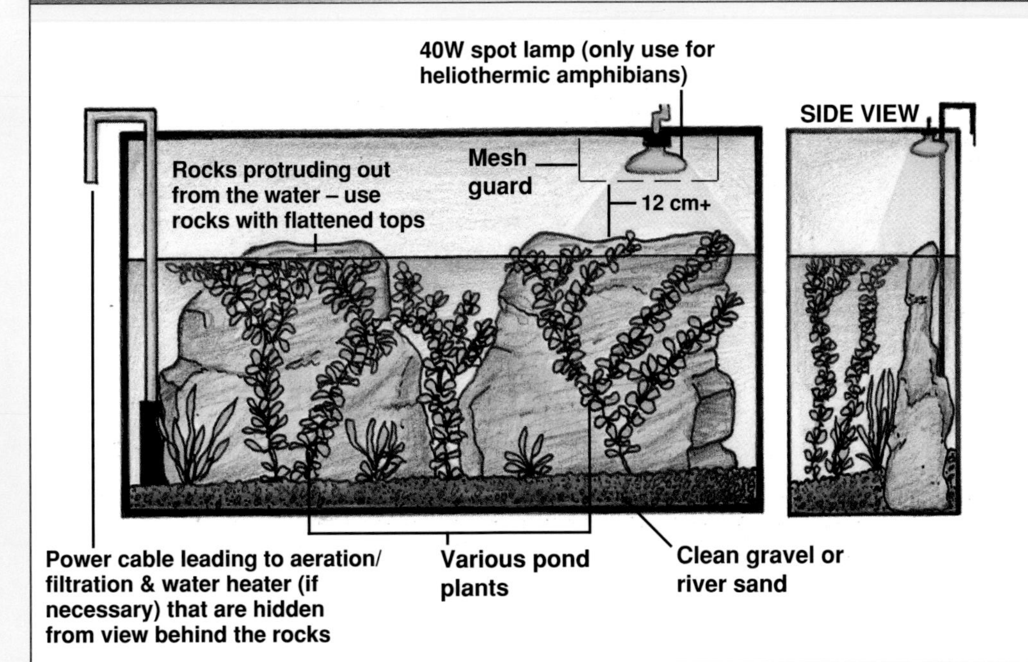

In the above aquaterrarium designed for largely aquatic amphibians, access to land is quite limited.

The shallow water and extensive land area of the aquaterrarium below provide safe surroundings for amphibians that need access to water yet swim poorly.

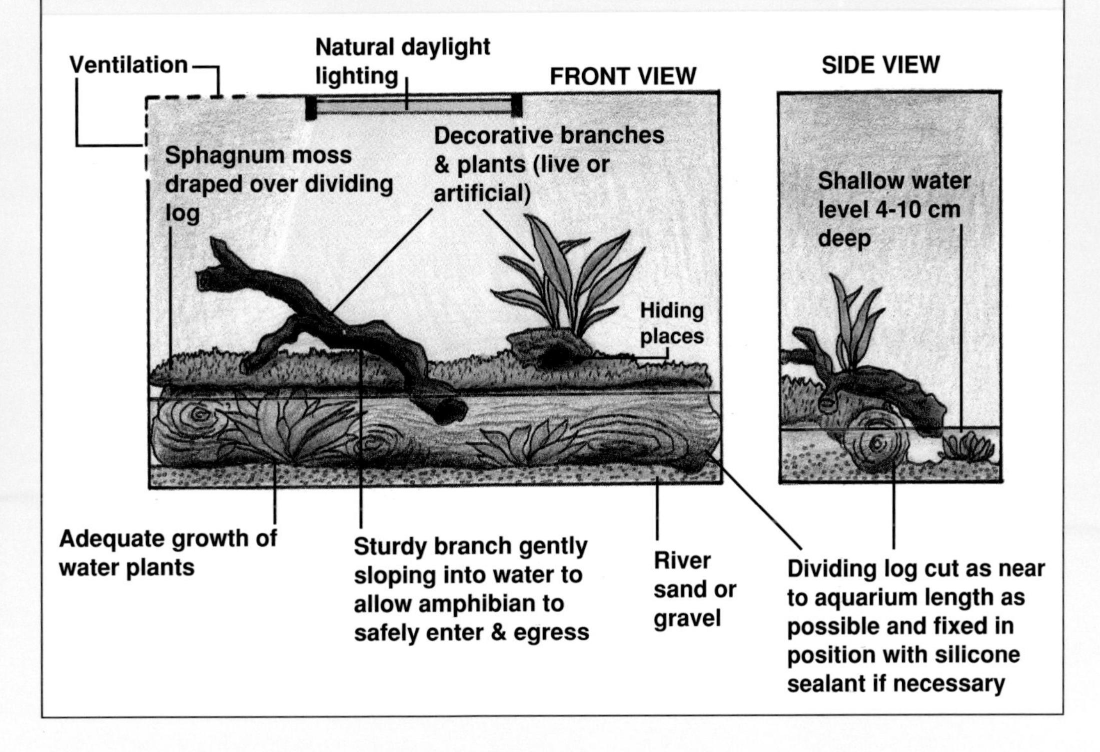

Many terrarium designs include a running stream or waterfall. For this you will need a strong, reliable aquarium pump and fittings. Photo courtesy of E. G. Danner, Inc.

and can then be decorated accordingly with moss, bark, etc.

Before incorporating a partition or shelf, the depth of the water must be considered because some amphibians lower just their abdomen into the water to deposit eggs, tadpoles, or larvae and are otherwise very inept swimmers. The aquatic side should be set up in the same manner as an fully aquatic setup, preferably including a filter that simultaneously aerates the water to ensure that it is kept relatively fresh. A number of water plants (i.e., *Elodea, Nitella,* and *Cabomba*) will oxygenate the water and absorb some of the excess nitrates. For deeper water reservoirs, include several weatherworn rocks such as granite, although generally avoid those with jagged edges that can inflict nasty injuries on the amphibian and those that slowly dissolve in water such as limestone and can cause excessive alkalinity.

THE SIMPLE TERRARIUM

However attractive the above terraria may appear, terrestrial planted terraria in particular need regular inspection and maintenance to preserve a clean, disease-free environment. For hobbyists who have limited

A very basic terrarium useful for rearing larger frogs. Notice the artificial substrate. Photo: M. Staniszewski.

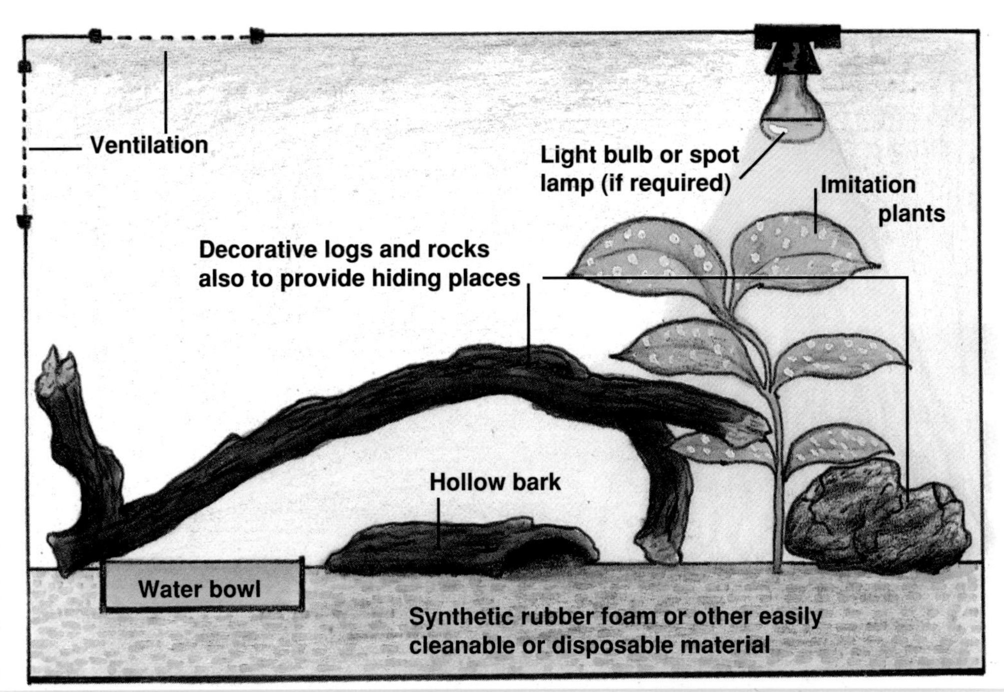

A simple hygienic terrarium suitable for horned frogs and African Bullfrogs, among others.

It's a good idea to invest in a small battery-powered air pump. These are useful in emergencies and also as intermittent sources of air for tadpole rearing tanks. Photo courtesy Hagen.

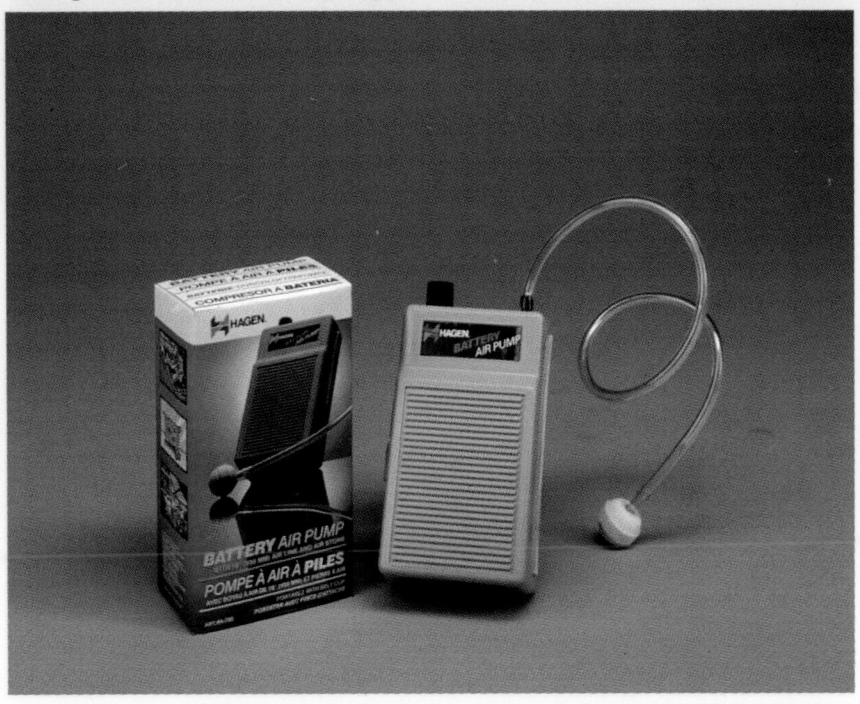

spare time or intend to maintain large numbers of specimens, alternative ways of keeping amphibians must be sought.

The container for this "laboratory-style" setup is at the discretion of the hobbyist, with plastic boxes, aquaria, and wooden terraria all serving the purpose adequately. The difference concerns the basic furnishing allowing easy removal and efficient cleaning, yet at the same time still providing the amphibian with its basic requirements. Sphagnum moss can be used as the base substrate because it is easily removed and rinsed. For the hygiene-conscious hobbyist, household items such as synthetic rubber foam, cotton material, and absorbent kitchen paper towels can be utilized. All provide a soft, moisture-retaining base and are easy to wash or dispose of and replace once soiled. Synthetic grass carpet (avoid the irritating long-pile type) can be used only for frogs originating from drier regions as it has little capacity to retain surface moisture. Even kitchen tiles that have a spongy PVC backing can be flipped over to form a comfortable smooth, dry surface.

This simple terrarium has proved sufficient to be used as a breeding setup for Golden Mantellas, *Mantella aurantiaca*. Photo: M. Staniszewski.

Decorations should comprise one or two nicely shaped rocks and hollow bark for the inhabitants to either retreat under or climb onto and a water bowl of sufficient size and depth. To give the setup a more natural feel, add a few artificial plants available from your pet shop and a piece of cork bark. In a simple aquatic setup plastic water plants that look strikingly real are good substitutes for the real thing.

ALTERNATIVE TERRARIA

A few hobbyists will have the space to construct a large-scale terrarium in the form of an outdoor enclosure, pond, or greenhouse. These exceptional terraria provide the opportunity to arrange an entirely natural environment in which can be kept a wide variety of different amphibian species. They also have the advantage of not requiring any form of lighting and heating unless species from warmer regions are to be kept. They only occasionally need maintenance and present few problems with regard to feeding because prey animals often will find their way into them and breed. Amphibians are more likely to breed and breed regularly in these outdoor setups, including some of the more difficult species.

The Outdoor Enclosure

An outdoor enclosure or amphibiary is limited with respect to the species of amphibians that it can maintain in that it depends entirely on the ambient climatic conditions. Hobbyists living in cold temperate regions will be able to keep only cold-temperate, cool-temperate, and possibly a few hardier warm-temperate species. Those living in warm-temperate regions may be able to keep only some cool-temperate, warm-temperate, and a few hardier subtropical species.

Most outdoor amphibiaries are built from bricks or concrete blocks, although sturdy smooth metal and thick, rigid PVC sheets can provide an acceptable substitute. The most important aspect to consider during design and prior to construction is to ensure that there are no potential escape points. Foundations should be fairly deep, in the region of 3 feet, while the height of the enclosing side walls depends on the amphibians to be kept, with around 2.5 feet for most salamanders and up to 4 feet for more agile ground frogs (hylids and other climbing frogs of course cannot be kept in an uncovered amphibiary). Where bricks or concrete blocks are cemented together it is wise to

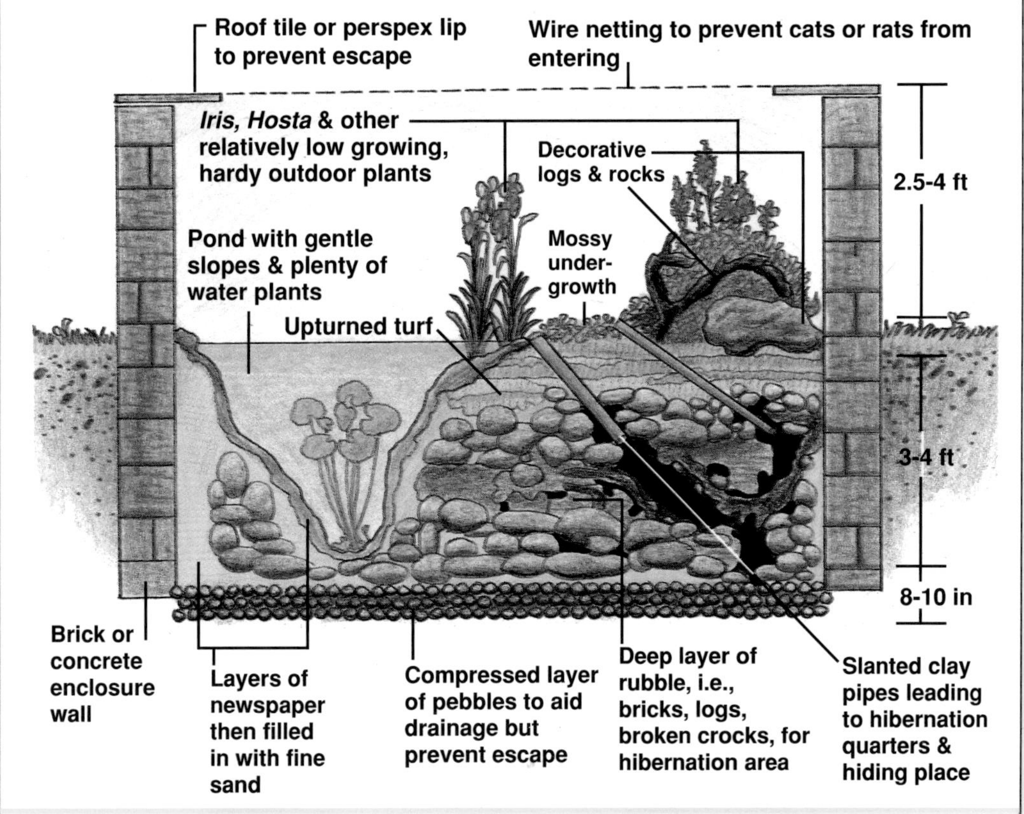

Diagrammatic cross-section of an outdoor enclosure for amphibians.

Top view of an outdoor enclosure.

Decorative logs and rocks

Chicken wire covering enclosure to prevent cats, rats & birds from entering

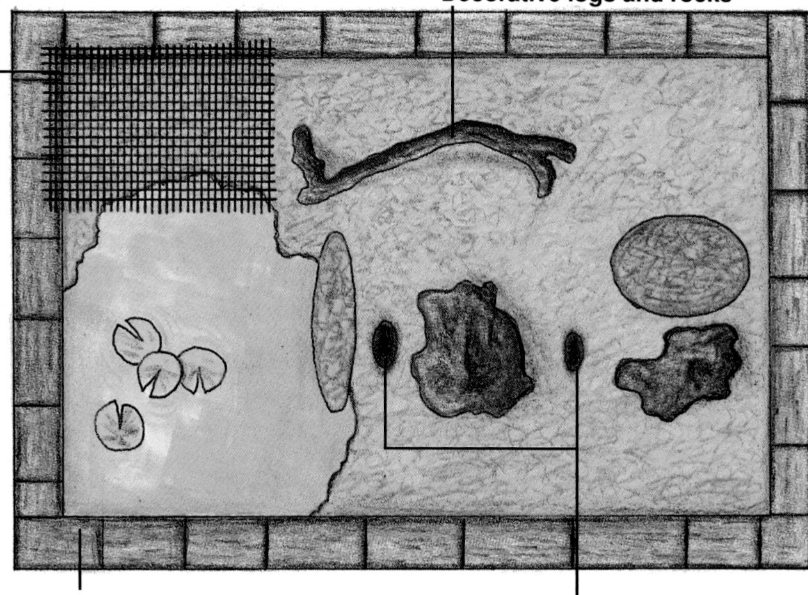

Overhanging “lip” made from roofing tiles or perspex concreted or screwed to top layer of bricks

Entrance via clay or concrete piping to hiding and hibernation quarters

add non-toxic hardening and waterproofing agents to the cement to increase its life, especially in places that experience frost, which causes brittleness. If plastic or metal sheets are used, they should be securely fixed with clips or screws at the corners and then sealed with silicone rubber. In terms of overall size, this depends on the number of species to be maintained. It is no use having a huge enclosure where only a dozen specimens are being kept as they will rarely if ever be seen. A good guideline is to allow 0.15 sq. m. of ground space for every amphibian the size of a Fire Salamander (i.e., a 3 m x 1.8 m enclosure could support around 36 adult Fire Salamanders).

An outdoor enclosure useful for temperate amphibians. Photo: M. Staniszewski.

Another necessity of an amphibiary is a overlapping lip on the topmost bricks or blocks. This can be in the form of roofing slates or bathroom tiles or wide strips of rigid PVC that should overlap by at least 6 inches and are fixed by cement and/or holding screws. To further decrease the risk of escape, a 6-inch PVC strip can be fixed to the inside of the wall about 3 inches below the overhanging lip.

Once constructed and before the substrate and decor have been incorporated, to aid the enclosure's drainage and prevent burrowing amphibia from tunneling through the base, spread a 4- to 6-inch layer of large stones or pebbles over the base and then compact these down.

The next stage involves determining the location of the pond, its overall size, and the material used to construct it. It is preferable to situate the pond in an area that receives half sun and half shade, although fringing plants can also be used as effective shading in full sun. Hobbyists living in warm regions will almost certainly need a pond that is in shade if cooler temperate species are to be kept, because otherwise the water may overheat and be unsuitable for breeding and egg and larval development. The size of the pond depends on the size of the enclosure and the aquatic tendencies of the species being maintained. Preformed pond materials come in many forms: PVC or butyl liners, prefabricated molds such as fiberglass or rigid plastic, old bathtubs and sinks, and concrete mixed with waterproofing agents. Liners are more flexible than others, and butyl in particular will have a long life. Concrete and prefabricated molds that look like rock pools are more natural, but in areas that experience harsh frosts they are liable to become brittle or crack.

The actual building of a pond is too complicated to go into here and is likely to appeal to only a small part of the reading audience. T.F.H. publishes many good books on various aspects of building and maintaining ponds and on the various plants that are used in and around them. See your local pet shop for these books if backyard ponds appeal to you.

Apart from ensuring that amphibians cannot escape, it is equally important to thwart potential predators such as rats, herons, and raptors (birds of prey) from entering the enclosure. Construct a wooden– or metal-framed wire assembly that fits neatly over the top of the enclosure. Where amphibian-eating snakes are common the assembly must consist of a small gauged chicken wire. For added protection in places that experience cold conditions, rigid plastic sheets can be placed over the whole enclosure.

The Greenhouse Amphibiary

In the outdoor enclosure the ambient outdoor climate restricts the number of species that can be maintained in this manner, but in an area totally confined within a glass or rigid plastic structure such as a greenhouse, climatic conditions can be artificially manipulated to enable less hardy amphibians to be maintained even in cold places. A greenhouse also is suitable for arboreal frogs such as hylids and rhacophorids that would otherwise escape from a walled enclosure. A greenhouse also provides better protection against extremely cold spells for temperate species.

Greenhouses come in varying shapes, sizes, and frame materials, but generally if it is solid and there are no missing or cracked window panes then with a little adjustment all these are suitable. All gaps and holes (i.e., where window panes join or reach a corner, or where the greenhouse sits on a base) must be sealed with silicone sealant or cement.

As with an outdoor enclosure, foundations should preferably be brick and reach a depth of 2 to 3 ft, and the pond or hibernation quarters are arranged in exactly the same way. Where decor is concerned, attempt to replicate the habitat of the amphibians intended to be kept. A greenhouse provides an opportunity to develop several microhabitats to keep a variety of species. An example of several temperate microhabitats within the boundary of one greenhouse could be a dry rockery (bufonid and spadefoot toads) from which begins a stream that is edged by various ferns and mosses (brook/gold-striped/red salamanders) and leads down to a large pond (many amphibians) encircled by bog plants such as irises and water marigolds (treefrogs). In a tropical arrangement there might be a swampy pond (many frogs

Partial side view and cross-section of a temperate greenhouse in which amphibians can be kept successfully.

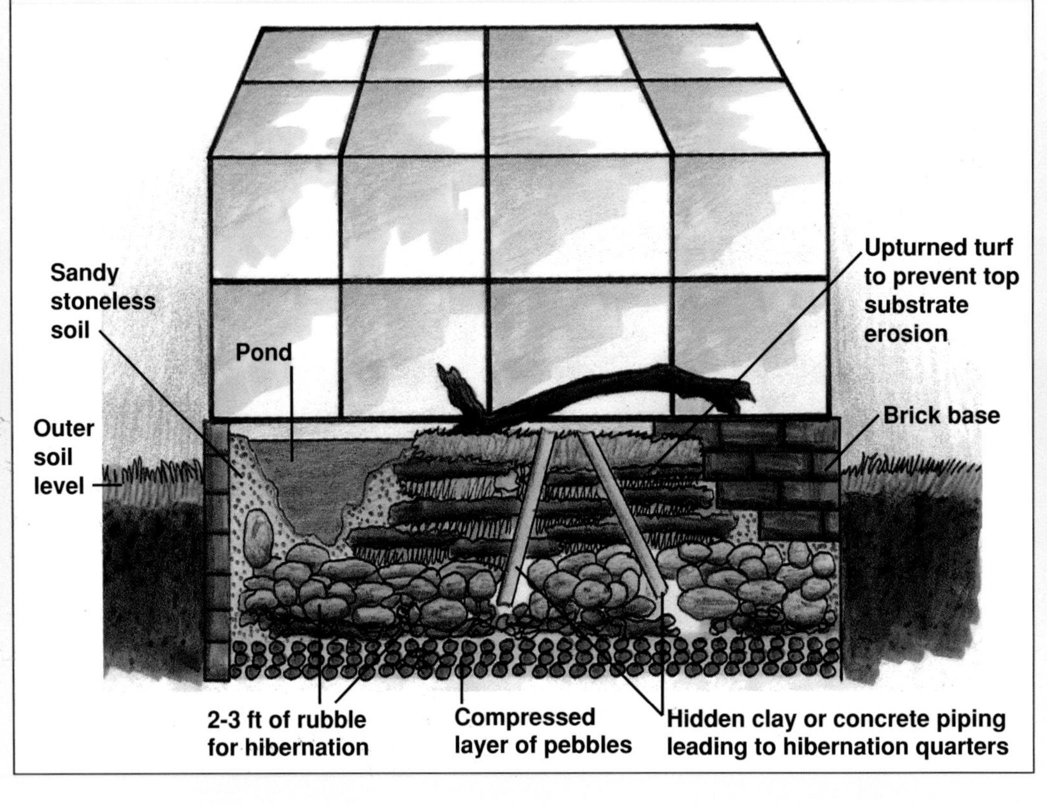

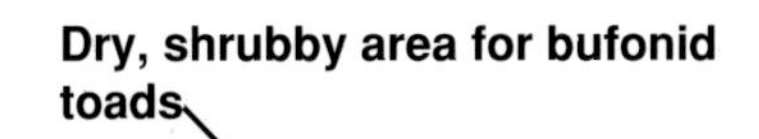

Diagram of a temperate to warm temperate greenhouse enclosure.

and aquatic caecilians) with high reeds (tree– and reedfrogs) in one corner and a humid leafy floor (woodland and burrowing frogs) in another.

Whatever the setup, the climatic conditions are of utmost importance. For instance, in a place where the ambient climate is relatively cool such as the northern USA, Canada, or western Europe, cool-temperate or even warm-temperate amphibians can be kept *in situ* without the need for supplementary heating because the greenhouse temperature will always be one or two degrees higher than outside. Yet if subtropical or tropical species are housed in a greenhouse located in a cold climate, then additional thermostatically controlled heating is required. This must be on standby all year round even during summer because nighttime or overcast daytime temperatures may fall to a level lethal to such amphibians. Electricity is a clean, efficient, and safe source of heating for greenhouses, with horticultural fans or convection heaters that are enclosed in a protective wire frame being the most suitable.

A problem with a totally enclosed greenhouse, even in cool-temperate regions, is that radiant heat from the sun is magnified and retained until temperatures are too high even for tropical species. Some form of shading is a necessity and can be accomplished by painting a translucent whitewash liquid onto the greenhouse roof or by using blinds or small mesh plastic netting. Some form of ventilation may still be required even when shading is present, therefore screen off door or window openings with insect netting or a small mesh chicken wire. Where there are no climbing amphibians, open a roof window during the day to allow insects passage into the greenhouse.

The greenhouse amphibiary. Photo: M. Staniszewski.

During cold spells the use of an insulating material such as sheets of bubble plastic fixed to the inside can cut down on heating costs where tropical species are being kept, and as a precautionary measure it is wise to have a back-up heater ready just in case the main heater fails. Most amphibians like moist humid conditions, so damping down the greenhouse regularly, particularly on very warm days, is critical. One method is to permanently fix a length of plastic hose pipe in an elevated position, seal the outlet end with a clip, and then puncture a series of 2-mm diameter holes along its length. Feed its trailing end through a hole drilled through the greenhouse base to which a separate hose pipe can be connected when watering is required. Water forced through the punctures creates a very fine spray without disrupting the decor and can be left on for around a hour or so to ensure a good soaking. In tropical setups that experience high humidity such an arrangement can be controlled by a humidity sensor.

Facing page: **A tropical greenhouse is able to support many different types of amphibians. Photo: M. Staniszewski.**

A greenhouse enclosure used for temperate amphibians. Photo: M. Staniszewski.

Whatever the setup, always try and keep one corner drier than the rest because even amphibians will sometimes wish to escape from incessantly damp conditions, particularly toads.

HEATING

Amphibians are ectotherms; that is to say, their body temperature is influenced by the temperature of their immediate surroundings. Different species have different critical body temperatures (the temperature at which activity and metabolic rates are at a peak). Outside these ranges an amphibian either becomes sluggish or hyperactive and may hibernate or estivate...or die. In captivity the hobbyist must provide either the correct critical temperatures for the species being kept or suitable hibernating/ estivating quarters. As a rule, amphibians originating from cold and cool-temperate regions need little or no supplementary heating whereas those found in regions that experience no excessively cold periods must be provided with a temperature suitable to maintain their own critical body temperature all year. Fortunately the range of equipment available today has made this once difficult aspect of successful amphibian husbandry much easier.

Types of heaters

• Tungsten light bulb and spot lamp usage as a heat source is severely limited for amphibians because higher wattage types in particular can damage an amphibian's thin epidermis very quickly even in species that have a relatively dry appearance. Where used they must be well out of reach or protected by a mesh guard. Many semi-aquatic amphibians such as fire-bellied toads, bullfrogs, and ribbed newts (*Pleurodeles*) are heliotherms (enjoy basking in sun) and benefit from a 40W or 60W lamp positioned toward one side of the terrarium so that they can seek out a cooler spot should they overheat. This is known as a thermal gradient.

Temperature ranges for amphibians from different climatic bands, indicating tolerance. Outside these ranges the amphibian either hibernates, estivates, or dies.

Climatic Conditions	Species Example	Lowest Temp	Highest Temp
Cold	Siberian Salamander (*Hynobius keyserlingi*)	0°C	20°C
Cool Temperate	Common Toad (*Bufo bufo*)	4°C	25°C
Temperate	Marbled Newt (*Triturus marmoratus*)	8°C	25°C
Warm Temperate	Green Toad (*Bufo viridis*)	10°C	28°C
Warm	Colorado River Toad (*Bufo alvarius*)	15°C	30°C
Subtropical	Cuban Treefrog (*Osteopilus septentrionalis*)	22°C	30°C
Tropical	Strawberry Poison Frog (*Dendrobates pumilio*)	25°C	32°C
Savannah	Argentine Horned Frog (*Ceratophrys ornata*)	12°C	35°C
Arid/Desert	White's Treefrog (*Litoria caerula*)	8°C	38°C

Correct heater power for water reservoir

Dimensions of Water Reservoir (either the aquarium or water bowl within a terrarium) **(Inches)**	**Approximate Power of Heater Required (Watts)**
9 x 10 x 10	15-30
18 x 10 x 10	30-60
24 x 12 x 12	75-100
36 x 12 x 12	100-150
48 x 15 x 15	120-180
60 x 18 x 18	150-210

Critical body temperatures of various amphibians

These ranges represent the temperature at which amphibians from different climatic areas show proper metabolism and normal behavior. Outside these ranges the amphibian will either hibernate, estivate, or die. Relative humidity levels may also have a similar influence on less tolerant species.

Climatic Condition	**Typical Species Example**	**Critical Body Temperature Range**
Cold Temperate	Siberian Salamander (*Hynobius keyserlingi*)	30 - 60° F
Cool Temperate	Leopard Frog (*Rana pipiens*)	43 - 75° F
Warm Temperate	Green Toad (*Bufo viridis*)	54 - 80° F
Subtropical	Running Frog (*Kassina senegalensis*)	68 - 85° F
Tropical	Uruguayan Atelopus (*Melanophryniscus stelzneri*)	75 - 90° F
Arid	African Bullfrog (*Pyxicephalus adspersa*)	62 - 95° F
Cave Dweller	Italian Salamander (*Hydromantes italicus*)	46 - 58° F

• Heater pads represent a good way of sustaining higher temperatures within the terrarium should temperatures outside become too cool. Most pads are placed beneath the base of the container on top of a layer of 5–mm styrofoam. For all but the lowest wattage models, some type of thermostatic control is recommended. Such pads also have the advantage of evaporating moisture in the substrate to create the humid atmosphere appreciated by many tropical anurans. Bear in mind that in the moist and planted terraria, the substrate directly above the pad will eventually dry out, so regularly spraying the terrarium is critical. For this reason never use a pad that covers the entire base of the terrarium. Also attempt to locate the pad away from shallow water bowls or ponds that will dry out too quickly. In tall planted setups sufficient heat may not rise to the upper reaches from pads located at the base, therefore fix one to the side of the terrarium.

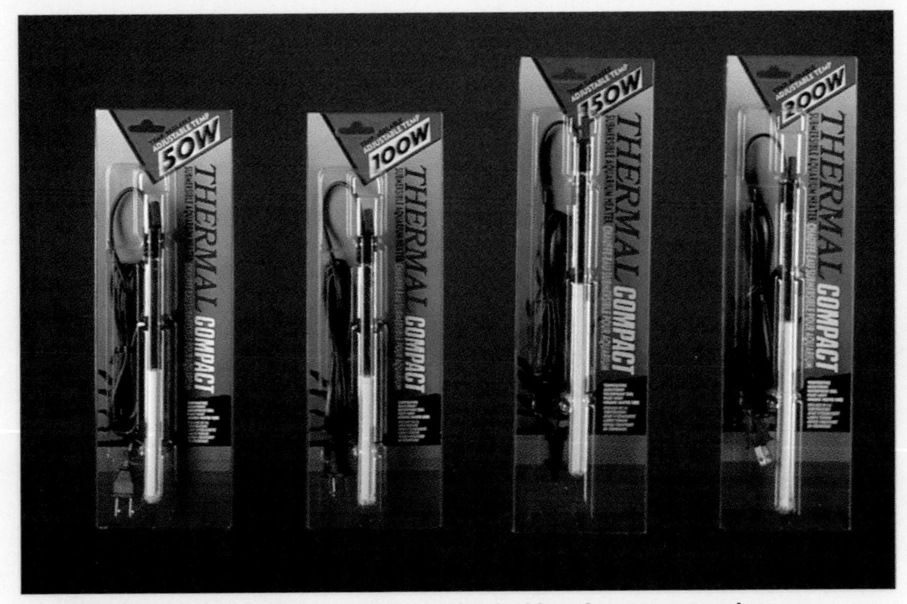

Aquarium heaters provide a simple method of heating any aquarium or aquaterrarium that contains a deep body of water. Photo courtesy of Hagen.

In arid areas where temperatures drop to near freezing at night, frogs will seek out and rest on large flat rocks that still radiate warmth from the heat of the day to maintain their critical body temperature. This interaction is known as thigmothermy (thigmo = touch, therm = warmth). To recreate this in captivity, low wattage pads such as 15W to 20W models that maintain a constant temperature of between 21 and 27°C (70 and 81°F) can be placed under a rock inside the terrarium. Fake rocks with heating elements hidden within are available from pet shops and are similarly effective.

Flexible horticultural heating cables used in seed germination can be utilized in the substrate of caecilians because they are both waterproof and do not get too hot.

• Water Heaters. Water temperature for those amphibians from warm temperate to tropical regions needs to be in the range of 22 to 28°C (72 to 82°F). For larger bodies of water such as found in aqua-terraria and aquatic setups, this is easily accomplished with a standard aquarium heater unit that is sealed in a watertight glass tube. For choosing the correct power, allow approximately 10 watts to 1 gallon (4.5 liters). Most models have a built-in thermostat that is adjusted by a knob or screw. Alternatives to tube heaters include the combined external power filter and heater units used for filtration and heating of large aquaria and heater pads placed beneath the aquarium.

• Cooling Units. Amphibians that occur in montane regions, caves, or cold climates will survive only below a certain temperature. It is possible to obtain a miniature air cooler that can fit inside the terrarium and works by fanning air over evaporation coils, cooling it in the process and also creating high humidity. Alternatively an old refrigerator, with a few adjustments such as a glass door and ventilation panel, could be utilized and converted into an excellent watertight cool terrarium.

• External Thermostats. Where a heating unit does not include a built-in thermostat, it is necessary to obtain a separate thermostatic device that allows temperatures to be adjusted. It is linked to the heater source via the heater's power cable and is controlled outside of the terrarium. Thermostats operate by incorporating a remote sensing cell on the end of a cable that is located within the terrarium, close to the heat source. Once the preset

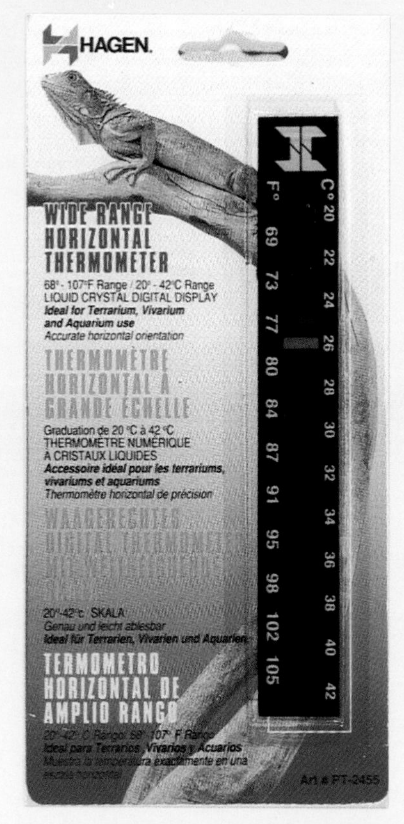

Every terrarium must have at least one thermometer. The liquid crystal strip thermometers work well and are available in temperature ranges suitable for amphibians. Photo courtesy of Hagen.

Correct photoperiod (daylight hours) for various amphibians

A correct photoperiod is essential in ensuring an amphibian behaves naturally and is not stressed by excessive or insufficient daylight length. The change of photoperiod through the four seasons should be accomplished gradually on a pre-determined graduated scale. Photoperiod also has a very important effect on stimulating breeding behavior especially in temperate species.

Climatic Conditions	Species Example	Season	Photoperiod
Cold Temperate	Boreal Chorus Frog (*Pseudacris triseriata*)	Summer Winter	10 hours 6 hours
Cool Temperate	American Toad (*Bufo americanus*)	Summer Winter	12 hours 7 hours
Warm Temperate	Spanish Newt (*Pleurodeles waltl*)	Summer Winter	14 hours 7 hours
Subtropical	Cuban Treefrog (*Osteopilus septentrionalis*)	Summer Winter	16 hours 10 hours
Tropical	Red-eyed Treefrog (*Agalychnis callidryas*)	Summer Winter	16 hours 13 hours
Arid	White's Treefrog (*Litoria caerula*)	Summer Winter	14 hours 10 hours
Cave Dwellers	Grotto Salamander (*Typhlotriton spelaeus*)	Summer Winter	0 hours 0 hours

temperature is reached the thermostat automatically cuts off the power supply to the heating unit, only reconnecting it once the temperature falls below the preset level. Such thermostats should not be used for light bulbs or spot lamps if these are the heat source because the constant switching on and off of the light creates an unnatural and stressful situation for the amphibian. When first using any type of thermostat or heater that already incorporates a thermostat, it is wise to give it a test run to see whether it is accurate and reliable. This involves setting the thermostat at different temperatures in increments of 5 or 10°C and checking these against a thermometer positioned very close to the remote sensor, or in the case of water heaters close to the heater itself. If the temperature is within about 3°C of thermostat setting then it can be considered suitable. It may also be of use to position two reliable thermometers, one near the heat source and one as far away from the heat source as possible, in order to keep a check on the thermal gradient.

LIGHTING

Although many amphibians are either nocturnal or dislike intense lighting, the photoperiod (hours of daylight in each 24-hour cycle) may influence their daily activity, feeding, and breeding behavior. Correct lighting also is extremely important for plants to flourish in a natural setup. The only situations where proper lighting is unnecessary are for terrestrial caecilians and cave-dwelling salamanders. For cave-dwelling and nocturnal species, low wattage blue or red coated light bulbs can be used in the terrarium or even in underground hollows to at least glimpse the rarely observed behavior of these creatures.

Types of Lighting

• Tungsten (Incandescent) Light Bulbs, Strip Lights, and Spot Lamps. Low wattage types (8 to 25 watts) are mainly used to light the cages of temperate species where no plants are present in the terrarium. Toads of the genus *Bufo* may benefit from a 25W or 40W spot lamp as both a lighting and occasional basking source. Wherever lamps that give out a fair amount of heat are used they should be fixed to the roof of the terrarium and positioned toward one side, never in the middle. Tungsten strip lights are best used in aquatic setups where there are no live water plants.

• Ultraviolet (UV) Lighting. Amphibians gain little benefit from the ultraviolet transmission of balanced natural daylight fluorescent tubes. However, this lighting is good in that it gives out very little heat, the UV light helps plants to flourish indoors, and the lighting significantly enhances the appearance of the display terrarium. Initial costs of purchasing such units can be expensive, but the life expectancy is in the region of 12,000 to 25,000 hours of continuous use, nine or ten times more than an average tungsten light bulb. Fluorescent tubes come in different colors or color temperatures (measured in degrees Kelvin), depending on their relative power at each wavelength in the visible spectrum. At the "cold" end of the

Almost every terrarium requires a good fluorescent light even if the amphibians never come out during the day. If you keep living plants you certainly need a good light. Photo courtesy of Energy Savers.

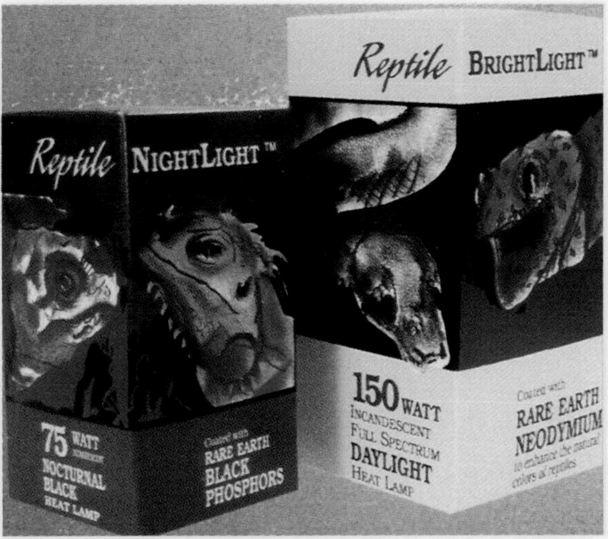

Basking lights are good accessories for some frogs, such as toads and White's Treefrogs, that like to bask occasionally. Be sure that the frog always has a cool, dark area to escape to, however. Photo courtesy of Energy Savers.

scale are models that emit a rather blue light, enhancing greens and blues in a terrarium. At the "warm" end are models that are yellow to pink and enhance the yellows, oranges, and reds in a terrarium. It is said that cooler types look more stunning in a planted terrarium, while warm colors enhance an aquatic setup. Some types emit more UV than others (which bears little significance for amphibian hobbyists) and some have a longer life, but these points aside, the choice of color-enhancing lighting is entirely up to the hobbyist.

UV spot lamp reflectors such as blacklights and reflectorized UV-A lights also are available, but because of the heat these give out they are not really suitable for amphibians.

• Rheostats and Timers. The sudden blinding flash of a light being switched on and the abruptness of being cast into complete darkness can be very alarming to an amphibian, possibly causing stress or even death in nervous or reticent species. Rheostats or dimmers can be implemented to form a natural and gradual exposure to light, and models are made that automatically dim or increase light over a preset time. Timers incorporating a rheostat are extremely useful units that gradually dim and switch off a light and at the same time operate over a 24-hour cycle so that an exact photoperiod can be preset.

TERRARIUM HYGIENE AND MAINTENANCE

To maintain a clean, disease-free environment, all terraria, whatever their arrangement, need to be inspected on a daily basis. This may just involve a change of water in a bowl, the removal of amphibian feces, uneaten or regurgitated food, or dead foliage from plants, or the replacement an expended light bulb. Specimens should also be observed regularly and if they show any signs of illness, they must be removed immediately and isolated to determine the cause of this indisposition.

The terrarium and its decor will need a thorough clean out every 5 to 14 days, although larger planted terraria and aquatic setups may not need such regular purges depending on how "messy" the inhabitants are and how often inspections are carried out.

In terraria containing live plants and artistic miniature landscaping in general, cleaning out can be a tedious task, yet it is an essential requirement of such a setup that should never be avoided. All decorations such as rocks, logs, and artificial (fiberglass, papier-mache) structures are removed and either soaked in a bowl of or washed down with a mild disinfectant solution. Disinfectants should be used with great care where amphibians are concerned. Household bleach (sodium hypochlorite) works well, but in

Cleaning frequencies for different terrarium setups

This table gives a guide to cleaning frequencies to prevent excessive levels of waste matter and detritus that may harbor potentially harmful molds, bacteria, and parasites. Cleaning refers to the use of a mild disinfectant to wash down the terrarium, all decorations and the basal substrate also being washed or discarded.

Terrarium Category	Terrarium Setup	Cleaning Frequency
Simple/Hygienic	Small container Large container	4 - 6 days 4 - 10 days
Terrestrial Planted	Small Large	6 - 10 days 7 - 21 days
Tall Planted	Small Large	7 - 14 days 10 - 21 days
Arid/Desert	Small & Large	10 - 21 days
Aquaterrarium	Small Large	7 - 14 days 10 - 21 days
Fully Aquatic	Small & Large	If the water is properly filtered, aerated and otherwise balanced this should be unnecessary up until the point where algal growth and scum become too dense and biowaste (nitrates/ammonia) levels become excessive.

a concentration of not greater than 1.5% (1.5 parts of bleach to 100 parts of fresh hot water). After disinfecting, ensure that decorations, particularly those of a woody nature such as logs and cork bark, are thoroughly rinsed with hot water several times to flush out any potentially harmful residues before being left to dry for a while. Artificial substrates, depending on the material, can either be discarded or washed in a soapy solution then rinsed. Compost and peat substrates are either steam sterilized or discarded, sphagnum moss is rinsed in running warm water, and sand and gravel substrates can be washed in boiling water.

The terrarium itself should then be disinfected with the same 1.5% sodium hypochlorite solution, making sure that all edges and corners in particular are properly cleaned. Then wash it down with clean water, dry, and return the substrate, decor, and water (if necessary).

In the case of aquaterraria and aquatic setups, complete clean outs are unnecessary if the water is correctly balanced, filtered, and aerated. It is wise to remove with a siphon any sediment that has collected on the substrate or in nooks and crannies. Also, a partial water change of 25 to 35% every four weeks may be beneficial. Green algae that cling to the glass and obstruct your view can be removed with a sharp razor blade scraper and the flakes siphoned up. Eventually algae, both on the glass and in the form of strands and matted layers entangling plants and submerged decor, may become so dense that a complete cleaning is inevitable.

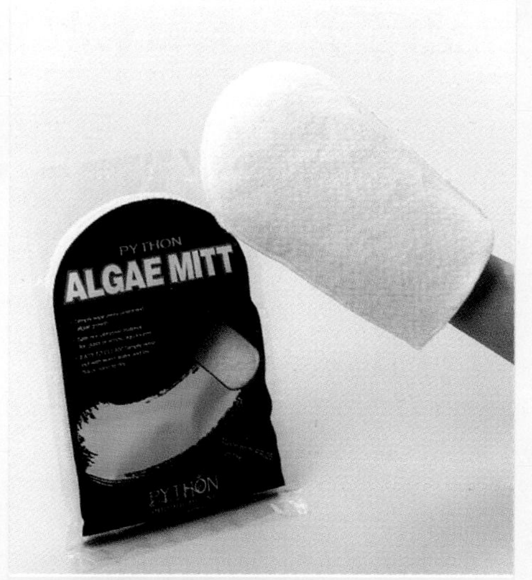

Keeping the aquarium glass clean requires a lot of work, but products such as this algae mitt make it easier. Photo courtesy of Python.

Electrical appliances in the terrarium also will need to be checked regularly to ensure that they are functioning properly and that all wires and cables are firmly attached.

Foods and Feeding

CAPTURING AND DEVOURING FOOD

Most anurans rely heavily on sight and to a lesser extent on smell to detect prey, which means they respond mainly to moving prey. Conversely, for the majority of salamanders and all apodans the sense of smell is much more important. The methods that amphibians display to stalk and capture their food may vary significantly among genera and even species of the same genus, providing the hobbyist with one of the most fascinating aspects in maintaining amphibians in captivity.

Physical Characteristics

• The Tongue. In most frogs and some salamanders the tongue is a fleshy extensible organ that is attached to the front of the mouth and points backward into the mouth cavity when withdraw. Upon locating prey the tongue is quickly and accurately flicked out toward its target. Heavily coated in a viscid mucus, the tongue immediately ensnares the food and is retracted into the mouth before the prey has any chance to react. Cave salamanders (*Hydromantes*) have a specialized extensible tongue that in addition to being viscid and very long ends in an inverted mushroom shape. This gives a larger surface area and therefore more chance of making contact with moving prey in the complete darkness of caves. Related lungless salamanders such as *Bolitoglossa* and *Batrachoseps* have a similar tongue. Other surface-dwelling amphibians have also evolved similarly shaped tongues but only to gain better purchase on larger prey.

• Fore Limbs. Anurans such as discoglossids and pipids have tongues that are fixed to the back of the mouth and cannot be flicked out, thus being functionally absent. Discoglossids appear rather clumsy when they try to capture prey because they simply lunge forward with a gaping mouth and then use their relatively muscular fore limbs to restrain and maneuver prey into the mouth. Aquatic pipids such as *Xenopus* use their fore limbs to stir up the muddy bottom of the pond or lake and then juggle prey such as small crustaceans into the mouth. The digits of the Surinam Toad's (*Pipa pipa*) fore limbs end in specialized star-shaped appendages containing highly responsive nerve endings that enable them to detect the prey before using the typical sweeping action of the arms.

• Teeth. The majority of salamanders and some frogs have a single row of pin-like teeth set in both the lower (mandible) and upper (maxilla) jaws that allows them to grasp even the slimiest of prey such as slugs and earthworms. Many frogs lack teeth in one or both jaws. In the

Food capturing technique seen in mushroom-tongued salamanders (*Eurycea, Hydromantes, Bolitoglossa*, etc.) of the family Plethodontidae.

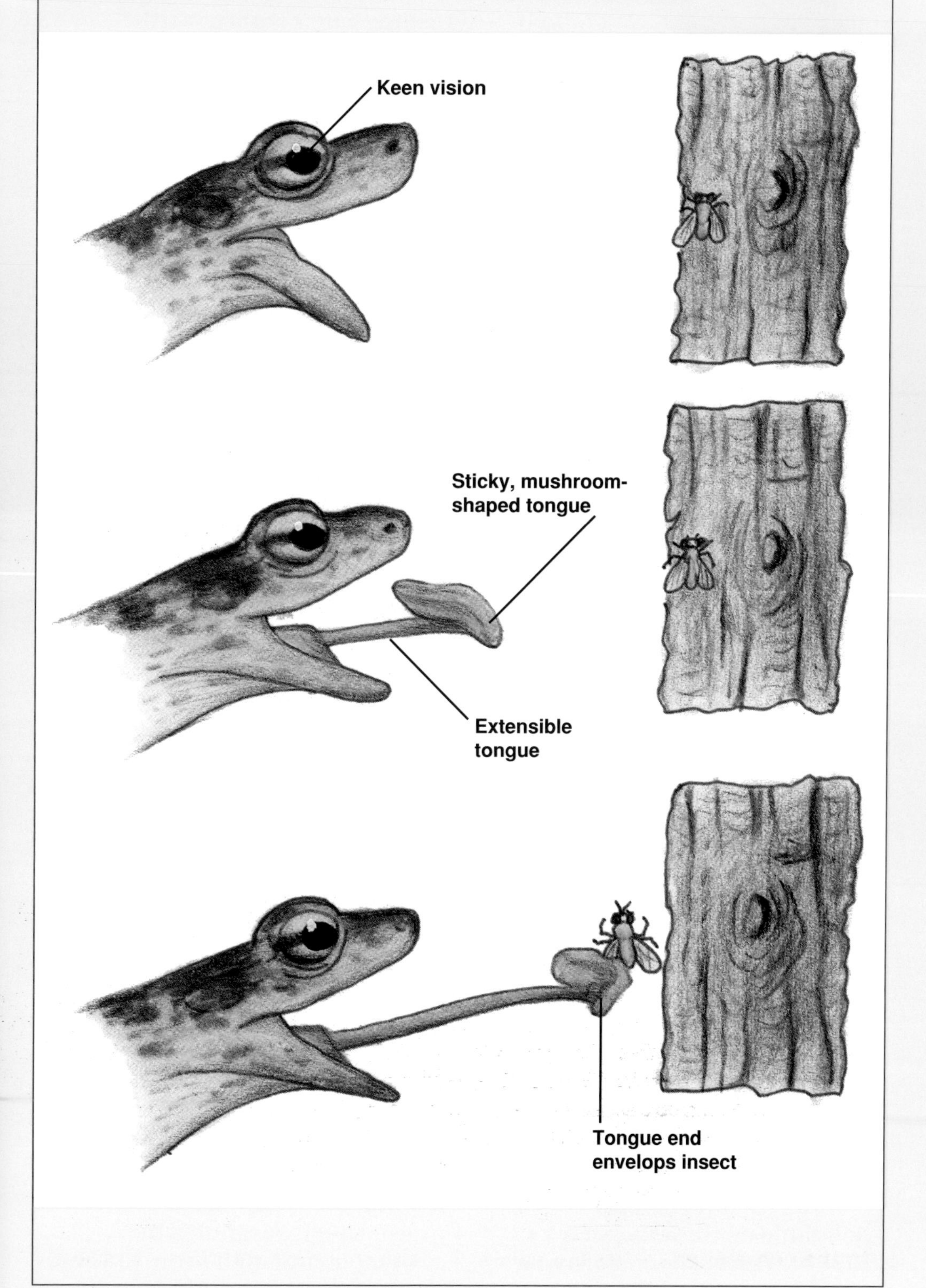

family Sirenidae teeth are completely absent and in their place are horny linings on both jaws, also a characteristic of some anuran tadpoles and the larvae of certain hynobiids and ambystomatids. In other anuran larvae the mouthparts (part of the oral disc) have series of concentric spicules (called teeth though technically different) leading to a centralized hard beak; these are used to scrape algae and bacteria from rocks or shreds of meat from dead animals.

The most well developed and prominent "teeth" are the odontoid formations seen in horned frogs (*Ceratophrys*) and the African Bullfrog (*Pyxicephalus adspersus*). Here several bony projections 5 to 10 mm high in adult specimens rise out from the lower jawbone itself. The incredibly strong jaws enable these pugnacious frogs to inflict a lethal hold on small mammals, allowing easier swallowing. They also have long saber-like teeth on the roof of the mouth ("daggers") that penetrate the heads of small animals and the fingers of unwary keepers.

Hunting Strategies

• The Stalk. This hunting technique, which involves physical movement to locate and capture prey, is displayed by the majority of amphibians, especially salamanders and aquatics. In temperate, warm-temperate, and desert regions stalking usually is influenced by favorable conditions such as rain at night. The majority of stalking amphibians have become nocturnal to avoid coming into contact with potential predators. Burrowing species such as apodans will follow the tunnels of earthworms or grubs to locate their prey, while the aquatic Hellbender lifts large pebbles and rocks to locate its favorite crayfish prey.

• Ambush or "Sit and Wait" Tactics. Besides using body coloration, patterning, and shape to camouflage themselves from would-be predators, frogs may also use this to capture their own food. In the case of treefrogs this may involve adapting the body color to match the flower, leaf, or bark of a tree so that when an unsuspecting insect lands nearby the frog is able to take it by surprise. Larger anurans, most notably the South American horned frogs and Asian *Megophrys*, display a phenomenon known as disruptive concealment or "crypsis" where their seemingly unnatural body outline allows them to remain virtually invisible against the leafy or mossy forest floor. They also may bury themselves in the same substrate with only eyes peeping out, their presence disrupted by fleshy horns. Attempting to stalk prey would be pointless for such bulky frogs because of their lethargic nature, but by using the element of surprise they are able to concentrate all their energy into leaping out when prey unknowingly stumbles by.

• Opportunistic Feeding. Some

of the more adaptive frogs, such as bufonids, microhylids, and larger ranids, may adopt both the previous techniques depending on the type of prey they are hunting. The Malaysian Painted Toad (*Kaloula pulchra*) sits near the entrance of ant or termite nests, picking off the insects as they walk across its path. It also will stalk larger prey in woodland areas and even enter human settlements to feed under street lights that at night attract an abundance of insects.

FEEDING AMPHIBIANS IN CAPTIVITY

In captivity, along with ensuring a clean and healthy environment, providing a diet that is nutritious and correctly balanced in carbohydrates, fats, proteins, vitamins, and minerals constitutes one of the most significant factors in the successful maintenance and breeding of amphibians.

In their adult form almost all wild amphibians are carnivorous, preying only on live food. The diet varies from species to species; some are opportunists preying on a variety of different food types, others are distinctly specific or fussy, preferring just one or two particular types of prey. Sometimes it may not be possible to mirror these feeding traits in the captive environment, at least on a regular basis, so other methods of providing a correctly balanced diet need to be taken into consideration such as supplementation of vitamins/ minerals or attempting to coax the amphibian into eating alternative foods. Captive-bred amphibians hold a distinct advantage over wild-caught specimens because they are not used to eating a certain selection of foods and can quickly be encouraged to take an alternative food (which in many species does not even have to be alive), while wild-caught specimens may take considerably longer to adjust, sometimes to the point of near starvation.

Obtaining Foods

Fortunately, over the last decade or so livefood breeding establishments have sprung up, particularly in North America, western Europe, and Australia, that have banished many of the problems associated with locating food all year around. Many of these foods are available at your local pet shop or can be ordered by the shop if you request it. Given sufficient time and space, breeding amphibian foods in the home is possible, although with certain types this may prove costly and not advantageous. On a seasonal basis probably the cheapest method of getting food is by collecting, although care must be taken to ensure that such foods are free from parasites, disease, and not contaminated with insecticides or pesticides.

Types of Food

Foods suitable for captive amphibians differ in shape, size, and availability. Obviously the smaller the amphibian the smaller the food required, and in general this means that larger amphibians are far easier to feed. Some foods are not taken by amphibians because they either are distasteful or are too hard for their soft palate. An amphibian may attempt to eat a certain food and dislike it so much that in the future such food is avoided on account of its appearance or smell. Wasps, bees, and brightly colored poisonous caterpillars are good examples.

Most tadpoles thrive on a diet of finely crushed fish flake foods. Always buy the highest quality flakes and try to get as much variety as possible. Photo courtesy of Hagen.

Below is a list of different foods, how they are obtained, and, if they are live, their potential for culturing in the home.

Foods for Anuran Tadpoles

• Infusoria. This is a term loosely applied to many microscopic organisms that provide food for almost all anuran tadpoles, one example being the soupy green algal growth in water. It can be obtained in the form of a concentrated, highly nutritious liquid, a drop or two of which can be added to the aquarium at two– to three-day intervals. Infusoria also can be cultured at home by placing slightly rotten (but not moldy) lettuce leaves or potato or banana skins in a pint of water that then is boiled and left out in a sunny position. Infusoria spores are always floating in the atmosphere and eventually some will settle on the water surface before rapidly multiplying. (The colony also can be started with a teaspoon of water from a ditch or an aquarium.) Tear off small sections of an infusoria-covered leaf or skin and place them in the aquarium.

• Raw Meat. Attach a small cube of clean, untreated raw meat such as steak or beef to a piece of string and submerse in the aquarium water. Carnivorous frog tadpoles enjoy sucking the blood and juices, while larger tadpoles such as *Ceratophrys* and *Pyxicephalus* actually tear off strips of meat. Meat should never be left in the water for more than 72 hours.

• Fish and Reptile Food Products. The availability of dried and moist canned food products directed at tropical and ornamental fishes and aquatic reptiles (especially sliders) has also served to increase the types of food available for the anuran larvae. As tadpoles are largely scavengers, they will feed on anything remotely edible, and

Raw meat and the bodies of small or dead siblings often are eaten greedily by toad tadpoles such as these *Bufo woodhousi fowleri*. Photo: R. T. Zappalorti.

the various flakes, pellets, and tablets composed of the dried, compressed bodies of krill, tubifex worms, brine shrimp, daphnia, or vegetable matter (which often are fortified with a multivitamin compound) all make excellent foods.

• Other Tadpole Foods. Tadpoles also will feed on bread and chopped earthworm. In species such as the Asian horned frogs (*Megophrys*), the specialized tadpoles feed only on decaying vegetable material and oils that float on the water surface. Tadpoles of some members of the North American spadefoots (*Scaphiopus*), horned frogs, and the pipid *Hymenochirus* are active carnivores attacking and devouring small crustaceans, fishes, other amphibian larvae, and even each other.

Your pet shop carries many types of freeze-dried worms and larvae that are good tadpole foods. Photo courtesy of Hagen.

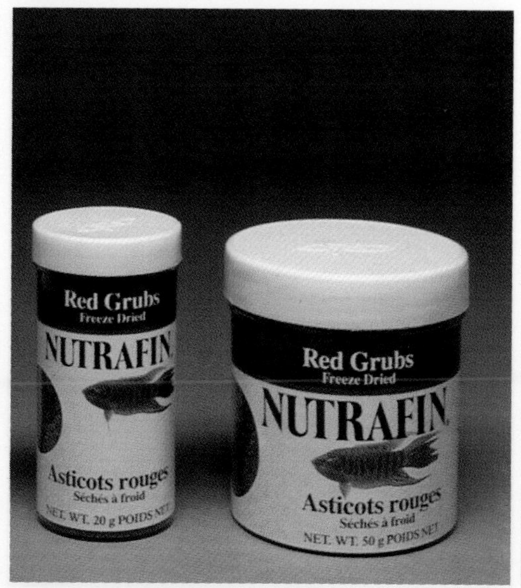

Foods for Salamander Larvae

• Paramecia. Live paramecia can be obtained in the form of a dried cake or tablets consisting of thousands of cysts (dried, inactive bodies of the single-celled animals that still are alive) of this protozoan. On introducing a section of the cake/tablet into water the cysts activate quickly, with the oblong microorganisms continuing to maintain a congregated formation. The shimmering movement caused by the spinning of their cilia-covered bodies entices salamander larvae to snap at large chunks of the now softened cake or tablet.

• Bloodworms and Tubifex Worms. Tubifex worms (also known as sludge worms) are true segmented worms related to earthworms, while bloodworms are the larval stage of chironomid midges (related to mosquitoes). They form the principal diet of many salamander and aquatic caecilian larvae and either can be collected from the silted bottoms of ponds and slow moving streams or, preferably, obtained from a pet shop, which provides cleaner specimens with much less effort on the part of the keeper. A specially designed floating holder can be purchased in which many small holes are perforated so that the clumped worms wiggle out singly and attract the larvae. Otherwise these worms are liable to tunnel into the aquarium substrate out of reach of the amphibian larvae and then die and eventually foul the water. Whatever the source of these worms, they must be cleaned

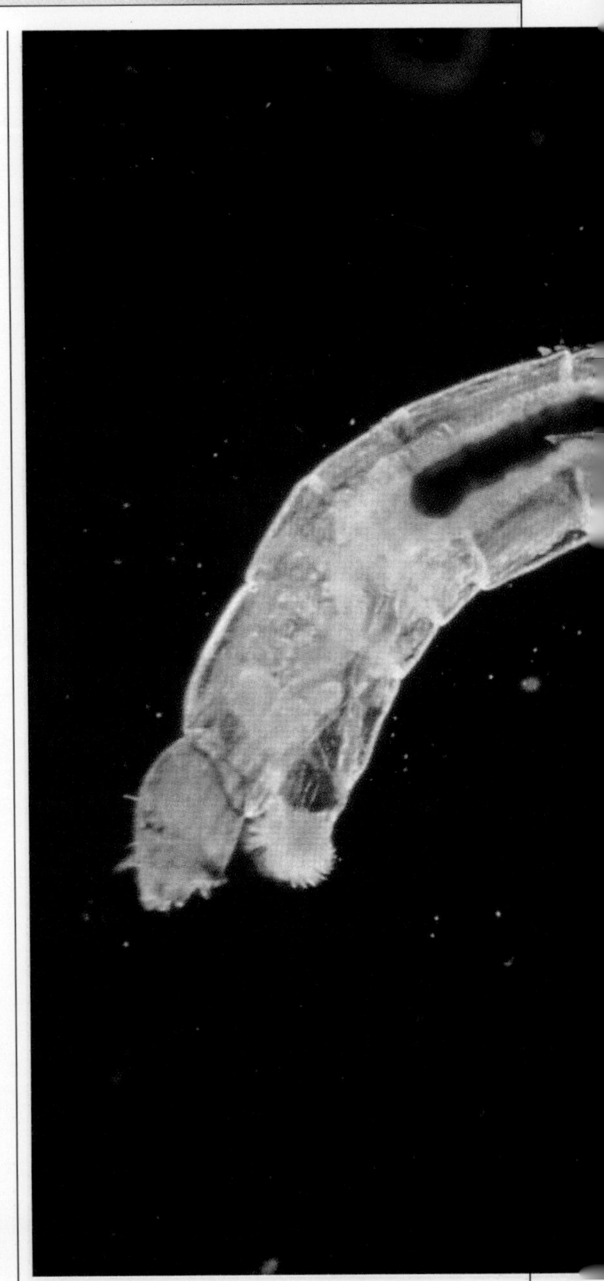

Bloodworms, the larvae of small flies called chironomid midges, are an excellent food for salamander larvae and even adults of many species. They are available live, frozen, and freeze-dried at almost any pet shop. Photo: D. Untergasser.

regularly by transferring the stock to a container of fresh water or trickling running water through their container until all the wastes run out. Bloodworms also make ideal foods for newly metamorphosed amphibians.

• Microworms (*Anguillula silusiae*). Starter cultures of these minute worms are obtained from pet shops. In nature they have an affinity for rotting wood, but a cleaner substitute is a sticky paste consisting of soy flour mixed with water and spread over a shallow tray that has a lid to prevent possible escape. The

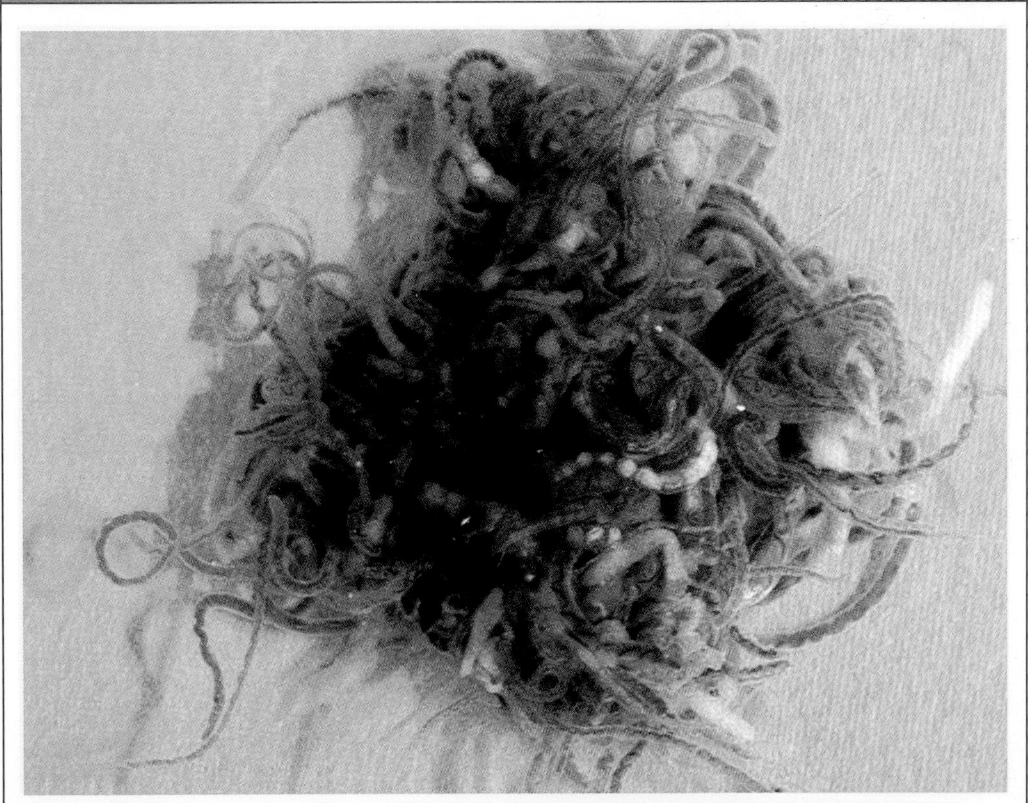

Above: **Tubifex worms are one of the easiest live foods to purchase. These worms are accepted by many larval and adult amphibians, especially aquatic salamanders and clawed frogs. Photo: R. Schreiber.** ***Below:*** **Though you could in theory collect your own bloodworms, it is easier, cleaner, and probably cheaper to buy them locally. Photo: M. Staniszewski.**

worms will burrow, feed, and breed in this mixture, but because they are so small it might be difficult to locate and separate them from the substrate. One method is to boil wooden lollipop sticks in water until they are softened and then plant these upright in the culture medium. Place the tray over a gentle heat source such as a radiator or stove pilot light for a few hours to force small masses of the worms up the sticks, which are then removed and swirled around the aquarium water where they detach and become a food for salamander larvae. An eighth of the worm substrate should be removed and placed in a batch of fresh mixture every four weeks to provide a fresh culture. The remainder should be discarded because mold eventually will render it unsuitable.

• Microcrustaceans (Daphnia and Cyclops). Mainly a salamander food, as with tubifex and bloodworms, waterfleas (daphnias) and copepods (cyclops) can be purchased from many tropical fish stores. They also are easily cultured in a well lighted spot at home by providing a one-gallon container of tepid rain water (not too acidic) to which is added either a quarter-liter of liquefied horse or cow manure, a handful of rotted leaves, or a teaspoon of liquid infusoria. By splitting up the daphnia or cyclops stocks every

Dredging through the detritus of the local lakes and streams may produce some usable food items such as small isopods, asellids. Though eaten by many amphibian larvae, they may be a source of parasites or chemical contamination. Photo: M. Staniszewski.

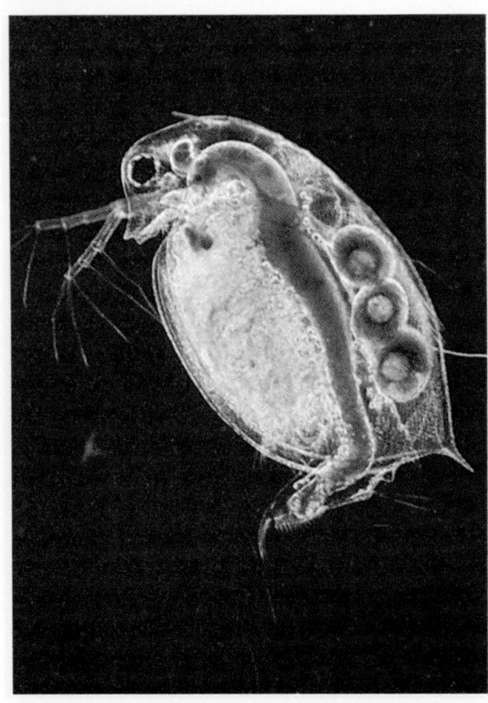

Many of the larger pet shops carry living daphnia ~~and similar~~ tiny crustaceans during the spring and fall. Photo: Engasser.

three or four weeks, huge quantities can be propagated. This is very useful where large numbers of salamander larvae are concerned. During cold weather daphnia and cyclops will die off, but many eggs are laid to hatch out with the onset of warmer weather, so do not discard the contents of the breeding tank.

• Brine Shrimp (*Artemia*). These small saltwater crustaceans (which are found in salt lakes and pans but not actually in the ocean) can be purchased in pet shops as well–developed 4 to 6 mm translucent orange larvae (nauplii) or in the form of sealed tubes or cans containing thousands of dried eggs. Eggs can be hatched in a solution of 30 to 35 grams of sea salt dissolved in a liter of dechlorinated water. About a teaspoon of the eggs is gently sprinkled over the water surface and the bottle of water is aerated

Mosquito egg rafts can be collected in the wild and hatched to feed small salamander larvae. Photo: R. Schreiber.

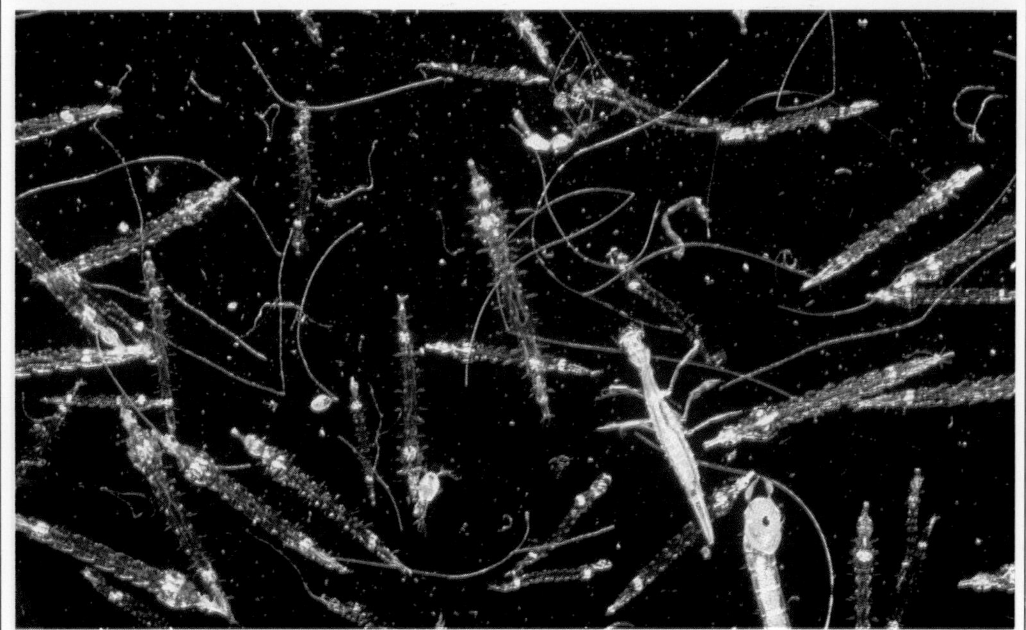

Glassworms (larvae of a small midge, *Chaoborus*) are an excellent food for small aquatic amphibians. Wild-collected worms may be contaminated with dangerous beetle larvae, however. Photo: M.P. & C. Piednoir.

The jerky movements of daphnia draw the attention of salamander larvae, promoting a lively chase and active, more healthy larvae. Photo: M. P. & C. Piednoir.

Mosquito larvae are easily collected (beware of pesticide contamination, however) or raised and provide an excellent food for both salamanders and frogs. Photo: R. Schreiber.

strongly with an air pump and bubbler. If the culture is maintained at a temperature of around 79°F (26°C), hatching of the nauplii will commence within 48 hours. Nauplii are attracted to a bright light and can be caught with a very fine net. They make a good starter food for salamander larvae (be sure to rinse out all the salt) in their early stages of development. Larger shrimp (which can be purchased or raised from nauplii on a diet of yeast or algae) are eaten by most aquatic amphibians. Brine shrimp do not live very long in fresh water, so it is wise not be over-zealous when feeding them to your specimens.

• Mosquito Larvae. Found in still and often stagnant water such as rainwater puddles, garden ponds, barrels, and cattle troughs, mosquito larvae are easy to recognize by their bulbous head and forked tail. They provide an excellent food for larger salamander larvae and adults of other aquatic amphibians. They are collected by skimming a net or, better yet, a ladle on a stick handle just below the surface of the water and should then be thoroughly rinsed in clean water before being used as food. They are present from mid-spring to the first frosts of winter in temperate areas and all year around in warmer countries.

• Aquatic Crustaceans. Freshwater

amphipods or scuds (usually *Gammarus* and *Hyalella* species) and isopods or water lice (*Asellus*) are abundant under stones at the edges of small water bodies and within the detritus of ponds and streams. They provide a good food supply for larger aquatic amphibians such as pipids, sirens, mudpuppies, and amphiumas. They can also be fed on the end of tweezers to some frogs—*Bombina* in particular enjoy them.

• Freshwater Fishes. Larger amphibians such as the Surinam Toad, Clawed Frog (*Xenopus laevis*), and Axolotl also include a large number of small fishes in their natural diet. Minnows and killifishes of various types (be sure to check all local fishing laws—you may need to purchase a license) can be caught with a net in local ponds, streams, or rivers. Alternatively and much easier, "feeder fish" such as Goldfish, Guppies, and Swordtails are inexpensive to purchase at the local pet shop and can even be bred in large quantities in the home if space permits. If you do not want to feed live fish, most aquatic amphibians will learn to accept strips of freshwater fish such as whitebait (smelt) and trout purchased from the supermarket or fish store. Saltwater fishes should not be fed to amphibians because they contain a chemical that may cause problems with the amphibian's metabolism.

• Other Foods. Some aquatic amphibians include various other creatures in their diet. The aggressive Hellbender will tackle mollusks, frogs, and even small rodents, but it has a particular affection for crayfish. Giant salamanders (*Andrias*) will even consume small freshwater turtles, as will large American Bullfrogs (*Rana catesbeiana*). Many larger frogs and salamanders will take frozen and thawed pinkie mice of the type commonly fed to snakes.

Though maintaining cultures of fruitflies (such as the wingless variety shown here) can involve a great deal of labor, these tiny flies remain the preferred staple diet for many small amphibians. Photo: M. Gilroy.

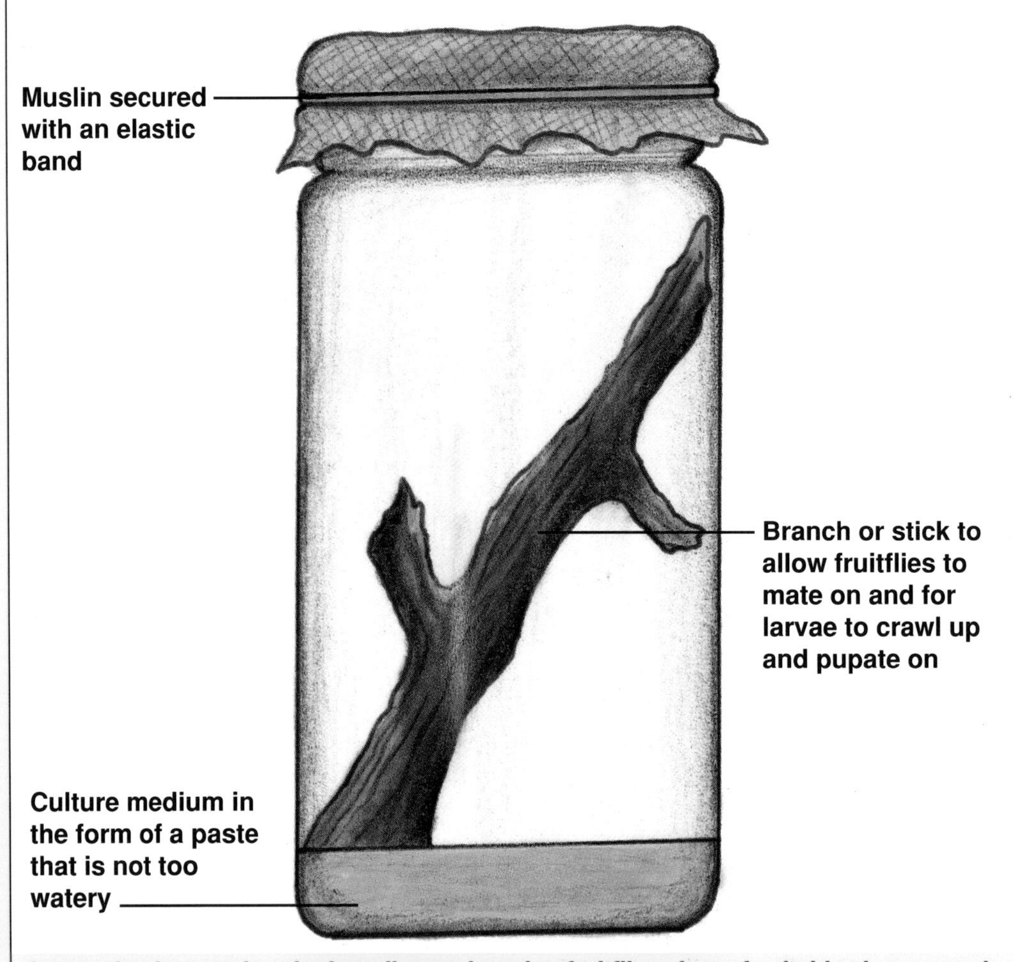

A very simple container for breeding and rearing fruitflies. Jars of suitable size covered with cheesecloth or muslin are used to hold the culture medium and a clean branch or stick is put in to allow the flies a substrate on which to mate. The branch also gives the larvae a place to crawl out of the medium to pupate. The jars may not look as neat as laboratory rearing containers, but they do work.

Foods for Newly Metamorphosed, Juvenile, and Very Small Amphibians

This includes frogs up to the size of about 2.5 cm (1 in) and salamanders and caecilians up to 5 cm (2 in).

• Fruitflies (*Drosophila melanogaster*). Fruitflies are an indispensable food source for those hobbyists intending to breed smaller anurans. Starter cultures of two different types, the winged variety and the vestigial-winged variety, are readily available. The former is useful for tiny species of newly metamorphosed treefrogs and reed frogs, while the latter is better for slower moving species and juveniles. Their nutritional value can be greatly increased by making up a culture medium from the following recipe (all measurements are approximate): 15 grams of oatmeal; 10 grams of agar jelly; 5 grams of cane sugar; 5 ml of multivitamin liquid; 150 ml of water. The ingredients then are thoroughly stirred into a fine paste and boiled in a saucepan for several minutes. While still hot the paste is poured into a glass jam jar until an inch or so deep. Any remainder can be stored in a freezer and heated again when required. Push a piece of clean wood (a lollipop stick) into the paste so that it protrudes 2 or 3 inches as this will provide the flies with a platform to mate. When the paste is cool, introduce around 20 or 30 flies then affix a piece of nylon stocking or similar fine mesh over the top and firmly secure it with a rubber band. Over a period of two to three weeks at a temperature of 74°F the culture will produce in the region of 200 to 500 new flies, most of which can be used as food, and another 20 or so to start a fresh culture in another jar. Liquefied fruit such as apple or the skins of bananas can be used as an alternative culture medium, but these are likely to mold much quicker.

Drawbacks of these flies are their small size, agility, and difficulty in capturing to transfer to a terrarium or another culture jar. They can be made lethargic by cooling down in a freezer for 60 seconds or killed by placing in a freezer for five minutes duration before being fed to small amphibians on the end of a moistened cocktail stick. It is surprising how many captive-bred juvenile amphibians learn to accept flies in this manner, and it allows for each individual to be offered similar portions of food.

• Aphids. Blackflies, whiteflies, and aphids are closely related tiny

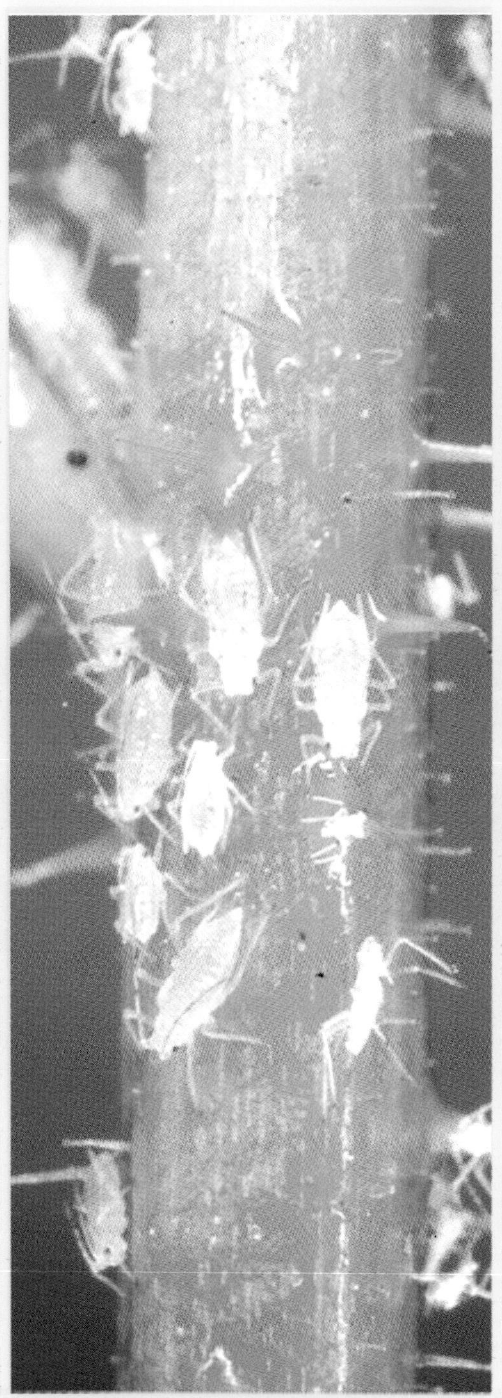

Aphids and closely related sucking plant pests make great food for small amphibians. Consider yourself lucky if your cabbages or roses are invaded! However, remember that the smallest trace of pesticides may be fatal to amphibians. Photo: M. Staniszewski.

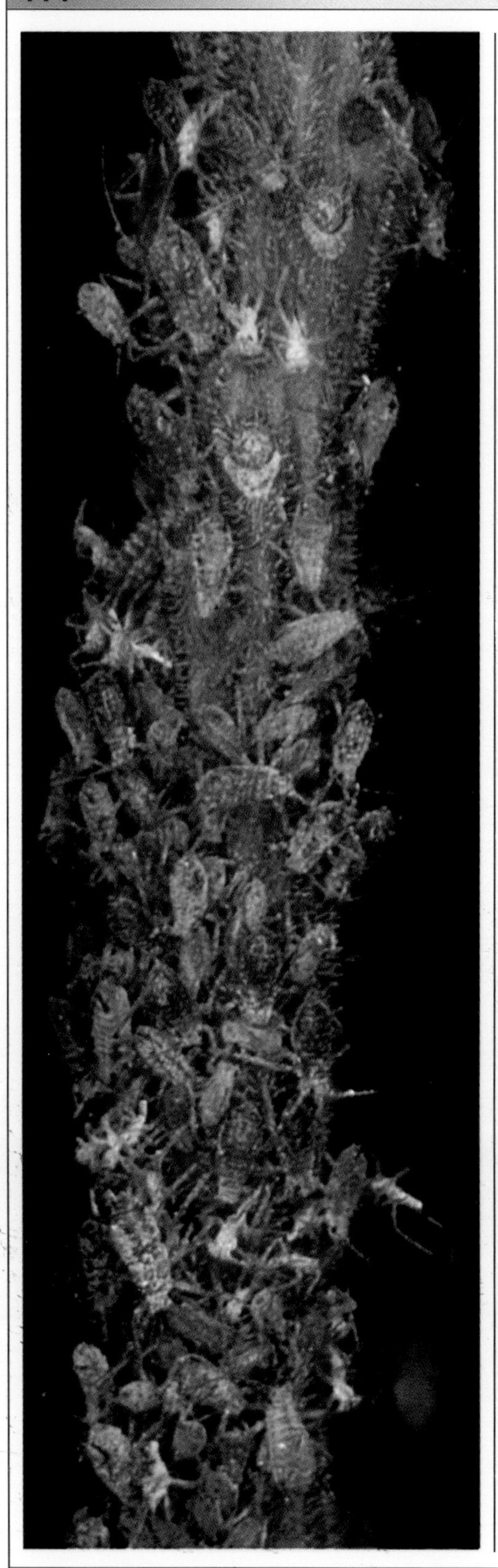

insects that are seasonal food sources plentiful in late spring to early autumn. Inspect the stalks of stinging nettles, bramble, and roses for aphids; whiteflies are plentiful on the underside of cauliflower, cabbage, and broccoli leaves. Blackflies tend to occur later in the year, even in the midst of freezing weather, and settle on the dying or dead leaves of apple trees and late vegetable plants. It must be ensured that such insects have not been previously sprayed.

• Sweepings. These represent a varied and therefore highly nutritional seasonal food supply and are collected during the warmer months by "sweeping" a fine-mesh insect net through grassy meadows or gently shaking the branches of shrubs and trees over a large square of white cotton material or into a bucket. A wide variety of small insects such as gnats, springtails, midges, moths, and caterpillars, as well as spiders and daddy longlegs, can be obtained in this manner.

Another method for obtaining very small insects and caterpillars in the middle of winter is to collect a handful of damp tree leaves and transfer them into a funnel that is directed into a glass beaker. A 60W spotlight is situated above so that it shines into the leaves and the radiant heat will gradually dry out the leaves, forcing the insects further down until they fall

Like aphids, greenflies make a desirable food for small amphibians. Photo: M. Staniszewski.

Many of the small invertebrates found in your back yard or garden will be eaten by small frogs and salamanders. Caterpillars of all types and of appropriate size should never be overlooked in your search for natural foods, while many amphibians are delighted to take small spiders. Photos: M. Staniszewski.

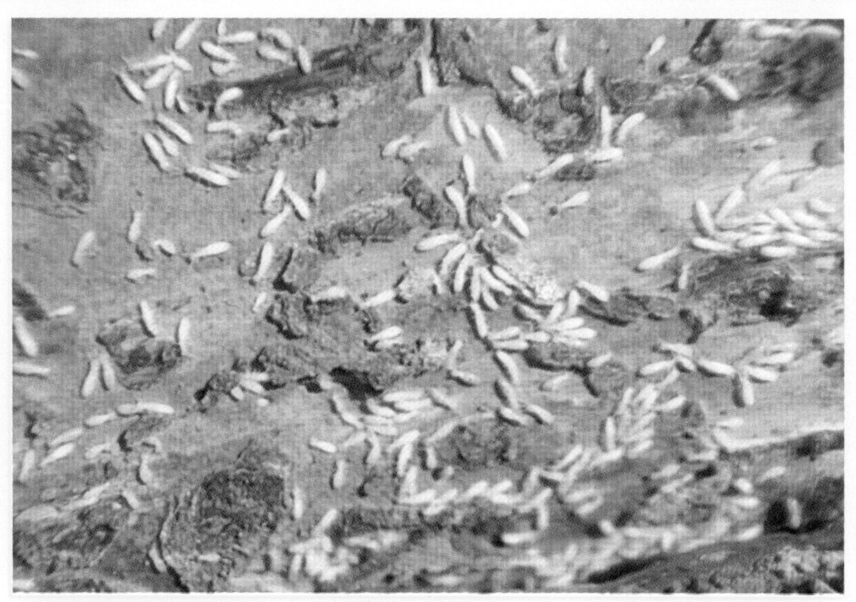

In many temperate and all tropical climates termites abound. The smaller workers (never the queens or large soldiers) can easily be collected for amphibian food. For many small frogs from the tropics termites are indeed the preferred food. Photo: W. B. Allen, Jr.

through the funnel into the beaker.

• Ants and Termites. Ants are disliked by most amphibians because they emit distasteful secretions and have a rather indigestible exoskeleton. Some caecilians, dendrobatids, and microhylids are among the few amphibians that include ants in their natural diet (though dendrobatids, at least, avoid ants in captivity). The European Common Toad (*Bufo bufo*) will gorge itself on ants, yet many closely related species will not even attempt them. Conversely, the larger winged queen ants that leave their nests in hot weather to form new nests elsewhere are eaten by a wide variety of frogs and some salamanders. Generally speaking, ants can be found all year around in warmer climates, but where cold weather is present for part of the year they disappear deep underground.

Termites are taken by many frogs and toads because they are relatively slow-moving, soft-bodied, and most do not exude any obnoxious secretions. Members of the family Microhylidae specialize in termites in the wild, with species such as the narrow-mouthed toads (*Gastrophryne*) from America often inhabiting termite mounds. In some regions, such as western Europe, finding a source of termites could prove difficult.

• Whiteworms (Enchytraeids).These 1 to 3 cm white, threadlike worms are similar to tubifex worms in size and provide an essential food for a host of newly metamorphosed and small amphibians, particularly newts. They are initially obtained in starter culture packs from a pet shop. A pack consists of a container filled with a loose peaty soil to which has been added leaf-mold to ensure it doesn't pack too tightly. The culture is fed with small strips of bread (preferably of the oatmeal variety) that have been soaked in milk and placed on the surface of the substrate. The container then is put in a cool dark place at a temperature of around 55°F. The worms quickly congregate beneath the strips of bread, where they multiply. Every three weeks around two dozen worms are moved to a container of fresh medium to begin another culture because the current medium will quickly become covered with mold. To feed individual worms to amphibians use a pair of tweezers to gently separate them from the substrate and then swirl in clean water.

Foods for Medium-sized Amphibians

This includes frogs between 2.5 and 10 cm (1 to 4 in) and salamanders and caecilians between 5 and 35 cm (2 to 14 in).

• Flies. A favorite food for many frogs and more agile salamanders is flies, which come in many different sizes ranging from houseflies (*Fannia* and *Musca*) to fleshflies such as the bluebottles (*Calliphora*). One type which must not be left in a cage (i.e., it must be eaten when you are observing), especially where bufonids are the occupants, is the greenbottle (*Lucillia*), which is liable to deposit its eggs in the toad's nostrils. The larvae will hatch and gnaw their

Sweeping uncontaminated foliage with an insect net will produce a variety of small moths and flies that make good amphibian food. Photo: G. Dingerkus.

Adult mealworm beetles, *Tenebrio molitor*. Small mealworm larvae make an excellent treat for larger amphibians. Photo: M. Gilroy.

A simple trap for capturing blowflies over a dish of spoiled meat.

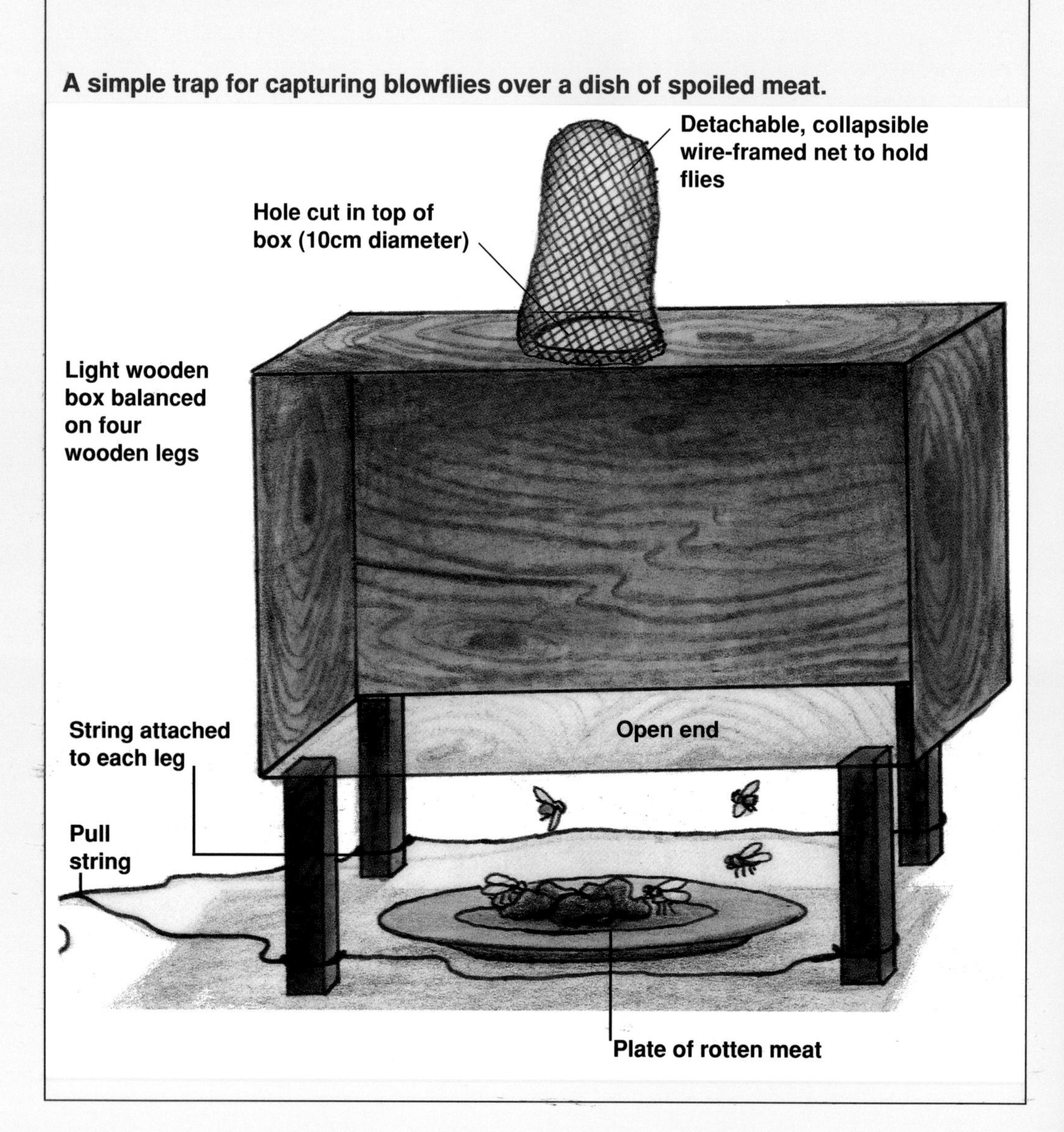

way through into the toad's brain cavity, ultimately killing it.

If you have quick reflexes flies can be caught with a net as they are basking during spring to late autumn. A bait of rotting meat or fish can be used to attract them under a small box (about 8 cm, 3 in, to a side) balanced over the bait. Flies are attracted to light, and when the box is dropped they will rush into a muslin or cheesecloth sleeve at the top of the box and can be collected into a jar. Slow them down in a refrigerator for a minute or so. Few people like to fool with rotting meat baits, however.

The cleanest and most efficient way is to purchase flies in larval form as maggots (sometimes called gentles or spikes) from bait shops (few pet shops carry maggots). These maggots are left to pupate and eventually will hatch out into flies that should be fed on a diet of honey fortified with a multivitamin solution prior to being used as food. The maggots themselves can be used as food, but because of their leathery skin and gnawing mouthparts, always slit the skin with a sharp instrument. Avoid maggots that have been dyed, as there is evidence to suggest that such dyes are carcinogenic.

• Mealworms. The high-protein larval forms of flour beetles are one of the most popular food types for amphibians and now are available in several different sizes: regular mealworms (*Tenebrio molitor*) are available in mini (up to 18 mm), typical (up to 30 mm), and giant forms (up to 40 mm); the super giant mealworm (*Zophobas atratus*) (up to 55 mm); and the small buffalo worm (*Alphitobius diaperinus*) (up to 14 mm). In terms of maintaining live mealworms for long periods all these strains require similar handling with a fairly deep smooth–sided tray filled with 1 to 2 inches of dry bran, oatmeal, or a similar food. There is no need to cover the tray because the mealworms are unable to climb up smooth sides and closing air off will create condensation and destroy the culture. In terms of storage temperatures, mealworms are best kept at normal room temperatures, while the other species require more warmth. To encourage quicker growth, place half a potato with the cut part face down for mealworms to feed on (beware of fungus!). Breeding cycles of mealworms (i.e., hatching, pupating, and mating) range from six to eight weeks in smaller types up to 24 weeks in super giant mealworms. Around 20 to 30 adult beetles should be moved to a different tray containing fresh dry bran and slices of potato each breeding cycle; here they will begin another culture producing about 50 new mealworms per pair. The remaining mealworms in the old tray should be used as food and the spent bran discarded.

Mealworms should not form the sole diet for amphibians because they contain very little in the way of usable calcium necessary for strong skeletal formation. One method for increasing calcium is to add bone meal (available from pet shops) to the bran. Their tough exoskeletons may be indigestible for many amphibians, in which case use freshly-molted mealworms, distinguished by their soft, white appearance.

• Waxworms and Tebos. Only in recent years have waxworms, the soft-bodied, inch-long larvae of the wax moth (*Galleria mellonella*) become a popular amphibian food. They are occasionally offered by pet shops and specialist suppliers of reptile foods. Starter cultures are available on occasion, containing a mixture of hatchling worms up to pupating stages. Although they are more nutritious and palatable than mealworms, some amphibians are reluctant to devour them because of a musty odor that is emitted. Also, their elastic skins are indigestible for some amphibians, so therefore make a small slit in the worm's body before feeding. Culturing these worms can be difficult, although once a good method is discovered they will give

Though hard to culture, waxworms, larvae of the wax moth *Galleria mellonella*, are accepted by many amphibians. They are easily purchased in the pet shop and make a good supplemental food. Photo: M. Staniszewski.

Tiny crickets are a readily available food for amphibians of almost all sizes. Photo: M. Staniszewski.

a continual food supply. The substrate can consist of finely ground oatmeal thoroughly mixed with a small amount of honey, then boiled to kill any mold and fungal spores. After letting it dry, the medium then is chopped up and used to fill a plastic shoe box to a depth of 2 to 4 inches. The lid should be firmly sealed to prevent escapes and should be given many pin-sized ventilation holes. Place the container in a cool (45°F), dark spot to prolong waxworm life. Any dead waxworms should be removed immediately as these will spoil the rest of the culture. At an inch in length the waxworms will encase themselves in cocoons. These should be separated to a warmer location where eventually wax moths will appear. In the wild, wax moths deposit their eggs in the honeycombs of bees. This can be mirrored by soaking tubes padded with cotton wool in a honey solution. Eggs hatch in five to eight days.

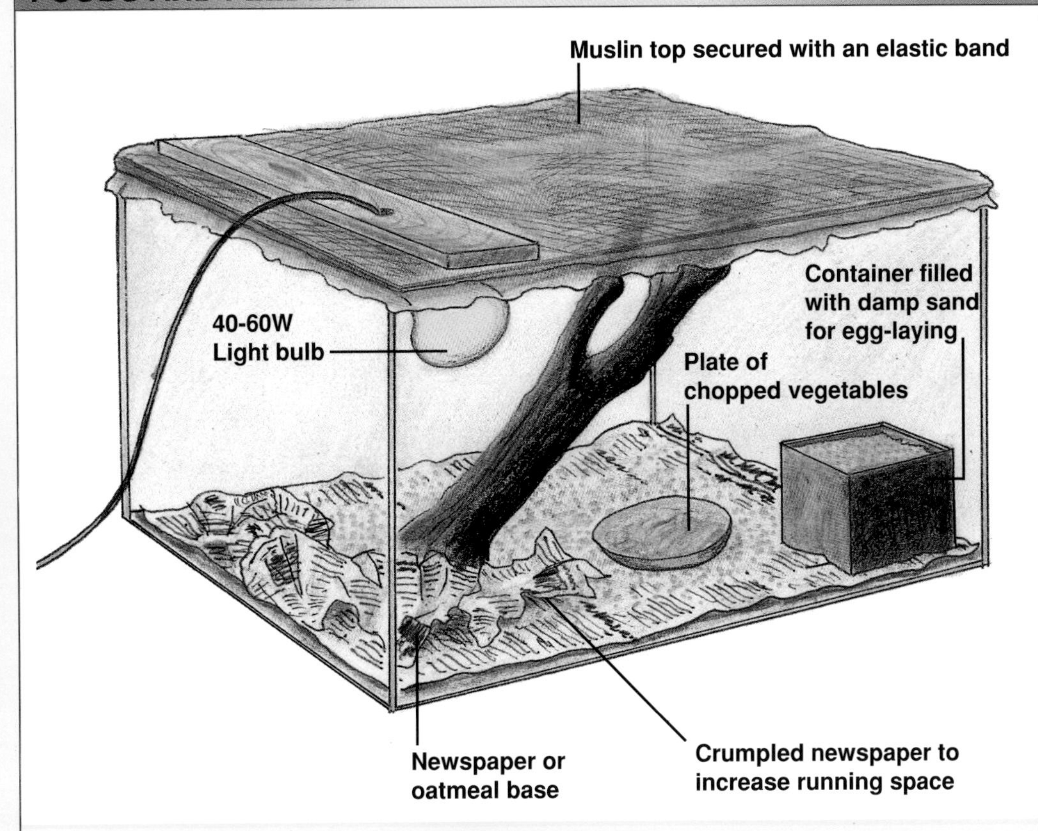

A rearing and holding container for crickets and locusts.

Tebos (butterworms) are the larvae of a larger species (up to 35 mm), the Chilean moth *Chilecomadia moorei*, and are treated in exactly the same manner.

• Crickets. At least two types of cricket are available from pet shops, the Gray or House Cricket (*Acheta domesticus*) and the field crickets (*Gryllus* species). Both are available in sizes ranging from 3 to 25 mm and offer an excellent nutritional food for amphibians of all sizes. In the United States only the Gray Cricket is commonly sold, many hobbyists thinking that field crickets are too large and heavy-shelled for most amphibians. Coupled with their year-round availability and relatively low cost, they have become the most popular amphibian food for most keepers.

Crickets are best stored at a temperature of 70°F in an ample container such as an old aquarium placed in a well-lighted location. As a guide, 100 crickets of mixed sizes can be accommodated per gallon of space (if given sufficient cover). The top will need a strong, well-ventilated lid that is tightly secured to prevent escapes. The base should consist of a dry substance on which they can feed such as chicken meal, bran, or crushed oatmeal crackers mixed with a multivitamin powder to further increase nutritional value. Pet shops sell special cricket food mixtures loaded with vitamins and minerals that assure the crickets will carry a good vitamin load to their amphibian predators. The addition of several pieces of scrunched up paper towels, newspaper, or paper egg cartons will increase living space and reduce cannibalism. Fresh vegetable peelings should be offered regularly in a jam jar lid but not allowed to fungus.

If adult crickets are present, tubes (old 35 mm film canisters) of moistened cotton wool should always be made available in which females will deposit their eggs. At weekly intervals the tubes should be replaced and transferred to a rearing container should you intend to begin a fresh culture. The eggs need a warm humid atmosphere (80 to 85°F) to develop quickly. Upon hatching the crickets are barely 2 mm in length. They can be fed immediately to newly metamorphosed frogs or allowed to grow at the same temperatures and fed on lettuce leaves and moistened bran.

Earthworms can be collected in sizes to suit the frog or salamander being fed. They also can be purchased from bait shops and sometimes from pet shops. Photo: M. Staniszewski.

A word of warning: Adult female crickets, distinguished by their egg-laying spike or ovipositor, should be used as food only after the spike has been clipped off. If left on this spike can easily lodge in an amphibian's esophagus or stomach and cause a blockage or actually penetrate the stomach lining and cause infection.

Collecting Medium-sized Foods

• Grasshoppers. Grasshoppers and wild crickets occur during warmer months in the dry grasses of meadows and hedgerows. They can be caught with a large butterfly net, but before using such an insect as food find out exactly which species it is. Some grasshoppers are rare and endangered and should be left alone. In North America grasshoppers are available from a limited number of suppliers, while in Europe locusts (large migratory grasshoppers) sometimes are sold and even cultured.

• Earthworms. Very few amphibians will not take earthworms of one type or another as part of their diet in captivity, even those species whose natural habitat contains no earthworms. The large nightcrawlers, which can attain 10 inches or more, appear on the surface of lawns and flowerbeds on damp nights to mate. Most earthworms are quite a bit smaller, however, often only 4 to 6 inches when fully grown. It is almost impossible to correctly identify earthworms without

Large toads (like this Western Toad, *Bufo boreas*) and salamanders often seem to enjoy wrestling with large earthworms. Earthworms, as long as they have been raised in uncontaminated soil and fed clean foods (no pesticides or herbicides) make an excellent treat for any amphibian that will take them. Photo: M. Staniszewski.

dissecting them or at least using high magnification, so don't worry too much about identification. All types of earthworms can be found by excavating in damp soil, overturning rocks and slabs, and in leaf litter and compost heaps. Avoid the red-ringed variety known as brandlings (*Eisenia foetida*), which may be distasteful or even lethal to smaller amphibians depending on their food.

A worm pen can be created by utilizing an old garbage can or similar container. The base is cut away to create a cylinder that is pushed into soft soil in a shady position. Using a mixture of finely chopped dead oak or maple leaves and loamy soil, the cylinder is filled to the brim and then firmed down. Finally it is thoroughly watered and the old garbage can lid is secured on top. The dark, moist surroundings encourage worms to feed and breed in the decaying leaves, and as long as the pen is kept damp it will provide a constant source of small worms even during hot, dry months.

• Slugs. Slugs are relished by salamanders in particular and are easily found crawling about on damp lawns, meadows, and vegetable gardens, under rocks, and in compost heaps. Several different varieties occur, with the small white or gray slugs (*Deroceras*) being more palatable than the brown garden slug (*Arion hortensis*). Very few amphibians except bullfrogs and large salamanders will tackle the huge black and spotted slugs because the viscid mucus they secrete is very distasteful.

Masses of the translucent-shelled eggs of slugs can be found under damp rocks and be removed to a hatching container.

Small brown garden slugs (such as the *Arion hortensis* shown here) are accepted by many burrowing salamanders and by toads. Do not attempt to feed large slugs even to large salamanders. Photo: M. Staniszewski.

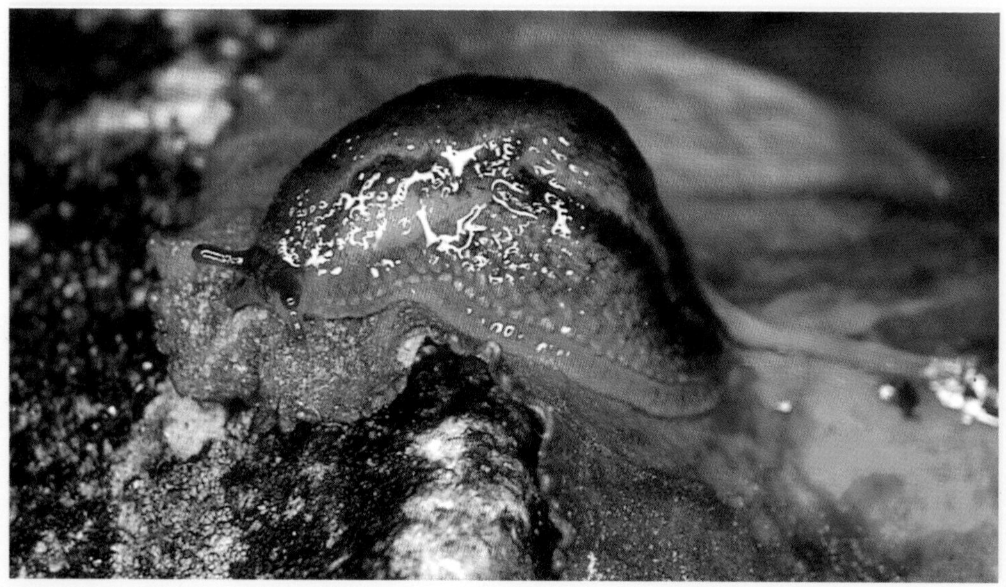

Weakly pigmented slugs (such as this *Deroceras*) are accepted by more salamanders than are brown slugs, but they are no more difficult to collect and hold than are less desirable types. Photo: M. Staniszewski.

The tiny 2 to 4 mm hatchlings make an ideal food for newly metamorphosed amphibians. The slugs can be grown to larger sizes by feeding them on lettuce leaves at a temperature no greater than 65°F.

Foods for Large Amphibians

These foods are for frogs within the range of 10 to 35 cm (4 to 14 in) and only the larger salamanders above 35 cm (14 in).

• Cockroaches. Because of the disdain with which most people view roaches, they are virtually unavailable as commercially bred food items. Additionally, it is unsafe to feed wild-collected roaches because of the probability that they have been treated with insecticides. Full-grown cockroaches have only limited use as food for the largest frogs and toads, while few salamanders except Hellbenders will attempt to tackle them. On the other hand, the young, known as nymphs, depending on their instar (hatchling nymphs molt 6 to 12 times before reaching adulthood; each molt is called an instar), make useful food for amphibians of all sizes.

Cockroaches are easily cultured but it cannot be too highly stressed that any escapees can give potentially disastrous consequences and this must be considered above all else. Once they escape they are extremely difficult to eradicate. Where escape-proof culturing containers are available, the standard

Old World locusts, such as the *Locusta migratoria* shown here, often are available in European pet shops though not often seen in American shops. Actually, any wild-caught or bred grasshopper will serve the same purpose, feeding large frogs and the occasional salamander. Photos: M. Staniszewski.

In Europe today locusts are bred in numbers and sold much as crickets are sold in America—by the box at various sizes from tiny "hoppers" (shown here) to large adults. Breeding locusts is a slow and time-consuming project that few amphibian keepers would find interesting if the grasshoppers where available commercially. Photo: M. Staniszewski.

method is to provide a dry base of chicken meal or bran. In the center a saucer containing scraps of vegetables and bread should be replenished on a regular basis. Scrunched up newspaper provides more running space and also a good egg-laying place. Room temperatures are sufficient to induce breeding. The females deposit many egg masses called ootheca, each containing up to 40 eggs. These should be removed to warm, humid containers, where the nymphs will appear 2 to 12 weeks later.

• Locusts. The African species *Schistocerca gregaria* and *Locusta migratoria* are now produced on a scale rivaling crickets by numerous commercial breeders in Europe. The 7-cm adults make an ample meal for giant frogs but are relatively expensive to purchase unless bought in bulk. The second and third instar nymphs, known as "hoppers," are eaten by most amphibians and are affordable if purchased by the hundred. Culturing locusts can be fairly expensive, and unless suitable temperatures are provided egg hatching and nymph development can be painstakingly slow and have a high mortality rate. An old aquarium can be used. The base should consist of either aquarium gravel or several sheets of newspaper. To provide necessary temperatures of 82 to 92°F when the container is kept in a room with average temperatures, a 60W or 100W bulb is needed for 14 hours daily, along with a 20W to 30W heating pad at night. Fresh grass provides both food and moisture and should be replaced on a daily basis. Several glass beakers about 10 to 15 cm (4 to 6 in) deep and filled with tightly packed damp sand provide the females with egg-laying sites. A branch should lead up to these beakers to allow access. The beakers are replaced every two days and removed to a separate hatchery where they are kept moist. At usual culturing temperatures the 5 to 7 mm hoppers will hatch out after two or three weeks. These are maintained in a similar fashion to the adults. Expect the mortality rate to be high for the first few weeks.

• Mice and Other Rodents. Although rodents are not an essential part of a large amphibian's diet, they are available from pet shops with their business aimed mainly at snake keepers. Typically they can be bought in sizes ranging from new-born mice (pinkies) and rats (pups) to small animals with first coats of fur (fuzzies) and juveniles that are fully independent of the mother (hoppers), as well as subadults and adults. Most conveniently, pet shops stock young mice and rats that have been humanely killed and frozen

As a general rule, red meats and chicken are not recommended foods for even the largest amphibians. However, African Bullfrogs and a few other very aggressive mouse-eating frogs and salamanders can be fed lean steak on occasion, especially if the meat is filled with vitamin and mineral supplements. Photo: M. Staniszewski.

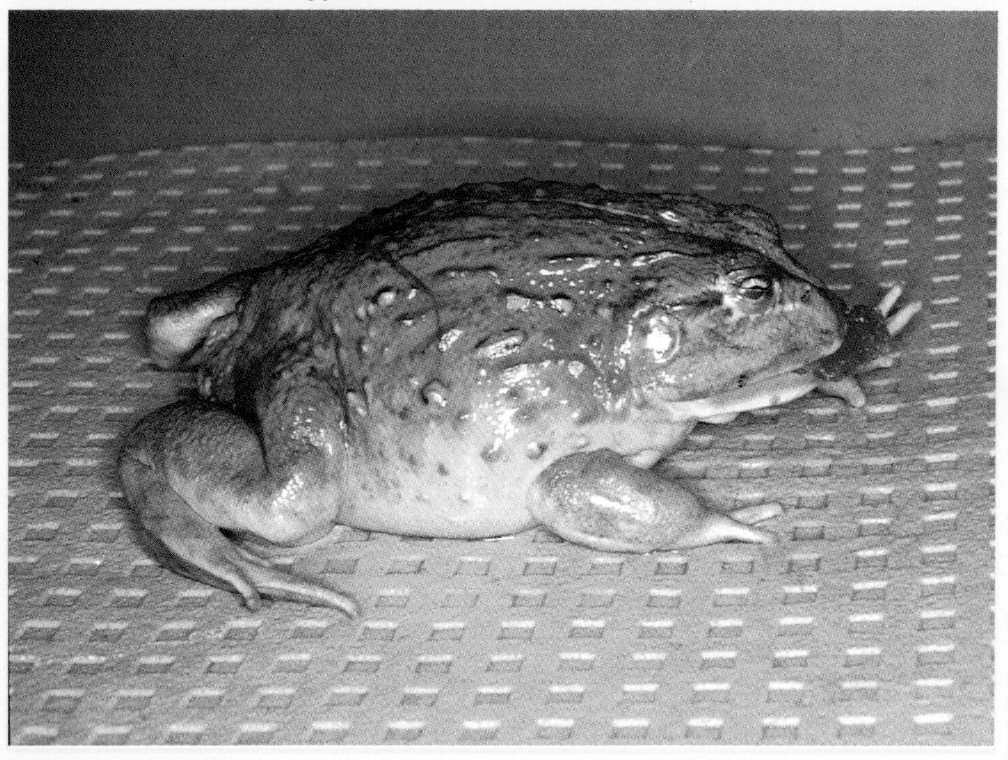

for storage until needed. Adult mice and gerbils are only suitable for larger anurans such as bullfrogs, horned frogs, White's Treefrogs, and Marine Toads, although giant salamanders may take small rodents. An adult African Bullfrog can overcome a large rat, but as these frogs are known to attack lions in the wild they must be an exception to the rule. Other larger salamanders such as the Tiger (*Ambystoma tigrinum*), the California Giant (*Dicamptodon ensatus*), and the aquatic Spanish Ribbed Newt (*Pleurodeles waltl*) will eat newborn mice in captivity, as will a whole host of medium-sized frogs.

Breeding rodents in the home is feasible only if there is space and time to feed and clean them out. A female mouse will produce a litter every five to eight days. The pinkies can be removed and killed for storage at any size, depending on the size of the amphibians to which they will be fed. In view of the moral issue of feeding live vertebrates to other animals, rodents should ALWAYS be killed before being used as prey, and indeed in some countries feeding live rodents to herptiles is against the law or at least frowned upon. In any event, it is possible that the tables will be turned, with the rodent attacking and maiming or even killing the amphibian. The most humane method for killing a rodent is to administer a sharp blow to the back of its head.

• Other Foods for Large Amphibians. In captivity many amphibians can be coaxed into accepting strips of raw meat. Use fresh, lean red meats such as steak, removing as many fatty deposits as possible. To encourage an amphibian to take the meat, attach a strip loosely to the end of a piece of cotton string and wriggle it about. Should an amphibian not seem interested in this, it may be because it dislikes the smell, so try rubbing the meat with a more favored food. Marine Toads eventually learn to take chunks of meat, including ground beef and dog food, from a dish because they habitually feed on carrion in the wild. Raw meat should not be used as the sole food source because it is deficient in certain vitamins and minerals and contains a high proportion of fats. Dust part of the meat with a vitamin/mineral supplement whenever possible.

FOOD SUPPLEMENTS

Amphibians sometimes may fall into a routine where they eat only one or two particular types of food, either because they refuse anything else offered or the hobbyist is unable to offer a varied choice. Inevitably this results in an unbalanced diet that is deficient in certain essential vitamins and/or minerals. Until recently amphibian hobbyists had little option but to use vitamin/mineral supplements formulated for popular household pets such as cats and dogs. This often culminated in many amphibians remaining deficient in certain vitamins that were not present in required quantities. Recently a number of multivitamin/mineral products aimed specifically at the herptile hobbyist have appeared on the market that are correctly formulated and therefore properly utilized by amphibians. Some products also include catalytic balancers such as vitamin D3 to correctly metabolize minerals like calcium. Liquid and tablet formats are of limited use to amphibians as food supplements, but powders can be dusted on the prey with an artists' brush or a small amount can be placed in a plastic bag containing a number of mealworms, crickets, locusts, etc., and the bag thoroughly shaken. There should be no need to use an excessive amount of supplements because any surplus is excreted and not utilized.

• Gut-loading. A very easy and successful method of assuring proper vitamin and mineral intake in captive amphibians is the process of gut-loading their prey animals. This technique works well with crickets and less well with mealworms. Simply put, the food eaten by the crickets is heavily dosed with a good vitamin/mineral powder each day or at least 24 hours before the crickets are harvested for feeding. Crickets eat the supplement with their normal food and retain high vitamin and mineral levels in their bodies (especially the gut and fat bodies) when they are fed to the frog or salamander. Vitamins and minerals eaten this way by the crickets are not digested and are freely available to the amphibian in a very natural manner.

Don't neglect prepared reptile foods from your pet shop when looking for treats for your amphibians. Some turtle foods, for instance, provide a very palatable, nutritionally well-balanced, and easy to store food for aquatic salamanders. Photo courtesy of Wardley Products.

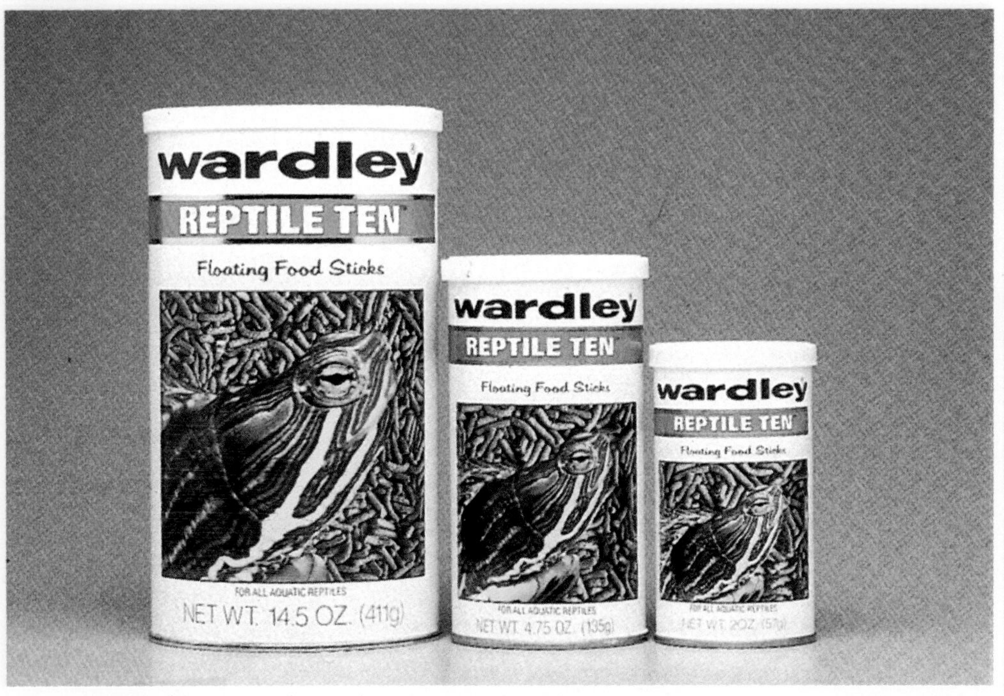

Breeding Amphibians

Discovering a small clump of frog spawn or several salamander larvae darting around a water bowl is one of the most satisfying aspects in keeping amphibians and gives an indication of how successful a hobbyist has been in providing a proper environment. Certain species of amphibians still cannot be bred due to conditions that govern their reproductive behavior in the wild and cannot be replicated in captivity without great expense, if possible to replicate at all. For instance, the European Alpine or Black Salamander (*Salamandra atra*) lives in the cold, rarefied atmosphere of high altitudes where temperatures rarely go above 65°F (18°C). Even in experiments conducted in specially constructed cabinets, this species refused to breed when climatic conditions apparently were perfect. Other factors such as diet, soil pH, or territory size may play decisive parts in encouraging such a species to breed. At the opposite end of the scale there are amphibians that prove very easy to breed, even in unsuitable or unfavorable conditions. Clawed frogs are examples of very tolerant amphibians.

Most species encountered in captivity fall into an area between these two extremes. Beginners to this hobby are advised to start off with easier species and gradually build experience until they are confident enough to attempt the more taxing species. Experience may reach the stage where a hobbyist is able to contribute greatly to the limited understanding of breeding behavior of those difficult (and inevitably rare) species.

Before attempting to breed any species of amphibian, there are a few necessary biological, conditional, and behavioral factors that have to be examined.

SEXING AMPHIBIANS

The phenomenon known as parthenogenesis or entirely female populations where unfertilized ova develop directly into new individuals does not occur in the amphibian world to the extent that it does in insects, fishes, and reptiles. Therefore, we can assume that in captivity at least one individual from each sex is required in order to produce fertile eggs. To distinguish one sex from another can be a difficult exercise, and in many species it might be necessary to use a magnifying glass for closer inspection. Often there are no visible external characteristics to suggest the sex, and three or four specimens may have to be obtained in order to secure a sexed pair. Urine and blood samples can also be used to determine sex, but very few dealers are likely to engage in such specialized activity. In other species sexual differences may become apparent only with growth to full adulthood or during the short courtship period. However, the sex of the majority of amphibians can be distinguished either by clear external characteristics such as crests, coloration, and size (which is known as sexual dimorphism), male vocalization (in anurans), or by closer examination of the cloacal region (area around the vent), skin texture, appendages on toes, etc.

CAECILIANS

Male and female caecilians exhibit no clear external differences outside of the breeding periods. The male's internal sexual organ (at least it acts like a penis) is everted only during copulation, with swelling of the cloacal region evident immediately prior to copulation. Unlike reptiles, caecilians cannot be internally examined by probing (the method of using a smooth, rounded tool that is pushed along the inverted sexual organ) because their sexual organ is actually a modified section of the lower gut.

SALAMANDERS

External sexual characteristics vary from family

Salamanders often are sexable by the condition of the cloaca. In males that are reproductively active the walls of the cloaca are greatly swollen, while in females and non-reproductive males (as shown here) the cloaca is small and not swollen. Photo of *Taricha torosa*: W. P. Mara.

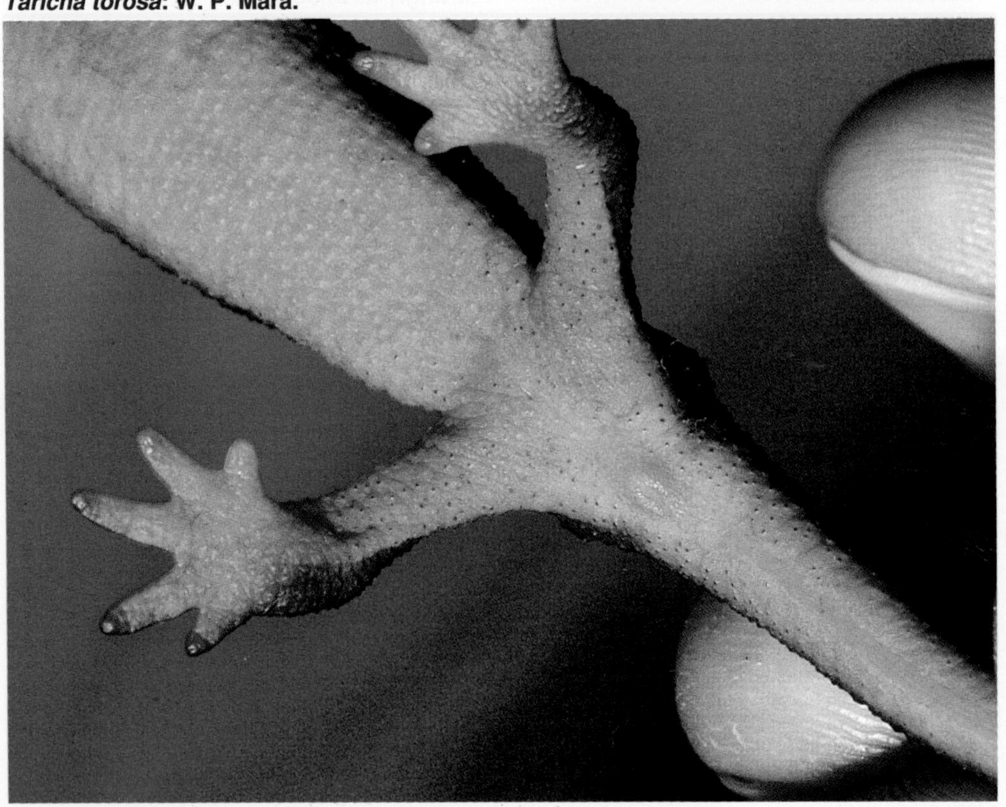

to family.

• Ambystomatidae (Mole Salamanders). In virtually all species the male has a longer tail and a visibly more swollen cloaca on which rectangular lobes may be present. In some species there may be distinctive coloration differences. For example, female Marbled Salamanders (*Ambystoma opacum*) have gray or dirty colored bands as opposed to white bands in the male.

• Cryptobranchidae (Giant Salamanders). In all species the female is considerably larger than the male.

• Hynobiidae (Primitive Salamanders). Physical differences are either difficult to determine or completely absent. Males sometimes have longer limbs and develop low ridges along the edges of the tail during the courtship period.

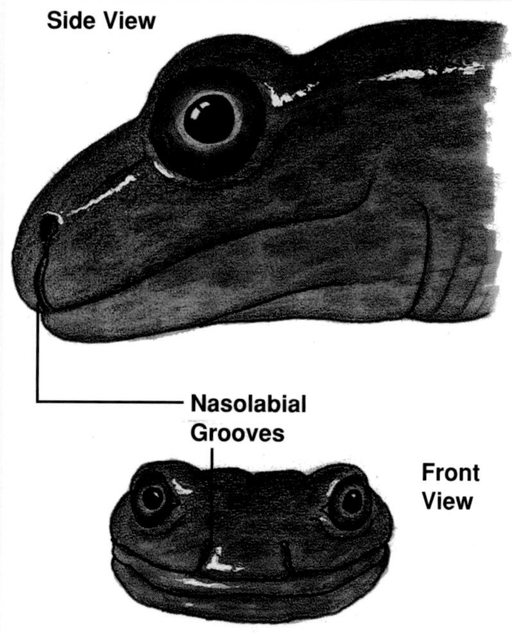

The family Plethodontidae is recognized, in part, by the presence of nasolabial grooves from the nostril to the mouth. Often male plethodontids have these grooves more strongly developed than in females.

• Plethodontidae (Lungless Salamanders). Since this is the largest and most diverse family, generalizations cannot be made to cover all genera and therefore it is better to look at the major genera individually:

Plethodon: Males have a broader head, a more pointed lower jaw, and a longer tail than females. On closer inspection the males of some species have a distinct tubercle at the end of the nasolabial groove on the upper lip and there may also be a large circular mental (scent) gland under the chin.

Desmognathus: Adult males sometimes are darker on the dorsal surface and have U-shaped or kidney-shaped mental glands on the chin.

Eurycea: Males often have conspicuous spike-like projections from the nostrils to the lip of the upper jaw called cirri.

Ensatina: The tail of the male tends to be longer and slimmer and the upper lip is larger than in the female.

Batrachoseps: Males have a blunter snout than females and their premaxillary teeth perforate (pass through) the upper lip.

Hydromantes: The teeth in the upper jaw of the male tend to project slightly out beyond the lip and there is an ellipsoid-shaped mental gland on the chin of the male.

Males of many *Eurycea* species (here *E. wilderae*) have the nasolabial grooves prolonged beyond the edge of the mouth as a distinct cirrus. Photo: R. D. Bartlett.

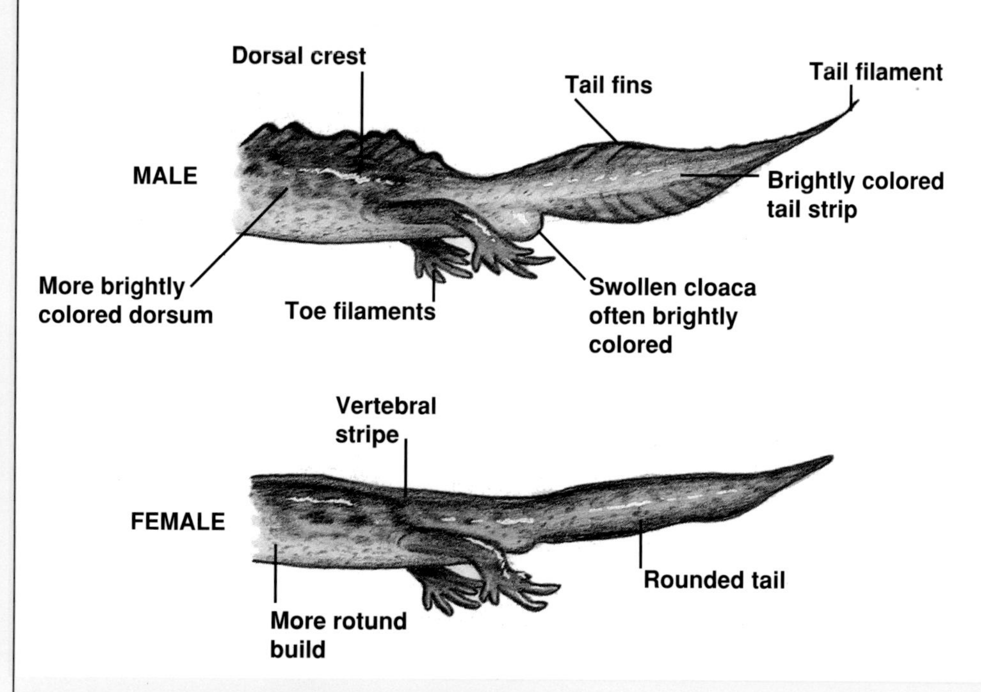

Comparison of sexual differences in the Marbled Newt, *Triturus marmoratus*.

Aneides: Males have an oval mental gland on the chin during the breeding season and a broader head than females.

• Salamandridae (Typical Salamanders and Newts). The most distinctive differences between male and female are seen during the courtship period when semi–aquatic newts of this family take to the water. Males go through several startling transformations: coloration, particularly on the ventral and lateral surfaces, becomes more vivid; they gain a high crest that extends from the head along the spine to the tip of the tail; and the cloacal region swells and sometimes intensifies in coloration. Females tend to remain rather drab, their crests are much lower, and they are noticeably more rotund than the male. At any stage other than courtship both sexes tend to be rather similar in terms of coloration, differ only slightly in size, and males may retain remnants of their crest in the form of a low dorsal ridge.

In other salamandrids, both semi–aquatic types such as the Italian Spectacled Salamander (*Salamandrina terdigitata*) and purely terrestrial types such as the Fire Salamander, adult females generally are more robust while in males the cloacal region remains swollen throughout the year. Male Pacific newts (*Taricha*) and Spanish Ribbed Newts (*Pleurodeles waltl*) have extremely rough skin during the

Vocalizing males, like this *Rana esculenta*, are perhaps the most positive way of sexing frogs. However, a few female frogs chirp noisily and some species have silent males. Photo: M. Staniszewski.

breeding season and also develop rough skin (nuptial pads) on the undersides of the feet.

FROGS

Apart from a handful of species, the male is nearly always smaller than the female, although this would be of help only when fully grown specimens are acquired. Intense coloration in breeding male frogs is not as apparent as in some breeding male salamanders because most frogs breed at night, when colors would be ineffective in attracting mates. Vocalization is a much better way of determining sex, but unfortunately it is of little help to the hobbyist attempting to acquire a sexed pair. Instead look for other slight differences related to vocalization, such as wrinkling and discoloration (usually gray, blue, or black) of the throat or loose skin below the tympanum of species in which males possess vocal sacs.

A common characteristic of frogs that breed in water is the presence of nuptial pads either on the digits, under the feet, or along the inner lower arm. These rough patches of skin allow the male to maintain a good grip when in amplexus (mating clasp) with the female.

Some frogs, such as hylids, hyperoliids, and certain ranids, can be sexed through the thin translucent skin of the underside when they are placed on a sheet of glass and held close to fairly strong lamp or, even better, a krypton bulb. Sometimes masses of developing eggs can be viewed in the lower abdominal cavity of females. In males two thin opaque tubes running alongside each other may be present, the ureters that connect the kidneys to the cloaca. In females these may be partially or completely hidden by the thicker uterus and oviducts.

A less common difference between sexes is the size of the tympanum in ranids such the American Bullfrog. In males it is larger than the eye, while in the female it is the same size as the eye or smaller. In the Tailed Frog (*Ascaphus truei*) from western North America, the male has a "tail" used as a copulatory organ.

PREREQUISITES FOR SUCCESSFUL MATING

Sex Ratio

In captivity a male and female will be sufficient for a mating to take place in the majority of amphibians, yet this is not

Sexual differences in the newt genus *Salamandra*.

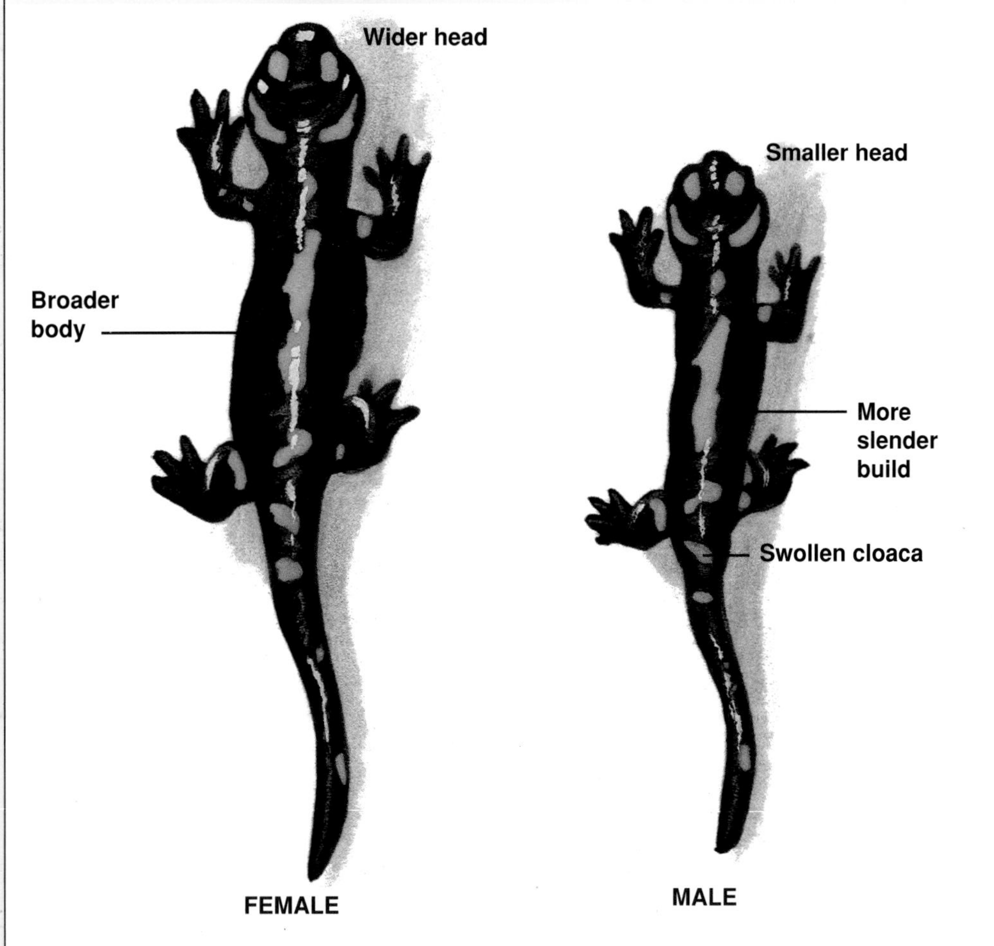

Male American Bullfrogs, *Rana catesbeiana*, have greatly enlarged tympana (eardrums), a character that can be seen even at a distance. Photo: M. Staniszewski.

Sexual differences in Argentine Horned Frogs, *Ceratophrys ornata*.

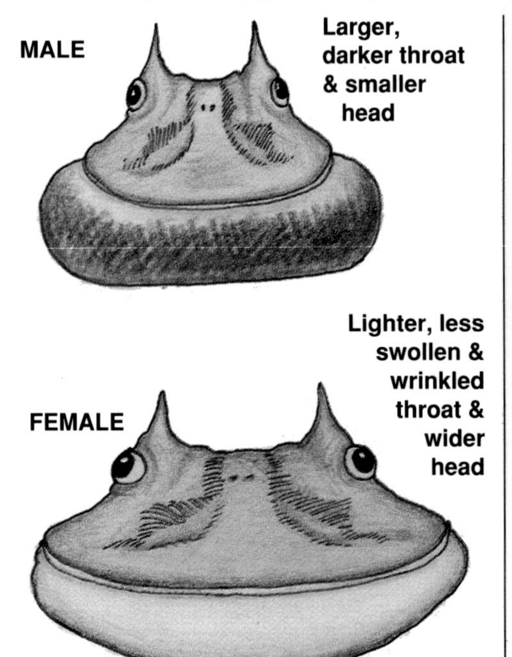

always a true reflection of what would be encountered in the wild. In amphibians that return to water to breed, males outnumber females sometimes on the order of 20:1. Often this not only creates a frantic rivalry and squabbling in order to secure a female (the sex drive of the males is so high that they will attempt to grasp other males, fish, plant stems, or even a hobbyist's finger), but consequently leads to a more vigorous pairing producing a more fertile spawning. Conversely, in fully terrestrial amphibians, most lead a solitary existence where there is minimal contact with other individuals and hence no rivalry. The limited space of a terrarium governs the ratio of males to females in a species that congregates to breed. Excessive numbers of male newts of the genera *Cynops, Paramesotriton, Taricha,* and *Triturus* always will fight in too small an aquarium, and this can lead to lost digits, limbs, and ends of tails and cause undue stress. Although anurans such as ranids and bufonids are not inclined to attack each other, in a small aquarium an overabundance of males will end up drowning either each other or the female.

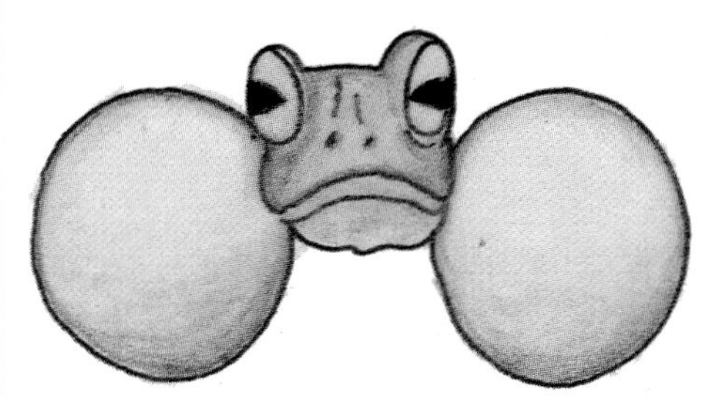

Paired vocal sac

Single vocal sac

Bi-lobed vocal sac

Some commonly seen vocal sac shapes in male frogs.

Stimulating Sexual Behavior

There are very few amphibian species that will simply mate and produce a fertile batch of eggs without any prompting whatsoever. The most important factor before any amphibian can begin the potentially exhausting ritual of courtship and copulation is that it should be healthy and well fed. Arousal, i.e., ovum production in females, sperm production in males, and sex drive in both, often is induced in response to changes in climatic conditions such as temperature, rainfall, and humidity, or in response to increased food availability. Recognizing and partially replicating such stimuli in captivity can have an advantageous effect in encouraging amphibians to breed, yet some species of amphibians can be induced to breed with the aid of stimuli that are completely alien to their normal existence. The characteristics and values of both are discussed below.

Natural Stimuli

<u>Climatic Effects</u>

• Cool-temperate to Temperate (Cyclic Breeders). During periods of the year when temperatures fall below 40°F, amphibians will seek out underground retreats such as holes beneath tree roots and disused rodent burrows (known as hibernacula) or bury themselves in the muddy bottom of ponds. Here they begin a period of inactivity during which their metabolism virtually stops, hibernation. When the temperature increases, hibernating amphibians are quickly aroused into sexual activity and immediately congregate in breeding ponds or seek mates. Hibernation should be simulated in captivity by using an old aquarium and filling it to near the brim with a loose, damp material such as chopped live sphagnum moss mixed with peat. Such amphibians are allowed to hibernate during a time that corresponds to a natural period of inactivity (between late autumn and early spring), being introduced into the aquarium to burrow into the medium. An escape-proof lid is secured in place and the aquarium is located in a cool, frost-free position such as an unheated garage, cellar, or attic. If a hobbyist lives in a region that does not experience cold conditions during any part of the year, plastic shoe boxes filled with the same medium can be positioned in a refrigerator at a temperature of no less than 38°F. (Be sure the refrigerator is ventilated and there is sufficient air entering the box for the

Other sexual differences in frogs. At left, anal papillae in female hyperoliids; at right, nuptial pads in many male frogs.

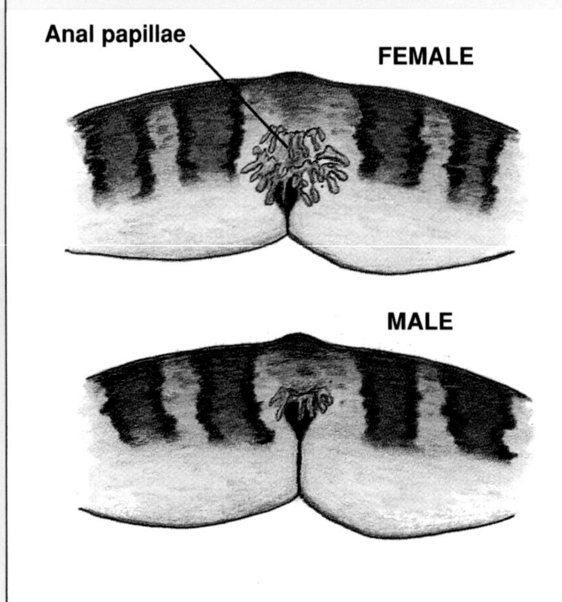

Sexual differences seen in some anurans (especially hyperoliids)

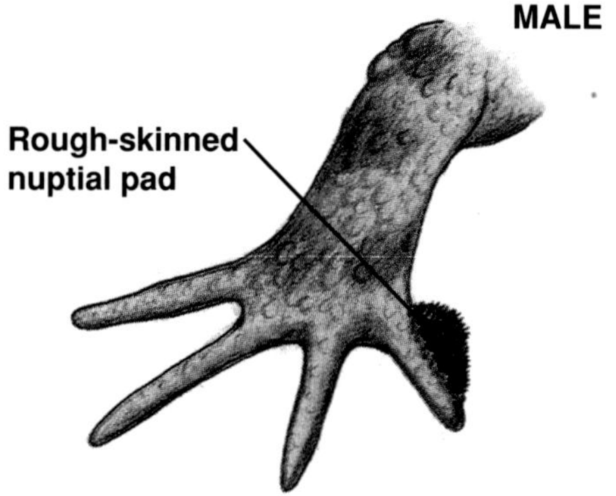

Front limb of the Yellow-bellied Toad (*Bombina variegata*) showing the horny nuptial pad also seen in many other anurans, especially bufonids, ranids, leptodactylids, and pelobatids

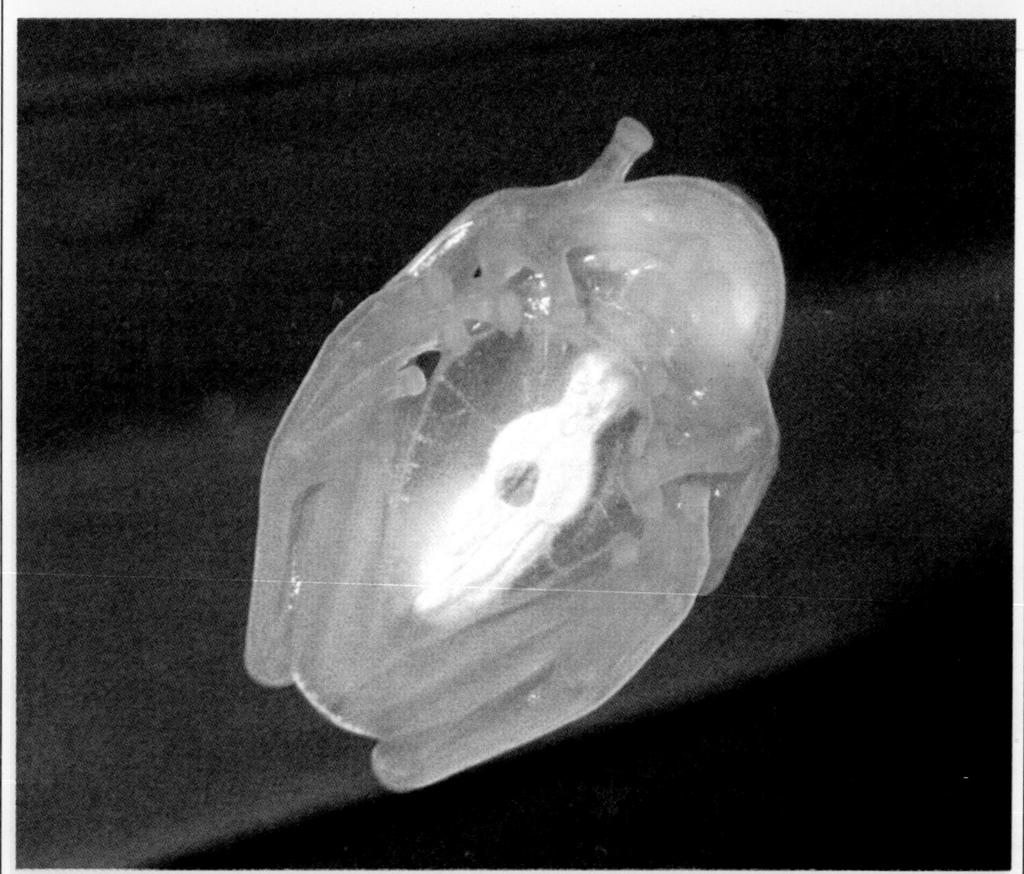

In centrolenids such as *Cochranella fleishmanni* and many small treefrogs the belly skin is transparent enough to allow important sex organs to be recognized in the living frog. Photo: R. D. Bartlett.

animal to breathe.) This hibernation period does not have to be as long as would be encountered in the wild. Six to eight weeks is sufficient for all but those species that hail from either very cold regions such as Siberia or from high altitude mountain habitats such as the European Alps, where 10 to 16 weeks would be more appropriate.

• Warm-temperate to Warm (Bicyclic Breeders). Species distributed within this climatic band are faced with two climatic stimuli and often they will breed twice a year. During the cool period temperatures fall to around 50 to 54°F, which is not low enough to halt activity but causes loss of appetite and low metabolism. In captivity this can be encouraged by gradually lowering temperatures and reducing photoperiod until the 50°F limit is reached and the lighting is completely switched off. After six to eight weeks the temperature and photoperiod are gradually increased. Hot, dry periods are also encountered in this climatic band, and then the amphibian will spend much of its time underground in cool, moist surroundings, occasionally venturing to the surface at night to feed. With the onset of rain amphibians leave their hiding places and begin to both feed and mate. For example, after rain Fire Salamanders appear by the thousands in southern Europe following a long, dry summer. Amphibians kept in greenhouses where summers are relatively warm will display this behavior.

• Subtropical to Tropical Forests (Regular Breeders). Many anurans that dwell in warm, moist equatorial forests do not experience such marked stimuli because temperatures, rainfall, photoperiod, and humidity levels are roughly constant throughout the year. Breeding can take place all year around and probably is influenced more by daily rainfall pattern than by annual changes. This can be duplicated in the terrarium by excessively spraying with water one day then reducing it the next. In some cases the sudden increase of migratory or seasonal insects for food can act as a stimulus; this could be carried out in captivity by offering larger amounts of insect food during certain times of the year.

• Savannah to Desert (Opportune Breeders). Fossorial anurans such as *Pyxicephalus, Ceratophrys ornata,* and Australasian burrowing frogs spend much of their time burrowed deep beneath the baked surface of the arid areas they inhabit. Here they shed several layers of dead epidermis that harden to form a waterproof membrane that retains sufficient moisture for life while the frog is completely inactive. Such inactivity may last several years if no rain falls and is known as estivation. When rain falls it tends to be so heavy that flood waters occur, enabling these anurans to push their way up through the now softened soil and immediately begin courtship. In captivity if the terrarium is kept warm (about 90°F) and dry, estivation will occur in these species even when no provisions are made for burrowing.

Food Availability

Anurans dwelling in drier regions such as rocky hillsides, savannahs, and semi-arid habitats may breed following a sudden but brief excessive supply of food that usually arrives in conjunction with rainfall. Energy derived from gorging on such prey can then be expended on mating, because when food is in short supply the frogs must conserve energy for capturing what little prey is available or must estivate. Such an existence has successfully been mirrored to a lesser extent in captivity with a number of species including Australian *Limnodynastes* and the African dwarf toad *Bufo taitanus*. The animals are offered food only sporadically for six to eight weeks and the terrarium remains fairly dry with no large body of water present. After this time the terrarium is misted in increasing regularity over a period of two to five days and then a water bowl of proper size is added. The final step is to introduce excessive amounts of food such as plant stalks crawling with aphids or plenty of caterpillars and the like. After the amphibians have gorged themselves, misting the terrarium is stopped, prompting the occupants to begin their courtship almost immediately.

Artificial Stimuli

Semi-aquatic anurans such as fire-bellied toads (*Bombina*) are easily stimulated into breeding by regularly and unnaturally spraying the aqua-terrarium or greenhouse pond with tepid water from a fine rose watering can up to ten times per day. It is not certain why this should stimulate breeding, but water freshness and the splashing sounds that encourage males to vocalize are possible answers.

An unusual but successful method for inducing more tolerant subtropical and tropical anurans such as mantellas, hyperoliids, and rhacophorids to breed is to lower the terrarium temperature by around 8 to 10°F and 20 to 40% relative humidity for a period of 5 to 12 days, day and night. The temperature then is gradually increased to normal levels and the terrarium is misted with greater frequency each day until mating occurs. In the wild such amphibians are acquainted only with very small differences in climate all year around, and it is quite surprising that this should be effective.

COURTSHIP BEHAVIOR

Once prompted into reproductive behavior, amphibians must be provided with an appropriate arrangement in terms of space and sometimes secluded places in which copulation can take place and cause minimal stress. Provisions should also be made for egg or larval deposition. Here we will look closely at the courtship behavior of each order.

Caecilians

Very little is known about caecilian breeding behavior, but it is thought that many species breed several times throughout the year. Copulation usually takes place on the soil surface at night, particularly after heavy rainfall, with the male entwining around the female before everting an intromittent organ at the tip of his body to deposit several sacs of sperm known as spermatophores inside her cloaca. Caecilians are among the few amphibians to display true copulation.

Salamanders

Salamanders can be divided into two groups, those that reproduce on land and those that reproduce in water. In the case of terrestrial types some manner of attracting a mate is essential because the majority of species lead secretive, solitary lives, rarely encountering other individuals of the same species. Females (and to a lesser extent some males) release strong natural body scents known as pheromones to lure a mate. Terrestrial salamanders that breed in water often migrate long distances to return to a pond or stream they themselves originated from, and here they meet up with many other individuals of their own kind. For males, vivid coloration and/or decorative body crests and toe webbing play an important part in enticing a female. Courtship displays are far more elaborate and frenetic than in terrestrial species because the males face greater competition from rival males in a smaller area.

Apart from a few species, actual copulation is strictly external because salamanders do not possess intromittent organs. Most salamander families adopt a method of internal fertilization where the male deposits one or more spermatophores that are cone-shaped and have a sticky surface or are covered in minute barbs; most have a sterile base and a sperm-containing cap. He then attempts to lure a female toward him either by ritualist dancing, using his snout to gently nudge her, or, in extreme cases, dragging her with his mouth so that her cloaca brushes against these sacs. The female picks up one or more spermatophores (or at least the caps containing sperm) with the lips of her cloaca and moves them into the body. The cap dissolves and the sperm are released to either fertilize the eggs or they swim to a pocket of glandular folds known as the seminal receptacle where they are stored for later use. A female often will mate with several males.

Fertilization in primitive families such as the Asian Hynobiidae, the Cryptobranchidae, and the Sirenidae is external. The males propel jets of sperm over eggs that have already been deposited either in water or on land. Hynobiid females produce often large egg sacks or cases containing the fertilized eggs.

Frogs

The main tool that many male anurans use to attract mates is their vocal ability. When he has successfully located a fertile mate, he then proceeds to clasp her around some region of her body with his forearms in a behavior known as amplexus. To enable him to spray sperm over the eggs as they are discharged and before the protective jelly over them swells, he must have his cloaca as close to the female's as possible to ensure that as many eggs as possible are fertilized. Amplexus typically lasts several hours until eggs are deposited. A male may mate many times with several different females, while a female may deposit several clumps of eggs fertilized by several males.

There are two main types of amplexus along with several slight variations and a few unusual isolated clasps known only from one or two species. The type of amplexus used by a species of frog can depend on the size of the female, the size of the male, the reach of the male's forearms, the girth of the female part clasped, and the habitat in which amplexus occurs.

• Axillary Amplexus. The male embraces the female by clasping her quite tightly beneath the armpits. Nuptial pads further hinder him sliding off, and because his cloaca is close to the female's there is no need for excessive maneuvering in order to fertilize eggs. This technique occurs in a wide variety of frogs, but particularly in the families Ranidae, Bufonidae, and Leptodactylidae.

• Lumbar or Inguinal Amplexus. A rather primitive technique found in primitive families such as Discoglossidae, Pelobatidae, and Pipidae, to name just a few, where the male clasps the female around the bases of her hind limbs. His cloaca may be positioned quite a distance from the female's, so he tends to significantly arch his back when eggs are being discharged.

• Fixed Amplexus. Males of the family Microhylidae such as *Breviceps* species release a mucilage from special glands located on the ventral surface that holds the male tightly to the back of the female. Any attempt to remove him can cause severe damage, and he is not released until the female sheds her skin.

• Other Types of Amplexus. A few species of dendrobatid frogs are known to clasp the female around the throat or chin in an embrace known as cephalic amplexus. Frogs of the tropical American genus *Atelopus* will stay in amplexus for days on end, sometimes weeks, because populations are so sparsely distributed over such a wide area the chances of a female meeting a male are slim, so he holds on to her from first contact until mating, no matter how long this takes.

Some frogs, such as a few *Eleutherodactylus* from the Caribbean Islands, fertilize the eggs internally by means of cloacal contact though there is no intromittent organ. Madagascan ranids such as the beautiful mantellas (*Mantella* species) lay eggs on land that are fertilized by the male secreting sperm over them even if they were laid several weeks earlier.

EGG DEPOSITION AND EGG CARE

If correct captive conditions prevail, then prior to, during, or following a successful pairing either eggs or larvae will be deposited. Amphibian eggs are laid on land or in water singly, in small clutches, in huge masses, in foam nests, or on some part of the parent's body. Whatever their location, the need for moisture is essential because as the embryo grows it will draw water from its surroundings. Although eggs of all amphibians are structurally very similar, they can differ in size, pole or nucleus coloration, and sometimes shape depending on where they have been laid. The size of the egg does not always bear a relationship to the size of the amphibian because larger amphibians usually lay lots of smaller eggs. Nucleus coloration usually is determined by climate

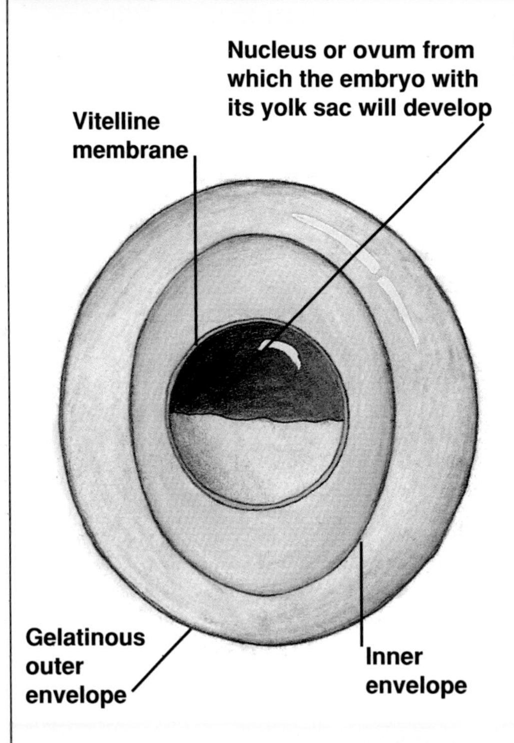

Cross-section of a typical amphibian egg.

and the surrounding environment. Eggs deposited in sunny locations such as those of mass–spawning temperate frogs and toads have a dark pole caused by a layer of pigment called melanin. This will both absorb heat to speed up embryonic development and protect the ovum from the sun's radiation. Usually as a camouflage measure the nucleus matches the color of the plant leaf, muddy pond basin, rock, bark, or soil the eggs have been attached to. As they are unable to alter their color, it is the female's task to ensure she has chosen a safe location.

Eggs Deposited in Water

Salamanders and some frogs that return to water to deposit their eggs are particularly choosy when it comes to finding a favorable location, especially in those species that lay them singly. A flexible plant leaf such as Canadian Pondweed (*Elodea*), eel grass, and even a blade of terrestrial grass bending into the water are the usual favorites. Some newts prefer to lay their eggs on thin strips of black plastic (as used for garbage can liners) made by cutting a dozen or so narrow strips (1 cm x 5 cm) that are then tied together at intervals along a piece of string. The end of the string is weighted and several are submerged in the aquarium or a pond, where they prove easy to remove and do not disturb any healthy plant growth. Such materials may even reduce the risk of fungal infections attacking the eggs.

Habitually heliothermic (basking) amphibians such as discoglossids and some hylids lay their eggs either singly or in small clumps very close to the water surface and where full sun is present. Warm temperatures present during the day promote rapid embryo development, allowing less time for predation of the defenseless immobile eggs. This situation can be reproduced in captivity by securely positioning an overhead 40W spot lamp approximately 12 to 15 inches from the water surface.

At the opposite end of the scale, some salamanders will lay their eggs only in cool, slow-flowing brooks and streams (*Chioglossa, Euproctus, Pseudotriton*), and this type of habitat must be present in

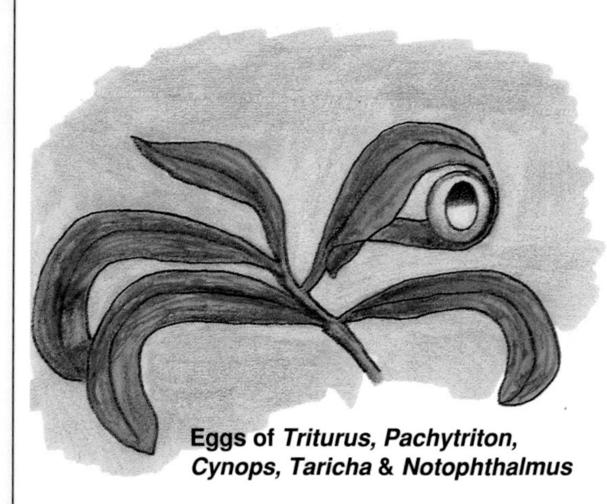

Eggs of *Triturus, Pachytriton, Cynops, Taricha* & *Notophthalmus*

Eggs of *Salamandrina*, some ambystomids and plethodontids (i.e., *Eurycea, Pseudotriton*)

Eggs of certain *Ambystoma* including *A. talpoideum* and the Axolotl, and many hynobiids

Eggs of cryptobranchids, sirenids, necturids and amphiumids

Examples of different types of salamander eggs and nests.

Eggs of many terrestrial plethodontids & certain ambystomids such as the Marbled Salamander (*A. opacum*)

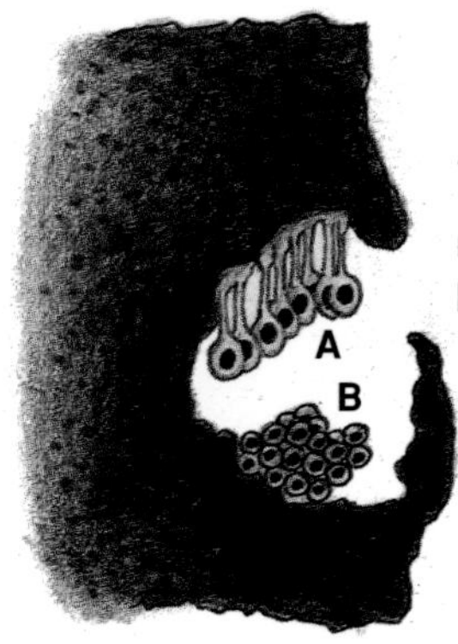

Eggs of:
A–*Aneides*
B–Arboreal neotropical plethodontids

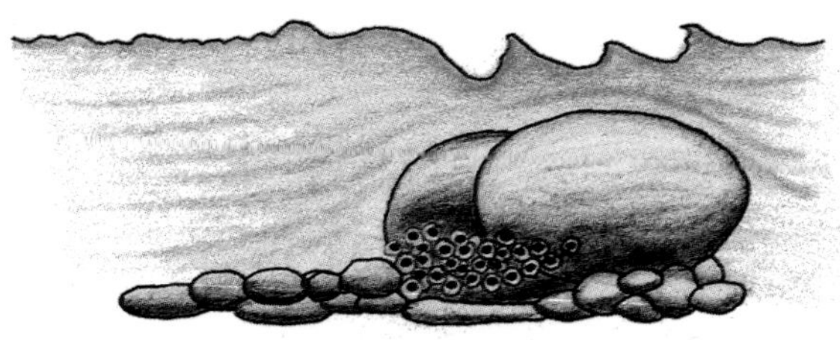

Eggs of *Euproctus, Chioglossa* & certain plethodontids (such as *Pseudotriton ruber*)

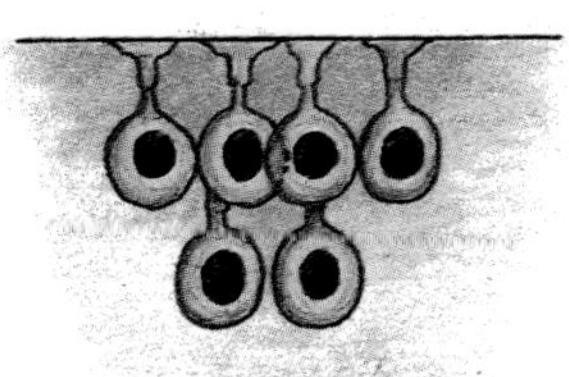

Eggs of *Rhyacotriton* (Rhyacotritonidae)

the setup if they are to breed successfully. The resultant larvae also live in moving water that contains a high proportion of dissolved oxygen.

Those amphibians that deposit mass clumps or strings of spawn tend to be quite perfunctory when choosing a spawning site and may drop spawn in any part of the water. Clawed frogs and Axolotls simply spread their spawn over the gravel bottom and rocks of the aquarium. In their natural environment many of the eggs would fall prey to a whole host of predators ranging from insects to various fishes, but because such huge numbers are produced, even if just 0.05% out of every batch (1 in every 2000 eggs) survives to produce a mature amphibian this would be sufficient to continue the existence of the species.

Once deposited in water, eggs should as soon as possible be transferred into rearing containers where they can be closely scrutinized and are free from predation (most salamanders and aquatic frogs will devour their own eggs and hatchling larvae). Even so, a few eggs will not develop. This is brought about by a number of factors. The most common cause, a fungal infection, can be a major problem especially where mass clumps of spawn are concerned. Fungus in itself is not always the source of the

Examples of different types of frog eggs and spawn.

Typical eggs of *Bombina*

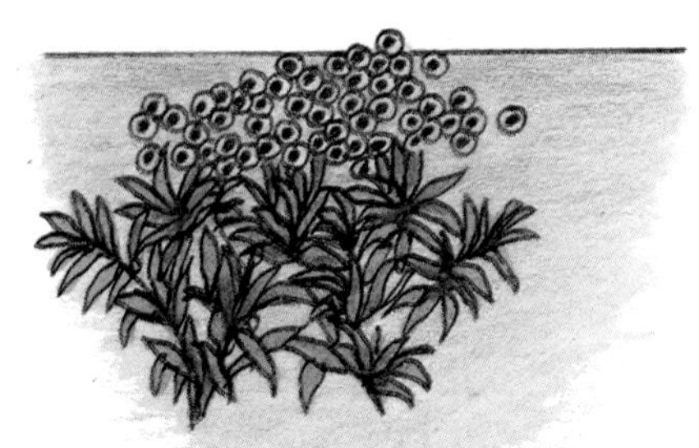

Eggs of *Discoglossus, Phrynomerus, Kaloula, Dyscophis*, & hyperoliids

Typical eggs of hylids & some microhylids

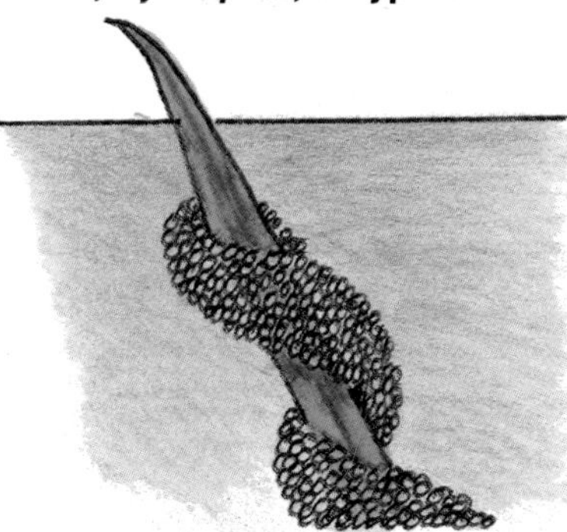

Typical eggs of *Pelobates* & *Scaphiopus*

Floating eggs of some microhylids & leptodactylids (including *Ceratophrys*)

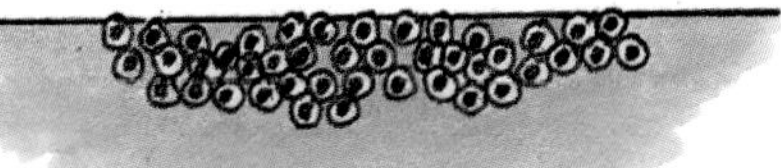

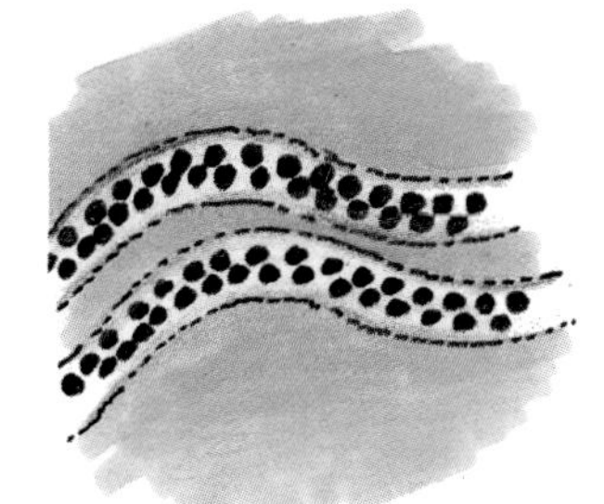

Eggs of bufonid toads usually are laid in double strings

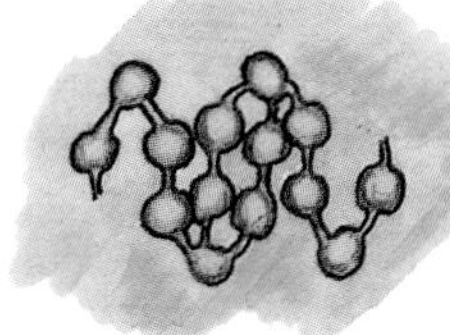

Hard, gelatinous-shelled eggs of *Alytes*

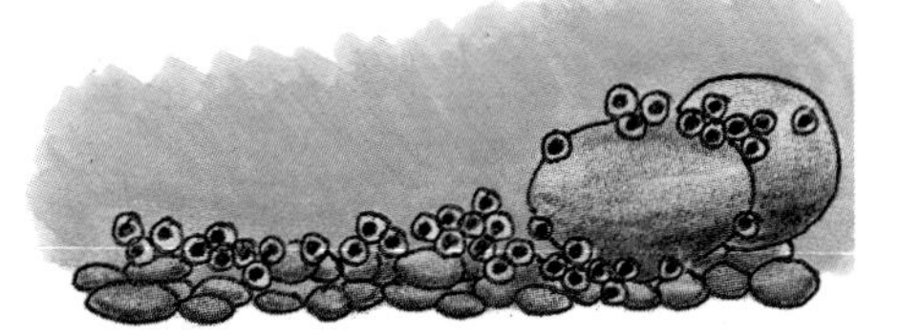

Eggs of pipids and some microhylids

Tadpoles drop into water

Eggs of some hylids

More examples of frog eggs and spawn.

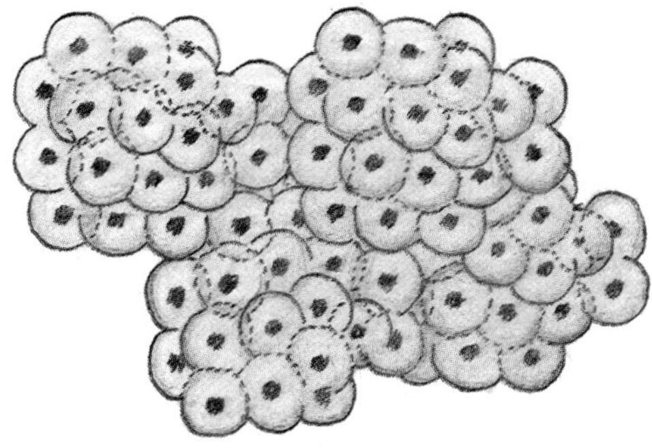

Eggs of typical ranids, many leptodactylids, some hylids & microhylids

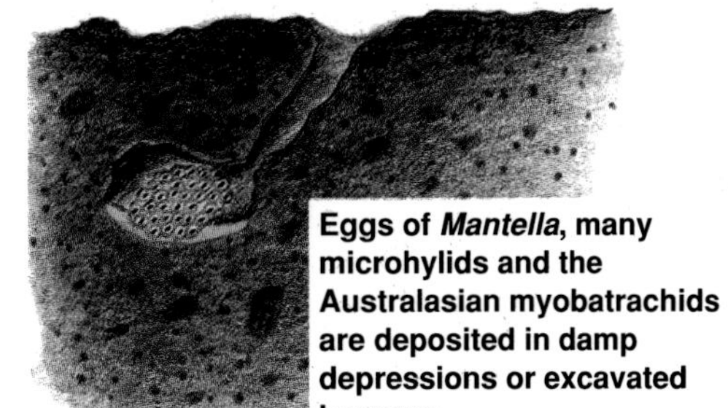

Eggs of *Mantella*, many microhylids and the Australasian myobatrachids are deposited in damp depressions or excavated burrows

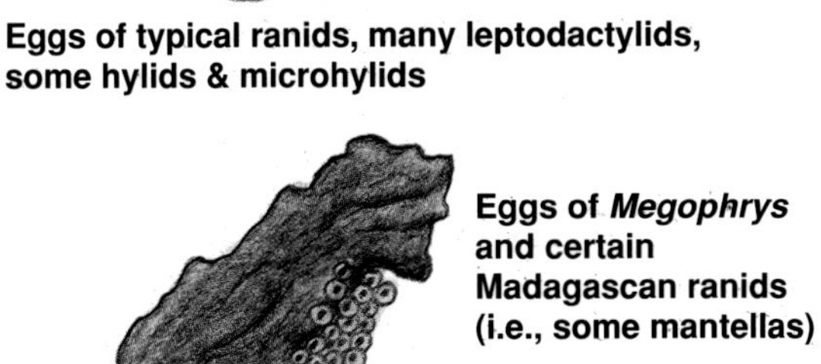

Eggs of *Megophrys* and certain Madagascan ranids (i.e., some mantellas)

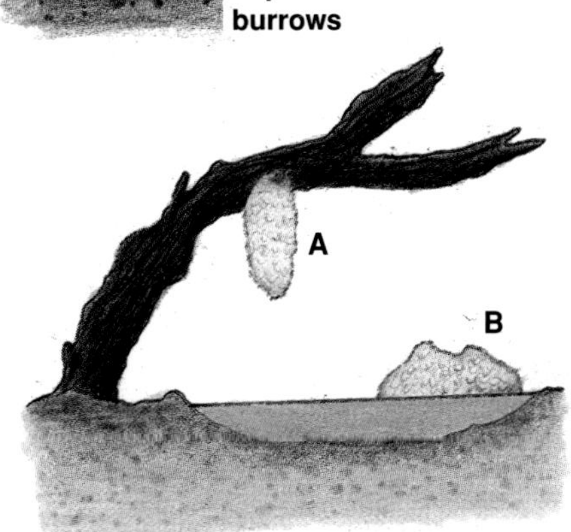

Eggs enclosed in a foam nest of: A–rhacophorids, B–*Limnodynastes*

problem and is more likely to be a pointer toward another underlying problem.

Causes of egg losses

• Infertile Eggs. This is caused by females voiding eggs even though no fertilization has occurred, in which case all of the eggs will eventually be inflicted with fungus. Where just a few eggs are infertile, fungus could develop and release spores that then infect healthy eggs.

• Unsuitable Rearing Conditions. Amphibian eggs requiring high temperatures for proper development are more susceptible to incorrect temperatures than are eggs from temperate species. The preferred temperature range for egg development is reflected in the climate the adults inhabit. High or low light intensities also can have adverse effects on eggs: those deposited beneath rocks or vegetation should be maintained in a dimly lit location; those deposited in open water should be maintained in a well lit location.

• Incorrect Water Quality. No amphibian eggs can withstand water containing high levels of chlorine or fluorine and will die in a few hours under such conditions. Water must either be dechlorinated by allowing to stand for 48 hours or mixed with a large proportion of boiled rain or pond water. Exact acidity or alkalinity is essential in some species, while others have a high tolerance. Even in the latter, preferred pH can mean healthier embryonic development. Insufficient levels of dissolved oxygen in the water can either kill the embryo or exacerbate the risk of anaerobic fungal infection.

• Bacteria. Nitrifying bacteria always are present in water no matter how well it is filtered and oxygenated. They are necessary for decaying vegetation and food particles to be broken down. Problems can occur when the water quality deteriorates or high levels of decaying vegetation and animal matter are in evidence. The bacteria will grow to such an extent that they will smother and begin to attack amphibian eggs.

• Embryo Collapse. This phenomenon occurs mainly in typical newts (*Triturus*) and ambystomatids that deposit their eggs in water. The embryo appears to be developing well right up to the point where it begins to hatch and then suddenly it collapses into an unrecognizable mess. The problem has been attributed to unusually high mineral levels and pollutants in the water, but it is just as likely that the adults that produced the eggs are of the same genetic strain and the embryos are extremely fragile or mutated.

Losses in batches of eggs can be reduced by dividing them into small clutches. Up to 75 can be maintained in an 18-inch aquarium well planted with oxygenating vegetation, and the water should be heavily aerated and filtered. If fungal infections still occur, a combative chemical treatment course such as Cuprazin should be administered.

Eggs Deposited on Land

Plethodons, ambystomatids, and many other American salamanders seek cool, moist places beneath logs and rocks or near edges of a water source in which to deposit small clutches of 25 to 80 eggs. As with aquatic eggs, these should be carefully removed to a rearing container and cared for under the same conditions as those from which they were taken.

Some frogs carry their spawn until the tadpoles are fairly well developed, at which point they are released into water. The male marsupial frog (*Gastrotheca*) maneuvers the freshly laid eggs into a pouch located in the female's lower back. Here the eggs hatch and the tadpoles live off their large yolk sacs. Midwife toads (*Alytes*) lay around 50 eggs held in a short string that the male wraps around his hind limbs. He frequently visits a body of water to moisten the eggs until a point when the developing tadpoles have outgrown their shell and the string is released into the water.

Mating rhacophorids construct foam nests attached to a branch or rock overhanging a pool by secreting mucus and beating it with their hind limbs. The outer surface of the nest dries to form a crust that protects the eggs and tadpoles from desiccation. When the tadpoles are well developed the outer crust is unable to hold their weight and breaks down, releasing them into water located below the nest. Some of the tropical rainforest treefrogs do not use foam and simply attach their eggs to the shaded underside of vegetation overhanging water where humidity is quite high. This method also is used by red-eyed treefrogs, *Agalychnis*. In the case of all the above frogs, eggs are best left *in situ* until tadpoles are released into the water, at which point they can be transferred to rearing aquaria. In the case of foam nesting species and the like, the adults should be removed to a separate terrarium as they are liable to accidentally damage the nest, especially in the confines of a terrarium. Once tadpoles emerge the adults then can be reintroduced.

Frogs such as many *Eleutherodactylus* and burrowing *Breviceps* have completely abandoned the aquatic tadpole stage by laying eggs from which non-feeding tadpoles develop. As with those salamanders that show similar behavior, eggs are best removed.

Fungal infections also can be a problem with land-based eggs but are easier to control because eggs can be irrigated directly with a weak formulation of Cuprazin. Infertile or diseased eggs can be removed from a clutch by carefully cutting them away with a fine scalpel if necessary.

HATCHING OUT

The time span from the first division of the fertilized embryo to a larva hatching out from its protective jelly coat depends on the species, the deposition location, and the surrounding temperature. Eggs of the

Siberian Salamander (*Hynobius keyserlingi*) take up to three months to hatch in the extreme cold of the lakes they inhabit, yet when exposed to warmer conditions this is cut drastically to just two weeks. Those eggs laid by desert frogs in the temporary pools brought about by flash floods must develop and hatch extremely quickly, often within hours, due to the water's evaporation rate. The speed at which they hatch is reflected in the high water temperatures, because if the same eggs are maintained in cooler temperatures in captivity, development time can be two or three times longer.

Normal development rates for aquatic amphibian eggs are within the 6 to 20 days range; 30 to 90 days is natural for eggs laid on land from which well developed larvae or tadpoles hatch out; and in those eggs from which hatch fully formed juveniles the time span is around 60 to 130 days.

OVOVIVIPAROUS AMPHIBIANS

In salamanders such as Fire Salamanders, the female retains her eggs in the oviduct where they develop until well-developed larvae later are released in shallow water. This may be one of the few instances where such a species will actually enter the water because they are very poor swimmers. Therefore, in captivity even shallow water must have a gentle slope with plenty of purchase so that the salamander can easily egress, otherwise she will inevitably drown.

AQUATIC LARVAE AND TADPOLE CARE

Most people are familiar with the life history of their common native frog tadpole from their school days, but the life histories of salamander larvae when compared to that of frog tadpoles are quite different. In the following discussion, the figures in brackets represent development time of each stage, the lower figure for those species that have a quick growth rate and usually inhabit warmer, drier areas, the higher figure for species that inhabit very cold regions and consequently have a very slow growth rate.

Stage 1: Hatchlings

• Anurans [1 to 3 days]. Tadpoles cling without moving to the outer jelly of their eggs using a ventral sucker. They have a pair of external gills that are not used until the mouth forms two or three days later, and no eyes are present. They remain in this stationary position for one to three days, during which time the remainder of the yolk sac is absorbed. When an aerator is present in the aquarium, do not have it bubbling too vigorously or you could dislodge tadpoles and larvae from their positions and cause them to drown.

• Salamanders [1 to 7 days]. Larvae are slightly more active that frog tadpoles, spending much of their time darting about until they bump into a rock, plant, or the glass side of an aquarium. The mouth is already evident and contains a number of teeth, but they do not feed.

Their feathery external gills are used actively upon hatching and the eyes are fully functional.

Stage 2

• Anurans [3 to 20 days]. The pair of external gills the tadpole had upon hatching gradually recede to become internal and are covered by protective flaps of skin called operculi. The body begins to fatten and tail fins begin to form. Small eyes and a mouth that has a central beak surrounded by "teeth" (the oral disc) appear. The herbivorous tadpoles are now very active and spend much of their time swimming up and down the rocks and glass aquarium sides scraping off microscopic layers of algal vegetation with the specialized mouthparts.

• Salamanders [5 to 20 days]. The larvae are immediately carnivorous, initially taking microscopic protozoans and worms. Small amounts of live paramecia can be introduced into the rearing container. Developing dorsal and ventral tail crests enable them to move very quickly, although they tend to spend much of their time resting on the aquarium bottom.

Stage 3

• Anurans [10 to 60 days]. Tadpoles now begin to develop hind legs from a region behind the specialized organ called the spiracle (this is an outlet for the water that is sucked through the mouth and passes over the internal gills, which extract the dissolved oxygen). Occasionally the tadpole will rise to the surface of the water to take a gulp of air. The mouthparts become developed enough for them to tear off strips of meat, and at this stage small chunks of raw red meat and fish pellets can be introduced into the aquarium. Some tadpoles never develop full mouthparts and always are restricted to fine algae as food.

• Salamanders [20 to 40 days]. Larvae develop wiry front limbs first and these initially act as balancing tools required for hunting, i.e., stalking small water crustaceans. Therefore, daphnia, cyclops, and brine shrimp nauplii should be offered. Like tadpoles, air occasionally is taken directly from above the water surface.

Stage 4

• Anurans [15 to 100 days]. The front limbs of the tadpole emerge from just below the opercula; in the common type of tadpole seen in ranids, bufonids, hylids, and many leptodactylids the left limb appears from the spiracle itself. Some tadpoles become entirely carnivorous, even attacking each other when food is in short supply. Air now is taken much more frequently from the atmosphere as rudimentary lungs are beginning to develop.

• Salamanders [30 to 140 days]. Hind limbs begin to appear. The pair of gills of caudate larvae now consist of three branches lined with many filaments that are tinged with red. This is caused by the high concentration of blood circulating near the surface that picks up oxygen and excretes waste gases. Air also is taken in and waste gases emitted more often via the water surface because of the presence of rudimentary lungs. At this stage the larvae may have to be split into even smaller groups of 15 to 30 if space permits because they are now highly aggressive and will attack each other, tearing off legs, gills, and tail parts. If this is not possible, add more water plants to the aquarium to reduce the amount of contact. Small chopped earthworms will satisfy the large appetites of the larvae, and food in general should be offered more regularly. Some species can remain in this stage of development for quite an extensive period or even reach sexual maturity (a phenomenon known as neoteny). This stage also is applicable for salamanders that deposit larvae directly into water, such as the Fire Salamander.

A fairly old larva of *Ambystoma maculatum*, the Spotted Salamander. This larva would be in a late Stage 4 in the broad classification used in this book. More specialized literature breaks the larval stages of amphibians into many more stages defined by characters that are hard for hobbyists to see in living specimens. Photo: R. T. Zappalorti.

Stage 5: Premetamorphosis

- Anurans [20 to 120 days]. In tadpoles the mouth begins to widen and the body becomes streamlined as it becomes more frog-like in appearance. Absorption of the tail begins and at this stage an easily accessible terrestrial area must be made available.

• Salamanders [40 to 150 days]. The external feathery gills and tail and dorsal crests begin to recede and the first dorsal coloration appears. Terrestrial areas should be provided, and be sure a tight-fitting aquarium lid is in place.

Stage 6: Metamorphosis

• Anurans [22 to 140 days]. Just before the tail is fully absorbed the newly-metamorphosed frog or toad will climb onto land (unless it is aquatic). At this stage it must be removed to a terrestrial rearing container that is kept thoroughly moistened. Tadpoles kept in very cool water may well take double the amount of time to reach metamorphosis and can grow two or three times larger than specimens of the same species kept in warmer surroundings.

• Salamanders [50 to 200 days]. Remove the young newts and salamanders, which now have no trace of external gills, to a rearing container. Here they will greedily devour small worms such as bloodworms, tubifex, and whiteworms.

PROBLEMS IN REARING AMPHIBIAN LARVAE IN CAPTIVITY

In all species except those that deposit small numbers of eggs or larvae, a fairly high mortality rate must be expected. Even in ideal conditions a success rate of only 5 to 15% reaching metamorphosis is the norm for fecund anurans (i.e., those producing above 5,000 eggs) or 25 to 75% for those species producing smaller clutches. In salamanders a higher rate of 50 to 75% is quite feasible.

Where possible, always try to rear the larvae of individual species separately from other species because all have differing growth rates, levels of aggression, and requirements in terms of temperature, water quality, etc.

Rules to follow when rearing amphibian larvae are quite straightforward. Oxygenate and filter the water freely to maintain good quality, with a partial water change of about 25% every fortnight. If it becomes too murky, a complete water change is necessary. It is possible to gauge the dissolved oxygen content of the water by how often the larvae take atmospheric air from the water surface. The less dissolved oxygen the more atmospheric air is taken; this may lead to excessive air being trapped in the spiracle region, causing the larva to float upside down at the water surface. Eventually it will die from starvation or lack of energy.

Remove any uneaten food and dead tadpoles or larvae immediately to decrease bacteria and possible infection. Salamander larvae can contract a fungal disease that destroys the feathery gills. If this occurs the aquarium must be completely cleaned out and all larvae treated with a careful dosing of Myxazin. Badly infected larvae must be isolated and treated accordingly. Feeding with contaminated food also can cause bacterial and fungal infections, although anuran tadpoles in particular are very tolerant.

Those larvae that appear not to be growing or in which movement is listless should be removed to smaller individual containers. If there are large numbers of such larvae, they are best destroyed so that your time and resources can be used in ensuring the remaining larvae are kept healthy.

NEOTENY

Neoteny occurs when an amphibian larva (almost exclusively salamanders) either temporarily or permanently continues to display larval features such as external gills beyond the normal development period. In permanent neoteny sexual maturity and breeding can successfully occur. Neoteny is not fully understood at present, but originally research pointed toward "temporary neoteny" being a trait of northerly species such as the Asian hynobiids or high altitude species. It was thought that the low water temperature and the high density of dissolved oxygen in the water of such places slowed down external gill absorption. Although this is partially true, there now is evidence to suggest that other factors, namely those occurring in "permanent neoteny," are more important. The lack of naturally occurring iodine-based chemicals in water and food inhibits endocrine glands such as the thyroid from producing cell-metabolizing hormones, particularly thyroxine. Consequently this suppresses gill absorption and lung development but still allows the reproductive organs to develop normally. The line of evidence was further substantiated by the fact that if iodine is added to iodine-deficient water containing neotenic salamanders, such amphibians will metamorphose and live normal terrestrial lives. Examples of "permanently neotenous" amphibians include the Axolotl, the European Olm (*Proteus anguinus*) and sirenids (*Siren* and *Pseudobranchus*).

VIVIPARITY

Some species, such as the Alpine Salamander (*Salamandra atra*), inhabit inhospitable regions where water is scarce. They therefore have an extremely long gestation period, up to two or three years, and then give birth to just one or two fully developed, miniature replicas of the parent that immediately begin a solitary life. Livebearing amphibians are very uncommon compared to the number of livebearing lizards and snakes.

CARING FOR YOUNG AMPHIBIANS

The initial few weeks following metamorphosis or being born alive represents the most crucial period of an amphibian's life, for how it adapts to captivity, feeds, and grows will govern its overall health and breeding potential later on. As a rule, frogs are more fragile than salamanders at this stage and may need a great deal more close attention.

Suddenly being faced with over 200 toadlets can present fresh problems in that it will be very difficult to provide correct conditions for each individual.

The only really common neotenic amphibians are the Axolotl, *Ambystoma mexicanum*, shown here, and some forms of the very similar Tiger Salamander, *A. tigrinum*. Axolotls will not transform to land-dwelling adults even under extreme conditions, living the entire life cycle in the water. Photo: P. Scott.

Large numbers can be disposed of by advertising in magazines or herptile newsletters, exchanging them for adults of other amphibians (some pet shops may be happy to oblige), or distributing them free among other hobbyists. If they are a species native to a region near the hobbyist's home it may be possible to release some into a suitable habitat (but remember that there is always the chance that a disease caught in captivity could wipe out a non-resistant natural population), but never introduce alien species into a place where they do not naturally occur; just look at the Marine Toad to see the disastrous effects this could have. An outdoor enclosure such as a greenhouse (heated for tropical species) could be constructed to house large numbers. Whatever the decision, the approach needed to initially rear the juvenile of a particular species depends mainly upon its temperament, appetite, and growth rate.

Cannibalistic Juveniles

Amphibians such as the African Bullfrog, horned frogs (including *Megophrys* and *Ceratophrys* species), Budgett's Frog (*Lepidobatrachus laevis*), and certain subspecies of the Tiger Salamander (*Ambystoma tigrinum*) will immediately attack and eat each other in the juvenile stage. This is an instinctive habit developed either because in the wild food would be in extremely short supply or they have very few natural enemies that would otherwise control their numbers. In captivity keep these species in isolation, sometimes for their entire lives except during breeding.

Terrestrial Salamanders

These are initially reared in plastic shoe boxes or ice cream buckets in groups of half a dozen or so. The container should have a layer of damp rubber foam or live sphagnum moss for a base and a few broken pieces of crockery and stones beneath which they can hide. With the exception of northerly and high altitude species, juveniles are best over-wintered for the first two years at a temperature of 50 to 60°F and should be offered tubifex, bloodworms, and chopped earthworms on a regular basis. As they grow the group should either be continually split up or transferred to progressively larger terraria.

Terrestrial Frogs

Most of the small to medium-sized ground-dwelling frogs are very small upon metamorphosis, within the 8 to 15 mm range. Directly prior to their metamorphosis it is wise to accumulate a good stock of fruitflies, aphids, and whiteworms. They are best reared in groups of two to four in small margarine tubs that have a moist paper towel or sphagnum moss substrate and a piece of crockery to hide under, but groups of up to 30 can be kept in a 12-inch terrarium with a similar base. Such frogs must not be allowed to dry out, and the paper towel should be replaced on a weekly basis. Rearing temperatures should be similar to those of the respective adults.

Treefrogs

Treefrogs can be grouped and reared in the same manner as ground-dwelling frogs, but the plastic containers should be taller than they are wide. Again use a moist substrate and also include a few twigs and branches on which they can climb. Groups such as the poison frogs (Dendrobatidae) need to be kept very humid, so regular misting of the containers is advisable. Separate weak or very small individuals into their own containers.

Aquatic Amphibians

Groups of 30 to 50 clawed frogs (*Xenopus*) or 15 to 25 Axolotls or the like can be reared in an 18-in aquarium, but should some start to outgrow others they are best separated to their own quarters until the remainder catch up.

Health and Disease

The chief methods by which nature controls the population of amphibians are predation, old age, and disease. Predation will occur in captivity only where there are large differences in the sizes of amphibians being kept together and in highly cannibalistic amphibians such as horned frogs. If common sense prevails, then predation should not be present. Death from old age is unavoidable, but where captive conditions and care are favorable, longevity often will be prolonged quite considerably.

It is disease that represents the most serious problems affecting the lives of amphibians in captivity and may even strike when all other aspects of their care seem to be perfect. Maintaining a hygienic regime in captivity will go a long way toward ensuring that an amphibian's tolerance level against disease is always fairly high. Besides cleaning out terraria on a regular basis, attention must be given to using uncontaminated food, providing a fresh water supply, and ensuring electrical appliances are working correctly and safely. The use of chlorinated water fresh from the tap as bathing water for juvenile to adult terrestrial specimens offers an excellent preventative remedy against many diseases because of its disinfection properties. Yet, no matter how clean a terrarium is kept or how well a specimen is provided for and nurtured, at any stage in its life it may fall a "little under the weather." This could be a short period of refusing food, regurgitating a previous meal, or appearing rather dull and sluggish. Yet an amphibian's powers of surviving major traumas such as the loss of a limb or recovering from a heavy parasitic infestation are considerably greater than those of many other animals.

The treatment ascribed to a sick amphibian is carried out according to the current health of the specimen concerned. Most of the time medicinal remedies are used. Many of these are available in the form of proprietary brands from pet shops, but some of the stronger drugs may require a signed prescription from a qualified veterinarian or must be administered by a veterinarian. Unless absolutely certain of the treatment, a hobbyist must never attempt to operate on or administer drugs with a hypodermic syringe to a live amphibian. Drugs in the form of solutions that are to be administered orally require a lubricated dispenser, a steady hand, and patience. Most amphibians have fragile jaws that could easily be broken or ripped. Also, the size of the instrument used to dispense oral solutions should be relative to the size of the amphibian. An eye dropper, a pipette, and a hypodermic syringe with a blunt needle are suitable for large, medium, and small amphibians, respectively.

The list of diseases and disorders affecting amphibians could perhaps furnish a book equal in proportions to this one, but many diseases rarely if ever crop up in healthy captive specimens. One way of discovering exactly what a specimen has contracted is to join a herptile club. Here there will be fellow hobbyists and experts who may either be familiar with the disease or who have had similar experiences and may even be able to offer their own successful methods of treatment.

The following section describes those ailments most likely to be encountered in captivity and the course of remedial action required. Whatever the disorder, if it keeps recurring or never quite seems to clear up always consult a veterinarian.

BIOLOGICAL DISEASES

Biological diseases are caused by living organisms, infections by which often are exacerbated by prevalent unhygienic conditions and using poor quality foods.

Fungal spores in a cyst on the American Green Treefrog, *Hyla cinerea*. Photo: Dr. E. Elkan.

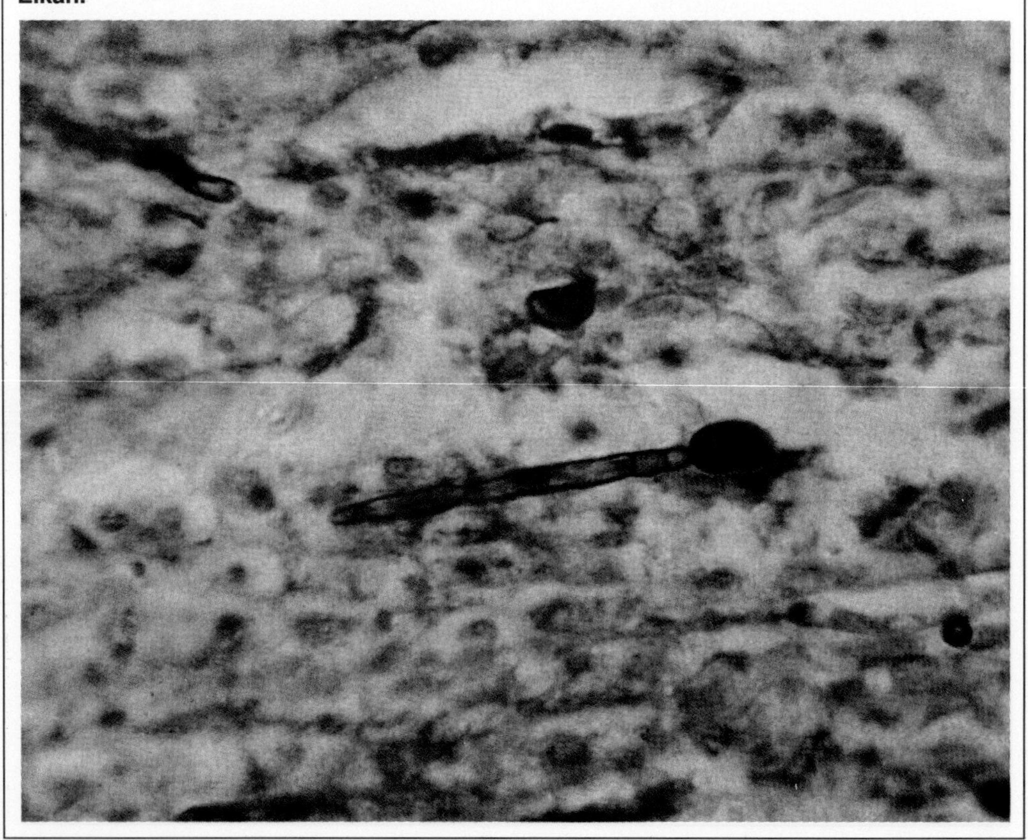

A fungal ulcer between the hind legs of a treefrog, *Smilisca baudini*. Photo: Dr. E. Elkan.

FUNGAL INFECTIONS

Due to the moist nature of their habitat, amphibians are more likely to suffer from fungal disease than any other animals apart from fishes, with semi-aquatic and aquatic amphibians being the most at risk.

General Fungal Disease

• Causes and Characteristics: The most common infections among temperate amphibians are those caused by fungi of various genera commonly known as saprolegnias, characterized by a pearly or creamy coating with a furry appearance in water and slimy on land. The fungus *Oodinium* is more likely to occur in amphibians hailing from warmer climes and tends to be velvety and more yellow in coloration. Both types of fungi usually occupy small sores and skin lesions, particularly around damaged external gills of caudate larvae and aquatic neotenous forms. Frog tadpoles and apodan larvae tend to be infected beneath the gill flaps. Terrestrial amphibians usually are infected in the regions around the eyes (known as sore eye), nostrils, ear openings, and cloaca. Saprolegnias and *Oodinium* thrive in water that has an excess of suspended biological material and in dirty environments where feces and dead uneaten food are not regularly removed. On infection the amphibian's health can deteriorate rapidly, and unless swift treatment is administered death occurs quickly and other specimens within the vicinity may be contaminated.

• Treatment: Fortunately, treatment in the early stages by applying hydrogen peroxide (diluted to 75% strength for adult amphibians, 50% for juvenile or small amphibians) to infected areas with a small paintbrush will give a good success rate. Aquatic species and larvae need to be immersed in a 0.05% solution of a traditional chemical remedy such as malachite green, methylene blue, or Mercurochrome for a period of 10 to 40 minutes (the smaller the amphibian the shorter the immersion period). Several proprietary brands more familiar to the tropical fish hobbyist are equally recommended.

Mouth Fungus

• Causes and Characteristics: Mouth fungus is apparent mainly in aquatic amphibians, attacking bruised or cut lips as a result of transportation or due to continually rubbing the snout against the glass of an aquarium in an attempt to escape. Specimens must be closely inspected before being acquired or the glass tank sides should be covered when specimens are not required to be viewed. Colorwise it is similar to saprolegnias but tends to be more fluffy in appearance. If left untreated it will quickly eat away at the skin tissue around the jaws, penetrating into the surrounding jaw bones and spreading to the palate and eventually lower brain cavity. When it has reached this stage, treatment is unlikely to be effective. Because it also is highly contagious, isolation and rapid preventative treatment of all specimens living in the same aquarium is of utmost importance.

• Treatment: Early treatment is by painting the infected area with hydrogen peroxide in the dosage described for the general fungal disease or by bathing the specimen in a highly concentrated salt solution of 50 to 80%. Such a concentrated salt solution may be deadly with small amphibians, however, and stressful to even large specimens, so extreme caution is advised.

BACTERIAL INFECTIONS

Relatively small and harmless numbers of bacteria are always present even in the cleanest terrarium. In aquatic setups nitrifying bacteria are essential for converting potentially toxic biological waste matter into a form that can be utilized by water plants. Yet when regular good hygiene is not practiced, i.e., cleaning out terraria/aquaria, changing water, and removing feces, dead food, and vegetation, bacteria begin to multiply very quickly and dangerous strains can develop that will quickly infect specimens. Feeding with contaminated foods or introducing non-quarantined and infected specimens to existing setups also is a way in which bacterial infections can start.

Facing page: **An African Clawed Frog, *Xenopus laevis*, with large lesions caused by red leg disease. Photo: Dr. E. Elkan.**

Red Leg

• Causes and Characteristics: This unpleasant and common disease usually is caused by the bacterium *Aeromonas hydrophilia*. As its name suggests, the disease is distinguished by a suffusion of red or orange on the thighs and ventral regions. This color is due to the actions of the bacteria causing red blood capillaries to expand and rupture. Unfortunately, properly diagnosing this disease in its early stages can cause confusion in that many amphibians naturally exhibit a similar coloration around these regions. When left unchecked, red leg proves fatal 100% of the time and curing it, even in its primary stages, is difficult.

• Treatment: The usual treatment involves bathing the whole body of the amphibian in a 1% solution of copper sulfate (sometimes in the form of the safer "chelated copper" products used by tropical fish hobbyists). Alternatively, tetracycline or oxytetracycline tablets can be dissolved in a small amount of hot water and administered orally via a dropper or pipette. The exact dosage depends on the size and metabolism of the amphibian concerned, and veterinary advice is essential. Additionally, hobbyist use of antibiotics should be restricted because of possible production of mutant resistant strains of bacteria if dosages and treatment cycles are not followed exactly.

Mouth Rot or Jaw Suppuration

• Causes and Characteristics: This disease is more familiar in reptiles but does occasionally crop up in terrestrial amphibians such as bufonids, plethodontids, and salamandrids. It is caused by a host of bacteria, including *Pseudomonas*, which in their normal existence are harmless. Poor hygiene, poor food quality, vitamin deficiency, and stress significantly increase the risk of infection of sores and minor tissue damage around the jaws, especially when teeth are lost. It brings about extensive swelling and causes the jaw to gape incessantly, sometimes coupled with a foul white or

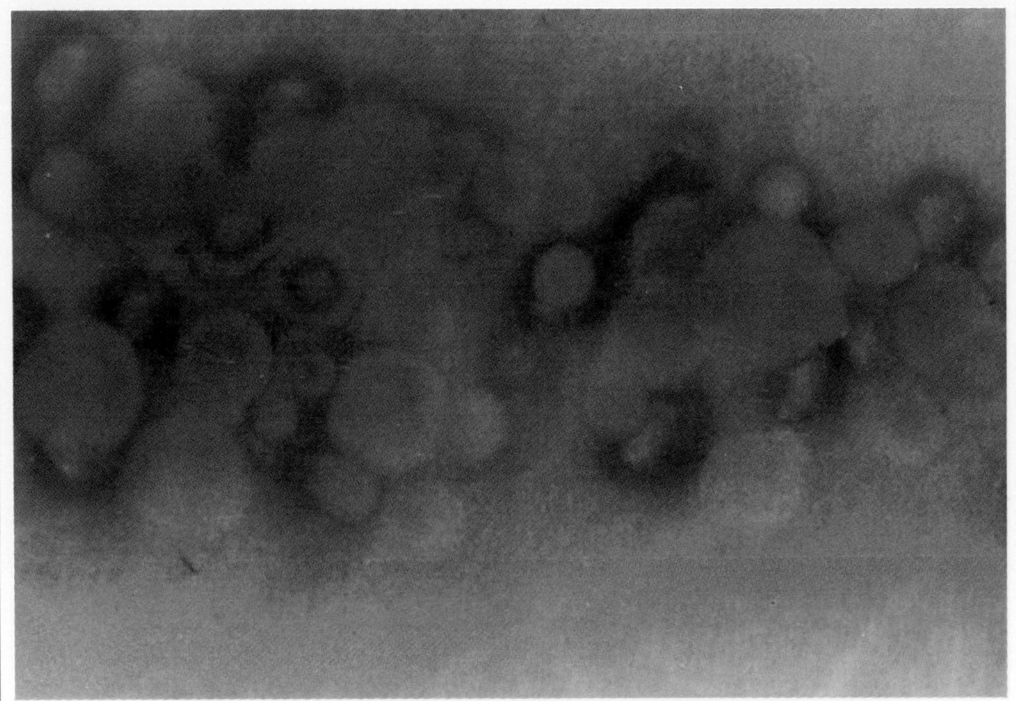

Bacteria of the genus *Aeromonas* are the main cause of red leg in amphibians. Several colonies are visible on this agar plate.

yellowish "cheesy" substance being exuded. In extreme instances the infection can spread throughout the amphibian's throat and into the brain cavity, resulting in "head rot." In such cases the specimen is best put out of its misery.

• Treatment: This should consist of a thorough cleaning of the terrarium and dusting of the infected areas with antibiotic powder containing sulfadimidine, prescribed by a veterinarian. Further treatment with a quarter-strength liquid iodophor (an iodine-based antiseptic) may be necessary. A multivitamin solution high in vitamin C should be administered via a dropper or pipette because the amphibian will almost certainly refuse food.

Amphibian Tuberculosis

• Causes and Characteristics: This results mainly from an amphibian eating food contaminated with the tuberculosis bacterium *Mycobacterium fortuitum*. Although related to the organism that can give humans tuberculosis, the chances of being infected are slim. Even so, extreme care is advised, with thin rubber gloves and a strict code of hygiene being applied when infected creatures are handled. The bacterium reaches the amphibian by being ingested and then is transferred to and primarily infects the liver or kidney, where living tissue is replaced by tuberculous granulomas. These waste-processing organs will begin to fail, resulting in rapid weight loss. The amphibian's own defensive system will try to eradicate the problem but carries the bacteria to combative organs, the lymph nodes. These in turn become infected. Eventually the point is reached where the whole body is riddled with the granulomas. At its peak the bacteria will find its way to the skin surface, causing lumps and "pop eye." The lumps eventually burst and can infect other specimens. Bacteria are also released via feces and urine.

• Treatment: Unfortunately, successful cures are almost unknown. Drugs such as doxycycline and Rifampicin merely serve to keep the infection in check. Absolute isolation of all infected and possibly infected specimens is required, then close observation to see which have developed the disease. Definitely positive cases are best destroyed. It might be best to check with a veterinarian as to the safest way to dispose of tubercular specimens—remember that this is a disease that at least theoretically is contagious to humans.

"Cotton Mouth" Bacteria

• Causes and Characteristics: This is primarily a fish disease that infects aquatic amphibians and in appearance bears a resemblance to real mouth fungus. The bacterium in question is *Columnaris*, which can

Numerous tuberculosis granulomas are visible in this dissected *Xenopus laevis*. Photo: Dr. E. Elkan.

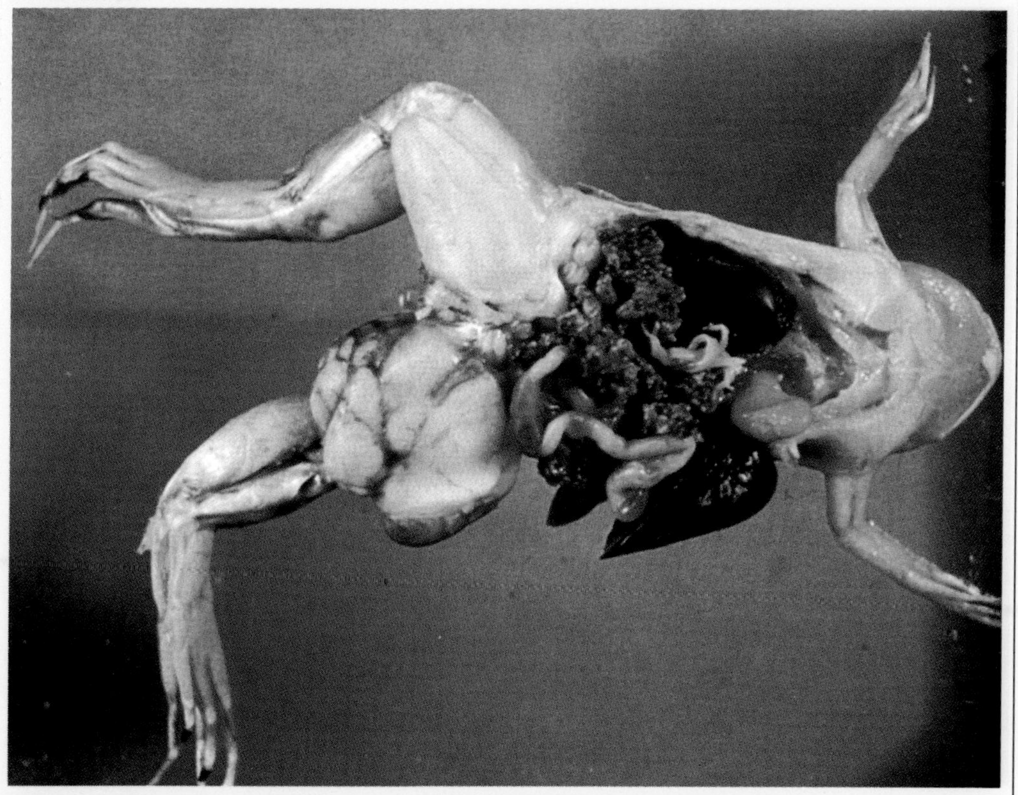

Numerous skin pustules caused by tuberculosis on the back of an African Clawed Frog, *Xenopus laevis*. Photo: Dr. E. Elkan.

affect broken skin, external gills, and tadpole gill flaps as well as the mouth. The white fluff that appears is actually the stacked bodies of flagellated bacteria that break down the underlying epidermal tissue.

• Treatment: Dip the amphibian in a solution of a proprietary quaternary ammonium compound for around 30 seconds three or four times daily. For systemic (internal) infections an aqueous sulfonamide solution should be administered orally as prescribed by a veterinarian.

Respiratory Infections

• Causes and Characteristics: These occur in the form of a mild infection when temperatures are too low for amphibians originating from warmer, humid environments such as tropical rainforests. Excessive water ingestion and terrarium drafts also can contribute to infection, with persistently low temperatures and drafts often resulting in a full-blown respiratory infection that proves difficult to treat. Characteristics include wheezing, frothing at the mouth and nostrils, and gulping for air.

• Treatment: Simply increase the temperature and reduce drafts. Serious infections may need an antibiotic course such as Aureomycin (chlortetracycline) as prescribed by a veterinarian.

PARASITIC DISEASES

In the wild, host amphibians often are loaded with internal parasites that in the main have little effect on their health. Most parasites use the host only as a way of increasing their own numbers with no intention of killing. Yet, as with bacterial infections, heavy infestations can severely weaken the host and problems can arise when the amphibian becomes injured or old age arrives. In captivity, amphibian parasites should be present in much smaller numbers where captive-bred specimens are concerned. Infection usually is linked to infected food, poor hygiene, and most commonly from introducing already infected specimens into a "clean" setup.

Protozoan Parasites

• Causes and Characteristics: In anurans the commonest protozoan is a parasitic species of the genus *Opalina* that lives within the gut. In those anurans that have returned to water to breed, *Opalina* begins to divide, forming cysts that are ejected along with the anuran's feces. The cysts are likely to be ingested by tadpoles, which will continue the life cycle. Entirely terrestrial amphibians are likely to ingest similar parasites from their prey or pick them up from their surroundings. Problems can arise in captivity when the cysts cause blockages in the gut and rectum, leading to rupturing and death. Similar protozoal parasites also occur in the bloodstream, respiratory system, and many of the major organs. All have a similar life cycle and are treated in exactly the same manner.

• Treatment: Proprietary

The swollen throat of this *Paramesotriton hongkongensis* probably is the result of a bacterial infection. By the time such a swelling is seen it may be too late to save the animal. Photo: W. P. Mara.

protozoacides are the most effective way of curing such an infestation. Myxazin and Cuprazin (which are also fungicides) are both excellent in this respect and are also recommended for use in preventative treatment (administering to newly acquired amphibians even if they appear not to show any protozoal parasites). Your pet shop and veterinarian should be able to steer you to other similar types of medications.

ECTOPARASITES

External parasites are relatively scarce in captive amphibians when compared to reptiles due to the moist skin and frequency with which these creatures enter water. Also, many amphibians secrete toxins that may prove fatal to parasites.

Skin Parasites

• Causes and Characteristics: Most amphibians have a soft, thin skin easily penetrated by various

A typical coccidian protozoan. Coccidians probably are found in the intestines of all animals but seldom are a problem if good hygiene is practiced. Photo: P. Freed.

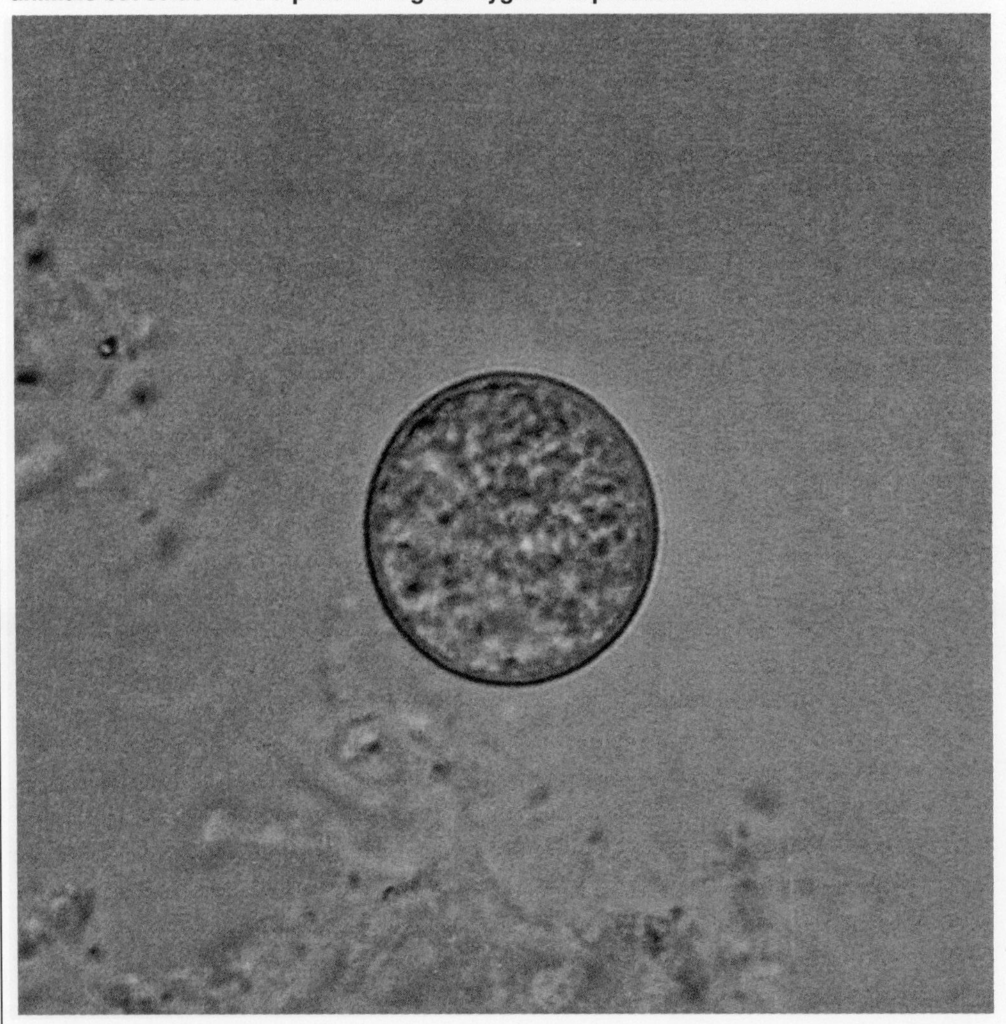

parasites. One genus in particular, *Ichthyophthirius* (called ich or white-spot in fishes), is caused by a protozoan that burrows beneath the skin, leaving white spots or cysts where the skin has loosened. This creates irritation and discomfort to the amphibian, which repeatedly attempts to flick at the irritated area with its limbs or rub its body against a rough object. If the disease is not checked this parasite will spread rapidly all over the dorsal region, stressing the amphibian to the point of death. Skin parasites can be accidentally introduced into the terrarium via improperly disinfected substrates and decor and will strike where there are regular sudden sharp rises or falls in temperature. Other specimens can be infected when the fully grown parasites fall off their host to multiply dramatically and then search for another victim.

Perhaps even more noxious is the aquatic trematode or fluke *Gyrodactylus elegans*, known as the "skin creeper," which can cause havoc in amphibian larvae and neotenous species from temperate regions. It attaches itself to a host, usually in the gill region, by secreting an adhesive substance and then drives a secondary anchoring device called an opisthaptor deep into the host's skin, sometimes proving fatal in itself to smaller amphibia. The skin creeper's mouthparts consist of a long tube covered in hollow spikes that draw up blood.

• Treatment: The most effective method for curing skin parasites is to use proprietary quinine products (either quinine hydrochloride or quinine sulfate) usually linked with curing the closely related tropical fish disease ich or white spot. These chemicals are highly toxic in large quantities and must be administered with care. A solution consisting of between 3 to 5 ml of quinine to every liter of water, depending on the extent of infestation, is applied to the skin by gently dabbing with a cotton swab several times daily. The terrarium substrate should be discarded, with all furnishings and the terrarium itself requiring disinfection with a strong solution of 4% household bleach followed by a thorough rinsing with hot water.

Leeches

• Causes and Characteristics: Frogs imported from the humid tropics sometimes have leeches attached to their belly, back, or rear limbs. Leeches live by feeding on the blood of their hosts and usually are dark brown or red in coloration (though a few may be black, green, or even bright blue). In most cases these flattened creatures are tiny and easy to remove with tweezers as long as the bitten region is subsequently painted with an antiseptic paste. Larger leeches are a different proposition, and no attempt should be made to detach them because this would result in the hooked mouthparts badly lacerating and disfiguring a specimen along with the possibility that infection and bacterial disease would ensue. Leeches are very tolerant of chemical treatment and difficult to exterminate, even being able to regenerate large sections of their bodies.

• Treatment: Unless dosages are applied that would prove fatal to an amphibian, chemical treatment may prove ineffective. Plain dry salt sprinkled over the body sometimes works, otherwise the best method is to wait until the leech moves to another region of the body and then flick it off before it manages to regain its hold. Aquatic leeches can be enticed away by leaving a lump of raw and bloody red meat in the water.

Mites and Ticks

• Causes and Characteristics: These arachnids very rarely attack amphibians because they dislike moisture. However, small (0.2 to 0.5 mm) orange mites commonly found on the ventral regions of fleshflies and beetles will occasionally infest the drier regions of bufonids and terrestrial salamanders that inhabit more arid habitats. Additionally, early larval stages of water mites may be found in large numbers on the feet of salamanders, where they may cause the loss of digits.

• Treatment: If an infestation is found in a terrestrial, dry-skinned amphibian, put a pea-sized piece of dichlorvos (a fly strip of

Notice the fully fed tick attached to the parotoid gland of this Marine Toad, *Bufo marinus*. Obviously you would never fail to notice a tick on your pet before it got so large. Photo: R. T. Zappalorti.

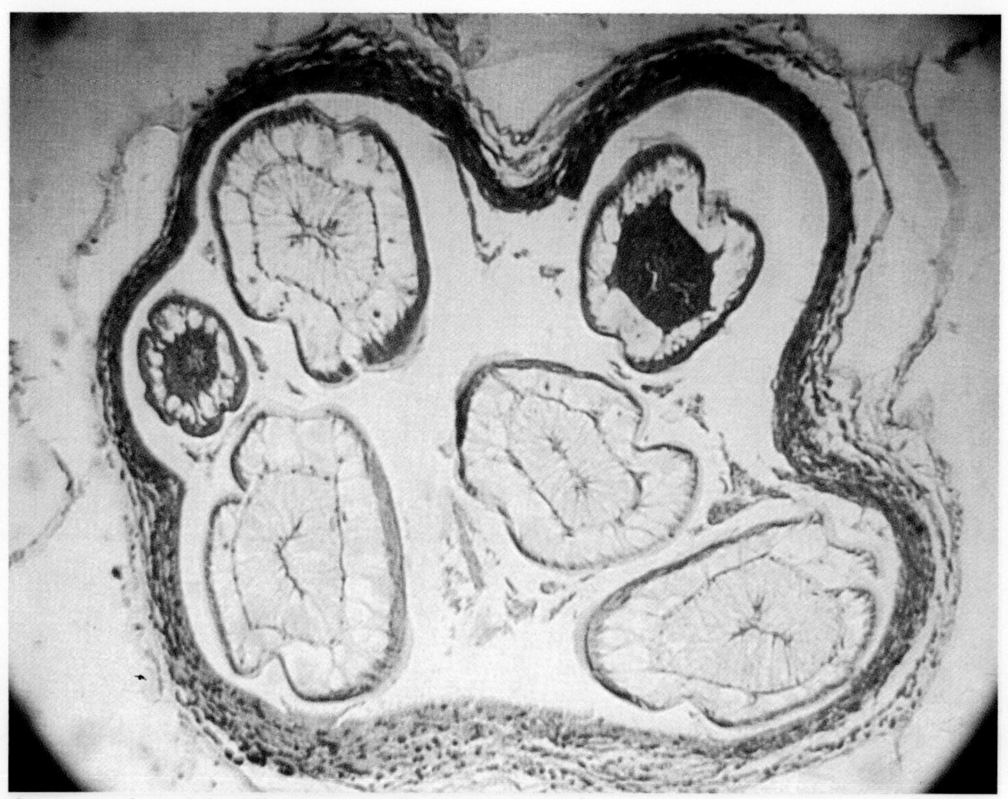

Cross-section of the bile duct of a *Rana* showing many nematodes partially blocking it. When nematodes infest small organs they can cause large problems. Photo: Dr. E. Elkan.

insecticide-impregnated plastic) in the terrarium for a period no longer than 24 hours, making sure it is suspended from the top and unavailable to the frog. Repeat the procedure once every three or four days until the infestation disappears. Mites on the digits of salamanders usually are considered incurable, though they can be picked off individually with pointed tweezers if the salamander is large enough, the wound then swabbed with a gentle antiseptic. However, the stress of being held for the procedure may result in death of the salamander, so most hobbyists just let the mites take their course. They cannot reproduce in the terrarium without other necessary hosts, fortunately.

ENDOPARASITES

Amphibians can be infested by a large number of internal parasites picked up by consuming infected water or food. Most are harmless, but several are particularly nasty and could in theory be passed on to humans.

Flukes (Trematodes)

• Causes and Characteristics: These flattened, unsegmented worms are classed as both endo- and ectoparasites, the previously described *Gyrodactylus* being an example of an external type.

Internal flukes enter into the amphibian body in infected live foods such as snails, blood-sucking insects, and worms or from water, but as the amphibian is probably only a secondary or tertiary host (i.e., adult flukes cannot develop within the body but must be passed on to another host), the fluke will be passed on to higher animals via feces and little damage is done. Most are like flattened cylinders in shape and possess elaborate arrangements of suckers and spikes used to puncture capillaries and organ tissue. Pathogenic quantities of the more dangerous flukes such as *Dactylogyrus* and *Schistosoma* can do a great deal of harm by secondarily infecting the amphibian with bacterial or protozoal diseases. Flukes also can incite irritation when they puncture tissue or capillaries, causing high levels of stress.

• Treatment: The best remedies are the orally administered specialized defluking preparations that are appearing on the market specifically aimed at herptiles. Defluking compounds used for cats and dogs can also be used, but these are considerably more concentrated and the exact

The lidded eggs of the fluke *Haemolychus*. This fluke is a common inhabitant of the lungs of many frog species. Photo: Dr. E. Elkan.

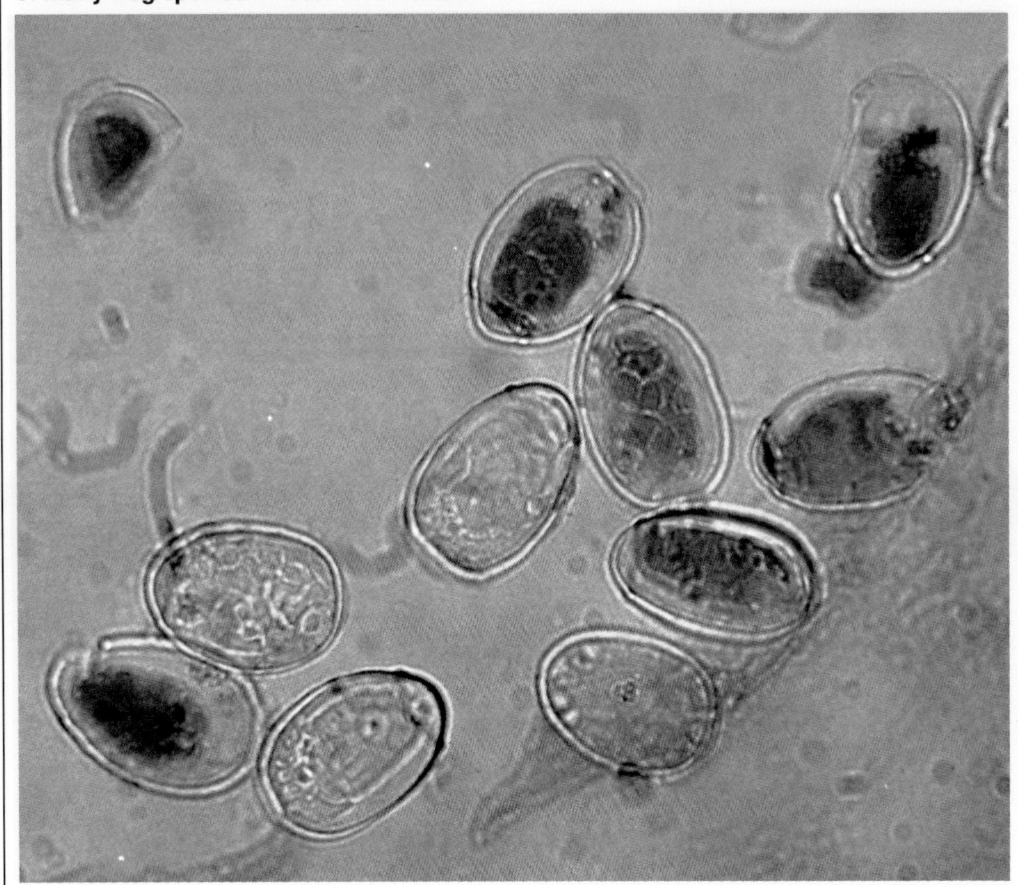

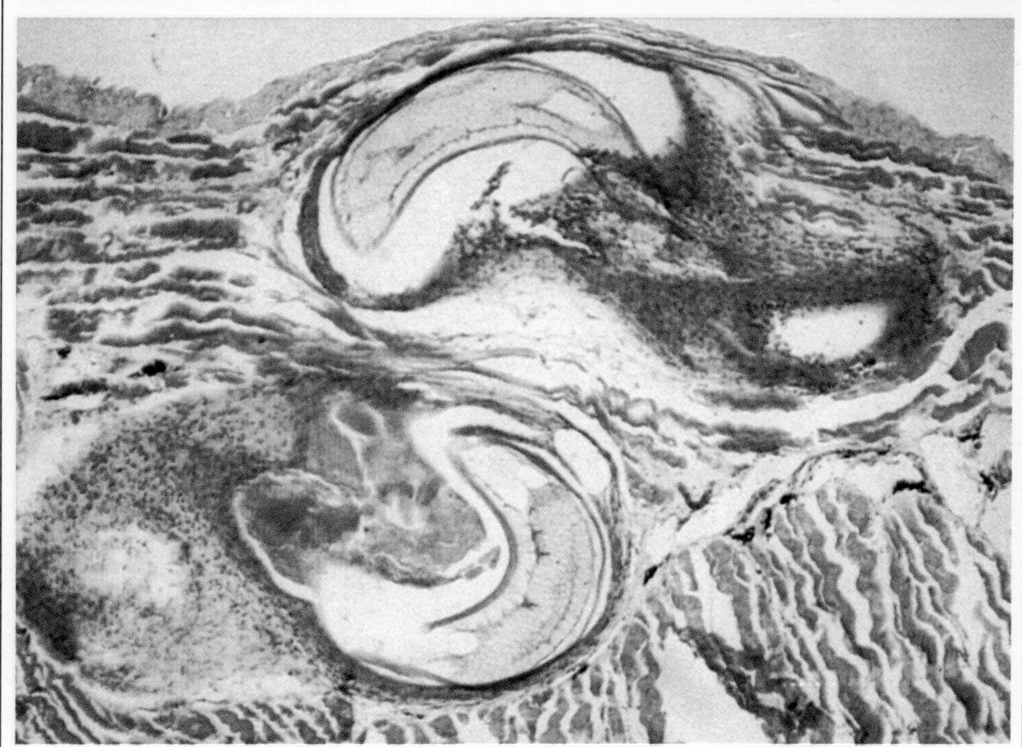

Cross-section of muscle tissue of *Rana* showing nematode worms embedded in the muscles. Photo: Dr. E. Elkan.

dosage is based on the size of the animal concerned; thus a 50-gram frog would require just 0.22% of the dosage required by a 50-pound dog.

Intestinal Worms (Nematodes and Tapeworms)

• Causes and Characteristics: Worms in the gut comprise a whole host of types ranging from microscopic threadworms to huge tapeworms that live off partially digested food and mucus traveling down the intestinal tract. The microscopic eggs of threadlike roundworms (*Enterobius*) are picked up from almost anywhere, even being passed on to specimens via humans. High infestations of these worms result in emaciation and extensive damage to the intestine wall.

One of the most common roundworms in amphibians is the microscopic *Rhabdia*, which occurs in isolated infestations through various parts of the digestive tract. Although not especially dangerous, they often induce the amphibian to regurgitate food, eventually leading to emaciation. The Swamp Hookworm (*Ancylostoma ranae*) is a widespread parasite of amphibians and reaches its host's intestines by penetrating the skin of the ventral region or limbs and traveling in the bloodstream. Once in the gut it digs in its two viciously curved hooks to lock itself to the intestine wall, where it feeds, grows, and produces huge numbers of eggs, most of which pass through the cloaca with the feces to hatch and locate other hosts.

The most dangerous worms for amphibians are the familiar tapeworms. These worms can attain one meter or more in the intestines of larger amphibians and, because of their size, they give a specimen the misleading appearance of being well fed (and, indeed, the specimen may still be feeding regularly). In reality, they induce starvation with resultant emaciation, and their relatively large hooks and powerful suckers can lead to huge lacerations in the gut wall causing infection, hemorrhaging, and ultimately death. Tapeworms reproduce rather primitively by shedding egg-filled body segments called proglottids. These are expelled from the host's body in feces, where they either are consumed or manage to slowly crawl into the cloaca of a new host and make their way to the gut.

• Treatment: Smaller nematodes are effectively destroyed with a mild aqueous solution (1% strength) of mebendazole (see your veterinarian), which should be carefully syringed down the throat of terrestrial species, but never in quantities of more than 2 ml. The usual cat and dog worming powders contain levels of piperazine that are far too strong for amphibians and must be drastically scaled down to 1 mg of powder per 10 g of amphibian body weight, a procedure requiring equipment unavailable to most hobbyists. This powder is either dusted on smaller food items such as insects or, in the case of larger, dead prey such as pinkies or fish, sprinkled into a small incision made by a scalpel.

For aquatic amphibians 1 g of methylene blue first dissolved in 0.15 L of water and then added at a rate of 1 cubic centimeter per gallon of aquarium water is particularly effective. Although the water takes on a blue tinge, this returns to normal clarity within a few days and there should be no need to repeat the treatment until two weeks later, when the next cycle of worms is due to hatch. The methylene blue will destroy these before they have a chance to reproduce.

Treatment of tapeworms presents difficulties arising from the fact that a fairly strong preparation is required to destroy them and can sometimes cause much discomfort to or even the death of the host amphibian. The most effective remedy is in the form of an orally administered chemical solution called bunamidine. Some amphibians intensely dislike both the taste of this solution and the effect it has on the digestive tract, making them edgy or aggressive for several hours. Veterinarians often use bunamidine for large snakes such as pythons and will prescribe a weaker dosage for amphibians based on body weight and metabolism. The dead tapeworm will be flushed out with the feces, but often a second course of the drug is necessary to expel proglottids that can still produce hatchling tapeworms.

Dissected stomach of a toad showing numerous spiny-headed worms, *Acanthocephalus ranae*, attached to the lining. These worms occasionally cause severe damage, but usually they are rare. Photo: Dr. E. Elkan.

ENVIRONMENTAL DISORDERS

Disorders caused by misjudgments or errors as a result of a misunderstanding of a species's requirements are commonplace, especially among beginners.

Poisoning

• Causes and Characteristics: Overcrowding is an unnecessary process of poisoning and is most prominent when either the terrarium containing amphibians is not cleaned out or the water source is not changed regularly. High levels of toxins generated in the amphibian's feces and urea gradually build up and after a period these are reabsorbed into the frog's bloodstream, resulting in poisoning. Symptoms include agitation, aggression, hyperactivity, and partial or total paralysis, especially of the lower part of the body. Anurans such as horned frogs (*Ceratophrys*) produce particularly large quantities of such toxins in their waste.

Incorrect pH and mineral content of water can account for a large number of deaths in amphibian larvae. Although some species tolerate a wide range of conditions, many species have a particular, if not strict, preference of water quality. Although adults may breed in substandard water, the resultant eggs may not hatch, larvae may grow to be badly deformed, or death may occur.

Poisoning can also occur when terraria or aquaria have been washed out with a disinfectant but were not rinsed properly. Amphibians may absorb or ingest the remaining traces and die very quickly.

Some amphibians (e.g., salamandrids, *Bombina, Phrynomerus*, dendrobatids, and the Pickerel Frog, *Rana palustris*) store in skin glands relatively virulent toxins that may be released when bathing. If several species are maintained in the same terrarium there is the likelihood that these toxins will be absorbed by the other species, causing paralysis or death.

• Treatment: Overcrowding is a deplorable and highly irresponsible way of maintaining amphibians. Cleaning the cage out regularly cannot be too strongly emphasized under any circumstances. Never leave traces of disinfectant. Always use "safe" antiseptic disinfectants labelled as harmless to children. Direct poisoning through water is more difficult to recognize, but thoroughly researching an amphibian's preferences or, if no information is available, dividing eggs up among test aquaria containing water of varying acidity, alkalinity, and mineral content to determine the most successful, usually works.

It is recommended to keep poisonous species separated from non-toxic amphibians. The toxicity of a species is highlighted in the species discussions wherever possible.

Stress

• Causes and Characteristics: Many salamanders, bufonids, and "squat frogs" tend to tolerate potentially stressful situations rather better than the majority of anurans because of their slower, more inactive lifestyles. In captivity stress can determine how well an amphibian lives and breeds and is caused by many factors. The majority of amphibians live rather quiet, sedentary lives and instinctively have a shy nature. Stress is induced when they suddenly are forced into situations that scare or intimidate them. Alternatively, stress may develop from situations that are accepted at first but gradually become intolerable the longer the amphibian has to endure them. Such causes of stress include but are not limited to the following.

1) Transportation;
2) Interference from the hobbyist by:
   i) Handling frequently
   ii) Tapping on the glass;
3) Cramped living conditions;

Facing page: **Notice the defective toes on the front feet of this fire-bellied newt, *Cynops*. This problem, sometimes called bumblefoot, can be caused by bacteria, mites, cold or heat damage, or bites and usually is ignored by the animal. Photo: W. P. Mara.**

4) An unsuitable terrarium setup in terms of:
   i) lack of retreats
   ii) too small or no bathing area
   iii) no basking area
   iv) lack of climbing facilities
   v) too damp or too dry;
5) Exposure created by an all–glass aquarium;
6) Bullying by other larger specimens;
7) Irritated by smaller, nuisance species or live foods such as locusts and crickets;
8) Irritation from internal or external parasites;
9) The sudden glare or darkness from lights being switched on or off;
10) Too powerful a light source;
11) A light source being left on for too long;
12) Overheating or insufficient heating;
13) Repeated offering of a single food;
14) Unhygienic living conditions.

Stress tends to have detrimental effects on specimens, with the usual symptoms including marked changes in disposition, where normally shy species become aggressive and snappy while ostentatious species may spend long periods hiding. Reproductive drive diminishes and courtship behavior may cease to exist for several years even after conditions improve. The overall alertness, coloration, and appearance of a specimen will suffer, with sluggishness, a dull, lackluster appearance, poor posture, and sunken eyes prevalent. A specimen also will tend to lose its appetite, resulting in emaciation and lack of energy when its immune system is unable to combat disease, or it will eventually die from starvation.

• Treatment: There are no instant proprietary cures for stress in amphibians. Common sense on the hobbyist's behalf usually provides all the answers and also suggests why it is so important to research and learn a species's requirements before it is added to a collection.

Injuries

• Causes and Characteristics: Agile frogs in particular can be troublesome in the terrarium, where they attempt to leap long distances and inevitably end up colliding with the terrarium sides. This can cause unsightly bruising or even broken jaw bones. Salamanders and caecilians initially have an annoying habit of attempting to escape through the transparent glass of an aquarium or a terrarium and can end up with red, raw snouts. Being bitten by other specimens is a common occurrence even with gregarious species, which may mistake their moving counterpart as food. Digits and crest filaments can be lost and skin can be badly torn.

• Treatment: For the first few days any open wounds should be treated with an mild antiseptic cream such as sulfanilamide or an iodophor-based preparation to stop infection setting in. Isolation of a badly injured specimen may be necessary. To avoid collision injuries associated with anurans, it may be necessary to cover the transparent glass sides of a terrarium or aquarium, at least until the inhabitants settle down.

Shedding Difficulties

• Causes and Characteristics: This problem can be caused by several factors, including an undetermined microorganism that feeds on the dead skin and whose waste by-products glue the living and dead layers together. More usual is a lack of sufficient water or air humidity, as well as low temperatures in more tropical species where an amphibian is too sluggish to loosen the outer layers of dead skin. Consequently the skin becomes hardened, irritable, and may hinder the amphibian's mobility. Unshed skin covering the eyes, known as corneal opacity, may encourage fungal infections to begin, eventually blinding the animal.

• Treatment: Increase humidity by regular misting of the terrarium or make the bathing area large or deep enough so that the specimen can immerse its whole body. For tropical species, higher temperatures are essential. Should a specimen still exhibit shedding (sloughing) difficulties, it is beneficial to thoroughly soak it in a bowl of slightly saline luke warm water, ensuring the head is kept above the water. After about ten minutes the skin can be gently—and cautiously!—detached with a pair of tweezers. For the treatment of bacteria-related sloughing syndrome a proprietary bactericide as used for tropical fish is the best chance of a cure.

Damaged snouts are common in captive frogs and usually are due to repeated escape efforts, the frog jumping into screen or glass tank tops. Not only is the damage unsightly, but it usually leads to bacterial infections and possible death. Photo of *Dendrobates tinctorius*: R. D. Bartlett.

DIETARY DISORDERS

The merits of providing captive amphibians with a varied and balanced diet are obvious. If basic guidelines are regularly followed, then dietary disorders will rarely if ever pose a problem. The introduction of multivitamin supplements to the pet market also has done much to lessen this problem, but at some point a hobbyist may acquire or purchase an amphibian that is showing signs of malnutrition either because it was previously incorrectly maintained or had been in transit without food for days or even weeks. Therefore it makes good sense to determine in exactly which nutrient the specimen is deficient.

Calcium:Phosphorus Imbalance and Avitaminosis D

• Causes and Characteristics: Some foods, such as mealworms and blood meats, have very little in the way of usable calcium. Juvenile amphibians fed largely on these show signs of deformation in the bone structure, such as kinks in the spine and twisted limbs, caused by disproportional amounts of phosphorus relative to calcium. In both juveniles and adults low calcium levels may increase the risk of rickets, reduce production of the protein precursor fibrinogen in the blood (essential as a clotting and healing agent), and hinder stimulation of the fibrilose contractile muscle tissue that allows movement and reflexes, leading to temporary or permanent paralysis. Even if sufficient calcium is provided, this is mainly in the form of insoluble salts that need to be processed and absorbed by the action of vitamin D in the intestine. Vitamin D deficiency results in most of the calcium passing through the digestive system being expelled as waste, with a calcium imbalance still prevalent. This same vitamin also plays a direct part in calcification of the skeletal structure, and if it is not present in sufficient quantities osteoporosis or weakening of the bones occurs.

• Treatment: Supplementary multivitamin powders with adequate levels of calcium and vitamin D usually are enough to combat this disorder. Extra calcium also can be offered in the form of finely ground cuttlefish bone. Vitamin D should never be offered in too large a quantity because it can overprocess too much calcium, leading to accumulations in the circulatory system and blockages in the heart, intestine, or bladder.

Avitaminosis A

• Causes and Characteristics: Mild symptoms of deficiency of vitamin A are fairly common, especially in terrestrial amphibians, and can be seen when lumps of an opalescent jelly-like substance congregate over and around the eyes. This is because excessive mucus is being produced in the film of eyewash that coats the cornea. Eventually it may harden, impairing the amphibian's vision, and can be difficult to remove without some damage occurring. The eyes themselves may also swell. A more dangerous symptom and often a difficult problem to reverse is loss of appetite.

• Treatment: Recently a proprietary antiseptic wash (given through an eye dropper and aimed primarily at the turtle market) that combats eye complaints quite efficiently has appeared. Using this together with increased levels of supplemented vitamin A in the diet reduces or eliminates eye problems. Appetite loss may by cured by a veterinarian by injecting a vitamin A solution directly into the stomach, but this would be dangerous for smaller amphibians.

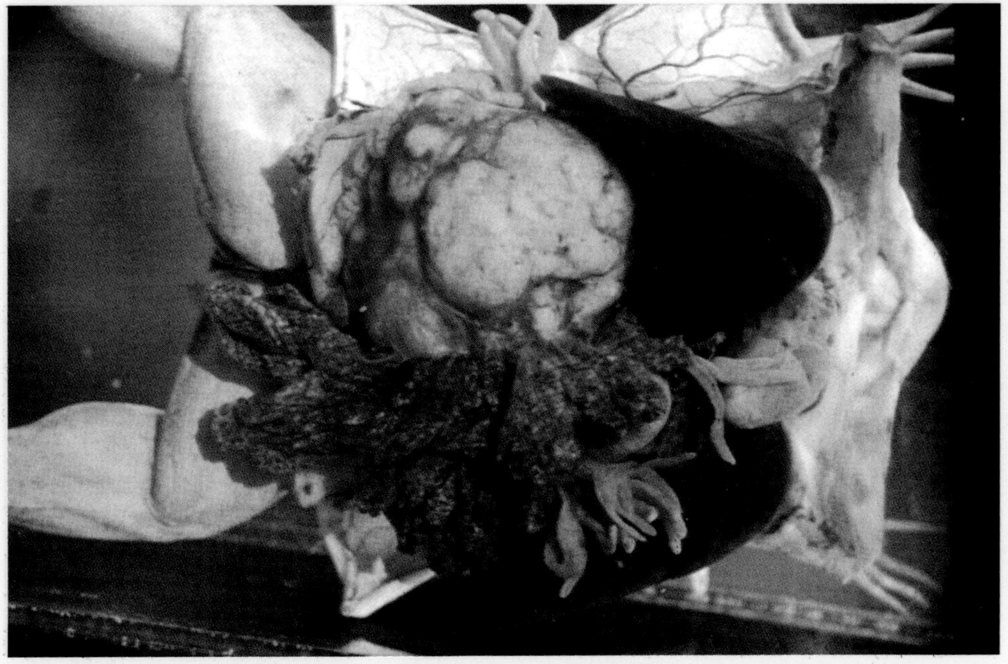

Though not cancerous, this large tumor has severely impinged on one kidney and obviously has to affect the health of the *Xenopus* carrying it. Photo: Dr. E. Elkan.

Other Vitamin Deficiencies

• Causes and Characteristics: Deficiencies in vitamins B, E, and more rarely K can occur in maltreated specimens. Vitamin B is prevalent in fairly high quantities in all live foods, so a deficiency is likely only in specimens that feed either very little or not at all. One of its functions is to promote proper cell division, so it is required in larger quantities by juveniles or females during egg production. Lack of vitamin B can cause infertility, improper metabolism, and deformation of living tissues.

Vitamin E is a precursor to red blood cell production, healthy muscle development, and hormones produced prior to and during reproduction. Deficient specimens become weak or listless and temporarily lose their reproductive drive.

Mild cases of avitaminosis K are likely to occur only in insectivorous amphibians where their prey contains little of the soluble animal fats and oils in which the vitamin occurs. Its main function is to synthesize the blood clotting catalyst prothrombin, where it may work together with the vitamin D complex in the intestine.

• Treatment: All of these potential disorders can be prevented by using multivitamin supplements. In very severe cases a veterinarian must be contacted.

Accidental Ingestion Disorders

• Causes and Characteristics: Complications arise when an amphibian ingests soil, sand,

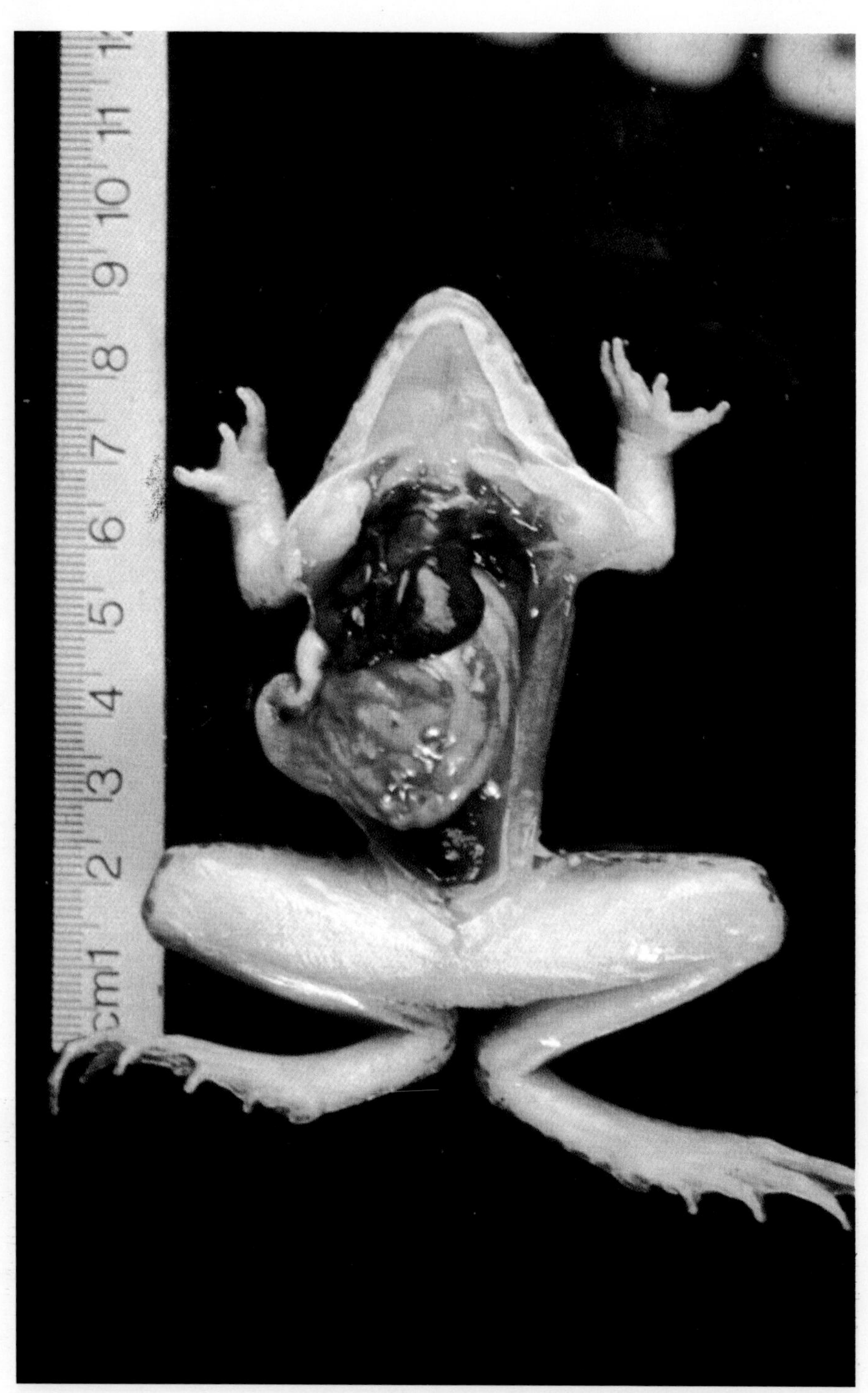

Death by mealworm! This *Rana tigrina*, Indian Bullfrog, ate almost 40 mealworms at one feeding. Mealworms and other heavily plated foods should be fed sparingly as treats, never freely. Photo: Dr. E. Elkan.

detritus, vegetable matter, or gravel either attached to the prey or adhering to the sticky amphibian tongue when it is flicked out. Although a large proportion of these indigestible particles pass harmlessly through the digestive tract, gradually small amounts accumulate in the stomach or gut to inhibit proper digestion, cause blockages, and increase the risk of biological disease. Vegetable matter can even ferment in the stomach or gut to release gases that can rupture the lining.

• Treatment: Ingestion disorders are more likely to be found in wild terrestrial and subterranean amphibians, especially those that live on forest floors. In captivity cleaning food such as earthworms or placing food on a clean area will reduce the risk. Avoiding the use of very small gravel as the substrate also is recommended. Accumulations can be surgically removed, but because of the small size of the typical amphibian, very few veterinarians would perform such a task.

Obesity

• Causes and Characteristics: Some amphibians, such as "squat frogs," White's Treefrogs, and giant salamanders, are naturally fat because they occur in regions where large amounts of body fat are needed for survival during periods of drought and lack of food. In captivity most amphibians are greedy if given the chance, and thus obesity is very easy to achieve. In a terrarium an amphibian may not be as mobile as in the wild. Food may be offered regularly and in large quantities, resulting in overweight specimens with unhealthy fatty deposits lining their arteries and heart. In such cases heart failure and respiratory disease are likely to occur.

A form of obesity in anurans that may be indirectly related to the hobbyist's actions originates from an osmotic disorder where too much water is absorbed through the skin. The elastic skin swells to accommodate this water, which cannot be quickly expelled, producing a balloon-like appearance. Research has shown that this syndrome is related to overfeeding or maintaining amphibians in fouled water where the kidneys are overworked to separate waste and eventually partially fail.

• Treatment: When feeding amphibians, stick to a strict schedule, offering healthy foods without excess fats at regular times and not whenever a specimen appears to be hungry. Fattening up specimens prior to hibernation or estivation and when females are producing eggs are the only exceptions to this rule. Water retention cannot be cured easily, but keeping a specimen somewhat drier and practicing good hygiene at all times are advantageous.

LONGEVITY

Just because an amphibian suddenly dies in captivity does not automatically mean that it was diseased. All living creatures have a natural life span, and amphibians are no exception. Even if the animal was recently purchased, it could have died from old age even though it looked quite healthy. The external appearance of an amphibian often gives no indication to its age. The longest life spans are seen in those species that are distributed through cooler climates and those that spend much of their time in dormancy such as estivation. In relative terms, the "active life span" of amphibians hailing from tropical regions is proportionally similar to that of amphibians from cooler regions because in the former up to 365 days of the year may be spent hiding, hunting, or mating, while in the latter as little as 40 days per year are accounted for in this manner. Hence the real life span of amphibians varies considerably across all three orders.

Salamanders contain the longest–living amphibians in terms of average life span, while frogs have the shortest average. Life spans of caecilians are largely unknown apart from specimens kept in captivity and are thought to be in between the two other orders. This does not mean to say that all anurans are short-lived. The African Bullfrog has been known to attain more than 40 years, while the European Common Toad has been accredited as living to 36.

In captivity, where correct conditions, a balanced diet, and proper general care are met, an amphibian will respond by attaining a greater age than would be expected in the wild. All amphibians reach a peak with regard to breeding potential that may persist for just a few years in certain dendrobatids or for over ten years in terrestrial salamanders such as the European Fire Salamander (*Salamandra salamandra* complex). After this egg or sperm production will deteriorate to the point where the specimen produces an infertile pairing or loses its reproductive drive.

Species Selections

INTRODUCTION

Aquatic amphibians generally are more widely kept than their mainly terrestrial counterparts, probably because they are more likely to be sold by numerous pet store outlets. Coupled with the fact that they tend to be less shy and are easier to maintain than most terrestrial species, the reasons for this favoritism are easy to see. Yet when we scrutinize the remainder of the order Amphibia, a vast array of colorful, bizarre, beautiful, and occasionally grotesque creatures is revealed. With over 4,000 species of amphibians currently known to science, it can be quite difficult deciding which type to keep. Some people gradually develop a specific interest in a single order, suborder, genus, or even a species, while many have a broad interest in all types of amphibians. Where beginners are concerned, initially keeping commonly available species is an essential aspect of this hobby for it provides the basic experience needed to tackle more desirable or difficult types. This section is designed to list and explain the wide range of species suitable for maintaining in captivity. Where possible it details specific care and breeding instructions and occasionally highlights difficulties associated with keeping a particular species.

Salamandra salamandra terrestris, one of the common forms of Fire Salamander. Photo: M. Panzella.

Order Apoda (Gymnophiona): The Caecilians

The number of caecilian species that are regularly maintained in captivity is surprisingly small. Many hobbyists are understandably apprehensive when the opportunity of acquiring caecilians presents itself, yet those species that are already in captivity have proved both relatively long-lived and hardy creatures. One reason for this reluctance lies in the caecilians's secretive nature, which has made them difficult to locate and study in their natural habitats. Consequently, literature documenting their behavior and preferred habitats, which could otherwise give clues as to what their requirements might be in captivity, is very limited. Recently, small-scale captive breeding successes of several species have brought about a slight surge in interest, and we can hope that this will result in the publication of more literature and hence make them more popular terrarium subjects.

No land caecilian is common in the terrarium hobby. Unusual species such as *Dermophis mexicanus* from northern Central America occasionally appear, however. Photo: K. Lucas.

Dermophis mexicanus sometimes is called the Mexican Violet Caecilian. Some specimens are strikingly beautiful shades of blue and violet. Photo: R. D. Bartlett.

FAMILY CAECILIAIDAE

Giant Caecilian (*Caecilia thompsoni*)

Distribution: Central and southern Colombia.

Length: Up to 140 cm (55 in) but usually around 105 cm (42 in).

Description: The largest of the described apodans, this shiny, gray-blue amphibian has a muscular body exhibiting very pronounced light blue annuli. The tiny, atrophied eyes are unusual in being functional, thereby allowing limited vision. Segments number between 95 and 120.

Availability: At one time some extremely unusual and interesting herptiles were exported from Colombia and neighboring regions, but during the 1980's wide-scale restrictions were imposed on the movement of all creatures, wild or commercially generated, from within these countries. Subsequently the only Giant Caecilians that can be obtained today are the remainders from occasional successful breeding attempts generated from those specimens acquired prior to 1980.

Captive Care: In the wild this species occurs in the humid leafy floors of rainforests. It is one of the very few apodans that occasionally ventures out from its subterranean burrows in daylight to hunt for worms, small frogs, and even reptiles such as ground geckos and skinks. Captive care is straightforward, with a fairly large aquarium (in the region of 48 inches for an adult pair) being required. The basal substrate should consist of around 20 inches of live sphagnum moss on top of which are rested large flat pieces of bark. A shallow water bowl in which these caecilians will often bathe and shed must be present. Temperatures need to be in the region of 78 to 90°F (21 to 32°C) with humidity maintained at about 80% through regular misting of warm water or via an electronic humidifier. The terrarium should never become too saturated through such misting. Food comprises large earthworms, caterpillars, or strips of raw red meat that have been fortified with a multivitamin supplement.

Sexual Differences: The adult male is slightly less rotund than the female and has a swollen cloacal region immediately prior to copulation.

Captive Breeding: Breeding can be sporadic in captivity, and it is not certain what triggers the mating response. Limited evidence suggests that keeping males and females separated for a period of six weeks before reintroduction sometimes may promote courtship activity. The female deposits between 18 and 50 yellowish eggs, 10 mm in diameter, in a moist terrestrial position close to water. To avoid being squashed or eaten these are best removed to a hatching container such as an aquarium with about 3 to 4 inches of water held at 86°F (30°C). They are positioned on a flat rock that rises just out from the water and then are covered with sphagnum moss to maintain a moist bed. Explosive hatching (all eggs hatch simultaneously) commences after six to eight weeks when the well–developed, cream-colored larvae with their bright scarlet external gills squirm into the water. The aquarium water must be clean, constantly aerated, and kept in dim light. If the larvae are fed well on daphnia and other small water crustaceans, metamorphosis is completed 6 to 12 weeks later.

Longevity: In the region of 6 to 12 years.

Other Species: The Blue or Mikan's Caecilian (*Siphonops annulatus*) is very similar in size to the unrelated ichthyophid caecilians but has a much stouter build. It occurs throughout the northern Amazonian region of South America and can be kept in the same manner as *Caecilia thompsoni.* The genera *Grandisonia* and *Hypogeophis* contain several species from islands in the Indian Ocean that include the smallest known apodans. They are best raised in small plastic shoe boxes or margarine tubs.

A Thai Striped Caecilian, *Ichthyophis kohtaoensis*. This truly unique animal appears on the market occasionally and does fairly well in the terrarium. Photo: Dr. W. E. Burgess.

FAMILY ICHTHYOPHIIDAE

Sticky or Striped Caecilian (*Ichthyophis glutinosus*); Yellow-striped Caecilian (*Ichthyophis kohtaoensis*)

Distribution: The Sticky Caecilian is very abundant in Sri Lanka, while the Yellow-striped is imported from Thailand. Other very similar species are found over all of southern Asia from India to Indonesia.

Length: 12 to 15 inches (30 to 38 cm) with a diameter of 1 to 1.3 cm (half an inch).

Description: Quite attractive dark blue or black animals that have a pair of distinctive yellow lateral stripes running along the body. When handled or molested the caecilian secretes an extremely viscid mucus from large glands located throughout the dorsal surface rather like the slime that earthworms produce. The slime serves both to deter predation and to aid movement through dry soils. Hobbyists probably cannot distinguish the various species of the genus.

Availability: This is the caecilian most likely to be offered by reptile dealers, mainly in the form of wild–collected specimens. They come from Indian, Sri Lankan, and Thai paddy fields during May to October, when they move to the surface in large

Close-up of the tail of *Ichthyophis kohtaoensis*. Photo: Dr. W. E. Burgess.

numbers following the floods of monsoon rains. Many are killed on sight because they are mistaken for snakes.

Captive Care: The Sticky Caecilian lives well in a small terrarium, requiring 8 to 18 inches of loamy soil where it can construct burrows. Sufficient moisture should be present, although drier conditions are tolerated by estivating in a water-holding cocoon of sloughed, dead skin and mucilage secretions. Temperatures of 77 to 86°F (25 to 30°C) are suitable, although lower temperatures of around 68°F (20°C) are tolerated at night. Prey needs to be small because of the small gape, so termites, small waxworms, earthworms, and caterpillars are ideal. Some individuals have an affinity for white slugs. The Yellow-striped Caecilian is similar.

Sexual Differences: There are no evident characteristics unique to each sex, so where possible it may be advantageous to acquire three or four individuals, ensuring at least one pair.

Captive Breeding: Breeding can be induced by reducing the moisture content of the basal

This model shows the inside of the nest of a Striped Caecilian, probably *Ichthyophis glutinosus*. Few hobbyists succeed in captive-breeding any caecilians. Photo: R. G. Sprackland.

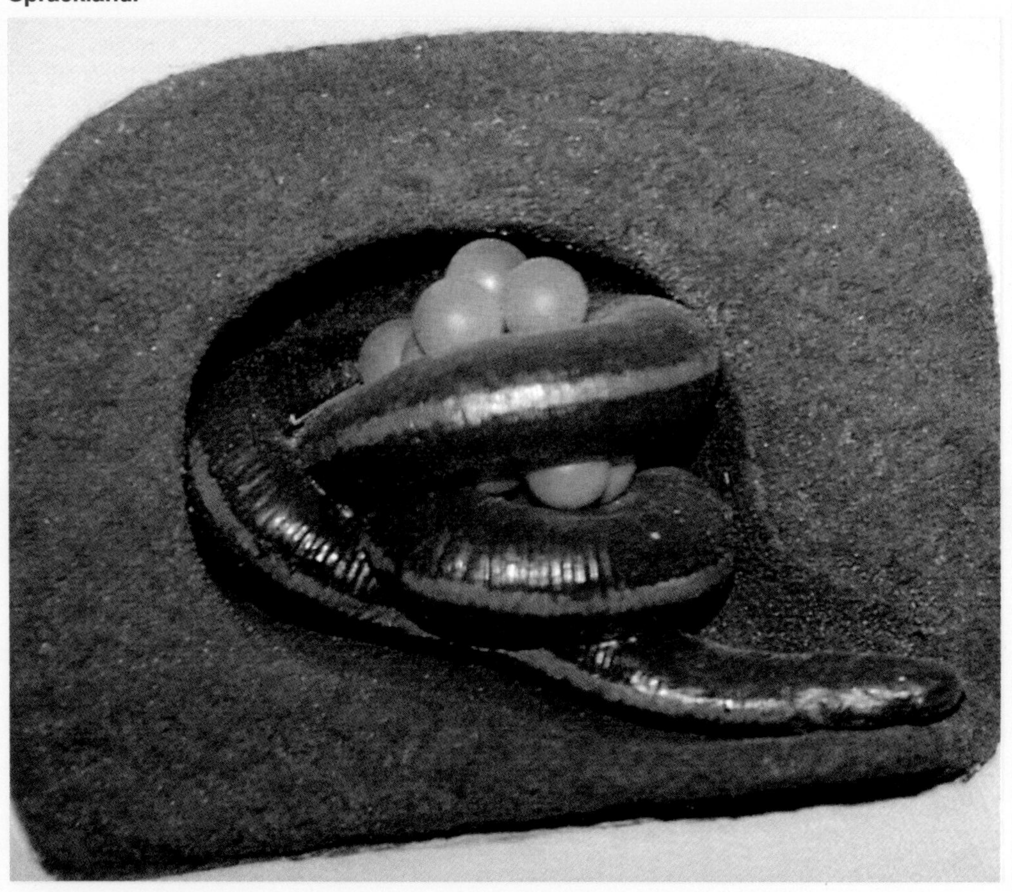

The various yellow-striped species of *Ichthyophis* (the generic name means "fish snake," in reference to the heavy slime) are virtually identical and cannot be told apart by hobbyists unless their point of origin is known for certain. Fortunately, all seem to be keepable in the same way. Photo: Dr. W. E. Burgess.

substrate by up to 75% for a few weeks and thereby persuading the caecilians to estivate. After a month or so the moisture content of the substrate is gradually increased until it is saturated and the caecilians will be aroused into courtship activity. The female deposits a glutinous chain of between 10 and 30 large yolked eggs in a hollow near the water's edge. These need not be removed because she protectively coils around them to maintain moisture by skin secretions and often will enter water to draw up moisture for this purpose. The larvae develop within the egg for up to four months, during which they will grow from 5 mm to 35 mm. On hatching the larvae lead a fully aquatic life for a further six to eight weeks, care being the same as for the Giant Caecilian. Newly metamorphosed Sticky Caecilians are about 7.5 cm (3 in) in length and the same color as the parents. They are best reared individually in plastic shoe boxes for the first two years and fed on whiteworms, hatchling waxworms, and chopped earthworms.

Longevity: At least 15 years.

FAMILY RHINATREMATIDAE

The 30-cm (12-in) Yellow Caecilian (*Rhinatrema bivittatum*) from tropical South America is perhaps the most attractive apodan and worth seeking. It prefers a leafy substrate and high humidity. Its care and breeding are similar to those of *Caecilia thompsoni.*

Scolecomorphus kirki **from Malawi. Though abundant in its homeland, it seldom is exported for the terrarium hobby. Photo: Dr. J. Visser.**

FAMILY TYPHLONECTIDAE

Colombian Aquatic Caecilian (*Typhlonectes natans*)

Note: This species often is seen in pet shops under very unusual common names, especially Sicilian Eel, often due to misunderstanding of the word caecilian, and Rubber Eel.

Distribution: Central and southern Venezuela, west toward central Colombia; actually, the species is recorded mostly from the Magdalena and Cauca Rivers of Colombia, the Venezuelan records being based on a virtually identical animal (*T. venezuelensis*) that probably is a synonym.

Length: 43 to 55 cm (18 to 22 in).

Description: With its blue-black to dark gray-black coloration and laterally flattened, finned tail this species is easily mistaken for a small eel. The mouth is recessed behind a rather long snout. The genus *Typhlonectes* contains truly aquatic caecilians that are extremely adept swimmers capable of quick, graceful movements. The skin is very loose and wrinkled, enabling them to pick up enough dissolved oxygen from the water to virtually forsake the need for surfacing for air (the lungs are greatly reduced). The eyes are small with poor vision. The strong muscles and heavy skin slime make this species very hard to hold. This species often has been called *Typhlonectes compressicauda* in the hobby literature, but that is a brownish species with a somewhat thicker body; it comes from the Amazon system and rarely is exported.

Availability: Most aquatic caecilians are exported from Trinidad and Colombia to tropical fish and herptile suppliers in the USA, who may distribute them elsewhere. They may be seasonally abundant in pet shops and very inexpensive.

Captive Care: In the wild, *Typhlonectes* frequent still or slow-moving water with rocky beds and fairly dense vegetation. This can be replicated in part in captivity, where a 36-inch aquarium filled with 20 inches of water should be furnished with a gravel base and plenty of rocks placed firmly over each other to form small tunnels and caverns. All rocks must be smooth-edged as the skin of this animal is very subject to cuts and following fungal infections. Water should be freely aerated, have an abundance of oxygenating plants, and be of high quality. *Typhlonectes* are expert at escaping, therefore a tight-fitting lid is essential. Water temperatures should be in the 77 to 86°F (25 to 30°C) range and the aquarium should be dimly lit with a low wattage "natural light" fluorescent tube. Preferred foods include aquatic worms, amphibian larvae, and small fish; in captivity thin strips of raw red meat attached loosely to a piece of cotton string are greedily taken.

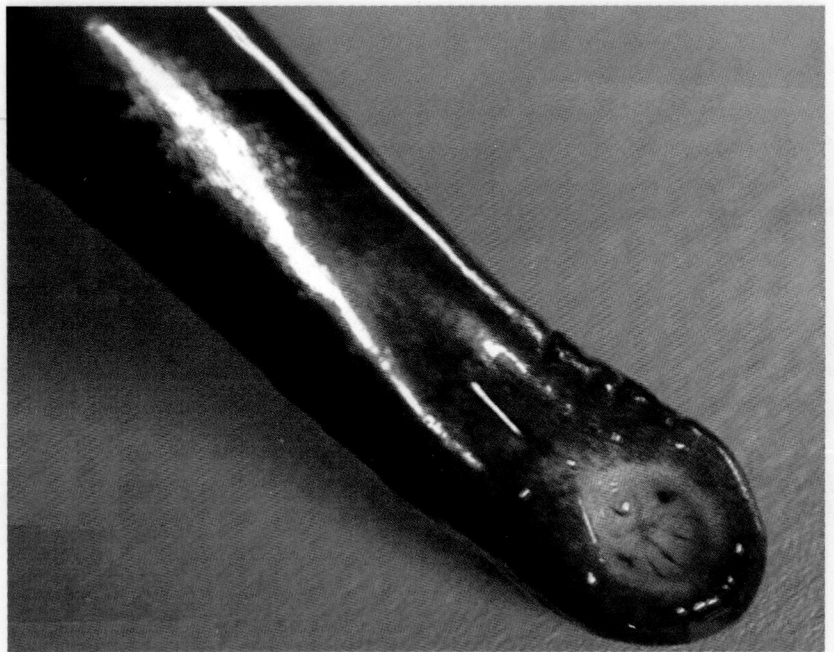

Close-up of the anal disc of the Colombian Aquatic Caecilian, *Typhlonectes natans*. The small papillae visible within the disc may include the penis if this is a male or the ends of the oviducts if it is a female. Photo: Dr. W. E. Burgess.

Sexual Differences: No obvious differences.

Typhlonectes natans is a blackish caecilian with dark blue-gray tones. The color distinguishes it from the rarely available distinctly brown *Typhlonectes compressicauda*. Photo: Dr. W. E. Burgess.

Captive Breeding: *Typhlonectes* is a caecilian genus that gives birth to live, well–developed young that number between 8 and 25, although breeding has until now rarely been achieved in captivity. Reproductive cycles may be governed by fluctuating water temperatures in their natural habitat, such as an increase in cool water due to rainfall or an increase in warm water due to evaporation. Suddenly raising or lowering temperatures by up to 10°F may prove effective in captivity. Pregnant females often are imported and give birth in the aquarium; these females often die soon afterward.

Longevity: Unknown. Many captives live less than a year in the aquarium.

Larvae of the Axolotl, *Ambystoma mexicanum*, just before hatching. Photo: M. Gilroy.

Order Caudata: The Tailed Amphibians

FAMILY AMBYSTOMATIDAE: THE MOLE SALAMANDERS

This predominantly North American (south into central Mexico) family includes some very popular terrestrial terrarium subjects in the form of the Tiger and Spotted Salamanders and what is probably the most popular aquarium amphibian, the Axolotl. Several other species often find their way into the tanks of hobbyists.

Axolotl (*Ambystoma mexicanum*)

Distribution: Lake Xochimilcho, Mexico (seemingly extinct in the wild).

Length: 18 to 30 cm (7 to 12 in).

Description: The axolotl is quite unlike most other ambystomatids because of its entirely neotenic form giving it the appearance of an overgrown newt larva. This sturdy creature has a large head from which sprout

A gorgeous Eastern Tiger Salamander, *Ambystoma tigrinum tigrinum*. Photo: R. T. Zappalorti.

feathery, three-branched gills. Coloration includes several phases ranging from pure white to dark brown or black or a mottled combination of light and dark colors.

Availability: The bizarre appearance has made this species popular with both amphibian and fish hobbyists. Currently it is by far the most widely kept species of salamander (and perhaps of amphibian), with many tropical fish shops now selling Axolotls because they are produced in such large quantities. It is difficult to imagine that this species is nearly (perhaps completely) extinct in the wild and classed as a CITES Appendix I species for wild–collected specimens. All Axolotls in the hobby are captive-bred and have been for many generations.

Captive Care: Axolotls are tolerant of a wide temperature range in captivity, from as low as 46°F (8°C) to a subtropical 78°F (26°C), although room temperature (68°F, 20°C) is preferable. In an enclosed area Axolotls will fight, therefore a 24-inch aquarium should not house more than one adult pair. Decoration need consist of only a smooth pebble base along with several large granite rocks or pieces of submerged driftwood. Live plants will be ripped apart and therefore are not recommended. Water should be dechlorinated, 18 to 24 inches in

An Axolotl, *Ambystoma mexicanum*. Photo: Dr. P. Scott.

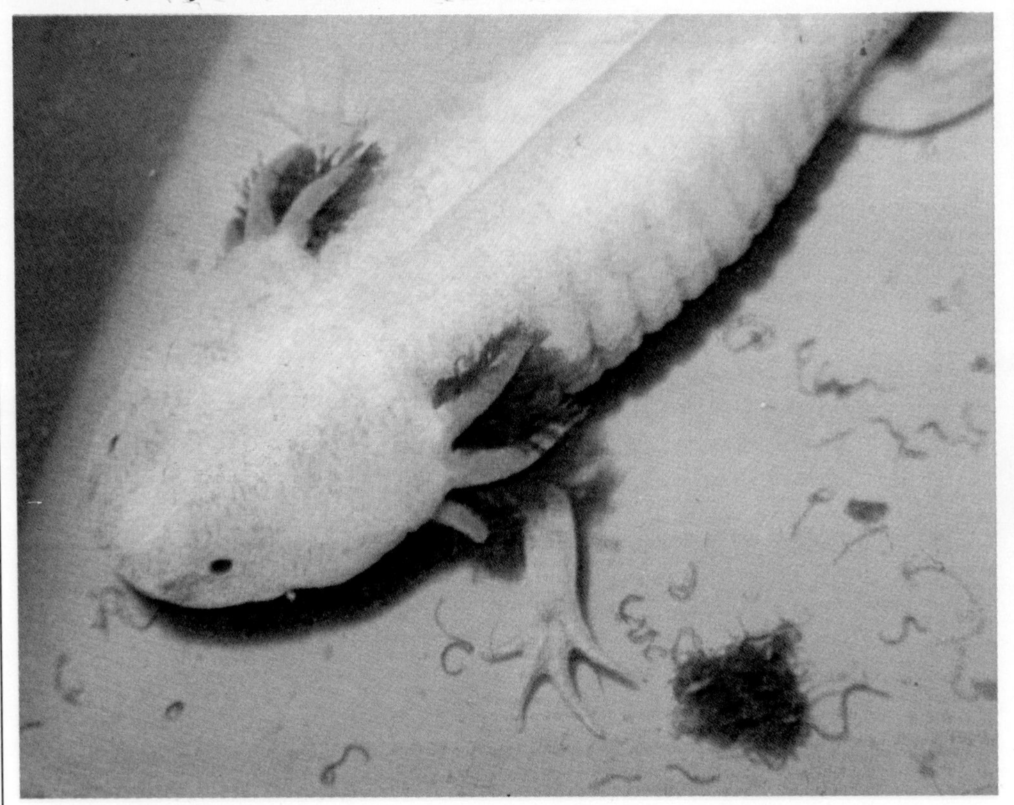

A rather dully patterned specimen of the Eastern Tiger Salamander, *Ambystoma tigrinum tigrinum*. Photo: M. Staniszewski.

depth, aerated, and filtered via an undergravel system to partially combat the production of large amounts of waste, uneaten food, and dead skin. Even then a setup will need a complete overhaul every four weeks. Food consists of aquatic crustaceans, earthworms, and other soft-bodied prey, but they also can be coaxed into taking raw red meat if it is gently rubbed against the snout. Only use small, thin strips of meat as large pieces may be regurgitated, especially where ambient temperatures are cool.

Sexual Differences: Males have a swollen cloaca.

Captive Breeding: This can commence after lowering the water temperature to around 46 to 50°F (8 to 10°C) for four weeks. After a temperature increase to 68°F (20°C) or so, the male Axolotl may attempt to entice the female toward him with rapid body movements and tail flapping. If she is receptive, the male produces spermatophores and leads her over them. Fertilization is internal, with a spermatophore cap being absorbed into the cloaca. A mass of 200 or more gelatinous eggs is laid and adheres to the surrounding

Detail of the head of *Ambystoma tigrinum*. Photo: M. Staniszewski.

pebbles and rocks. These should be removed to separate rearing tanks to prevent adults from devouring them. Incubate at 60 to 70°F (16 to 21°C). Hatching occurs 12 to 18 days later. The larvae will grow at a rate of 1 to 2 cm per month. In the latter stages of proper larval development, cannibalism is displayed; although it can be avoided by separating the young Axolotls, such behavior may ensure that only the strongest specimens survive. Maturity is achieved after 7 to 13 months. If the water remains fairly deep, metamorphosis will be arrested permanently even though the animals are sexually mature. Shallow water coupled with higher temperatures may induce metamorphosis into a fully terrestrial mole salamander that is quite drab and secretive in comparison to the more familiar aquarium animal.

Longevity: Twelve to 20 years.

Tiger Salamander (*Ambystoma tigrinum*)

Note: From six to almost a dozen subspecies are recognized, most difficult to distinguish. One, *A. t. californiense*, often is considered a full species, the California Tiger Salamander, while some of the Mexican subspecies also may be entitled to species rank.

Distribution: Tiger Salamanders are found in a wide

One of the most striking Tiger Salamanders is the Barred, *Ambystoma tigrinum mavortium.* Good specimens of this subspecies can be mostly bright yellow with black bars. And yes, a large Tiger will most definitely take small mice. Photo: K. T. Nemuras.

Larval Tiger Salamanders, *Ambystoma tigrinum*, usually are muddy brown animals with a pattern of irregular black spots. Only several weeks after metamorphosis do the more brightly colored subspecies attain the more colorful adult pattern. Photo: A. Norman.

variety of damp habitats throughout southern Canada, the central and eastern U.S.A., the Great Plains and Southwest, and California, south into central Mexico. Because larvae are widely collected as fishbait, they have been introduced into many lakes and rivers outside the natural range, and it may be impossible today to correctly identify subspecies by geographical data.

Length: Recognized as the largest terrestrial salamander, attaining 15 to 22 cm (6 to 9 in), with records to 33 cm (13 in).

Description: A robust salamander showing considerable variation in pattern and coloration even among individuals of the same subspecies. Generally it is boldly marked with cream or yellow blotches or broken bars on a brown to black background. In some subspecies and local populations the pale spotting is diffuse and fades into the background. The broad head ends with a rounded snout and the eyes are small with round pupils. The feet often have horny tubercles on the undersides, and the tail is long and flattened.

Availability: Most tiger salamanders offered to hobbyists are either adults collected from their breeding sites during early spring, well–developed larvae collected from ponds, or recently metamorphosed juveniles produced as a result of intensive breeding programs in American research laboratories. Entire populations have been depleted as a result of over-collecting of larvae for use as fishing bait or by the introduction of carnivorous game fishes such as basses into breeding pools. Wild-collected larvae often are in poor condition and should be watched for fungal infections. This species is protected in several eastern states of the U.S. where natural populations have almost disappeared.

Captive Care: A medium to large terrarium is required, with a soft base of either sphagnum moss or a synthetic foam that remains uniformly moist. Robust pieces of bark and caves constructed of sturdy rocks are necessary for hiding places because initially these salamanders tend to be shy. Avoid live plants because Tiger Salamanders will dig them up either to hide or to locate prey. A large water bowl that enables a specimen to completely submerge itself also is necessary. Normal daytime temperatures for northern forms should be no more than 72°F (22°C) during most of the year, while southern USA and Mexican forms can tolerate 79°F (26°C) but are best kept cooler. Lighting should be dim to moderate but not radiate much heat. As they are extremely greedy

In California the Tiger Salamander has a yellow-spotted pattern on brown or black and is quite attractive. Because this subspecies, *Ambystoma tigrinum californiense*, does not occur near other subspecies and also differs in some aspects of its reproductive biology, it often is considered to be a full species. Photo: A. Norman.

A large larval Tiger Salamander, *Ambystoma tigrinum*, makes a good pet. They are hardy animals that feed well and accept a broad diet. Photo: K. T. Nemuras.

amphibians (hence the ease with which they adapt to captivity), food consisting of waxworms, earthworms, pink mice, strips of raw red meat, and small fish (minnows, strips of whitebait) should not be offered too frequently. Larvae can be kept much like Axolotls but may need a larger tank. If the water is deficient in iodine, the larvae may not metamorphose.

Sexual Differences: Males have a prominently swollen cloacal region often surrounded by frilly edges. Females are generally more rotund.

Captive Breeding: Breeding is feasible only in a large terrarium containing an expanse of deep water. A better proposition is the outdoor amphibiary. For northern forms a 10-week dormancy period at 38°F (3°C) will stimulate breeding. Temperatures just 2°F above this can stir tiger salamanders into activity, following which successful courtship will be likely. Southern subspecies tend to retreat into cool underground burrows where they semiestivate for up to three months. This should only be attempted in captivity where a definite vertical thermal gradient can be achieved; i.e., warm above the surface of the substrate and cool below it. Tiger Salamanders enter water very early in the year when ambient temperatures are as low as 40°F (4°C). A water depth of 25 to 40 inches is recommended in captivity where, in common with many ambystomatids, a brief courtship period involving internal fertilization will result in 180 to 250 eggs being deposited. These occur in small packets numbering 8 to 15 that the female affixes to submerged plants, twigs, or pebbles. Remove these packets to rearing tanks filled with an equivalent depth of water. To ensure healthy development, the water must be kept cool, filtered, and aerated. Hatching commences after 52 days at 45°F (8°C) or as little as 18 days at 75°F (24°C), but resultant larvae tend to be weak and listless, seldom living more than a few days. Healthy larvae grow steadily from 10.2 mm to a premetamorphosis size of 90 mm (3.5 in) in 54 to 112 days depending on how often they are fed and the food's nutrition content. In the later stages of development and on metamorphosis, fighting and cannibalism are commonplace unless individuals are separated into their own plastic containers. Maturity will occur after a further three to five years. In the wild, western subspecies often are neotenic because of the absence of iodine in water sources. This is unlikely to occur in captivity.

Longevity: Sixteen years or more.

Spotted Salamander (*Ambystoma maculatum*)

Distribution: Very moist areas from southern Canada to the northern part of Florida and west toward Texas.

Length: 11 to 20 cm (4.5 to 8 in).

Description: A fairly slender,

Though one of the most beautiful North American salamanders, Spotted Salamanders, *Ambystoma maculatum*, often do not fare well in captivity and have a poor reputation among many keepers. Photo: M. Staniszewski.

broad-headed salamander uniformly colored black to blue-gray, over which run two rows of fairly regular yellow or orange round spots on the upper sides and continuing to the tip of the tail. Costal grooves are quite pronounced, numbering usually 11 or 12.

Availability: A very widely kept salamander, the bulk of which are adults that have been collected from their breeding ponds in early spring. This species is said to be difficult to produce commercially.

Captive Care: Requirements are very similar to those of the Tiger Salamander, although the Spotted inhabits somewhat damper conditions. It also is much more secretive, spending almost its entire terrestrial life underground or beneath damp logs and rocks. Due to its preference for moist areas it is quite susceptible to fungal infections, especially around the snout, eyes, and lips. Increasing ventilation may prove effective. Temperatures of 57 to 75°F (14 to 24°C) are suitable.

Sexual Differences: Males always have a more swollen cloaca.

Captive Breeding: Breeding this species requires considerable persuasion and is likely to occur only in a large aqua-terrarium or outdoor amphibiary. The main stimulus appears to involve heavily watering the terrarium with warm (70°F, 21°C) water immediately following an eight– to ten-week hibernation period. The salamanders immediately search for and congregate in cool water. After fertilization the female lays several clumps of 20 to 75 eggs. Rearing conditions for eggs are exactly the same as for *A. tigrinum*, although larvae grow to a smaller premetamorphosis size of 7 cm (almost 3 in). Cannibalism among juveniles is rare, and this salamander is quite gregarious in its behavior. However, all mole salamanders should be looked upon as potentially cannibalistic and the terrarium never overcrowded.

Longevity: Twelve to 18 years.

Marbled Salamander (*Ambystoma opacum*)

Distribution: Found throughout the eastern U.S.A. in many different moist or relatively dry habitats, including gardens, parks, and wasteland.

Length: 8 to 11 cm (3.5 to 4.5 in).

Description: A rather small but plump salamander attractively marked with broad alternating bands of white or silvery gray and black or dark brown.

Availability: Another species that often is collected in large quantities when they move to the surface following heavy rains, usually in the autumn. Seldom bred in captivity.

Captive Care: This species will live quite happily in a small terrarium where conditions are similar to those for the Tiger Salamander, apart from its preference for somewhat drier conditions except during the autumn and winter.

Sexual Differences: Males have whiter bands, whereas in females these are light gray. The male's cloaca also is more swollen.

The number of yellow spots varies considerably in the Spotted Salamander, *Ambystoma maculatum*. Some specimens have bright orange spots on the head. Photo: A. Norman.

Unlike most mole salamanders, the Marbled Salamander, *Ambystoma opacum*, lays its eggs in the autumn and waits for the water levels to rise. Photo: R. T. Zappalorti.

Marbled Salamanders, *Ambystoma opacum*, make interesting though rather secretive pets. Their color pattern is unique among common salamanders, and though the colors are not bright, they are attractive. In the photo above, the male is the smaller, brighter white animal. Often females have the white or silvery banding greatly reduced and partially replaced by gray. Photos: M. Staniszewski.

Captive Breeding: Unfortunately this little salamander is not regularly bred in captivity. Its breeding behavior is unusual among the ambystomatids, with egg deposition taking place in damp depressions during autumn. Here the female guards her 75 or so eggs until rain forms a puddle into which the larvae hatch in late autumn. If the depression remains dry, larval development continues within the egg capsule, with larger young hatching out the following spring. In either case metamorphosis is reached 130 to 160 days later.

Recently metamorphosed Marbled Salamanders, *Ambystoma opacum*, don't look much like their parents. The color pattern takes several weeks to develop even in a weak fashion. Photo: K. T. Nemuras.

Long-toed Salamander (*Ambystoma macrodactylum*)

Note: Five subspecies generally are recognized, distinguished in part by color pattern. One, the Santa Cruz Long-toed Salamander, *A. m. croceum*, is among the rarest North American salamanders, being restricted to a small area of Santa Cruz and Monterey Counties, California, where it is protected.

Distribution: Pacific Northwest, U.S.A. and Canada.

Length: 15 to 23 cm (6 to 9 in).

Description: An attractive, highly variable salamander distinguished by a solid dorsal band of green to gold or yellow or the band broken to appear like yellow to orange blotches and spots on a blackish back.

Availability: Rarely available commercially, although it is quite abundant across most of its range. Well worth seeking.

Captive Care: See Tiger

Salamander. In the aquatic breeding state adults consume huge numbers of aquatic crustaceans such as scuds and isopods.

Sexual Differences: Males have a swollen cloaca and a slimmer build than females.

Captive Breeding: Courtship takes place after a relatively long hibernation period (up to three months in northern subspecies), with still, shallow (6 to 12 inches deep), or slow-moving water preferred. In excess of 150 eggs are deposited, either singly or in small clumps. Larvae are slow-growing in cool conditions and may not metamorphose until the following spring. Southern subspecies may not come into breeding condition until early winter; they remain in water for up to five months, making this one of the most aquatic mole salamanders.

Jefferson Salamander
(*Ambystoma jeffersonianum*)

Note: The Jefferson and Blue-spotted Salamanders hybridize in portions of their range to produce all-female hybrids sometimes considered to be full species: *A. platineum* and *A. tremblayi.*

Distribution: Central and northeastern U.S.A.

Length: 10 to 18 cm (4 to 7 in).

Description: Rather plain, slender species colored dark gray or black with relatively few whitish to silvery gray spots and a pale belly (or at least not black).

Availability: Commonly offered by dealers and often exported to Europe, where there is some demand.

The Long-toed Salamander, *Ambystoma macrodactylum*, is one of the most attractive mole salamanders. Not every specimen has such a nice dorsal stripe, however. Photo: A. Norman.

Captive Care: Moist woodland terrarium with temperatures around 65°F (18°C).

Captive Breeding: The breeding season is somewhat later than in most other species, usually when the water reaches 48°F (9°C). Adults remain in water for only two to four weeks. Around 150 eggs are deposited. Their care is much like that of the Tiger Salamander. Seldom bred in captivity.

Blue-spotted Salamander
(*Ambystoma laterale*)

Distribution: Northeastern and north-central U.S.A. and adjacent Canada.

Length: 10 to 14 cm (4 to 5.5 in).

Description: Black body flecked with many blue and white spots, the belly black or at least dark.

Captive Care: A very hardy species that should be kept cool at about 60°F (16°C). Hibernation

Several of the American mole salamanders could be described as basically brownish gray with brighter gray or bluish mottling. These species sometimes are hard to distinguish on sight and may require consideration of number of costal grooves, toe length, and head shape. Above is the Jefferson Salamander, *Ambystoma jeffersonianum*, while below is the Smallmouthed Salamander, *Ambystoma texanum*. Photo: above, R. T. Zappalorti; below, K. T. Nemuras.

is essential for breeding, which occurs in temporary ponds. Fifty or so eggs are deposited, these slow to develop.

Mole Salamander (*Ambystoma talpoideum*)

Distribution: Southern U.S.A.

Length: 7 to 10 cm (3 to 4 in).

Description: A short-bodied little species with the head appearing too large for the body. Usually grayish or blackish with blue and white spots and mottling especially dense on the lower sides.

Availability: Often collected at the breeding ponds.

Captive Care: Prefers slightly acidic woodland terraria. Breeds from December to February, depositing up to 200 eggs. This

The Blue-spotted Salamander, *Ambystoma laterale*, is a rather plainly colored salamander that does well when kept cool. It hybridizes with the Jefferson Salamander, and the two often are very hard to distinguish. Photo: R. T. Zappalorti.

Ambystoma talpoideum, the Mole Salamander, looks like a squashed Smallmouthed or Blue-spotted Salamander. The short trunk and large head are characteristic. Photo: W. B. Allen, Jr.

species is very secretive and spends most of its life in burrows or under debris. You seldom will see it except at night if the terrarium is properly furnished. Often feeds well on earthworms.

Ringed Salamander (*Ambystoma annulatum*) and **Flatwood Salamander (*Ambystoma cingulatum*)**

Distribution: Ringed: Ozark Plateau and Ouachita Mountains of Missouri, Arkansas, and Oklahoma. Flatwood: Southeastern U.S.A.

Length: Ringed: 14 to 18 cm (5.5 to 7 in). Flatwood: 9 to 13 cm (3.5 to 5 in).

Description: Ringed: Rather elongate for a mole salamander, the black body ringed with bright yellow. Flatwood: Black, with bright golden to silvery frosting that may be restricted to the lower sides or produce narrow rings over the back; a beautiful animal.

The scarce Ringed Salamander, *Ambystoma annulatum*. Photo: K. T. Nemuras.

Availability: Rarely offered for sale. Adults are collected at breeding ponds. Because these animals have small areas of distribution and are believed to be declining in numbers, their commercial capture has been controlled to some extent and they may be given more complete protection later. Neither species could be called common unless the breeding ponds are found.

Captive Care: A medium to large, cool, moist woodland terrarium kept at 60 to 65°F (16 to 18°C) will do for both species. They are very secretive.

Captive Breeding: Breeding can be stimulated by completely flooding the terrarium in autumn with warm water (70°F, 21°C). Don't be afraid of these salamanders drowning; they adapt to an aquatic state very quickly, although it is wise to create a shelf of dry land onto which they can crawl. Eggs number as few as 50 but hatch very quickly. Eggs should be removed to a shallow aquarium maintained at room temperature. The larvae will develop rapidly, metamorphosing in as little as six to eight weeks.

Though it is one of the most beautiful of the salamanders, the Ringed Salamander, *Ambystoma annulatum*, seldom is available because it is protected. It is found only in a few populations in the Ozark Mountains of Missouri and Arkansas (and adjoining areas). This is one of the species that might be seriously hurt by repeated collecting from the breeding ponds. Photo: K. T. Nemuras.

The Flatwood Salamander, *Ambystoma cingulatum*, is found only in the southeastern United States and seldom is common. Some specimens are rather dull, while others are covered with a beautiful bluish silvery network. Photo: R. T. Zappalorti.

FAMILY DICAMPTODONTIDAE: COPE'S SALAMANDERS

Though the giant Cope's salamanders often have been considered members of the Ambystomatidae, recently they have been split into their own family, of which *Dicamptodon* is the only genus. Relationships with the Olympic salamanders (*Rhyacotriton*) are obscure, so that genus also has been recognized as a full family by most American workers. The number of species of Cope's salamanders is uncertain.

California Giant Salamander (*Dicamptodon ensatus*)

Note: The description that follows applies to a composite of *Dicamptodon ensatus* and *D. tenebrosus*, species that seem externally almost indistinguishable.

Distribution: The Pacific coast and moist interior forests of north-central California (*D. ensatus*), north through the Pacific Northwest into British Columbia (*D. tenebrosus*).

Length: The second largest terrestrial caudate after the Tiger Salamander, attaining 22 to 33 cm (9 to 13 in).

Description: An impressive salamander that is even more robust than the Tiger Salamander. It is distinguished by its proportionally large head and a marbled patterning comprising irregular black blotches on a dark green, brown, or purplish background. This is one of the few vocal salamanders, emitting a low rattle-like sound when disturbed.

Availability: Wild-caught adults occasionally find their way into pet shops to be wrongly labeled as Tiger Salamanders; the species are protected to some extent, especially in California.

Captive Care: The setup is the same as for the Tiger Salamander, although better lighting and a large container filled with 5 to 10 cm of cool water should be provided. The California Giant Salamander also enjoys climbing, so integrate a large sturdy branch into the setup along with several piece of cork bark beneath which it can retreat. Ideally, temperatures should be between 60 and 68°F (16 and 20°) and the terrarium should be misted freely to create humidity. They make interesting captives because they are showy creatures and often are active by day. Specimens seem to respond to feeding by leaving their hiding places after a light is switched on or the terrarium door is opened. Feeding presents few problems, with strips of raw meat and a wide variety of invertebrates, small fishes, and pink mice being readily accepted.

Sexual Differences: Loose cloacal flaps in males.

Captive Breeding: See Tiger Salamander for conditioning. Mating and egg deposition occur in cool, shallow, slow-flowing waters, and by simulating these conditions with an integrated pump/filtration/aeration system, breeding commences in late

***Dicamptodon ensatus*, the California Giant Salamander, makes an unusual addition to the collection. The male (top) is smaller and more slender than the female. Photo: M. Staniszewski.**

The various species of giant salamanders are distinguished by molecular biology, not by structure, and are best identified by locality. This *Dicamptodon ensatus* came from central California. Photo: M. Staniszewski.

summer to late autumn. Several clumps containing 15 to 55 eggs are attached to the undersides of submerged rocks. A fertile egg has the nucleus a light brown and measures 3 mm in diameter. The eggs hatch after eight weeks, the larvae 5 to 8 mm long when they emerge. In cool water, development can be painfully slow, sometimes as long as two years, when larvae may measure 18 cm (7 in). True neoteny is prevalent in some populations (which now mostly are identified as *Dicamptodon copei*). Giant salamanders reach sexual maturity after five years.

Other Species: Formerly only a single species, *Dicamptodon ensatus*, was recognized, with a range extending from central California to Idaho and over the rest of the Pacific Northwest. Recent studies of the molecular chemistry of this salamander yielded results that indicate to some workers that three species, externally identical or nearly so, should be recognized: *D. ensatus*, California Giant Salamander, central and northern California; *D. tenebrosus*, Pacific Giant Salamander, northern California over rest of Pacific Northwest; *D. aterrimus*, Idaho Giant Salamander, northern Idaho and adjacent Montana. Many specialists, however, recognize only one species, *D. ensatus*, then called the Pacific Giant Salamander, and feel the other two names should be treated as synonyms. However, there is a second morphologically distinct and recently described species of Cope's salamander:

Dicamptodon copei, Cope's Giant Salamander. Rarely seen in captivity, this species is neotenous and requires very cold, highly oxygenated waters. In captivity they can be subjected to thyroid (iodine) treatments and induced to metamorphose into adults that adapt well to cool, humid woodland terraria. Attaining about 7.5 in (19 cm), Cope's Giant Salamander has a yellowish back speckled with clusters of curious white skin glands. Preferred food is the same as the California Giant Salamander and breeding is similar apart from the totally aquatic existence.

FAMILY PLETHODONTIDAE: THE LUNGLESS SALAMANDERS

The salamander family with the largest known number of species paradoxically contains very few species that are regularly kept in captivity, even though many of them are extremely abundant. One reason for this is their highly secretive behavior that presents difficulties in locating sufficient numbers for the pet trade. Additionally, many hobbyists may be discouraged by the lack of practical information regarding captive care. However, some plethodontids are attractive and colorful amphibians and well worth looking for. Documenting behavior and breeding could even safeguard the threatened future of many species. In captivity, because of their lack of lungs and specialized respiratory system, all species demand good ventilation to ensure fresh air or high levels of dissolved oxygen in water. They are unable to tolerate warm, dry conditions. Two subfamilies are recognized, one (Desmognathinae) for the dusky salamanders and their allies and the other (Plethodontinae) for the remaining species. Dusky salamanders are able to lift the upper jaw while the lower jaw is heavy and rigid, an adaptation for burrowing.

Dusky Salamander (*Desmognathus fuscus*)

Note: As is so common among the salamanders, there is considerable controversy as to the number of subspecies of Dusky Salamander and its relationship to several very similar forms.

Distribution: Southeastern Canada south over much of the central and eastern U.S.A. Found in moist meadows, swamps, river and stream edges, moist rocky screes, and woodlands.

Length: 6.5 to 12 cm (2.5 to 5 in).

Description: A small, chunky salamander showing considerable variation in color, with gray, light brown, or sometimes black being evident. Pairs of coppery, clay-colored, or yellow spots on each side of the backbone sometimes fuse together to produce a broad pale stripe down the middle of the back with dark, scalloped edges. The tip of the tail is sharp-edged above, not rounded. Distinguishing any one species of

A female Mountain Dusky Salamander, *Desmognathus ochrophaeus*, guarding its egg clutch. Such guarding is typical of all *Desmognathus* species. Photo: R. T. Zappalorti.

Desmognathus from the others can prove frustratingly difficult.

Availability: This species occasionally is offered by American amphibian dealers as wild-caught juveniles or adults throughout most of the year except the summer months. Often specimens are labeled as just "dusky salamanders," so it may prove wise to discover the origin of a specimen and run it through the appropriate field guides.

Captive Care: Being relatively small salamanders, this along with all other similar species is best housed in a small, humid terrarium containing a sufficient layer of live sphagnum moss and a large, shallow (2 to 3 inches) water dish. The smallest species, the Pigmy Salamander (*Desmognathus wrighti*), has been successfully housed and bred in plastic sweater boxes. In terms of temperature, lowland species prefer temperatures of 60 to 75°F (16 to 24°C), while 50 to 60°F (10 to 16°C) suits mountain dwellers.

Sexual Differences: Older males tend to be darker and in some species a mental gland is present on the chin. Males often have more robust heads and legs.

The species of *Desmognathus* are found only in the eastern and central United States, where they can be very abundant. All look much alike at first glance and often are hard to distinguish just by looking at shape and color patterns. The Mountain Dusky (above), *Desmognathus ochrophaeus*, often looks like a small, rather cleanly patterned version of the more common Northern Dusky (below), *Desmognathus fuscus fuscus*. The two species often are found together. Photos: W. P. Mara.

Captive Breeding: Hibernate *Desmognathus* for six to ten weeks from February to April to induce a brief courtship, which may involve the male nudging and nipping the female. She deposits a small clutch of large, gelatinous eggs numbering 15 to 60 (depending on her age) in a very moist location, usually the edge of the water or a damp depression. Here she actively coils around the eggs until they hatch and if necessary frequents water before returning to secrete moisture over them. This behavior is thought to be unique to plethodontids, and her secretion is known to give some protection against egg fungus. The larvae often will remain in the egg capsule for a full four to seven months, but if placed in shallow water they will hatch and lead a normal larval life. Either way the juveniles are 25 to 35 mm long when they begin their fully terrestrial life. Their colors and patterning are significantly more vivid than in adults.

Southern Dusky Salamanders, *Desmognathus auriculatus*, can be very plainly colored animals; most have blackish bellies. Often they are found in the muck at the edges of cypress swamps. Photo: Dr. D. Green.

Southern Dusky Salamander (*Desmognathus auriculatus*)

Distribution: Southern U.S.A.

Length: 7 to 13 cm (3 to 5 in).

Captive Care: A species of stagnant or slow-flowing waters and their edges. Prefers an aqua-terrarium setup with shallow, slightly acidic water

Desmognathus apalachicolae **is closely related to the Dusky Salamander and differs mostly in its biochemistry. The range is very restricted, mostly the Apalachicola River drainage of the Florida Panhandle and adjacent Georgia. Photo: R. D. Bartlett**

Mountain Dusky Salamanders, *Desmognathus monticola*, often have a great number of small white specks on the head, a feature that helps distinguish the species from the more common Dusky Salamander. Photo: R. D. Bartlett.

containing plenty of water weed. Temperature range 60 to 72°F (16 to 22°C). Females deposit clumps of 22 to 40 eggs beneath rotten logs and other debris in mid-spring.

Seal Salamander (*Desmognathus monticola*)

Distribution: Appalachian Mountains from Pennsylvania to Florida.

Length: 8 to 15 cm (3 to 6 in).

Captive Care: A predominantly montane species that is highly nocturnal and seeks out cool, humid caves between rocks. Maximum temperature 66°F (19°C). The female attaches her 18 to 26 eggs to the moist walls of a cave. In nature this species frequents ravines and similar cool, humid environments.

Blackbelly Salamander (*Desmognathus quadramaculatus*)

Distribution: Appalachian Mountains from West Virginia to Georgia.

Length: 10 to 18 cm (4 to 7 in).

Captive Care: The largest desmognathine apart from the rare Red Hills Salamander (*Phaeognathus hubrichti*), this species likes flowing streams with many large boulders and is extremely hard to handle. Often appears during the day to sun itself on damp rocks. Temperatures range from 60 to 65°F (16 to 18°C). Eggs are

Close-up of the Blackbelly Salamander, *Desmognathus quadramaculatus*. Photo: R. D. Bartlett.

deposited near the edges of streams.

Pigmy Salamander
(*Desmognathus wrighti*)

Distribution: Restricted to certain mountains from southwestern Virginia to southwestern North Carolina in the Appalachians.

Length: 4 to 5 cm (about 1.5 to 2 in).

Captive Care: A dweller in cool, damp mountain forests, this is one of the smallest salamanders known and makes an excellent captive for the small terrarium as long as the temperature does not rise above 65°F (18°C). Males have a large U-shaped mental gland under the chin. Females lay clumps of 8 to 14 tiny eggs during favorable wet weather. There is no free larval stage, the babies hatching out as fully developed specimens lacking gills.

If you look closely, you can see the nasolabial groove running from the edge of the nostril of this Blackbelly. Photo: M. Staniszewski.

Northern Two-lined Salamander
(*Eurycea bislineata*)

Note: This name formerly was used for what is now considered to be a group of as many as five species that externally are very similar and differ mostly in biology. *Eurycea* species often are called brook salamanders.

Distribution: Northeastern U.S.A. and adjacent Canada.

Desmognathus quadramaculatus **is a big, husky, dark-bellied salamander that likes it wet. It is very slippery and hard to handle. Photo: M. Staniszewski.**

Length: 6 to 9.5 cm (2.5 to 4 in).

Description: Slender, long-tailed, waxy species with a bright yellow to greenish tan stripe down the middle of the back, bordered by two broad black lines on the sides; belly translucent yellow.

Captive Care: One of the most widespread small plethodontids (especially if all the related species are included), usually found along and in cool, highly oxygenated streams and seepages. Temperatures around 60°F (16°C) are fine for this species, with the more southerly species of the group (including especially *Eurycea cirrigera*, the Southern Two-lined Salamander) tolerating temperatures to over 68°F (20°C). To breed it needs hibernation for a month or more and cool, moving water to lay its eggs. Twelve to 30 eggs are deposited.

The Northern Two-lined Salamander, *Eurycea bislineata*, is the most commonly seen brook salamander. This group of species is found mostly in the wet vegetation at the edges of streams and springs. They have a waxy orange coloration that is quite attractive. Photo: A. Norman.

Long-tailed Salamander (*Eurycea longicauda*)

Distribution: Most of eastern U.S.A. and adjacent Canada.

Length: 10 to 16 cm (4 to 6.5 in).

Description: A bright waxy brown species. The broad pale brown stripe down the middle of the back is bordered by broad black stripes or rows of large

black spots; the center of the back stripe may have a row of black spots or a narrow black stripe.

Captive Care: In the wild the Long-tailed Salamander is an inhabitant of streams, cool ponds, and leaf litter in moist, shady woods. Occasional wild-caught specimens are sold between March and June. It cannot tolerate warmth, with 52 to 60°F (11 to 16°C) being preferred. An escape artist that climbs well and will go up moist glass sides. Eight to 25 eggs are deposited singly on submerged vegetation in shallow ponds and streams.

Long-tailed Salamanders, *Eurycea longicauda*, are found over much of the eastern United States and are quite variable. The obvious dark stripe down the center of the back of the two specimens shown here indicates they belong to the southern subspecies, *E. l. guttolineata*, often called the Three-lined Salamander. Photos: top, M. Staniszewski; bottom, A. Norman.

Dwarf Salamander (*Eurycea quadridigitata*)

Distribution: Southern U.S.A.

Length: 5 to 7.5 cm (2 to 3 in).

Description: Like most *Eurycea* this dwarf species has a pencil-thin body and long tail. The dorsal coloration is coppery with a series of dark spots or short lines leading from the head to the middle of the tail. There are broad dark stripes on the sides, and the belly is yellowish. The head is small with large eyes. There are only four toes on the hind feet (five in other *Eurycea)*; for this reason and some differences in larval biology, the species once was placed in the genus *Manculus*.

Availability: It is surprising that the brook and Dwarf Salamanders represent some of the most abundant U.S. amphibia and yet they are infrequently available.

Captive Care: More tolerant of a range of habits than most plethodontids, Dwarf Salamanders can be found far away from water (though always in moist substrates) or in and near streams and ponds. An aqua-terrarium is the best setup for this and other brook salamanders, with a shallow water area not more than 4 inches in depth. Some species prefer running water, so a pump system may need to be integrated to create a small stream, which in a small terrarium may not be possible, but such niceties are not necessary for Dwarf Salamanders. Air temperatures can reach 81 to 86°F (27 to 30°C), but the water must remain around 65°F (18°C).

Sexual Differences: Males have a small spike called a cirrus (plural cirri) projecting downward from each nostril. (Gently brush a finger up the snout or use a magnifying glass.) The male cloaca also is more swollen.

Captive Breeding: In captivity southern species such as the Dwarf Salamander must be estivated for a few months to induce more vigorous breeding in late summer or autumn. *Eurycea quadridigitata* tends to breed in still shallows of slow streams and ponds, where 8 to 20 clumped eggs are hung at the water surface by means of a gelatinous stalk. They hatch within four to eight days at a temperature of 60°F (16°C). Development of the long, thin juveniles is completed after eight weeks. Whiteworms, bloodworms, and fruitflies patiently offered on the end of a cocktail stick provide the staple diet for the fragile 20– to 25-mm young.

Clouded Salamander (*Aneides ferreus*)

Distribution: Wooded, often fairly dry regions of coastal California and Oregon, U.S.A., plus Vancouver Island, Canada.

Length: 12.5 to 16 cm (5 to 6.5 in).

Description: A delightful little salamander with the back brown, mottled with gray or coppery markings. The skin is

Clouded Salamanders, *Aneides ferreus*, can display unusual green tints. Photo: K. H. Switak.

heavily granulated and the toes are unusually square at the ends, to help the salamander secure a better purchase during climbing. Clouded Salamanders are also fairly vocal, squeaking at night when they are hunting prey or are alarmed.

Availability: The Clouded and the Arboreal Salamanders (*A. lugubris*) are occasionally available usually in late spring, when adults moving from the vicinity of their hiding places to find a mate are collected from the wild. Demand for these and other unusual or colorful plethodons is increasing, but few populations could withstand heavy collecting pressure, meaning that captive–breeding will have to increase before the salamanders become common pets.

Captive Care: Requires a fairly tall (30+ inches), cool, humid terrarium where it is best maintained in small groups of four to ten. *Aneides* will not tolerate continually damp conditions, so a shallow water pan and the occasional brief spraying of part of the terrarium are quite sufficient. A sturdy, gnarled branch that is not placed in too vertical a position gives these salamanders a chance to show off their excellent climbing abilities. Several large holes should be drilled in this branch to provide hiding and egg-laying sites. Ideally, temperatures should be around 62 to 70°F (17 to 21°C),

The obviously expanded toe pads are an indication that the Arboreal Salamander, *Aneides lugubris*, is a climber. Color patterns in *Aneides* species can be very variable. Photo: Dr. D. Green.

decreased to 50 to 55°F (10 to 13°C) during December to early March. This is a fairly agile species that hunts and captures moths, flies, spiders, and caterpillars in a lizard-like fashion. In the wild it is known to scrape off and eat certain fungi on the bark of trees by using specialized protruding teeth in the upper jaw.

Sexual Differences: Males have a broader head than females and a heart-shaped mental gland (oval shaped in *A. lugubris*) on the chin.

Captive Breeding: Breeding in captivity is possible following a "cool period" when humidity is decreased. The smaller space within the terrarium makes contact between specimens far more frequent than in nature, and eventually a female and male that are sexually receptive will have a successful mating. Following courtship, the female *Aneides* seeks the holes drilled into the tree branch, which should now be laced with damp sphagnum moss. Alternatively she may excavate a depression in the basal substrate beneath a rock. If such conditions are not provided, eggs may be abandoned beneath a water bowl, where they will desiccate. A small clutch of 12 to 30 gelatinous eggs with light brown nuclei is laid. The eggs are cared for and moistened by the female, although such behavior may be neglected in captivity. When she does tend to her eggs she will guard them

Two views of the Santa Cruz Black Salamander, *Aneides flavipunctatus niger*, of California, the juvenile below. Photos: M. Staniszewski.

jealously, biting and squeaking at would-be predators. Larval development takes place completely within the capsule, and 12 to 18 weeks later the 3.5– to 4-cm (1.5-in) miniature *Aneides* crawl out. These must be separated to prevent cannibalism and to more closely control feeding.

Ensatina (*Ensatina eschscholtzi*)

Note: Currently seven subspecies are recognized, but many workers feel these represent several distinct species.

Distribution: The Pacific coast of North America including California, Oregon, and Washington north to southern British Columbia.

Length: 8.5 to 16 cm (3.5 to 6 in).

Description: Extremely attractive salamanders that show a wide variation in color over the different subspecies, which once were classified as separate species (and may be again). All forms have a waxy brown ground color that may be plain, marked with large blotches or bands of yellow or orange (sometimes green in young), or profusely speckled with pale yellow, orange, or rust spots; there may be orange on the flanks and ventral surface. The bulbous, dark eyes are huge, while the fairly short tail thickens noticeably in the center and has a constriction at the base.

Availability: Occasionally available in the U.S.A., unfortunately not available elsewhere.

Captive Care: The normal moist woodland terrarium applies,

The beautifully marked Large-blotched Ensatina, *Ensatina eschscholtzi klauberi*. Photo: A. Norman.

Above: A Monterey Ensatina, *Ensatina eschscholtzi eschscholtzi*, perhaps the plainest of the Ensatinas. *Below:* A male (at bottom) and female Sierra Nevada Ensatina, *Ensatina eschscholtzi platensis*. Photos: M. Staniszewski.

Yellow-eyed Ensatinas, *Ensatina eschscholtzi xanthopicta*. In the photo below, a large male (top) can be compared with the smaller female. Photos: M. Staniszewski.

A Sierra Nevada Ensatina, *Ensatina eschscholtzi platensis*, from the Giant Sequoia country of California. Photo: M. Staniszewski.

and in cooler conditions this species tends to be very active even during daytime. Temperatures should be around 55 to 60°F (13 to 16°C), except for southern forms that prefer it 5 to 10°F warmer. It is an excellent prospect for the temperate outdoor enclosure. When molested it exhibits an intriguing defensive display of arching its back and waving its tail in the air like a cat. Earthworms, slugs, grubs, and caterpillars constitute its normal diet, but it particularly enjoys waxworms.

Sexual Differences: Males have a longer, less enlarged tail and are more slightly built than females.

Captive Breeding: Hibernation at 40°F (5°C) is necessary. Ensatinas are entirely terrestrial in their breeding habits. Several small clutches of 6 to 12 eggs, each 3.5 mm in diameter, are deposited and abandoned in sodden, live sphagnum moss. As the larvae develop the eggs swell to almost 8 mm, and after 14 weeks the brightly colored 3-cm young emerge. Eggs or young must be removed from the adults's terrarium as they are likely to be devoured.

Red-Backed Salamander (*Plethodon cinereus*)

Distribution: Inhabits cool woodlands throughout eastern U.S.A., the Great Lakes, and much of southern and southeastern Canada.

Length: Rarely grows to more than 12 cm (5 in) and usually around 6 to 10 cm (2.5 to 4 in).

Description: A slender, short-legged, long-tailed little salamander with dark sides and usually a bright red stripe down the middle of the back. The name is slightly misleading in that several phases exist that have either a lead gray or yellowish dorsal stripe instead of red. In all phases the belly is heavily mottled in black and white spots.

Availability: Red-backs are one of the most commonly kept plethodontids in North America but are not widely available elsewhere. Their small size and burrowing habits discourage most collectors from keeping them as pets.

Captive Care: A secretive salamander that seeks dark, damp habitats, especially rotting logs or slabs of upturned turf. Small terraria are suitable, with plenty of plants present plus regular misting to help maintain the necessary humidity. They virtually never surface during the daytime, but the night hours are actively spent pursuing small worms and slugs. Tubifex and bloodworms are relished. They can climb vertical glass walls if the glass is wet, so don't be misled by the small size of their legs.

Sexual Differences: In common with most *Plethodon* species, the males have a large circular mental gland on the chin.

Captive Breeding: The Red-back is a cyclic breeder with courtship commencing in spring after a 10– to 14-week hibernation period. The male may secure a small territory that he patrols and wards off trespassing males.

Red-backed Salamanders, *Plethodon cinereus*, are abundant and attractive salamanders, but the problem is that they are too small to appeal to any but the more advanced hobbyists. Photo: J. Dommers.

Many small *Plethodon* species lives in the eastern United States, and they can be very difficult to identify. This "lead-backed" specimen probably is a Ravine Salamander, *Plethodon richmondi*, but you would have to see the belly to tell for sure. Photo: A. Norman.

Should a female enter this zone, he exhibits some fairly complicated movements including nipping her neck, cloaca, and tail. The usual spermatophore is produced by the male, who guides the female over it to pick up the cap containing sperm. Eight to 16 large eggs are deposited, almost always under a rotten log. The female broods over and moistens them, giving them protection from fungal infection. The larvae develop within the egg case, and after four to ten weeks 30-mm young hatch out that are exact replicas of their parents. These are best raised individually in plastic containers with damp sphagnum moss, where they achieve maturity within 18 to 30 months.

Northern Slimy Salamander (*Plethodon glutinosus*)

Note: This name now is considered to be part of a gigantic complex of very similar species that are restricted to rather small ranges over the eastern and central U.S.A. The group of "slimy salamanders" represents some 13 species that are best identified by geography. The most common, and only one in the northeastern U.S.A. and adjacent Canada, is *P. glutinosus*.

Distribution: Northeastern U.S.A. and adjacent Canada, replaced to the south and west by similar species.

Length: 12 to 20 cm (5 to 8 in).

Description: A large, robust

Slimy Salamanders belong to a complex of virtually identical species formerly all called *Plethodon glutinosus*. Locality data are important to assure a correct identification. Photo of a real New Jersey *P. glutinosus*: R. T. Zappalorti.

black salamander with sparse to heavy white to silvery and brassy speckling and frosting at least on the sides; belly pale. When molested they secrete a sticky slime that is difficult to wash off the hands and may actually seal the mouth of a predator.

Availability: Often collected and sold at low prices. Southern species are just as likely to be available as the true *P. glutinosus*, so check a field guide to identifications if you care about the proper name.

Captive Care: Prefers damper conditions than many other plethodons (but varies considerably with the other related species) and may frequent stream edges in warm conditions. A hider under rocks and debris in woodlands and ravines. Easily bred in the terrarium after a long hibernation. The female lays about 30 to 44 eggs (3.5 mm diameter) under a damp rotten log or similar debris and coils about them while they develop, as in most other land-laying plethodons. Males have a conspicuous round gland under the chin and a more swollen cloaca.

Variability also is the name of the game for the Appalachian Mountains *Plethodon jordani*, Jordan's Salamander. This is the "red-cheeked" form, almost certainly a full species. Photo: M. Panzella.

Jordan's Salamander
(*Plethodon jordani*)

Distribution: Southern Appalachian Mountains, U.S.A.

Length: 9 to 13 cm (3.5 to 5 in).

Description: A small, attractive mountain species that occurs in a bewildering variety of color patterns, from solid black to black with bright red cheeks and legs. Seldom heavily spotted with white, but may be heavily covered with brassy mottling. Typical of the tremendous variety of Appalachian plethodons that seldom are available to hobbyists.

Captive Care: Inhabits mossy screes and leaf litter in humid, high-elevation forests. The terrarium should be damp but without standing water. Needs cool, humid conditions at

Another form of *Plethodon jordani*, this time the "red-legged" type. Jordan's Salamander probably is a complex of six or more species according to recent research. Photo: M. Panzella.

around 52 to 60°F (11 to 16°C). Females lay between 18 and 45 eggs in damp moss and guard them until they hatch in 60 to 75 days.

Western Red-backed Salamander (*Plethodon vehiculum*)

Distribution: Humid coastal forests from Vancouver and British Columbia to southern Oregon.

Length: 8 to 16 cm (3 to 6.5 in).

Description: A very slender salamander much like *Plethodon cinereus*, except the stripe on the back (which is straight-edged) tends to be yellowish to pale orangish.

Availability: Like most western plethodons, its restricted range prevents it entering the hobby on a regular basis.

Captive Care: Prefers relatively dry conditions and does well in a humid, rocky terrarium with a shallow water dish and a temperature between 65 and 75°F (18 and 24°C). Its agile movements allow it to capture small crickets, spiders, and flies.

Red Salamander (*Pseudotriton ruber*)

Note: Four very similar subspecies usually are recognized in the Red Salamander, though recently one, the Blackchin Red Salamander, *P. r. schencki*, has

Western Red-backed Salamanders, *Plethodon vehiculum*, are fairly typical of the small plethodons of northwestern North America. Photo: Dr. D. Green.

been proposed for full species rank.

Distribution: Much of U.S.A. east of Mississippi River except the southeastern coast and Florida peninsula.

Length: 10 to 15 cm (4 to 6 in).

Description: The Red Salamander ranks as one of the most desirable of all amphibians because of its salmon pink to bright red coloration often heavily speckled with dark spots. The eyes are very prominent. The stocky build and rather short tail are vaguely comparable to the mole salamanders and the European genus *Salamandra*.

Availability: Widely available in small numbers across the U.S. both as wild-caught adults and captive-bred young. Elsewhere occasionally available from sporadic imports of wild-collected adults.

Captive Care: The Red Salamander and its relative the Mud Salamander (*P. montanus*) demand high humidity that, if not provided, will cause loss of appetite and stress. Therefore, the terrarium must either be briefly sprayed four to six times per day or a miniature fountain/waterfall must be integrated into the setup. If correctly cared for, *Pseudotriton*

Red Salamanders, *Pseudotriton ruber*, may be the most brightly colored salamanders. Many young adults are truly bright coral red. Photo: R. T. Zappalorti.

The spring salamanders, *Gyrinophilus*, include several neotenic species and subspecies adapted to subterranean rivers and caves in the Appalachian Mountains. This is the Tennessee Cave Salamander, *G. palleucus*. Photo: R. S. Simmons.

species adapt well to captivity, where they live happily in a large aqua-terrarium with plenty of mossy growth, leafy plants, and damp bark and rocks beneath which they will hide. A third of the terrarium must consist of well oxygenated, filtered water 8 to 15 cm (3 to 6 in) deep. Maximum temperatures for the northern and southern subspecies of *P. ruber* should be 64 and 70°F (18 and 21°C) respectively. The Mud Salamanders (except *P. montanus floridanus*) are very hardy but do not tolerate warm conditions, 58 to 64°F (15 to 18°C) being ideal.

Sexual Differences: Males have a swollen cloaca and less rotund build than females.

Captive Breeding: Unlike most other lungless salamanders, Red Salamanders breed in water, hence the scientific name *Pseudotriton*, meaning "false eft." After a hibernation period of 8 to 12 weeks at 37 to 39°F (3 to 4 °C), they enter cool waters (slow-

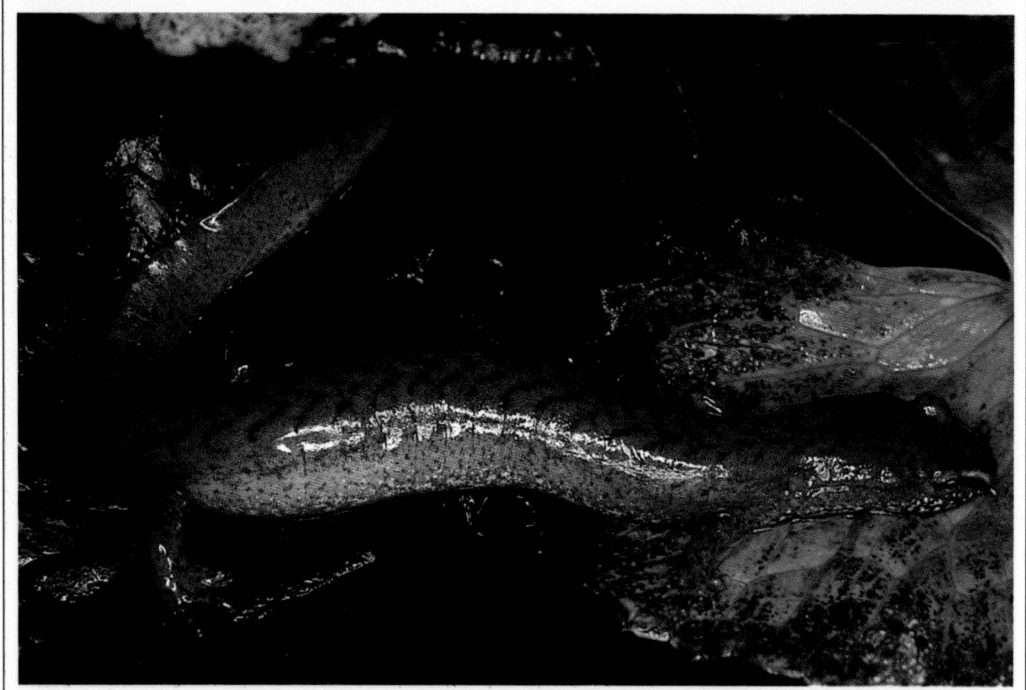

Many eastern American lungless salamanders are notable for extreme variation within a single species. Recent research into the molecular biology of many of these "subspecies" and variations have shown they really are full species. It has been suggested that the Blue Ridge Spring Salamander, *Gyrinophilus porphyriticus danielsi* (above), is distinct enough from typical Spring Salamanders (below) to be considered a full species. Photos: Top, M. Staniszewski; bottom: K. T. Nemuras.

moving shallow streams in the wild) for two to six weeks, although captive-bred individuals may breed in clean, still water. Adults feed heavily on aquatic crustaceans such as isopods when in this aquatic state. Large numbers of eggs (over 100 in *P. ruber*) are deposited singly or in small clumps. These must be maintained in well oxygenated water. After three to six weeks the larvae emerge. As they grow they are best separated into groups of 10 to 15 to avoid fighting. These are among the slowest developing larvae of all caudates and may not metamorphose until the second summer as 40-mm youngsters or even the third summer at 60 to 85 mm (1.5 to 3.5 in). They mature within 18 to 30 months if given a proper diet.

Longevity: A Red Salamander has been kept for over 17 years in captivity.

The small legs and long bodies of the slender salamanders, such as this *Batrachoseps attenuatus*, the California Slender, give them a particularly worm-like appearance. Photo: K. H. Switak.

California Slender Salamander (*Batrachoseps attenuatus*)

Note: A southern California subspecies, *B. a. nigriventris*, sometimes is recognized as a full species, the Blackbelly Slender Salamander.

Distribution: Humid woodlands and forests along the Pacific coast of California and into southwestern Oregon, east to the Sierra Nevada.

Length: 7.5 to 13 cm (3 to 5 in).

Description: An elongate body and tail with tiny limbs and head make this one of the smallest salamanders in the world. The basic color is dark brown or black, speckled (depending on locality) with orange, brown, or red spots; specimens from the Sierra Nevada may have a broad red band. The head has a blunt, flat snout and relatively large, soulful eyes. Premaxillay teeth are very evident projecting through the upper lip and can be felt by brushing a finger gently along the snout. All the members of this genus have only four toes on the hind feet (five in *Plethodon* and most other plethodontids).

Availability: This is perhaps the most common amphibian native to California, being found anywhere damp, even suburban gardens. Small numbers find their way into captivity, as do some of the other species of the genus. An excellent captive that is both fascinating and easily bred.

Captive Care: Due to its small size, it is content with a relatively small terrarium. However, after maintaining this species for several years I have found that males are territorial and will patrol a small area for food and potential mates. Therefore, where more than one male is maintained, a 3-foot terrarium is advised. There should be plenty of leaves and chopped bark (the forest bark used as mulch is ideal)

Notice the tiny feet on this California Slender Salamander, *Batrachoseps attenuatus*. In this genus there are only four toes on the hind feet and the toes of the front feet may appear to be partially fused. Photo: M. Staniszewski.

Though they are small, males of the California Slender Salamander, *Batrachoseps attenuatus*, are territorial and must be provided with a large terrarium if you plan to keep more than one male per tank. Photo: M. Staniszewski.

along with a water bowl that contains a pad of cotton or a dish towel (to prevent drowning accidents). A few hollowed sections of tree branches should be present. The whole terrarium should be sprayed at least twice a day. Ventilation should be good to reduce growth of algae, fungi, and bacteria. Temperatures should be in the 50 to 70°F (10 to 21°C) range. Food can consist of small crickets, worms of various sorts, sweepings, wingless fruitflies, and small waxworms.

A note of caution: Do not grasp the tail. This will be shed at the slightest touch and, although a new one eventually regrows, it is never the same size or color. When molested, slender salamanders will display the bizarre behavior of curling up and catapulting into the air like a watch spring.

Sexual Differences: Males are smaller than females and have a blunter snout with more prominent premaxillary teeth than in females.

Captive Breeding: Success is gained by increasing temperatures to 70 to 74°F (21 to 24°C) during July and August, at the same time reducing terrarium misting to once a day (so that complete desiccation does not occur). In September the temperature should be allowed to drop to around 55 to 65°F (13 to 18°C) and misting can be increased.

Mating and egg production are entirely land-based, with 4 to 25 small (2 mm) sand-colored eggs being deposited in cool, moist hollows during October to December. Both sexes may attend the eggs intermittently to moisten them. Larval development occurs entirely within the egg case. Prior to hatching in spring, the eggs measure 6 mm in diameter, swelling from absorbed moisture and growth of the embryo. The 15-mm juveniles that emerge look like strips of pencil lead and are extremely delicate. Raise them in individual margarine tubs filled with damp sphagnum moss and feed them whiteworms, bloodworms, and hatchling crickets of appropriate size. Sexual maturity occurs in about two years.

Longevity: Ten years maximum.

Other Species: The Channel Islands Slender Salamander (*B. pacificus*) is confined to islands off the southern California coast, where it is extremely common. It has distinctive brick-red dashes along its flanks. The pale, sometimes white, Garden Slender (*B. major*) has the most southern range and is the largest *Batrachoseps*, attaining 16 cm (over 6 in). The Relictual

A slender salamander tentatively assigned to *Batrachoseps relictus*, the Relictual Slender Salamander. The species of this genus are difficult to distinguish by color pattern and structure and can be expected to change in the next few years as more research on their biochemistry is published. Photo: M. Staniszewski.

Slender Salamander (*B. relictus*) occurs with the Channel Island species on Santa Cruz Island and is very common in Del Monte Forest in Monterey. I even found one near the eighteenth green on the Pebble Beach golf course! This is the species from which the others are thought to have evolved, yet it was not described until 1975. The Oregon Slender (*B. wrighti*) is found in a small area of northern Oregon and is not common anywhere; there are reports of other populations in Washington and British Columbia. All the preceding species occasionally are available in captivity and can be cared for like the California Slender.

The 9-cm (3.5-in) bizarre maroon Desert Slender Salamander (*Batrachoseps aridus*) from Riverside County, California; the bronze and black mottled 12-cm (5-in) Kern Canyon Slender (*B. simatus*); and the 12-cm (5-in) Tehachapi Slender (*B. stebbinsi*) from the mountains of Kern and Tulare Counties, California, and with distinctly webbed feed adapted to rock-climbing habits, all were discovered in the 1960's and are strictly protected by federal and state laws due to their limited ranges in often very isolated spring and scree areas.

Andean Salamander
(*Bolitoglossa altamazonica*)

Distribution: Colombia to Bolivia in the eastern foothills of the Andes. Isolated populations exist in the upper Amazon valley, western Brazil.

Length: Males to 9 cm (3.5 in), females to 16 cm (6.5 in).

Description: A wonderfully patterned species with gold or copper striations on a black or chocolate-brown back. In shape these salamanders, like most tropical American species, look like *Batrachoseps* but are larger and far more stockily built. The tail is long and prehensile and, as in most *Bolitoglossa*, the feet are heavily webbed to act as suckers for climbing.

Captive Care: The Andean Salamander prefers a tall, planted terrarium bordering on the temperatures and humidity of a subtropical rainforest. High humidity is the key to successful South American plethodontid husbandry. However, temperatures should not be allowed to get too high, and a range of 68 to 75°F (20 to 24°C) is favored. Misting should be frequent. There should be plenty of leaf litter, in which these agile salamanders often explore for food. Most of its time is spent climbing and resting in cool, moist tree hollows. Mainly nocturnal, it preys on most small insects, treefrog tadpoles (those developing in bromeliads), and (in captivity) waxworms. It uses its long, mushroom-like tongue to snare moths and other flying insects.

Sexual Differences: Males are smaller and have obvious premaxillary teeth and a swollen cloaca.

Captive Breeding: Breeding

Andean Salamanders, *Bolitoglossa altamazonica*, seldom are available to hobbyists. They must be kept fairly cool to do well. Photo: R. T. Zappalorti.

can occur several times throughout the year. There is no single stimulus, and mating can be triggered by a number of factors such as increased rainfall, increased food supply, and even tiny downward shifts in temperature. After mating, females almost always look for a suitable depression in the basal substrate where 8 to 15 large (4.5 mm) whitish, gelatinous eggs are laid. She constantly attends them, leaving only to search for food. Larval development takes place within the egg, and two months later jet black juveniles 25 mm (1 in) long hatch out. The distinctive pattern develops in the second year.

Other Species: Hobbyists occasionally can obtain specimens of *Bolitoglossa* and *Pseudoeurycea*, just two of about a dozen plethodontid genera restricted to tropical America. *Bolitoglossa* species are found mainly from southern Mexico to central South America, while *Pseudoeurycea* species are typical of the central and southern Mexican highlands. Exportation restrictions and rather limited distributions for the species (as well as difficulty of access of many of their habitats) mean that only a small number filter through to the hobby in the U.S.A. and an even smaller number reaches European markets.The species most likely to be seen include the Venezuelan Salamander, *Bolitoglossa adspersa*, a small copper-colored tree-climber that prefers cool temperatures (65 – 70°F, 18 to 21°C), and the Palm Salamander, *Bolitoglossa subpalmatus*, a 9-cm (3.5-in) ground-dweller from the high mountains of Costa Rica that is attractively mottled in black and white flecks. It makes sense to keep adult Neotropical salamanders segregated from juveniles as they will inevitably be eaten if not separated.

Climbing Salamander (*Bolitoglossa mexicana*)

Distribution: Veracruz, Mexico, south into northern Honduras. Occurs in cool, moist mountain forests.

Length: 12 to 22 cm (5 to 9 in).

Description: Attractively marked in black and pale yellow stripes and blotches. The feet have heavy webs and the tail is semiprehensile.

Availability: One of the few Neotropical salamanders regularly offered by dealers.

Captive Care: A specialist tree-climber. Extremely agile and capable of jumping, it requires a tall planted terrarium. Keep it cool and humid. Between 14 and 22 eggs are attached to the undersides of damp bark or leaves at any time of the year. Like many other Neotropical plethodontids, a cooling-down period is necessary.

Notice the strongly webbed toes of this *Bolitoglossa dofleini*, one of the more heavily built tropical salamanders. Such feet aid climbing, and most of the species are distinctly arboreal. Photo: K. T. Nemuras.

Though many tropical salamanders are dully colored, some are quite attractive. ***Above: Bolitoglossa subpalmata.*** Photo: P. Freed. ***Below: Bolitoglossa platydactyla.*** Photo: R. S. Simmons.

Bolitoglossa striatula has an interesting pattern of delicate dark brown lines and points on a rich tan background. Photo: R. S. Simmons.

Tlaconete Salamander (*Pseudoeurycea belli*)

Distribution: Mountains of central and southern Mexico, inhabiting damp pine forests and damp open grasslands.

Length: 19 to 28 cm (7.5 to 11.5 in).

Description: A striking black salamander of robust build with many red or bright orange bars or paired spots across the back.

Captive Care: Mainly nocturnal, the Tlaconete demands a cool (65°F, 18°C) terrarium with high humidity and plenty of hiding places. In nature it spends much of its time beneath fallen trees in search of centipedes, earthworms, slugs, and juveniles of its own and other salamander species. Females are considerably larger than males. Breeding occurs several times each year. The 25 to 50 eggs (3.5 mm diameter) are laid in damp depressions or rotting wood.

FAMILY CRYPTOBRANCHIDAE: THE GIANT SALAMANDERS

Hellbender (*Cryptobranchus alleganiensis*)

Distribution: Appalachian and Ozark Mountain regions of U.S.A.

Length: Usually 30 to 50 cm (12 to 20 in). The largest American amphibian, males can attain 68 cm (27 in), females 74 cm (29 in).

Description: These powerful and grotesque-looking, fully

Pseudoeurycea is a fairly large tropical salamander genus with species that vary greatly in color patterns and body shapes. Almost the only species likely to be seen by hobbyists, however, are the Tlaconete Salamander, *Pseudoeurycea belli*, and its close relatives. Top: *Pseudoeurycea gigantea*. Photo: R. D. Bartlett. Bottom: *Pseudoeurycea belli*. Photo: R. S. Simmons.

aquatic flattened salamanders have an enormous head with small eyes. The loose, wrinkled gray to olive-brown skin forms frills down the torso, legs, and tail. Typically there are small black spots or blotches over the body.

A fairly typical Hellbender, *Cryptobranchus alleganiensis*. The spotted pattern varies greatly in intensity. Photo: R. T. Zappalorti.

Availability: Unlike its relatives from the Orient (*Andrias*), Hellbenders are still fairly common over much of their range and are offered on a frequent basis, usually as a result of specimens being accidentally caught by anglers. Captive breeding also provides a small but steady supply.

Captive Care: Hellbenders adapt very well to captivity, but it is important to provide a suitably large aquarium. A 48-inch tank filled with 18 to 24 inches of water will house one pair, but there must be sufficient caves constructed from rocks to reduce interaction between specimens or fighting and injury may result. The base should consist of 4 to 6 inches of gravel or washed river sand. Full filtration and oxygenation are essential. Water temperatures of 55 to 60°F (13 to 16°C) are suitable. Foods include worms, fish (especially small eels), and crayfish, in addition to pieces of lean raw meat. Once caught the food is violently thrashed about and care must be taken to avoid two Hellbenders latching onto the same item.

Sexual Differences: Males are smaller than females.

Captive Breeding: Breeding is possible only in a large aquarium and if temperatures are reduced to 45°F (8°C) for eight weeks. Upon warming to normal temperatures, the male constructs a nest by excavating gravel from beneath a suitably large rock. He attracts the female by nudging her toward the nest. Once she has laid her long strings of up to 600 eggs near the nest opening, she plays no further part. The male disperses sperm to fertilize the eggs, pushes them into the nest, and guards the entrance aggressively. It is wise to remove the female to a separate aquarium during egg incubation. Larvae emerge in 8 to 12 weeks, have external gills, and are 25 to 30 mm long. Although the male still protects them, he also may devour a large proportion of the clutch, so remove a large number to another aquarium. Larvae reach the adult stage in 18 to 24 months, when their filamentous gills are absorbed and they have reached 9 to 12 cm (3.5 to 5 in) in length. They can be kept in groups of 10 to 15 until they reach 30 cm (12 in) or so.

Longevity: Reaches more than 24 years in captivity.

The greatly flattened form, small eye, and many skin folds make the Hellbender, *Cryptobranchus alleganiensis*, a truly unique salamander. Photo: R. T. Zappalorti.

FAMILY HYNOBIIDAE: THE PRIMITIVE SALAMANDERS

Siberian Salamander (*Hynobius keyserlingi*)

Distribution: The largest range of any amphibian, occurring throughout Siberia west of the Urals, northern Mongolia, and northeastern China.

Length: 8.5 to 12 cm (3.5 to 5 in).

Description: A chunky, smooth-skinned species that has black flanks and a pair of bronze stripes cut by a vertebral groove. The eyes are very prominent and set forward to give a short, rounded face. The tail is shorter than the body and laterally flattened. The 11 to 16 costal

The Japanese Giant Salamander, *Andrias japonica*, is a bit less flattened than the Hellbender and has a much rougher skin. Photos: W. P. Mara.

In the Ozarks of Missouri and Arkansas the Hellbender, *Cryptobranchus alleganiensis*, tends to be darkly blotched rather than more finely spotted and is considered to be a distinct species or subspecies, *C. a. bishopi*. Photo: K. T. Nemuras.

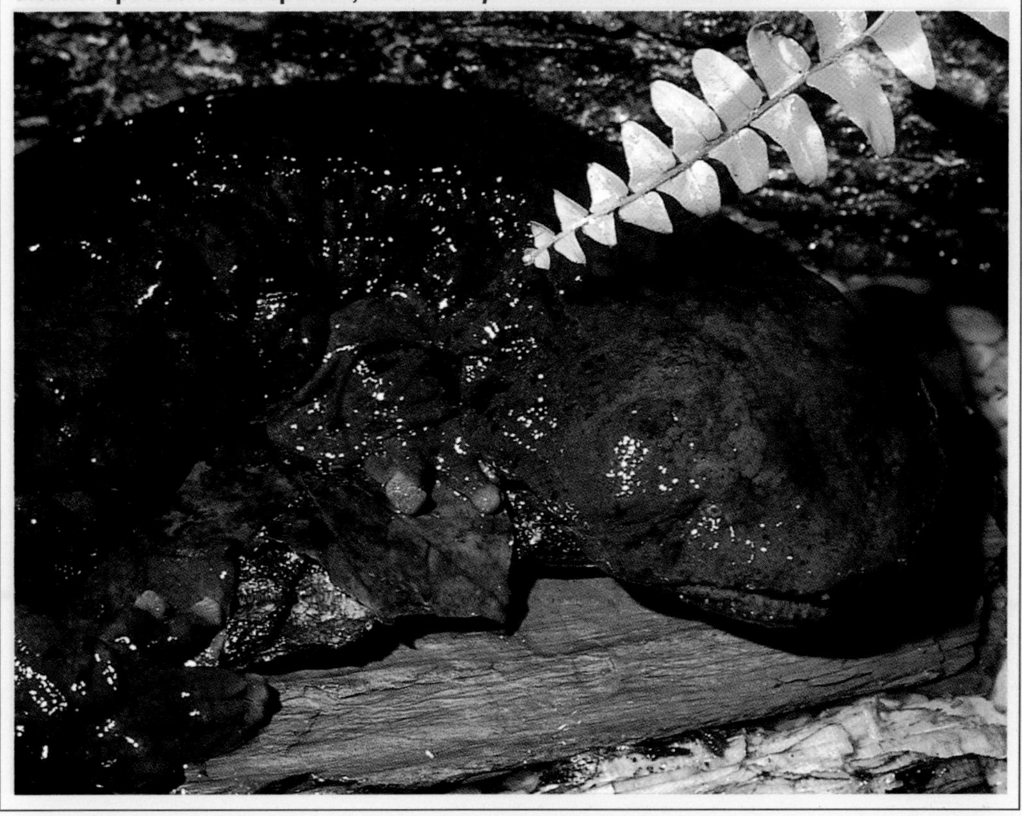

Hynobiids are uncommon in the terrarium hobby and few are attractive. Their behavior is poorly known, but certainly their reproductive habits, including laying a large egg sac, make them of interest to hobbyists. Top: *Hynobius nebulosus*; bottom: *Hynobius* species. Photos: Dr. D. Green.

Onychodactylus fischeri **from Russia and Siberia is one of the few hynobiids that has a somewhat colorful pattern. All hynobiids appear to need cold water and cannot tolerate heat. Photo: S. Kochetov.**

grooves are very evident even in young specimens.

Availability: Hynobiids are seasonally available in Europe but rarely are offered elsewhere.

Captive Care: Hynobiids are best kept in the outdoor terrarium, where they should have access to deep underground burrows and a pond of 30 to 40 inches. If they are maintained indoors, the terrarium must be located in a cool room with a north-facing window. Temperatures above 75°F (24°C) are not tolerated, and utilizing an old freezer may be necessary in warmer regions. Other hynobiids such as *Onychodactylus* and *Ranodon* are far more tolerant and will live happily at room temperature. A 36-inch terrarium decorated with plenty of moist moss, damp logs, and a fairly deep water pan will house several specimens. Food consists of all the normal invertebrates; worms in particular are relished.

Sexual Differences: Males have longer limbs than females, and ridges form on either side of the tail during the breeding season.

Captive Breeding: An extended hibernation period of 12 to 18 weeks at near-freezing temperatures during December to February is essential in encouraging breeding. In regions that are not subjected to harsh winters, this may be possible only by utilizing a freezer set to a temperature of 33°F (1°C); make sure the freezer is not air-tight by removing a section of the door seal. Specimens have been found alive in solid blocks of ice in the wild. Other hynobiids are less hardy, with 38°F (4°C) being the preferable low. On "warming" to around 36°F (2°C), adult Siberian Salamanders become active and often are seen bathing in water at night. They should be transferred to a large aquarium containing deep and slightly acidic (pH 5.7) water at 38°F (4°C). The female lays a large spindle-shaped gelatinous egg sac attached to submerged pond plants, floating debris, or a rock; this contains up to 60 eggs. To fertilize them the male releases his sperm over the sac, which may even be grasped in his jaws and swirled around. On hatching three to eight weeks later, the larvae remain in the protective sac for the first few days until it disintegrates. Once free, the 13– to 16–mm larvae are excellent swimmers, but because the mouth consists of a horny beak-like structure they can only feed by scraping algae, bacteria, and microscopic infusoria from rocks. They grow quite slowly, but in climates warmer than their native homeland they always metamorphose by late summer to early autumn when they are 25 to 38 mm in length. Young Siberian Salamanders are initially very dark and fairly slender.

FAMILY SIRENIDAE: THE SIRENS

Lesser Siren (*Siren intermedia*)

Distribution: Southern U.S.A. from Rio Grande River and Mississippi valley to Virginia.

Length: 20 to 65 cm (8 to 26 in).

Description: These entirely aquatic, elongated, blue-black or slate-gray creatures are eel-like in appearance but distinguished by the pair of feathery red gills located behind the head. The head itself contains degenerate eyes and the mouth has horny linings instead of teeth. Costal grooves number 30 to 35 (36 to 40 in the virtually identical Greater Siren). Only the front limbs are present, each possessing four toes. The tail is short but has well-developed fins.

Availability: Sirens are available throughout the year, with spring and early summer being the most likely times to encounter these amphibians.

A young Lesser Siren, *Siren intermedia*. The strongly marked mucous pores are typical of small specimens of this species. Photo: R. D. Bartlett.

Generally speaking, the Lesser Siren, *Siren intermedia* (top) is a more slender, colorful animal than the darker, coarser Greater Siren, *Siren lacertina* (bottom). In life the two species often are very difficult to distinguish. Photos: R. D. Bartlett.

Captive Care: Temperatures from 38 to 80°F (4 to 27°C) are tolerated, with the middle 60's F (about 18°C) being preferred. Sirens require a large aquarium containing 8 to 20 inches of fresh, oxygenated water over a coarse river sand or fine gravel base. Several rocks should be present along with a number of stronger cold-water plants that are firmly secured beneath rocks. A low wattage fluorescent tube will enhance the whole setup immensely. Although this mainly nocturnal creature is naturally shy and edgy, it will become bolder and venture out in daylight more frequently with time. Food must be provided regularly to reduce fighting among the occupants. This should consist of earthworms, fish, shrimp and other freshwater crustaceans, and raw meat. Prey is ambushed from the entrance of the hiding place and when seized is violently thrashed about. Sirens are able to utter clicking noises when molested, angered, or excited.

Sexual Differences: Sexing is very difficult outside the breeding period, when the male's cloacal region is noticeably swollen.

Captive Breeding: Breeding often is achieved in captivity and commences after the water has evaporated to leave a shallow pool that is then replenished to the normal level to simulate flooding. Fertilization is external, with the female constructing a bowl-shaped nest from mud, gravel, and detritus into which she deposits 100 or more eggs. The male then releases his sperm in jets and may swim around the nest in rapid circular movements to ensure good fertility. The eggs develop slowly, and the 5-mm larvae initially remain around the nest for up to two weeks. During the larval stage the juvenile is light bluish gray with red bands running laterally down the body,

Dwarf Sirens, *Pseudobranchus striatus*, make satisfactory aquarium inhabitants. All the subspecies (recently the single species has been split into two) are similar in size and shape and look like large dark worms at first glance. Photo: R. D. Bartlett.

Close-up of the anterior body of *Pseudobranchus striatus*. This species usually has a distinctly striped pattern. Photo: R. D. Bartlett.

but as it matures the body becomes darker. They prey on daphnia, tubifex, and bloodworms.

Longevity: Very long-lived amphibians often attaining 25 years of age.

FAMILY SALAMANDRIDAE: THE NEWTS

This large family comprises many distinct genera that are popular with amphibian hobbyists all over the world. Many species are easily bred within the terrarium, but other species have proven difficult, sometimes impossible, even to maintain successfully and continue to tax even the most experienced herpetoculturists.

Japanese Fire-bellied Newt (*Cynops pyrrhogaster*)

Distribution: Throughout the mountainous regions of Japan.

Length: 8 to 12 cm (3 to 5 in).

Description: The back is a fairly drab dark brown, sometimes with a green tinge, and the skin tends to be heavily granulated with prominent cream tubercles on the sides. A poorly developed crest is present throughout the year. It is the ventral coloration that gives this species appeal; as the common name suggests, it is a vivid scarlet or orange-red, often interrupted here and there by dark blotches.

Availability: Readily available throughout the world, now in the form of captive-bred stock as

***Cynops pyrrhogaster*, the Japanese Fire-bellied Newt, is not always easy to find on the American market, but it does show up on occasion. The belly pattern and color are very variable. Photo: B. Kahl.**

opposed to the mainly wild-caught specimens available until the early 1980's. Tropical fish stores are the most likely source of supply.

Captive Care: All *Cynops* species are extremely hardy and easy to maintain in the aqua-terrarium. Although most of their time is spent swimming, a damp shelf extending above the water level and consisting of rocks and mosses should be provided, especially where juveniles are concerned. The setup should contain 12 to 20 inches of cool, oxygenated water (maximum 65°F, 18°C) abundantly planted with water weed. During winter the water temperature should be

In good condition, the Japanese Fire-bellied Newt, *Cynops pyrrhogaster*, is a study in brilliant black and scarlet. Photo: M. Staniszewski.

lowered to around 40°F (5°C) for 10 to 16 weeks, during which time the newts are sluggish and feed sparingly. During warmer conditions these newts feed voraciously on anything from daphnia, bloodworms, and amphipods to chopped earthworms and strips of raw lean red meat.

Sexual Differences: Males generally are smaller than females, and prior to courtship they develop a purple iridescence along the flanks and tail.

Captive Breeding: *Cynops* species breed erratically in captivity, breeding clearly depending on the individual's willingness to mate. Should a compliant pair be present, breeding will take place regularly if the hibernation rule is followed. Other individuals may steadfastly refuse to breed, and in such cases it is worth experimenting with water temperatures, moving water to simulate a stream, and increasing/decreasing water plant concentration or even trying different water plant species. Eggs, which are laid in spring, number 170 to 300 and are 2.5 mm in diameter with a light brown nucleus. The female attaches them to water plant foliage but rarely bends a leaf around them like more typical newts. At a temperature of 60°F (16°C) the 3–mm larvae hatch in 14 to 18 days and require a further 14 to 20 weeks to metamorphose into 35– to 40-mm newtlets. Initially they are best kept in aquaria containing cool water at a depth of 2 to 3 in and fed frequently on tubifex and bloodworms.

Longevity: Twenty years, often longer.

Golden Fire-bellied Newt (*Cynops ensicauda*)

Distribution: Japan (Ryukyus) in cool, slow-flowing mountain streams and still pools.

Length: 12 to 14 cm (5 to 5.5 in).

Facing page: **The Golden Fire-bellied Newt, *Cynops ensicauda*, is even more colorful than the Japanese. This specimen belongs to the subspecies *popei*. Photo: K. T. Nemuras.**

Hobbyists should be on the look out for *Cynops ensicauda* and other unusual newts that may be imported from the Orient on a more regular basis today. Photo: K. T. Nemuras.

Description: A larger and more attractive species than *Cynops pyrrhogaster*. The rough-skinned back is lightly sprinkled with yellow or gold speckles, giving this species its familiar name "Gold-dust Newt." A slightly smaller subspecies, *C. e. popei*, sometimes is available. Care is as for *Cynops pyrrhogaster*.

Chinese Fire-bellied Newt (*Cynops orientalis*)

Distribution: Eastern China in still, well-vegetated pools.

Length: 10 to 12 cm (4 to 5 in).

Captive Care: This is a very aquatic species spending almost its entire life in the water; it sometimes may be neotenic. It is more of a lowland species than the others mentioned and is able to tolerate a wider temperature range (38 to 78°F, 4 to 26°C) than other *Cynops*. It demands a well-oxygenated, densely planted aquarium setup.

Spot-tailed Newt (*Pachytriton brevipes*)

Distribution: Southeastern China in mountain streams.

Length: 12 to 16 cm (5 to 6 in).

Captive Care: This black, smooth-skinned species spends its entire life in running water and therefore such conditions must be integrated into the terrarium. It requires a temperature below 65°F (18°C) during most of the year, with a drop to 38°F (4°C) for several months to induce breeding. A closely related species, *P. labiatus*, sometimes is offered by dealers.

Spot-tailed Newts, *Pachytriton brevipes*, are not common in the terrarium hobby as yet. They have a distinctive "chubby" shape and smooth skin that, in combination with the broad tail, make them easy to identify. Photos: K. T. Nemuras.

Sardinian Brook Salamander (*Euproctus platycephalus*)

Distribution: Cool mountain streams of the Italian island of Sardinia.

Length: 9 to 14 cm (3.5 to 5.5 in).

Description: A slender salamander with a flat head, depressed snout, and prominent eyes. The dorsal color of plain olive or brown occasionally is spotted with light green, and sometimes a brick-red vertebral stripe is present. The skin itself is granular, and vestigial parotoid glands are barely evident. The underside and throat are creamy yellow and heavily spotted, especially in males.

Availability: The various *Euproctus* species rarely are offered, mainly because they are strictly protected in their countries of origin. Most specimens come from specialist breeders in Europe and the U.S.A.

Captive Care: Of the three described *Euproctus* species, the Sardinian Brook Salamander presents the fewest difficulties in captivity. In the wild it occurs at altitudes from 120 m to around 6000 m, with lowland individuals in particular adapting successfully in a cool terrarium. Most of its time is spent in and around cold, shallow (typically around 2 in), slow-moving waters, and creating a stream to provide clean, fresh water is crucial to the survival and breeding of this species. The terrarium needs to be fairly extensive to contain such a layout and should not be positioned anywhere that gets direct sunlight. A maximum temperature of 70°F (21°C) is endured, with 52 to 60°F (11 to 16°C) being more desirable, down to a low of around 42°F (6°C) for several months during winter. Obviously the most favorable way to maintain *Euproctus platycephalus* is the temperate outdoor amphibiary (not greenhouse), where very deep refuges will remain cool and damp even in hot summers. Food is the normal soft-bodied invertebrates.

Sexual Differences: Males have conspicuous rounded spurs on the hind limbs and the cloaca is conical in shape (rounded in females).

Captive Breeding: Breeding will occur under optimum conditions, including suitable temperatures and water and air quality. Adults enter water in the spring, although if they have estivated during a hot summer a secondary breeding may occur thereafter. The fascinating courtship behavior involves the male grasping the female's neck with his jaws and coiling his tail tightly around her lower abdomen such that his body is beneath hers. Sperm are transferred directly into her cloacal opening, making *Euproctus* one of the few caudates to exhibit true amplexus (lasting up to 30 hours) and internal copulation. After a further 5 to 18 days the female deposits 50 to 75 large eggs (5 mm diameter) in shallow water where the current is not too swift, such as a recess in the bend of a stream. Dissolved oxygen levels in the water must be high. These

A Corsican Brook Salamander, *Euproctus montanus.* These newts need cool, running water in which to thrive and seldom do well in the terrarium. Photo: G. Baumgart courtesy Dr. D. Terver, Nancy, France.

hatch in 20 to 35 days at 52°F (11°C). After a further 12 to 18 weeks the highly active, voracious larvae emerge, transforming into docile, shy little salamanders that are treated like the adults.

Other Species: The 17-cm (7-in) Pyrenean Brook Salamander (*Euproctus asper*) and the 7– to 9-cm (3 to 3.5 in) Corsican Brook Salamander (*E. montanus*) occur in high montane habitats of the regions suggested in the common names. Both are difficult to keep in captivity because temperatures cannot be allowed to go above 65°F (18°C), the water and air must be very fresh, and the humidity must be very high at all stages.

Yellow-spotted Newt (*Neurergus crocatus*)

Distribution: High Middle East plateau, Iran and Iraq into Turkey and then into Israel.

Length: 10 to 14 cm (4 to 5.5 in).

Description: A striking species that, on first impression, appears similar to a small Fire Salamander. However, on closer inspection the skin is seen to be more like that of aquatic newts, being highly granular. The back is jet black and covered with many yellow spots, while the mouth has peculiar pink lips. The belly is gray-cream in color. Invariably a streamlined newt, when mature

Will the Yellow-spotted Newt, *Neurergus crocatus*, be the next newt to take the hobby by storm? Certainly its bright colors and ease of keeping are advantages in its favor. Photo: M. Staniszewski.

The several species and subspecies of *Neurergus* are all from the Middle Eastern area and have been virtually unavailable until lately. Currently *N. crocatus* seems to be the only species in the hobby. Photo: M. Staniszewski.

the male possesses a low black and yellow barred crest. If attacked, the body is flattened to accentuate the pointed ribs, which, as in *Pleurodeles*, can penetrate the flanks. Strangely, males exhibit less webbing and filamentation than any other semiaquatic to aquatic newts, possibly due to the fact that the stunning color is present throughout the newt's lifetime.

Availability: This species has become available only recently, after a population was discovered in Lake Vai in southeastern Turkey and other pockets were found in Israel. Specimens are just becoming available after several successful breeding projects in Germany.

Captive Care: Being a mountain-dweller, this species prefers cooler temperatures. It is highly aquatic, inhabiting both shallow rock pools and deep ponds that usually are fed by cold meltwater or seasonal springs for all but a month or so of the year. An aqua-terrarium with about 4 inches (minimum) of cool, fresh water with some vegetation (but not excessive) and an easily accessible land area should be provided. Lighting should be low-wattage fluorescent. Yellow-spotted Newts tend to be active throughout the year except for a short period in mid-summer when temperatures force them to estivate deep underground unless a deep, cool water hole is provided. It will feed on chopped earthworms, pieces of raw meat, waxworms, various small crustaceans, and aquatic worms such as tubifex and bloodworms. Frequently it remains suspended near the surface of the water, anticipating stray insects that fall within its reach. It also will climb onto land in pursuit of crickets and spiders, which it stalks and traps with the long sticky tongue. Specimens that remain primarily aquatic grow at a rate three times faster than those kept on land. Sexual maturity can be attained within 18 months in specimens kept in water.

Sexual Differences: Males are smaller than females and develop a low crest during the breeding season. They also have a swollen cloaca and tend to have wider "pinkish" lips.

Captive Breeding: In nature, the breeding stimulus is the presence of icy meltwater trickling into the breeding ponds after an estivation period. An attempt to simulate such conditions in the terrarium should lead to success. A complex courtship ritual occurs, with males and females dancing, nudging each other on the flanks continually, and even nipping each other. Approximately 70 to 100 small light brown eggs are scattered randomly among the rocks and pebbles and between the leaves of the vegetation. Larval development lasts for two or sometimes three months, during which the dark brown to blackish larvae consume large quantities of microorganisms, daphnia, and tubifex. When the 3-cm newtlets

A not-so-red eft or land stage of the Eastern Newt, *Notophthalmus viridescens*. These bright little salamanders vary greatly in color with age and diet. Photo: M. Staniszewski.

climb onto land they are miniature replicas of their parents. Within a month they should be allowed to return to water to resume a largely aquatic existence. Longevity is not known at this time.

Eastern Newt (*Notophthalmus viridescens*)

Distribution: Southeastern Canada throughout central, southern, and eastern U.S.A.

Length: 6 to 12 cm (2.5 to 5 in).

Description: Much variation is evident throughout the range of this species, and four subspecies are recognized. The back of typical Eastern Newt adults is olive green or orange-brown, peppered with many small dark spots that also spread down onto the yellow belly. A row of four to six or more large red spots ringed in black occurs on each flank, which gives these newts their more familiar name, Red-spotted Newt. This coloration applies to the typical northeastern subspecies. Of the other subspecies, the Florida Peninsula Newt (*N. v. piaropicola*) is the darkest above and usually lacks spots, the Broken-striped Newt (*N. v. dorsalis*) tends to have elongated red stripes rather than spots, and the Central Newt (*N. v. louisianensis*) may lack red spots and their black outlines. *Notophthalmus* has an unusual developmental stage known as the "red eft." When the young metamorphose and leave the water, they live an entirely terrestrial existence for often two to four years before returning to water permanently to live and reproduce. Efts have very granular, dry skin, a protection against the often rather dry environment in which they live. The eft has stunningly brilliant orange coloration and iridescent red spots, at least in the northeastern U.S.A. Efts of the other subspecies may be uncommon or locally absent and

A female Eastern (Red-spotted) Newt, *Notophthalmus viridescens viridescens*, with a somewhat reduced spotted pattern. Photo: M. Staniszewski.

This eft shows the pair of bony ridges on top of the head that help separate the genus *Notophthalmus* from several other newt genera. Photo: M. Staniszewski.

often lack the red spots. Efts may return to the ponds in which they were hatched in tremendous numbers at the same time.

Availability: Commonly available in pet shops. Most of the subspecies are available as wild-caught specimens that are not distinguished by the pet trade.

Captive Care: If handled roughly these newts will secrete a toxin that can cause irritation of the skin, inflammation in cuts, and great pain if it gets into the eyes, nose, or mouth. Handle these newts gently with wet hands or use thin plastic gloves. Never let a child put a newt in the mouth. The terrarium setup depends on the newt's stage of life. Efts require a medium-sized terrarium provided with plenty of damp hiding places, while adults are mainly aquatic but occasionally come ashore to feed so need an aqua-terrarium. Water should always be clean, filtered, and aerated, with a dense growth of oxygenating plants. Preferred temperatures are around 62°F (17°C), with specimens from southern regions tolerating water temperatures of 75 to 80°F (24 to 27°C). Although Red-spotted Newts are hardy creatures, efts and adults are susceptible to fungal diseases, especially in outdoor terraria, and may survive no longer than three or four years. In the indoor terrarium the hobbyist will be able to control the conditions more tightly, and regular purges of the complete setup may be necessary to ensure survival.

Sexual Differences: Land-

Notophthalmus viridescens viridescens, the Red-spotted subspecies of the Eastern Newt, slowly attains the bicolored (tan above, yellow below) adult pattern before returning to water from spending a year or more on land as an eft. Photo: M. Staniszewski.

The Broken-striped Newt, *Notophthalmus viridescens dorsalis*, of the southeastern United States is even more colorful than the other subspecies of Eastern Newt. Photos: Top, A. Norman; bottom, K. T. Nemuras.

dwelling male efts and adults have a noticeably swollen cloaca. In full-breeding condition aquatic males have a high, beautiful yellow or olive crest and rough dark growths on the hind limbs.

Captive Breeding: Healthy specimens will breed regularly in cool (50°F, 10°C), well-lit water abundantly planted with *Elodea* and *Myriophyllum*. In northern forms, a 6 to 12 weeks hibernation period at 38°F (4°C) is required prior to breeding, but southern subspecies such as *N. v. piaropicola* are best cooled down to only 45°F (8°C). Courtship is a vigorous affair although females may need much persuasion before accepting a male spermatophore. Around 350 eggs (2.5 mm in diameter) that have a light brown nucleus are laid either wrapped individually in an *Elodea* leaf blade or small clumps are stuck to the axis of the stalk and branch of the same plant. Eggs must be removed to separate rearing quarters, where larvae hatch within four to seven days, growing quickly to metamorphose after seven weeks if abundant supplies

Black-spotted Newts, *Notophthalmus meridionalis*, are rather thickset newts with a reduced color pattern compared to the Eastern Newt. The black spots are more numerous, but there are no round red spots on the sides. This is not a well-known species. Photo: P. Freed.

Red Eft stage of *Notophthalmus viridescens viridescens*. Art: J. R. Quinn.

of daphnia, copepods, and tubifex are provided. Larval and juvenile mortality rates can be fairly high. Juveniles are initially sandy brown with reddish spots before developing the red eft characteristics and grow well on their favored whiteworm and hatchling cricket diet.

Longevity: Ten years plus if kept clean.

Black-spotted Newt (*Notophthalmus meridionalis*)

Distribution: Southern Texas and northeastern Mexico.

Length: 7 to 11 cm (3 to 4.5 in).

Description: An attractively marked light gray-green newt with black spots on the back and belly that are much larger than in the other American newts. The belly is bright orange. Rarely seen except during winter and spring rains, this species seldom is collected (it is protected in Texas) and rarely makes it to the hobby. It prefers shallow, muddy pools with little vegetation. Males may be fairly aggressive toward each other.

Striped Newt (*Notophthalmus perstriatus*)

Distribution: Restricted to southern Georgia and adjacent Florida, U.S.A.

Length: 5 to 10 cm (2 to 4 in).

Description: An unmistakable little slender newt with continuous red stripes along the middle upper back. Red spots on the side may be quite faint, and the belly usually is rather dull yellow. In nature it inhabits small, clean bodies of water without fishes. It accepts the usual newt foods in captivity. Now protected but declining in numbers.

Hong Kong Newt (*Paramesotriton hongkongensis*)

Distribution: Confined to Hong Kong and adjacent mainland China.

Length: 13 to 18 cm (5 to 7 in).

Description: A stocky newt with a dark brown back that either is plain or marbled with lighter blotches of brown. A high vertebral ridge is always present, while the ventral surface is black and abundantly blotched in orange or yellow. Parotoid glands are very evident, as are skin tubercles that form a series of small ridges along the flanks.

Availability: A commonly kept terrarium subject throughout the world; likely to be seen in tropical fish stores.

Top to bottom: Notophthalmus viridescens dorsalis, **Broken-striped Newt; *N. v. piaropicola,* Peninsula Newt; *N. perstriatus,* Striped Newt; *N. v. viridescens,* Red-spotted Newt. Art: J. R. Quinn.**

***Top: Notophthalmus viridescens louisianensis*, Central Newt. *Bottom: Notophthalmus meridionalis*, Black-spotted Newt. Art: J. R. Quinn.**

Captive Care: Very similar to *Cynops* in demanding a cool aqua-terrarium and a strict hibernation period from August to October (use a refrigerator cooled to a temperature of 40°F, 5°C). Food consists mainly of earthworms, waxworms, and water crustaceans, although small fishes and raw lean red meat are equally relished.

Sexual Differences: Males are small and less rotund than females and have a purplish streak along the tail during breeding.

Captive Breeding: Hibernation and cool, oxygenated water are the keys to success in breeding. This species also favors deeper water than *Cynops*, with 12 inches minimum but preferably 14 to 24 inches. This species is not as dependent as *Cynops* on abundant waterplant growth and often may breed in ponds devoid of vegetation. Even so, the water should still be richly oxygenated and filtered. The 100 to 130 eggs are about 3.5 mm in diameter and somewhat elongated. They are attached to rocks, gravel, or plant stalks. After three weeks the 8-mm larvae hatch out, by which time the adults are less aquatic. The larvae later become extremely cannibalistic and should be split up into groups of 15 to 30 in well-planted aquaria. Metamorphosis occurs 25 to 30 weeks later at 35 mm, with juveniles being patterned in light brown and green blotches.

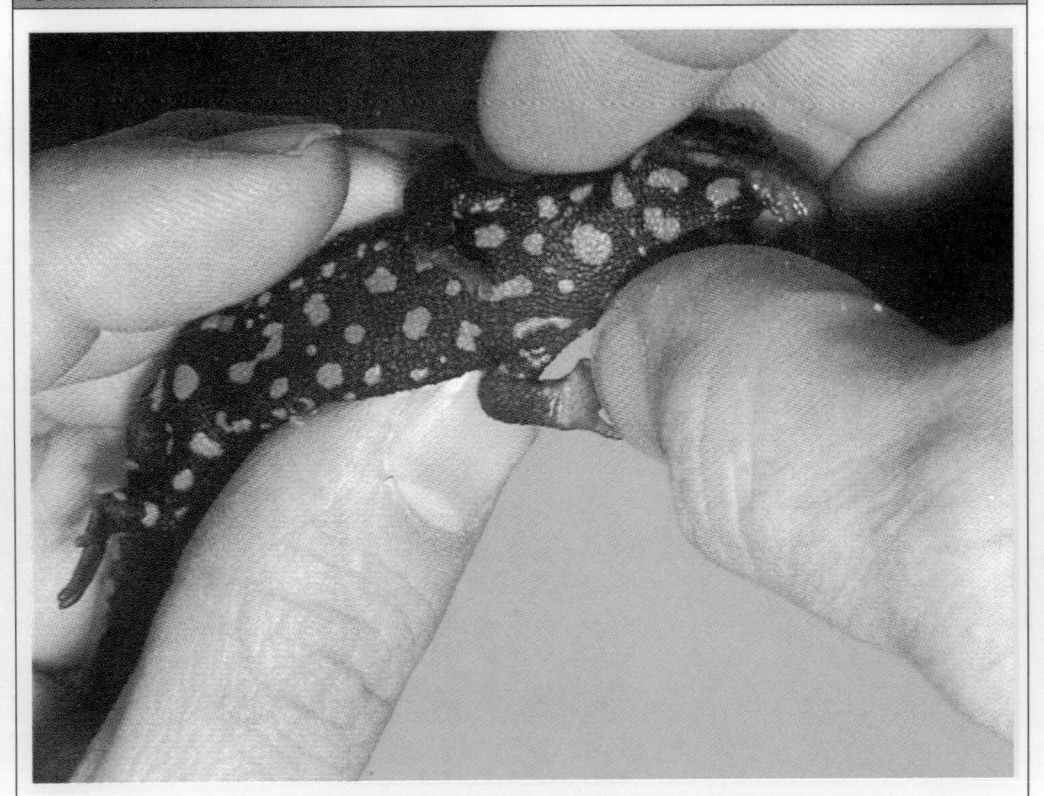

Above: Belly view of the Hong Kong Newt, *Paramesotriton hongkongensis*. This species is much more likely to be found on the American market than is the Japanese Fire-bellied Newt. Photo: W. P. Mara. *Below:* An adult Hong Kong Newt, *Paramesotriton hongkongensis*. Photo: M. Staniszewski.

The Spanish Ribbed Newt, *Pleurodeles waltl*, is one of the most fascinating newts though not especially colorful. Photo: R. D. Bartlett.

Chinese Warty Newt (*Paramesotriton chinensis*)

Distribution: Southern China in mountain streams.

Length: 12 to 16 cm (5 to 6.5 in).

Description: A very rough-skinned newt with a uniformly brown back and black belly sprinkled with many orange or red spots and a laterally flattened tail. Males develop white bars on either side of the tail during courtship. This highly aquatic species can be kept much like the Hong Kong Newt.

Chinese Brown Paddle-tail Newt (*Paramesotriton caudopunctatus*)

Distribution: Southern China in damp, hilly regions.

Length: 11 to 15 cm (4.5 to 6 in).

Description: Very similar to the Chinese Warty Newt, but is more tolerant to high temperatures and more terrestrial in its habits. The venter also is more heavily blotched in red or orange.

Spanish Ribbed Newt (*Pleurodeles waltl*)

Distribution: Portugal, central and southern Spain, and northern Morocco. A rarer, smaller, and more aquatic species called *Pleurodeles poireti* occurs in central and southern Morocco.

Length: To 35 cm (14 in), but usually 25 to 28 cm (10 to 11 in), which makes it the largest European salamander.

Description: Along with

Above: A larval specimen of the Spanish Ribbed Newt, *Pleurodeles waltl*. Photo: M. Staniszewski. *Below:* A mating pair of Spanish Ribbed Newts. Photo: R. D. Bartlett.

Juvenile Spanish Ribbed Newts, *Pleurodeles waltl*, give little idea of the distinctive newt they will grow into. Photo: M. Staniszewski.

Tylototriton species, this robust newt is one of the few species able to protect itself against predation—with the aid of sharp protruding rib ends. The back is mottled in brown and olive, with a series of yellow or orange tubercles running along the flanks through which the ribs may sometimes protrude. The underside is pale yellow or cream and speckled with dark spots. The highly granulated skin is quite thick, offering good water conservation, while the head and body are flattened, enabling this newt to seek damp, narrow rock crevices during drought periods.

Availability: There should be little difficulty in obtaining this species as it is bred in large numbers, but it is not especially common on the American market.

Captive Care: Ribbed newts will thrive in a large aqua-terrarium (30 inches or more) comprising two-thirds tepid water at a depth of 4 inches and profusely planted out. The terrestrial part should consist of a damp, rocky, mossy bank onto which is directed a 40W spot light for around two to six hours each day—the adults are one of the few heliothermic caudates. Adults feed voraciously on most living creatures but should not be fed too regularly to guard against obesity.

Sexual Differences: Males are slimmer than females and have both a visible red excrescence over the dorsum and a swollen cloaca during courtship.

Captive Breeding: Once a healthy, mature sexed pair is put into an aqua-terrarium with sufficient water at room temperature, breeding will occur almost at any point. Hibernation is not recommended, although a "cooling down period" where adults are kept at 50°F (10°C) for four to six weeks will invigorate breeding and egg laying. In the wild estivation is frequent in ponds that dry up, and this too can act as a breeding tonic. Courtship takes place within water, the male initially depositing one or more triangular spermatophores. He then swims upside down under the female and hooks his front limbs, equipped with black nuptial pads, over her fore limbs and drags her across the spermatophore. Up to 350 small eggs are deposited within a mass of gelatinous envelopes from which larvae hatch within two to five days. Adults will devour both eggs and larvae, therefore remove eggs as they appear. Larvae remain in the water for 8 to 14 weeks, where they devour enormous amounts of infusoria, daphnia, aquatic

A fairly typical Fire Salamander, *Salamandra salamandra salamandra*. Photo: M. Staniszewski.

worms, and slivers of raw meat. On crawling onto land they measure 5 to 7 cm and are more brightly colored than the adults. At this stage they are liable to drown easily even in shallow water and should be kept in containers of damp sphagnum moss. Maturity is attained after three years, when the 15-cm nocturnal newts return to water to live an aquatic, diurnal life.

Longevity: Fifteen to 22 years.

Genus *Salamandra* (Fire Salamanders)

This small genus contains one of the most popular terrarium subjects, and it also includes species that are almost impossible to maintain successfully because of the requirement for high–altitude conditions. The species of *Mertensiella* formerly were included in this genus but now are held to be quite distinct.

Fire Salamander (*Salamandra salamandra*)

Distribution: Central and southern Europe and North Africa, with relict populations existing from eastern Turkey to northern Iran.

Length: 15 to 25 cm (6 to 10 in).

Description: An unmistakable species where the only difficulties may arise in identifying the dozen named subspecies. Typical Fire Salamanders are vividly marked with yellow, orange, or (rarely) red spots, blotches, bars, or stripes on a black background. The

The Striped Fire Salamander, *Salamandra salamandra terrestris*, is common in the terrarium hobby and also is one of the most attractive subspecies. Photo: M. Staniszewski.

Juvenile *Salamandra s. terrestris* have more yellow than the adults and often appear to be less distinctly striped. The short tail is typical of the subspecies. Photo: M. Staniszewski.

smooth skin usually has between 9 and 14 well–defined costal grooves. Open pores called cutaneous gland ducts, through which poison is released, are clearly visible especially over the yellow regions and on the pair of swollen parotoid glands behind the large, dark eyes. The well-developed, strong limbs are able to hold the whole body and most of the tail off the ground, with the tail itself being relatively short and cylindrical. When molested, Fire Salamanders exude a toxic, sticky white secretion that has a distinct vanilla odor. If it enters a cut or scrape, the ensuing symptoms include intense irritation and swelling; obviously care should be taken when handling Fire Salamanders.

Availability: Widely available throughout Europe and occasionally elsewhere in the form of captive-bred pets and occasionally as wild-caught Iberian specimens.

Captive Care: Fire Salamanders are easily maintained in a cool (maximum 68°F, 20°C), moist, and fairly spacious terrarium. Plenty of hiding places, rocks, and a loose substrate such as live sphagnum moss should be made available, along with a wide but shallow (1 to 3 inches) water dish. Lighting should be subdued, with a low wattage fluorescent tube being

The larva of *Salamandra salamandra terrestris* is not very different in appearance from most newt larvae even though the mother deposits well-developed larvae in the water, not eggs. Photo: M. Staniszewski.

most suitable. By misting the terrarium each evening, the salamanders will be enticed from their hiding places to hunt for prey or a mate. White and gray slugs are relished, with earthworms, waxworms, and even snails also being devoured.

Sexual Differences: Males are much slimmer and smaller than females and have a more swollen cloaca throughout the year.

Captive Breeding: Breeding is easily accomplished both in the terrarium and particularly in the outdoor or greenhouse amphibiary. A three-month hibernation period is essential and should begin in November, although during warm spells salamanders often leave their hibernacula to hunt for food. Their behavior is strictly nocturnal and terrestrial, with courtship being no exception and possible throughout the year. Fertilization is internal, and the female may store the sperm in seminal receptacle folds for up to four months until conditions for egg development become more favorable. Eggs and developing larvae are retained in the female's body. After a gestation period ranging from two to four months, she seeks shallow and cool, fresh water. It must be ensured that she cannot drown while laying; be sure slopes into the water are gentle and have sufficient purchase. Twenty-five to 75 well-developed, inch-long dark brown larvae complete with feathery gills and four fragile limbs are deposited. If this happens in a terrarium they are best removed to a 24– to 36-inch aquarium filled with around 2 to 3 inches of gently aerated and filtered water. They are immediately carnivorous, hunting and devouring any small aquatic life, and within three to six months, depending on water temperature and food volume, they begin to metamorphose. At this stage larvae are liable to drown very easily due to the absence of webbed feet and dorsal fins. Losses can be avoided by removing to a new container those larvae that are showing gill absorption and on whose back light brown or gold blotches are appearing. This aqua-terrarium should contain land and water at a depth of no more than an inch. Here the 5-cm juveniles can safely leave the

The Black or Alpine Salamander, *Salamandra atra*, of the Swiss and Italian Alps and other high altitudes of southern Europe is even more terrestrial than the Fire Salamander. At least some populations give birth to fully developed, metamorphosed juveniles. Photo: K. H. Switak.

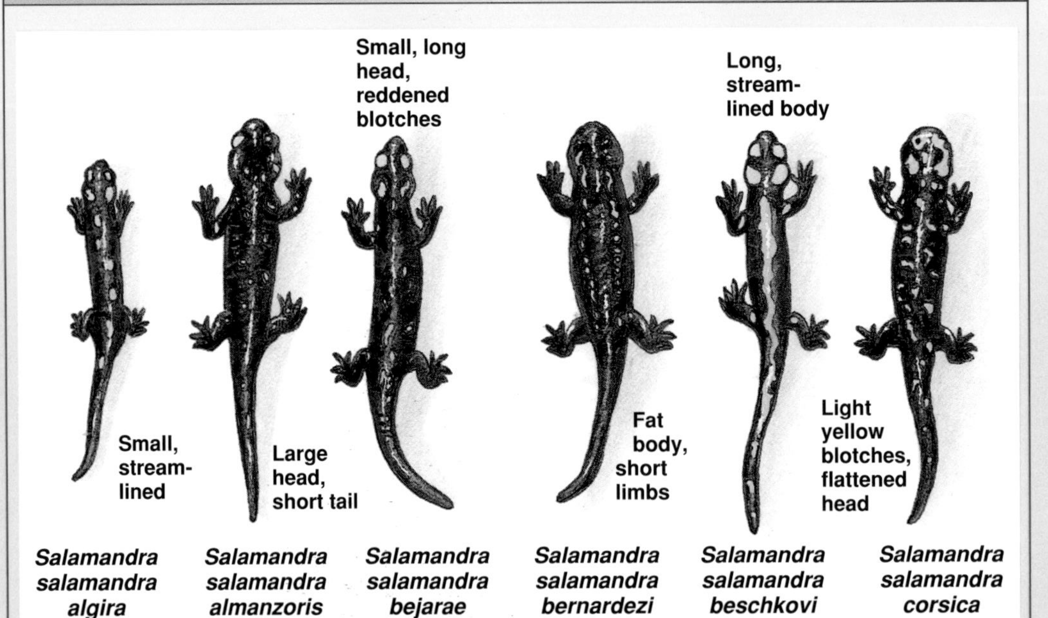

Comparison of the subspecies of *Salamandra salamandra*. All the drawings are very generalized; expect much variation within animals of any single subspecies.

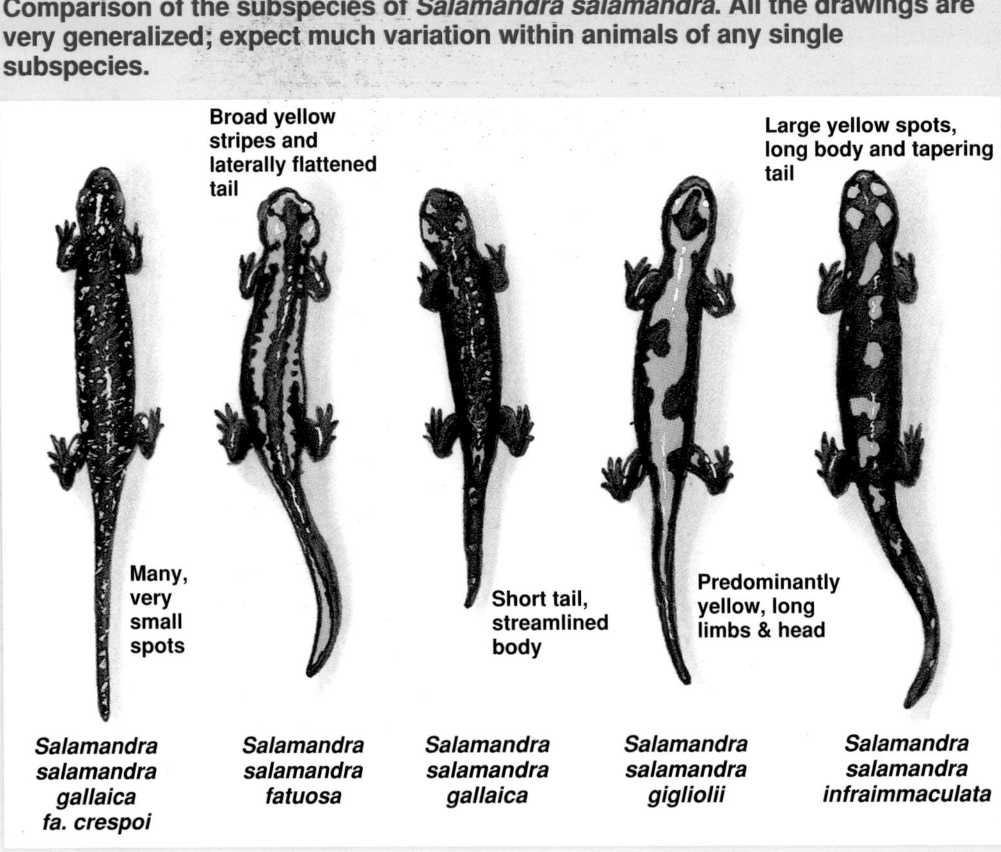

The Subspecies of the Fire Salamander *(Salamandra salamandra)*

Subspecies	Range	Size and Characteristics
Common European Fire *(S.s. salamandra)*	Central & southeastern Europe	20–24cm; Small irregular and sparsely distributed yellow or orange blotches, a broad body and wide head
Algerian Fire *(S.s. algira)*	Northwest African coastal region	16–22cm; Very slender with a narrow head and few cream-yellow spots. Live-born larvae develop extremely quickly
Central Spanish Fire *(S.s. almanzoris)*	Central Spain	13–15cm; A dwarf form whose predominantly black dorsum has very few dull yellow spots. Laterally compressed tail. It is the most aquatic member of the genus
Spanish Fire *(S.s. bejarae)*	Central & southern Spain, eastern Portugal	14–18cm; A robust form with large, distinct "n" or "w" shaped yellow blotches freely intermingled with red blotches
Bernardez's Fire *(S.s. bernardezi)*	Restricted mountainous region around Bilbao, northern Spain	13–16cm; Dorsum is heavily covered in large areas of bright yellow. Body is robust and head is rounded. Deposits fully developed young (viviparous)
Balkan Fire *(S.s. beschkovi)*	Southern Bulgaria	18–25cm; A slender form usually with a single unbroken yellow stripe along the dorsum and yellow legs
Corsican Fire *(S.s. corsica)*	Corsica	16–20cm; Robust form whose dorsum exhibits many small yellow spots while the head is heavily marked in yellow
Pyrenean Fire *(S.s. fatuosa)*	Pyrenees & northern Spain	12–14cm; Variable dwarf form with either broad or pencil thin yellow stripes. Body is almost obese and the tail is very short. Needs a cool terrarium due to its high mountain range
Portuguese Fire *(S.s. gallaica)*	Portugal	14–18cm; Frequently encountered in captivity. The yellow, orange or red blotches are elongate and wavy while background may be black with a red sheen. A finely spotted subspecies from southern Portugal called *S.s. crespoi* may exist
Italian Fire *(S.s. gigliolii)*	Western & central Italy	14–17cm; Short-elongate pear-shaped body, very swollen cloacal region and large parotoid glands. Large yellow blotches sometimes fusing together to form completely yellow areas
Caucasian Fire *(S.s. infraimmaculata)*	Western Caucasus & eastern Turkey	16–18cm; An agile, well-built form with large rounded, yellow blotches on the dorsum. The tail is long and laterally compressed
Israel Fire *(S.s. semenovi)*	Northern Israel mountains	14–19cm; A very long, thin body with a tapering tail. The dorsum may be completely black or have many tiny grayish yellow spots
Striped or Lined Fire *(S.s. terrestris)*	Northwest and western Europe	14–20cm; The most popularly kept subspecies, with a relatively slender body and a series of broken or continuous, broad or thin bands running dorsolaterally. The head is relatively compact and the tail short

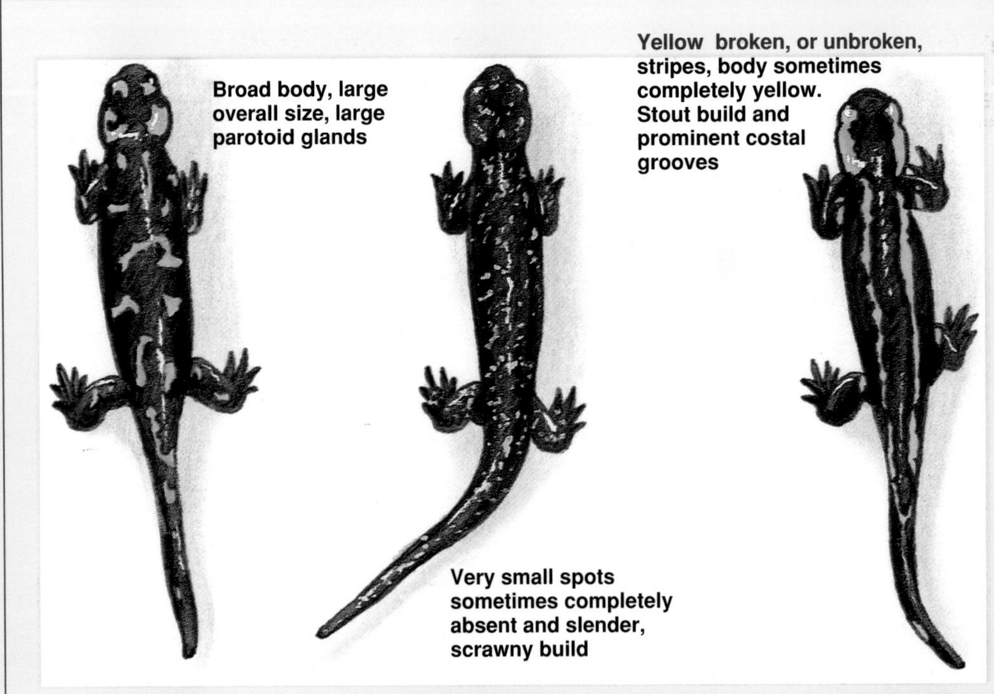

Comparison of other subspecies of *Salamandra salamandra.*

water, by which time they are exhibiting those familiar striking markings. In captivity it is wise to overwinter the young salamanders at 55 to 60°F (13 to 16°C) for the first year. Maturity is achieved in the fourth year.

Longevity: Eighteen to 35 years.

Luschan's (Turkish) Salamander (*Mertensiella luschani*)

Distribution: Hilly pine forests of southwestern Turkey and several Greek islands, such as Karpathos.

Length: 8 to 17 cm (3 to 6.5 in).

Description: An unusual, rarely seen nocturnal species that has at least seven subspecies ascribed to it. The head is large, flattened, and has prominent eyes. The slender body is sandy brown to orange, the limbs are long and well-developed, and the tail is short. In males, a 3– to 6-mm fleshy spike develops on the back near the tail base during the breeding season.

Captive Care: In captivity a relatively dry woodland terrarium is required, with temperatures in the 60 to 68°F (16 to 20°C) range.

Captive Breeding: Mating occurs on land at any time of the year. The female has a lengthy gestation period of four to six months before giving birth to one to four young about 3 cm long. To stimulate breeding, an estivation period at 75°F (24°C) surface temperature for 12 weeks during summer is followed by a lengthy damp period (to mirror natural rainfall). Mating is a vigorous affair, with males securing a small territory. This species will almost certainly become quite popular with hobbyists within the next few years.

Other Species: The Caucasian Salamander, *Mertensiella caucasica*, comes from the Black Sea region of Turkey and grows to about 20 cm (8 in). It is more rotund than *M. luschani* but has a much longer tail. Its back is black with a series of broken cream or yellow stripes. This is a more aquatic species than the Turkish Salamander and requires a moist terrarium. Little is known of its behavior and breeding requirements.

Spectacled (Italian) Salamander (*Salamandrina terdigitata*)

Distribution: Western Italy in the Apennines Mountains.

Length: 7 to 11 cm (3 to 4.5 in).

Description: A small, slender, and secretive species that rarely is available to hobbyists outside continental Europe. The long tail often is mottled on the sides with dull orange, while beneath it is bright red, as are the undersides of the legs and the area around the cloaca. Heavy tubercles mark the midline of the back and a row on each side of the body. There are only four toes on the hind feet.

Captive Care: In nature this species occupies cool woodlands

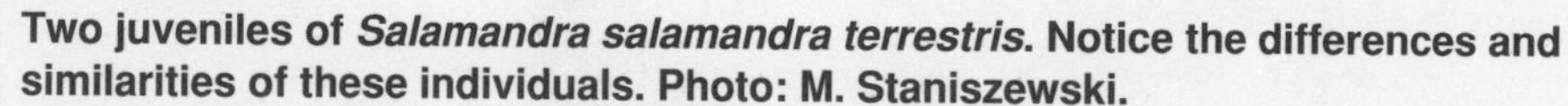

Two juveniles of *Salamandra salamandra terrestris*. Notice the differences and similarities of these individuals. Photo: M. Staniszewski.

The Striped Fire Salamander, *Salamandra salamandra terrestris*. Photo: A. Norman.

and streams of the upland regions, and in captivity it must be kept similarly. Keep it in a woodland terrarium with a shallow water area, but after hibernation at 38°F (4°C) for three months it should be moved to an aqua-terrarium for mating. The water needs to be about 5 inches deep, 50 to 58°F (10 to 15°C), slightly acid, and ideally slowly but continually moving with the aid of a pump. Plenty of plants such as *Elodea* and *Vallisneria* must be provided. This is an excellent subject for the unheated greenhouse.

Captive Breeding: After hibernation and the move to the aqua-terrarium, mating may occur both on land and in the water. The female attaches small (6 to 14 eggs) clumps of whitish eggs about 2 mm in diameter to plants in the aqua-terrarium. A total of 45 to 60 eggs is laid. Adults may spend two to four weeks in the water, while the juveniles emerge six to eight weeks later at 2 to 2.6 cm in length.

Gold-striped (Portuguese) Salamander (*Chioglossa lusitanica*)

Distribution: Western Spain and northern central Portugal.

Length: 9 to 15 cm (3.5 to 6 in).

The Gold-striped Salamander, *Chioglossa lusitanica*, bears a striking resemblance in structure and color to many North American plethodontid salamanders. Photo: M. Staniszewski.

Though one of the most sought-after of the European salamanders, *Chioglossa lusitanica*, the Gold-striped Salamander, has a small range, is uncommon to rare, is protected by various laws, and is not especially easy to maintain or breed in the terrarium. Photo: M. Staniszewski.

Description: A very slender little species with an elongated body and tail and small limbs. The middle of the back and tail is marked with a broad golden stripe.

Captive Care: Native to cool, moist valleys and streams, this species is difficult to maintain successfully indoors. It requires fresh air along with high humidity and cool temperatures (no greater than 65°F, 18°C), a difficult combination of parameters. It also requires semihibernation at 46°F (8°C) for several months prior to breeding plus estivation during the warmer months. This species can shed its tail when caught and regenerate a new one eventually.

Captive Breeding: Breeding may occur twice a year, in spring and autumn. Provide a terrarium like that for *Euproctus*. Mating takes place on land, but the female partially enters the water several weeks after collecting a number of spermatophores. She attaches 40 or more large (2.5 mm) eggs to rocks and vegetation just below the surface. Hatchling larvae are elongated and excellent swimmers. At a size of 4 cm, they metamorphose six to ten weeks after hatching and are immediately agile creatures capable of capturing small insects with their tongues.

Rough-skinned Newts, *Taricha granulosa*, are common pet shop newts. Notice that the lower eyelid is dark, not yellow like the upper lip. Photo: P. Freed.

Rough-skinned Newt (*Taricha granulosa*)

Distribution: Pacific North America from southeastern Alaska to central California.

Length: 14 to 18 cm (4.5 to 7 in).

Description: A large newt with a dorsal coloring of plain to dark brown. In the terrestrial phase the skin is heavily granulated with pointed tubercles. The underside is a vivid orange or yellow, and a thin orange crest runs along the entire lower tail. The legs are well developed, while the head tends to be more flattened than in other newts. An irritating poison is exuded even when these newts are handled gently, therefore a net or surgical gloves are recommended for safety. Breeding specimens (especially males) develop very smooth skin and high tail crests. The lower eyelid is dark.

Availability: Along with the similar California Newt (*T. torosa*), this species is widely seen throughout the world in pet shops.

Captive Care: Rough–skinned Newts are hardy, adaptable, and make excellent subjects for the terrarium even in a centrally heated room, although like most salamanders they do better at cooler temperatures of around 60°F (16°C). The terrarium should consist of a sphagnum moss or synthetic foam base that is misted frequently to give a high humidity (especially in a

California Newts, *Taricha torosa*, are not common pet shop newts because most populations in California are protected from commercial collecting. They show a great amount of variation in color depending on season and probably individual populations from which the specimens were collected. Notice that the yellow color of the upper lip includes the lower eyelid, a feature that helps distinguish this species from *T. granulosa*, which has the lower lid dark. Photos: A. Norman.

centrally heated room). A 36-inch terrarium will comfortably house two pairs and should be segregated into two-thirds land and one-third water that is 4 to 6 inches deep. Both sturdy branches on which they will climb and plenty of crockery and bark for hiding places should be provided, although *Taricha* are partially diurnal, often searching for prey ranging from woodlice, slugs, and worms to strips of raw meat offered on forceps.

Sexual Differences: Outside the breeding season, when males have dark nuptial pads on the hind limbs and an enlarged cloaca, sexing can be problematic.

Captive Breeding: Hibernation is a prerequisite to successful breeding. A typical woodland setup, allowing Pacific newts access to water, is likely to be too small for breeding purposes. Instead transfer them to a large aqua-terrarium containing 14 inches of water abundantly planted out. This newt's courtship behavior is less spectacular than in many other newt species. *Taricha granulosa* differs from the other *Taricha* species by depositing each of its 150 eggs individually on leaves of *Elodea*. When the larvae show signs of transforming, the water level should be gradually lowered to around 4 inches. The larvae should be treated exactly

A late larva of the California Newt, *Taricha torosa*. Photo: Dr. D. Green.

***Taricha rivularis*, the Red-bellied Newt, is the third species of the genus *Taricha*, but it seldom is seen in the terrarium. Art: J. R. Quinn.**

as for Fire Salamander larvae.

Other Species: The California Newt, *Taricha torosa*, is a large (14 to 19 cm), attractive species from coastal California that makes an excellent, long-lived terrarium subject. In nature it occurs near most types of water from sea level to 2,000 meters. The back is light to medium brown and covered with tiny spines (though smoother than the back of the Rough–skinned Newt), while the belly is bright orange. As in the Rough–skinned, breeding males have very smooth skin and high tail crests. The lower eyelid is yellow. This species preys on smaller amphibians and the usual array of soft-bodied invertebrates. Semi-

A breeding male (top) and female of the Marbled Newt, *Triturus marmoratus*. Art: J. R. Quinn.

A stunning male Marbled Newt, *Triturus marmoratus*. Is there any doubt why newts are such popular terrarium animals in Europe? Photo: M. Staniszewski.

aquatic in habit, it returns to water in winter to breed. Females deposit around 300 eggs in small clumps numbering about 15 eggs each. Easily bred in captivity once it settles down.

Genus *Triturus* (Typical Newts)

Triturus is a European, North African, and West Asian genus whose members are similar in size and habits but differ greatly in coloration, abundance, and hence desirability. All species are excellent candidates for the outdoor and greenhouse amphibiary.

Marbled Newt *(Triturus marmoratus*)

Distribution: The Iberian Peninsula and France west of the Rhone Valley.

Length: 12 to 17 cm (5 to 7 cm).

Description: Along with the Banded Newt (*Triturus vittatus*), this large, robust species is the most beautiful member of the genus. The upper parts of the body, legs, and tail are boldly marbled and spotted with green and black, while the venter is mottled in gray, pink, black, and cream. This coloration tends to be more vivid in terrestrial newts, with males showing very bright greens while juveniles and females have a conspicuous orange or yellow stripe running down the back. Older individuals may become relatively drab. The skin of this newt has a velvety texture on land and is smooth and shiny in water. Like most *Triturus* species, if the newt is

Even the female Marbled Newt, *Triturus marmoratus*, is a beautiful animal. Additionally, this species is not especially shy in the terrarium. Photo: M. Staniszewski.

A well-developed egg of the Marbled Newt, *Triturus marmoratus*. Photo: M. Staniszewski.

molested, a creamy toxin is secreted from ducts located all over the dorsum. The toxin can cause irritation and swelling.

Availability: The Marbled Newt frequently is bred in captivity and is widely available, especially in Europe.

Captive Care: Most typical newts require very similar captive conditions when in their terrestrial stage, with the Marbled Newt tending to spend less time in water than other species. A medium-sized, predominantly terrestrial terrarium maintained at around 58 to 65°F (15 to 18°C) and given subdued lighting is suitable. The preferred substrate consists of a 4-inch layer of damp (but not waterlogged), loose live sphagnum moss on which are rested a few rocks, bark, and logs. A small water pan with 2 inches of water must be present because newts will often enter water to shed their skin. Prey consists mainly of soft-bodied invertebrates, although small fishes and tadpoles are consumed in the water.

A poorly documented disease that sometimes occurs in captive typical newts is "head-rot" syndrome caused by a fungal pathogen. This attacks the brain cavity, causing skull disintegration, and ultimately ends in a slow, painful death. If detected, all newts should be isolated immediately, treated with a systemic fungicide, and the terrarium thoroughly disinfected.

Sexual Differences: Females have a conspicuous orange dorsal stripe. Males have a swollen cloaca even in the terrestrial stage and develop high, barred, black and white dorsal and tail crests during breeding, the dorsal crest visible as a low ridge the remainder of the year.

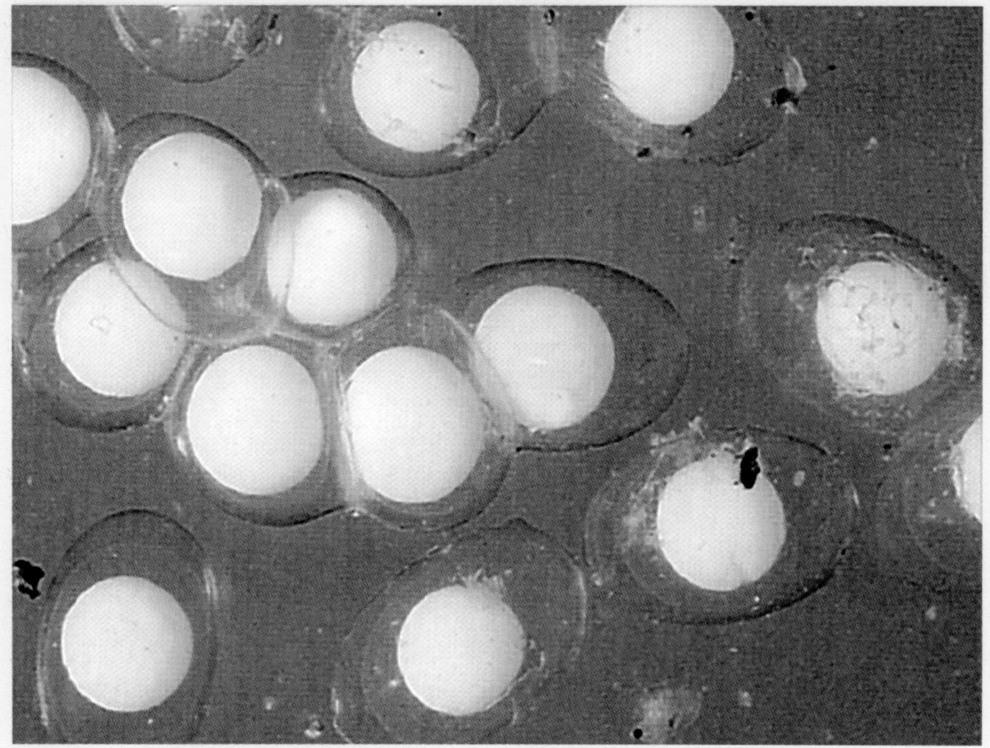

The eggs of *Triturus marmoratus* are laid individually and usually hidden under a small plant leaf or blade of grass. Photo: M. P. & C. Piednoir.

Captive Breeding: The breeding pattern of the Marbled Newt is typical of the genus, differing only in the type of water preferred, male courtship movement, and egg deposition locations. Essential is a lengthy hibernation within a container filled with a loose mixture of damp peatmoss, chopped live sphagnum moss, and straw. Put the container in a cold (36°F, 2°C) but frost-free location such as an unheated garage or refrigerator. After 12 to 16 weeks the newts are transferred to a large aqua-terrarium maintained at a temperature of 50 to 65°F (10 to 18°C). Females may enter water immediately, while males remain terrestrial for two to four weeks until their breeding adornments are fully developed. After a courtship lasting three to eight weeks, the females begin to search for suitable egg-laying spots, tending to favor submerged reed/grass blades, dead leaves, and especially strips of thin plastic sheeting.

Development of the Marbled Newt, *Triturus marmoratus. Above:* A two-month-old larva. *Below:* Juveniles look much like the adult female. Photos: M. Staniszewski.

Elodea is rarely utilized. About 150 to 230 eggs (2.5 mm diameter) that have a white (with a hint of pale green) nucleus are deposited individually. Using her hind limbs, the female will maneuver the egg into position before gently bending the leaf blade or plastic to enclose and protect the egg. Eggs are best kept cool (maximum 55°F, 13°C). The 6-mm larvae hatch 12 to 18 days later. Initially they hang inanimately from vegetation or the aquarium side, absorbing the large yolk sac. For the next 10 to 18 weeks they are active carnivores, initially seeking and devouring microscopic infusoria and progressing to daphnia, tubifex, and larger prey as the front then hind limbs appear. Later they are voracious creatures, often attacking each other, and are best divided into smaller groups. On metamorphosis the beautifully colored juveniles are 4 to 5.5 cm in length. They take three or four years to reach maturity on a diet of earthworms and slugs.

Longevity: Up to 20 years.

Banded Newt (*Triturus vittatus vittatus*)

Additional Subspecies: Caucasian Banded (*T. v.*

***Triturus marmoratus pygmaeus*, a Marbled Newt from the southern Iberian Peninsula. Photo: M. Staniszewski.**

A male Banded Newt, *Triturus vittatus vittatus*. This spectacular animal seldom is available to the terrarium hobby but certainly deserves more attention and efforts at captive-breeding. Photo: M. Staniszewski.

ophryticus); Syrian Banded (*T. v. syriacus*).

Distribution: At altitudes of over 2,000 ft throughout Turkey, Israel, and the northern Middle East.

Length: 14 to 16 cm (5.5 to 6.5 in).

Description: The subspecies differ quite considerably, with the nominatc form, *T. v. vittatus*, being a relatively slender newt with a long, laterally flattened tail, extremely long digits, and an overall greater length. The ground color is a gray-green, with the male being heavily speckled with black-ringed white spots. The venter tends to be a white or creamy yellow with faded blue-gray speckles and lines. *T. v. ophryticus* and *syriacus* are bulkier subspecies having larger dorsal speckling, stronger limbs, a broader head, a more cylindrical tail, and a bright orange belly with few spots. In all subspecies the most conspicuous feature is the broad pearl band running along either side of the flanks; this band is most evident during the breeding period.

Availability: Less commonly offered than other newts, with *T. v. ophryticus* the most likely to be seen. In terms of demand and

Above: The eggs of *Triturus vittatus ophryticus* are often but not always laid on plant leaves. *Below:* Even females of *Triturus vittatus ophryticus* are readily distinguished; notice the broad white stripe just above the belly. Photos: M. Staniszewski.

Above: The juvenile *Triturus vittatus vittatus* bears a vague resemblance to the Marbled Newt. *Below:* Male Banded Newts, *Triturus vittatus vittatus*, are stunning enough to put most other newts to shame, but even they are overshadowed by other subspecies. Photos: M. Staniszewski.

appearance this is one of the most desirable newts.

Captive Care: A hardy species preferring relatively drier conditions than more typical newts, it should be given access to both dry and damp areas. Otherwise care is as for the Marbled Newt.

Sexual Differences: Male Banded Newts represent one of the most bizarre amphibians during the breeding season, when they develop two high denticulate crests patterned in cream, green, and black bands, one along the back, another on the tail. (*T. v. vittatus* has a much lower crest.) Crests also appear along the hind feet and lower legs. Out of water look for the males to have more swollen cloacas and larger hind feet than females.

Captive Breeding: Breeding is stimulated in the same way as for the Marbled Newt, but the Banded Newt prefers deep water, 24 to 40 inches, which is fresh, cool (maximum 60°F, 16°C), and sparsely planted with vegetation. These newts intensely dislike warm water and will not breed under such conditions. In the wild they often occur in deep limestone pools with little or no vegetation. Courtship activity is particularly lively and may last up to 12 weeks, with males being territorial and highly aggressive toward each other. A dominant male usually fends off other males who enter the pool and subsequently often leave the water early. The number of eggs deposited ranges from 50 to 80 in *T. v. vittatus* or up to 250 in *T. v. ophryticus*. Females are not always inclined to wrap leaves around their eggs, often securing them to rocks or pushing them into gravel. Where plants are used, particular favorites include *Aponogeton, Elodea densa*, and

A male *Triturus vittatus ophryticus* in his full glory. Even the species of the Crested Newt complex are not more spectacular in color and "finnage." Photo: M. Staniszewski.

Ludwigia (*Elodea canadensis* usually is ignored). Adults will devour their own two-tone gray and white, 2-mm eggs and the resultant 10-mm larvae, which should be removed to aquaria containing deep, well-aerated water. Metamorphosis occurs 8 to 18 weeks later when the newtlets are 3 to 4 cm in length. They reach maturity in two or three years if fed well on their favorite prey of spiders, small crickets, and small worms.

Alpine Newt (*Triturus alpestris alpestris*)

Additional Subspecies: Italian (*T. a. apuanus*); Spanish (*T. a. cyreni*); Yugoslavian (*T. a. lacusnigri*); Montenegran (*T. a. montenegrinus*); Bosnian (*T. a. reiseri*); Greek (*T. a. veluchiensis*). Except for the Italian, these subspecies consist mostly of relict populations occurring in high mountain lakes. Other isolated subspecies are recognized by some authors.

A male Common Alpine Newt, *Triturus alpestris alpestris*, in full breeding color is one of the few truly blue amphibians. Photo: M. Staniszewski.

Distribution: Northern and central Europe and western Russia.

Length: 10 to 13 cm (4 to 5 in).

Description: An attractive species with the male having a dark blue or occasionally black dorsum with a silvery blue, black-speckled band along each flank. Females are quite drab in comparison, often being brown or olive. The ventral color is a uniform deep orange and, in all but the Italian subspecies, dark speckles are absent from the throat.

Male (top) and female Banded Newts, *Triturus vittatus ophryticus.* Photos: M. Staniszewski.

Larva (top) and juvenile of the Common Alpine Newt, *Triturus alpestris alpestris*. Notice the extremely blunt tail of the larva. Photos: M. Staniszewski.

Breeding males of the Italian Alpine Newt, *Triturus alpestris apuanus*. This smaller subspecies closely resembles the Common Alpine Newt in all features and often is captive-bred. Photos: M. Staniszewski.

Female Alpine Newts (here the Italian subspecies, *Triturus alpestris apuanus*) remain rather drab even during the breeding season. One unfortunate aspect of newts as terrarium animals is that beautiful colors and "finnage" may be shown for only a few weeks each year. Photo: M. Staniszewski.

Availability: The nominate and smaller Italian forms are widely offered in Europe.

Captive Care: A very hardy species capable of tolerating a wide range of waters including frozen, stagnant, polluted ponds. They are also by far the most aquatic true newt (triton), with the Italian Alpine actively spending almost its entire adult life in water. In captivity they live happily in the standard cool (60°F, 16°C, maximum) semi-aquatic setup.

Sexual Differences: Males develop a very low, smooth dorsal keel that is yellow with a series of black spots. The male's blue and orange cloaca remains swollen throughout the year.

Captive Breeding: Water temperatures should drop to around 36°F (2°C) in winter, although the newts remain active. Females deposit 300 to 400 eggs on most types of aquatic plants throughout the year. Males hierarchically develop distinct but small territories that they defend from other males by nudging and biting. Hatching and larval development can last just eight weeks in warm water or as much as 40 to 80 weeks in very cold water, with metamorphosed newts measuring from 3 to 8 cm depending on development time. Maturity is achieved in as little as 18 months in the Italian Alps, but three years is more normal.

Longevity: Twenty years.

Newts of the Crested Newt complex. Top to bottom: Male and female Caucasian Crested Newts (*Triturus karelini*); male Danube Crested Newt (*Triturus dobrogicus*); male Alpine Crested Newt (*Triturus carnifex*). Art: J. R. Quinn.

Italian Newt (*Triturus italicus*)

Distribution: Central and southern Italy in lowland waterways and damp woodlands.

Length: 5 to 8 cm (2 to 3 in).

Description: One of the smallest salamanders, this species is distinctly more yellow both above and especially below than is *Triturus vulgaris*. A body crest is completely absent in breeding males. Do not let the common name allow this species to be confused with the Italian subspecies of *Triturus alpestris*.

Captive Care: A normal woodland terrarium can be used for the terrestrial stage. It cannot stand cold temperatures, so maintain it at 60°F (16°C) and hibernate at 40°F (4°C) for two months prior to breeding.

Captive Breeding: An aquarium or pond containing just 3 to 5 inches of water is all that is needed for breeding this species. It tends to breed earlier than any other European tritons, usually in January or February. Eggs may be scattered over the substrate if plants are absent, but females are particularly fond of wrapping their eggs in *Egeria densa*. Around 120 eggs are deposited. The 6-mm larvae may need only six weeks to metamorphose.

Bosc's (Spanish) Newt (*Triturus boscai*)

Distribution: Portugal and eastern Spain in brooks and shallow ponds in mountains.

Length: 6 to 10 cm (2.5 to 4 in).

Description: A rather dull brown little newt with a pale to bright orange belly. There is a white stripe or row of tiny specks along the edge of the belly running onto the tail. Both sexes have a tiny filament at the end of the tail.

Captive Care & Breeding: For some reason this newt can be quite difficult to maintain in captivity. A temperature of around 66°F (19°C) must be provided. It rarely will hibernate successfully and is best given a cool period of around 44°F (6°C). Breeding commences in April in cool, shallow, weed-filled waters that are slightly acidic, especially if fed by running water. About 250 eggs are deposited. Unless the water is maintained in pristine condition, there will be a high egg and larval mortality rate.

Carpathian Newt (*Triturus montandoni*)

Distribution: Carpathian Mountains of eastern central Europe in cool ponds and damp woodlands of higher elevations.

Length: 7 to 12 cm (3 to 5 in).

Captive Care & Breeding: This is a sought-after species that is tolerant of low temperatures and a variety of water conditions. Adults are unusual in being the only newts to properly hibernate at the muddy bottoms of ponds. Coloration is an attractive orange-brown with a darker brown marbling. Males are smaller than females and have a low (1.5 mm) yellow-orange crest during the March to July breeding season. It favors cold (36 to 45°F, 2 to 8°C), slow-flowing waters although it will

Top pair: **The Alpine Newt, *Triturus alpestris*, male above. *Bottom pair:* Bosc's Newt, *Triturus boscai*, male below. Art: J. R. Quinn.**

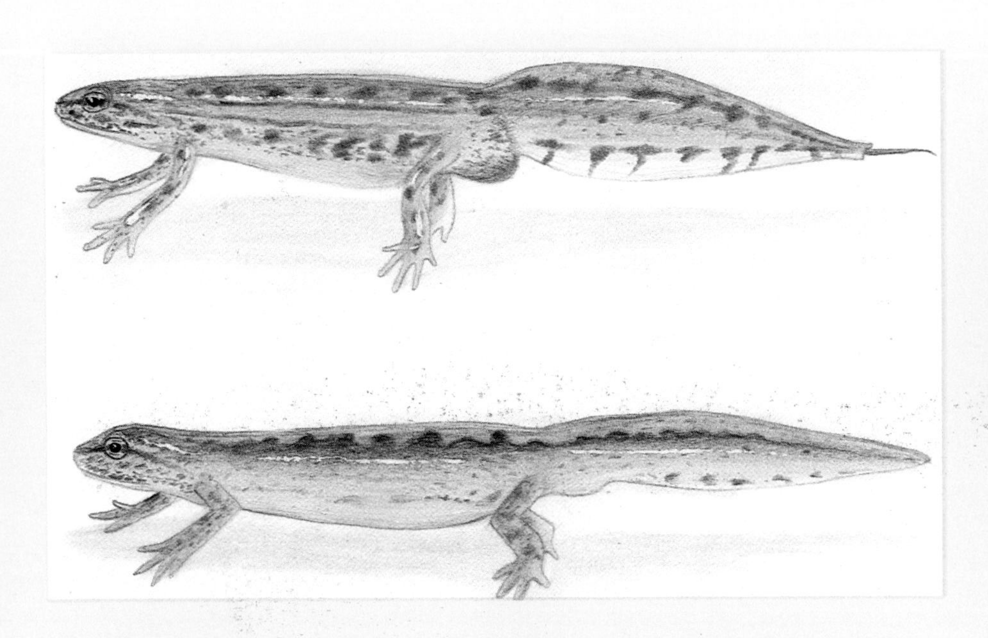

Top pair: The Carpathian Newt, *Triturus montandoni*, male above. *Bottom pair:* The Palmate Newt, *Triturus helveticus*, male above. Art: J. R. Quinn.

Top pair: **The Common Smooth Newt, *Triturus vulgaris*, male above. *Center:* A Greek Smooth Newt, *Triturus vulgaris graecus*, male. *Bottom:* Common Banded Newt, *Triturus vittatus vittatus*. Art: J. R. Quinn.**

Top pair: Caucasian Banded Newt, *Triturus vittatus ophryticus*, male above. *Bottom pair:* Italian Newt, *Triturus italicus*, male above. Art: J. R. Quinn.

Northern Crested Newt, *Triturus cristatus*, male above. Art: J. R. Quinn.

breed in relatively deep, warm, still water if necessary. Around 300 eggs are simply scattered around. The larvae take two to six months to metamorphose.

Palmate Newt (*Triturus helveticus*)

Distribution: Much of western and northwestern Europe.

Length: 7 to 10 cm (3 to 4 in).

Description: Two subspecies are recognized, the nominate being widely distributed over northwestern Europe and the smaller (to 7.5 cm, 3 in) Iberian (*T. h. sequeirai*) being restricted to northwestern Spain and northern Portugal. The species is distinguished from the similar *Triturus vulgaris* by having cranial grooves. The Iberian subspecies is more yellow than the nominate form. In both forms the belly is pale yellow to whitish, the male has a tail filament, and the back and sides are light brown with scattered spots and mottling of darker brown, the spots extending onto the tail as rows of spots or stripes at the edges.

Captive Care & Breeding: It prefers shallow water (5 to 7

Like most female newts, the female Palmate Newt, *Triturus helveticus*, is quite plain. Photo: M. Staniszewski.

The male Palmate Newt, *Triturus helveticus*, is relatively unadorned. Notice, however, the long tail filament and the black lining of the hind foot. Photo: M. Staniszewski.

inches) with dense growths of *Elodea* in which it will breed from early March to later June. Males are distinguished by the hind toe fringes, small crest, tail filament, more conspicuous spotting on the head, and prominent glandular pad running along the flank. The 300 to 400 black, 1.5-mm eggs are wrapped singly in elodea leaves. The Iberian subspecies breeds in cool lowland ponds in winter.

Smooth Newt *(Triturus vulgaris*)

Distribution: England across central and northern Europe (not in southern France and the Iberian Peninsula) into Russia and the Balkans, south into Turkey.

Length: 6 to 13 cm (2.5 to 5 in).

Description: A brown triton with (usually) a high, scalloped dorsal crest extending onto the tail without a break. Typically there is a dark line through the eye and another on the upper jaw with a paler stripe between. The

A newly metamorphosed Turkish Smooth Newt, *Triturus vulgaris schmidtlerorum*. Photo: M. Staniszewski.

A non-breeding pair of Southern Smooth Newts, *Triturus vulgaris meridionalis*, the male with heavier spotting. Photo: M. Staniszewski.

belly usually is yellow with large round black spots, and the lower edge of the male's tail is bright blue in breeding season. The hind feet are strongly webbed. Many subspecies are recognized. The above description applies mostly to the nominate subspecies of most of northern and central Europe into Russia. The more minor subspecies tend to be from the Balkan region and include:

•Romanian *(T. v. ampelensis)*, upland Transylvanian Plateau of Romania. Lower crest and more conspicuous rear toe filaments.

•Yugoslavian *(T. v. dalmaticus)*, central and southern Yugoslavian area. Small crest and well-developed dorsolateral ridges.

•Greek *(T. v. graecus)*, southern Yugoslavia into Greece. A slender, highly spotted form with a poorly developed crest and long tail filament in the male.

•Northern Turkish *(T. v. kosswigi)*, Black Sea coast of northwestern Turkey. A little-known form with peculiar dorsolateral ridges and a thin, squarish body; lays only 80 to 140 eggs, and the larvae develop extremely quickly given adequate food.

The heavily spotted belly of the Southern Smooth Newt, *Triturus vulgaris meridionalis,* is typical for the species. Photo: M. Staniszewski.

•Caucasian *(T. v. lantzi)*, northwestern Caucasus. The male's crest is very denticulated and has a series of black bars. This is one of the least aquatic forms.

•Southern *(T. v. meridionalis)*, Swiss Alps to central Italy. A common form that tends to breed in shallower, somewhat warmer

The extent of the bright color on the belly of a male Smooth Newt, *Triturus vulgaris*, varies considerably both geographically and individually. This male has the brilliant orange restricted to a rather narrow stripe down the center of the belly. Notice also the bright orange stripe just behind the cloaca, typical of the species. Photo: P. Freed.

The Turkish Smooth Newt, *Triturus vulgaris schmidtlerorum*, though only recently described, holds great promise as a terrarium animal. The non-breeding pair above (male at top) show the very lizard-like appearance of the subspecies and indicate the great change that takes place when the male is ready to breed (below). Photos: M. Staniszewski.

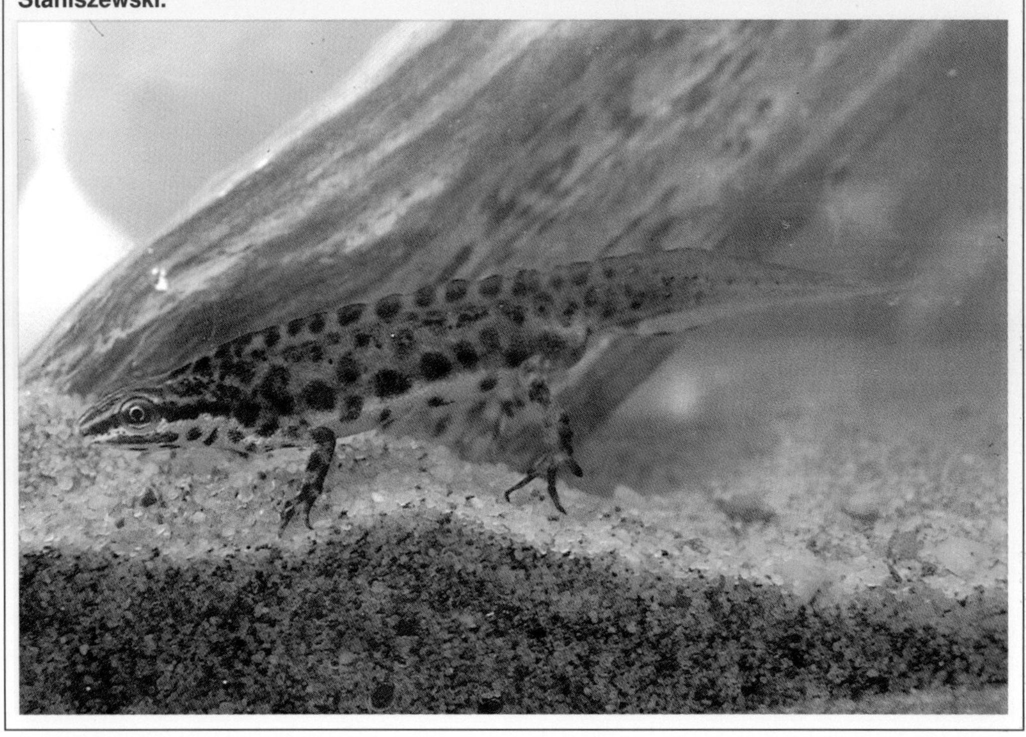

water than other forms and breeds from January to mid-April.

•Turkish *(T. v. schmidtlerorum)*, western Turkey. The smallest and most unusual subspecies, described only in 1988. Very lizard-like in movement and able to capture small insects with its tongue. The body is held high off the ground and the digits are extremely long. Well worth seeking.

More subspecies are recognized by specialists.

Captive Care & Breeding: An easy and long-lived terrarium subject suitable for most damp setups and fairly tolerant of a wide temperature range. It generally prefers shallow water with plenty of water weed in which to breed. Males have the high, bright crest well-developed during March to June or July, when the females lay their eggs. The 300 eggs are wrapped individually in elodea and similar leaves. Adults will devour both eggs and larvae if given the chance.

This breeding male *Triturus vulgaris schmidtlerorum*, the Turkish Smooth Newt, shows the striped head pattern characteristic of the species. Photo: M. Staniszewski.

Alpine Crested Newt *(Triturus carnifex)*

Note: Intensive research into the biology, genetics, and geographical distribution of the crested newts (formerly all *T. cristatus*) has resulted in the four subspecies recognized earlier being assigned specific status.

Distribution: Much of Italy and the southern Alps of Yugoslavia.

Length: 11.5 to 18 cm (4.5 to 7 in).

An adult female Alpine Crested Newt, *Triturus carnifex*. This female is in the land phase and shows the rough skin typical of most terrestrial crested newts. Photo: M. Staniszewski.

Description: Of the crested newts, this species is the most robust. White or light gray speckling along the flanks, neck, and dark throat is largely absent, and the skin is more finely granulated in the terrestrial stage. The back tends to be a dark brown with many barely evident dark blotches that are more conspicuous on the distinctive orange belly.

Availability: Strictly protected in the wild across much of its range, so only captive-bred specimens are likely to be offered.

Captive Care: This is the most aquatic crested newt, but its general care is similar to the Marbled Newt.

Sexual Differences: The slightly smaller, slimmer males develop a high, jagged crest during the breeding season and are more highly colored with a vivid orange, swollen cloaca. Females have an unbroken yellow vertebral stripe.

Captive Breeding: Following a necessary hibernation, this species remains on land until spring or early summer when the water has warmed slightly to around 42°F (6°C). They prefer deeper water than most newts, particularly water that is rich in elodea and other plants. The 100 to 350 pale gray eggs produced should be removed to separate rearing quarters, where they

Above: **This three-month-old larva of the Alpine Crested Newt, *Triturus carnifex*, shows a long tail filament. *Below:* Not all Alpine Crested Newt larvae mature in one year. This eight-month-old larva overwintered in the larval stage. Photos: M. Staniszewski.**

hatch in 7 to 12 days. The larvae must be offered large amounts of tubifex and daphnia to prevent fighting. After 10 to 25 weeks, at a size of 4 to 6 cm, they metamorphose into shiny black newtlets that have prominent yellow vertebral stripes, which gradually fade in the males.

Longevity: Eighteen years plus.

Northern Crested Newt
(Triturus cristatus)

Distribution: Northern and central Europe into Russia.

Length: 14 to 17 cm (5.5 to 7 in).

Description: A large, impressive species with the breeding male adorned with a high, denticulated crest, a bright orange belly with many large black spots, and a pearly stripe running along the tail. The lower

A breeding pair of Alpine Crested Newts, *Triturus carnifex*. Photo: K.-D. Kuehnel.

An adult female Northern Crested Newt, *Triturus cristatus*. Notice the extent of the white speckling low on the sides. Photo: L. Wischnath.

Above: A recently transformed Northern Crested Newt, *Triturus cristatus*. The yellow middorsal line is typical of most young and female crested newts. Photo: M. Gilroy.
Below: A breeding pair of Northern Crested Newts, *Triturus cristatus*. Again, notice the fine white speckling low on the sides and on the lower jaw. Photo: L. Wischnath.

A breeding male Northern Crested Newt, *Triturus cristatus*. Not all males have high crests or brilliant colors. Photo: B. Kahl.

sides are covered with fine white specks.

Availability: An excellent species for the outdoor amphibiary, but remember that the collection of wild *Triturus cristatus* is prohibited over much of its range. Some captive-bred specimens are available.

Captive Breeding: This hardy species is quite choosy about its breeding waters. A deep (minimum 12 inches), well-planted aquarium or pond is necessary, as is a strict two to three months of hibernation. Some 250 eggs are deposited from March to July, females showing a preference for strips of thin plastic or wide-leafed water weeds rather than elodea. Larvae attain 35 mm before metamorphosis three months after hatching. Both adults and young feed voraciously and are protected by a milky poison.

Danube Crested Newt *(Triturus dobrogicus*)

Distribution: Danube Basin of central Europe.

Length: 11 to 15 cm (4.5 to 6 in).

Description: The smallest and most slender crested newt. Breeding males exhibit a low but denticulated crest. The belly and sides (even of the tail) tend to be more orange than brown, even red. A pearly tail stripe is evident but has a bluish tinge, while the yellow vertebral stripe is absent in juveniles and females.

Captive Care: This is a species of lowland woods and open grasslands in the vicinity of water. It can tolerate fairly high temperatures (to 75°F, 24°C) but prefers 64°F (18°C). Only 120 to 150 eggs are produced from February to July.

A breeding male Danube Crested Newt, *Triturus dobrogicus*. Photo: K.-D. Kuehnel.

Caucasian Crested Newt (*Triturus karelini*)

Distribution: Northern Turkey and the western Caucasus region in mountains.

Length: 14 to 21 cm (5.5 to 8.5 in).

Description: The most robust crested newt. The breeding male has a low and less denticulated crest than the other species and the belly is pale orange or yellow. The sides of the throat are mottled with black and white.

Captive Breeding: Females produce between 200 and 450 eggs from December to May. The larvae develop quickly, transforming into 4-cm newtlets within ten weeks.

Emperor (Mandarin) Newt (*Tylototriton verrucosus*)

Distribution: Yunnan Mountains of southwestern China west into India, south into Burma, and east to Thailand and Vietnam in the mountains.

Length: 16 to 20 cm (6.5 to 8 in).

Description: An attractive member of a widespread Asian genus that is closely related to the genus *Pleurodeles*. The broad and flattened body has a broad, bony orange/yellow vertebral ridge and a series of enlarged orange/yellow tubercles along the flanks into which the rib ends protrude and where toxins are produced. The tail, limbs, and head are an orange or orange-brown, while the sides are black or a purple-brown. Large parotoid glands are evident on the head.

Availability: An increasingly popular terrarium subject that is exported from Burma and Thailand in large numbers, so large that it may soon become extinct. Increased captive breeding must be the answer to reducing this unnecessary pressure and assuring future supplies.

Captive Care: Emperor Newts are maintained in a similar

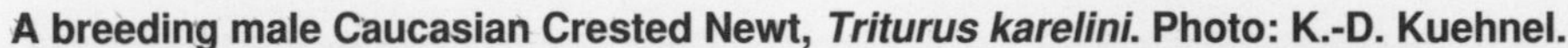

A breeding male Caucasian Crested Newt, *Triturus karelini*. Photo: K.-D. Kuehnel.

One of the most striking newt imports of recent years is the Emperor, Mandarin, or Crocodile Newt, *Tylototriton verrucosus*. Photo: K. T. Nemuras.

So far the majority of Emperor Newts, *Tylototriton verrucosus*, offered for sale have been wild-caught imports, but it appears that wild populations are nearly depleted. If not captive-bred in commercial quantities, this newt may disappear from the hobby. Photo: A. Norman.

manner to ambystomatids, for outside the breeding season they are largely terrestrial. Their lively behavior and gregarious nature make them interesting captives, with a large terrarium capable of housing four to six adults being required. Plenty of damp hiding places should be arranged on a moss or foam base, and a large water bowl containing 2 or 3 inches of cool, fresh water must be available. Temperatures near 65°F (18°C) are preferred. Food consists of the usual invertebrates, but snails are also taken and crushed between the powerful jaws.

Sexual Differences: Females are considerably larger, often by 2 to 4 cm.

Captive Breeding: Hibernation for four to eight weeks will induce breeding in cool (55°F, 13°C), shallow water from February onward. Males are quite aggressive toward each other. After mating, females deposit 75 to 160 eggs singly on aquatic vegetation, each 2.2 mm in diameter. Larvae hatch in four days but are slow growing and will not tolerate warm waters with poor oxygen content. They feed mainly on water crustaceans and later on each other. Metamorphosis occurs in 8 to 11 months, when they are 5 cm long.

FAMILY AMPHIUMIDAE: THE AMPHIUMAS

Two-toed Amphiuma (*Amphiuma means*)

Distribution: The coastal plain of the southeastern U.S.A.

Length: 50 to 110 cm (20 to 43 in).

Description: Amphiumas are strange, snake-like salamanders comprising only three species. This species has the long, thick, rounded body and short tail typical of the family. It is uniform dark gray on the back, gradually fading into a lighter gray on the belly. The head ends in a flattened snout rather like a duck's bill, while the eyes are minuscule and poorly functional. No external gills are present, but gill slits are visible just behind the head. The common name is derived from the four tiny, almost vestigial limbs, each of which has just two toes.

Availability: Not as popular as other aquatic amphibians due to their pugnacious disposition and nocturnal habits, as well as lack of color. Sometimes sold in

Close-up of a Two-toed Amphiuma, *Amphiuma means*. Notice the tiny two-toed foot behind the head. The legs are virtually useless remnants that often cannot even touch the ground. Fighting amphiumas often grab an opponent's leg and literally twist it off. Photo: R. D. Bartlett.

pet shops, but more available from biological supply companies (the blood cells are exceptionally large, making this a popular physiology laboratory animal).

Captive Care: A surprisingly easy species to maintain in a relatively large (at least 36 inches) and deep (20 inches or more) aquarium containing slightly acidic water at around pH 5.5 to 6. Supplementary oxygenation and filtration prove beneficial, especially at the preferred water temperature of 72°F (22°C), but are not essential. As with sirens and hellbenders, live rooted water plants are unlikely to last, but ensure plenty of hiding places constructed with rocks (not limestone) to create nooks and caves are present. Too many specimens residing in one aquarium may result in fighting and death. Even when just two are kept together, sufficient food consisting of earthworms, mollusks, small fishes, raw meat, and even canned dog food must be offered to reduce aggression. Capturing an amphiuma to clean out the aquarium can be tricky even with the aid of a fishing net because they possess sharp teeth capable of inflicting a nasty bite. Swiftly grasping the back of the head while using soft leather gloves and arm protection is advisable.

The small *Amphiuma pholeter*, the One-toed Amphiuma, was not named until 1964. It is specialized to live in deep muck beds near cypress swamps in Florida and adjacent areas. Photo: R. D. Bartlett.

Though sometimes kept because they are the only members of their family and thus a novelty, amphiumas (here the Three-toed, *Amphiuma tridactylum*) are drab, aggressive animals that find little favor with hobbyists. Photo: P. Freed.

Sexual Differences: Differences are few, with adult females sometimes being longer and more robust than males.

Captive Breeding: Breeding is feasible only in a large setup where the female is able to construct a nest without interference from other specimens and the hobbyist. Mating follows an extended cool period of three to five weeks at 55°F (13°C). The nest usually is a deep depression in mud or gravel. Fertilization is internal after the male places a spermatophore in her cloaca. The female releases 30 to 180 very large (8 mm) eggs in a mass like pearls on a string. She guards her nest aggressively, coiling around the eggs until they hatch 160 to 200 days later. The resultant larvae are 4 to 7 cm in length (depending on egg incubation time), black above, olive below, and have large, red feathery gills. Tubifex worms and daphnia are devoured in great quantities until the larvae achieve the 10– to 13-cm juvenile stage four to six weeks later. Larvae and juveniles are best separated from the adults into shallower aquaria.

Longevity: Twelve years, sometimes longer.

FAMILY PROTEIDAE: THE OLM AND WATERDOGS

Two subfamilies, each with a single genus, are known. The genus *Proteus* of the subfamily Proteinae consists of only the European Olm (*Proteus anguinus*), a unique and strictly protected species from caves of Yugoslavia. It is a permanent larva, lacks most coloration (though pale tan spots and stripes have been recorded), and has only two toes on the hind feet. In contrast, the subfamily Necturinae of North America contains the waterdogs and mudpuppies, often seen in captivity.

Mudpuppy (*Necturus maculosus*)

Distribution: Ranges over the Great Lakes area of northern U.S.A. and southern Canada south into the lower Mississippi River valley.

Length: 20 to 35 cm (8 to 14 in).

Description: Mudpuppies and waterdogs form an aquatic genus of about five species that have a permanently neotenous (larva-like) body form. The Mudpuppy is the largest species and is quite a robust salamander with well-developed limbs and a short, laterally

Mudpuppies, *Necturus maculosus*, make interesting and attractive additions to the aquarium. Small specimens have two golden stripes on the back and look quite different from adults. Photo: K. T. Nemuras.

The Alabama Waterdog, *Necturus alabamensis*, is one of several spotted southern *Necturus* that occasionally are available. All are rather small and make interesting aquarium animals. Photo: R. D. Bartlett.

flattened tail on a somewhat cylindrical or flattened trunk. The body color is gray or brown with a scattering of dark blotches. Deep red feathery gills are most prominent in still, stagnant ponds, tending to become paler and smaller in highly oxygenated waters.

Availability: This and the smaller Alabama Waterdog (*N. alabamensis*) are collected in large numbers throughout their range and shipped all over the world, though many are destined for physiology and anatomy laboratories.

Captive Care: Mudpuppies can be kept in setups based on that of the family Sirenidae or the Axolotl, although oxygenation can be slightly reduced to encourage growth of the attractive feathery gills (but remember that this may stress the salamander). River sand is the favored substrate. A common mistake among hobbyists where *Necturus maculosus* is concerned is keeping the water too warm. About 55 to 60°F (13 to 16°C) must be the upper limit, otherwise loss of appetite and stress are likely. Species that have more southern ranges can be kept at somewhat higher temperatures, but even they usually come from cool, flowing rivers and streams. Mudpuppies will eat almost any small water animal, from shrimp and crayfish to snails and small fishes, as well as worms and bloodworms.

Sexual Differences: There are no obvious differences except during breeding, when females are more rotund.

Captive Breeding: Breeding will not occur in warm water or if hibernation at 38°F (4°C) is omitted. Mating is seen in autumn, after which the female stores the spermatophores until the following spring, when she constructs a small hollow mound from vegetation, twigs, and detritus. She then attaches around 150, 5-mm eggs to its inner roof and guards the nest until the 20-mm larvae hatch 8 to 12 weeks later. Larvae are olive brown with two broad yellowish stripes on the back. They are very adept at capturing insects that fall onto the water surface as well as the usual small crustaceans and aquatic insect larvae. Adults will devour larvae given the chance, so separate most to rearing tanks. Maturity is slow to be reached, sometimes taking five or six years. Generally speaking, captive-bred Mudpuppies are far more tolerant of captive conditions than are wild-caught specimens.

Longevity: Ten to 16 years.

The African Clawed Frog, *Xenopus laevis*. Though other species of the genus occasionally become available, this is the only species that most hobbyists see. Photo: G. Dibley.

Order Anura: The Frogs and Toads

The protruding eyes set high on the head and far forward on the snout of *Xenopus laevis* are typical adaptations of frogs that spend much of their time loafing just below the water's surface. Photo: Dr. J. P. Bogart.

FAMILY PIPIDAE: THE TONGUELESS FROGS

This family comprises some of the most popularly kept and bizarre frogs. All species are almost entirely aquatic and are distributed in generally warmer climates.

African Clawed Frog (*Xenopus laevis*)

Distribution: Southern and central Africa. Small colonies have been established throughout the world, even in western Europe, and may be very destructive of native aquatic animals. In California they have become a menace.

Length: 7.5 to 14 cm (3 to 5.5 in).

Description: A large, plump frog with powerful hind limbs equipped with well-developed webbed feet to aid swimming. The main purpose of the smaller, fairly rigid front limbs is to stir up mud while looking for prey and also to compensate for the absence of the tongue by juggling food into the wide mouth. The eyes are set on top of the head, enabling the frog to keep watch for surface predators. The dorsal color ranges from a uniform dark gray to a reticulate pattern of brown or olive. The flanks possess a series of crisscross tubercles, and the cream or gray-white undersides contrast sharply with the dorsum. The common name is derived from the hard claws on the toes of the hind feet. Tadpoles are nearly transparent and have two long barbels extending from the corners of the mouth.

Availability: Clawed frogs are among the most common amphibian pets and are available from virtually all tropical fish outlets unless prohibited by local laws.

Captive Care: A very tolerant amphibian species able to withstand near-freezing temperatures and, in the case of my own specimens, being nearly "boiled alive" at 132°F when an aquarium heater thermostat broke down! For these reasons clawed frogs should never be released intentionally into the wild, where they could easily survive to reproduce and devastate native amphibian populations. Temperatures of around 70 to 78°F (21 to 26°C) should be maintained (use a thermostatic water heater) in an aquarium containing 10 to 16 inches of slightly acidic water (pH 5.7) along with a base of river sand or fine gravel. Rocks and lumps of bogwood/weighted driftwood will enhance the aquarium's overall appearance, although very few plants will be able to withstand the frog's destructive food searching habits. A tight-fitting (but well ventilated) lid must be present because *Xenopus* are prone to wander. A flat rock protruding out of water, onto which is directed a 40-watt spot lamp, should be provided and will be frequented as a basking spot for a few minutes at a time, especially after a heavy feeding session. Unless the whole aquarium is cleaned out fortnightly, undergravel filtration is necessary to prevent the build

Pipids in general (and *Xenopus laevis* in particular) have a rather primitive style of amplexus in which the male holds the female just in front of the hind legs rather than by the front legs. Clawed frogs have an elaborate egg-laying behavior. Photo: R. Zukal.

A rather nicely patterned female African Clawed Frog, *Xenopus laevis*, showing not only one of the large claws on the hind foot, but the ring of tubercles around the cloaca typical of breeding females. Photo: G. Dibley.

up of biological toxins. In addition, allowing only one adult pair to a 24– to 36-inch tank will restrict a rapid increase in such toxins. Clawed frogs have a prodigious appetite, consuming anything edible, and obesity can cause problems. Restrict feeding with earthworms, fish, or strips of fish and raw meat to twice weekly, although a few amphipods or isopods can be offered daily to keep them content.

Sexual Differences: Adult females are considerably larger than males and have papillae (skin protrusions) around the cloaca.

Captive Breeding: Breeding is easily induced with commercially available hormonal kits, but preferably this and other *Xenopus* species should be allowed to reproduce naturally, often with considerable success. Gradually decreasing water levels to a minimum of 5 inches and increasing water temperatures to 85°F (30°C) will encourage females to develop eggs. The water is suddenly increased to its previous level with cold water (50°F, 10°C) or by adding ice cubes at regular intervals to simulate flooding. As a result, male courtship activity becomes frenetic, with limb quivering being most apparent when the male is approached by another clawed frog. Only when the female is ripe with eggs will she allow the male to clasp her. To scatter her spawn over a wide area the female, with the male now in lumbar amplexus, swims in looping somersaults. Every so often she releases 4 to 12 eggs, which the male sprays with his sperm. A total of 500 to 600 eggs is laid to settle between gravel and rocks on the bottom. It probably is easier to remove the adults rather than the eggs, at least until the tadpoles are large enough to be captured. In their early stages of development up to 80% of the fish fry-like tadpoles may succumb, with those that survive growing quickly on a diet of suspended food particles. Several drops of liquid fish fry food added to the water daily will aid growth. Metamorphosis into 2-cm miniature clawed frogs is reached 8 to 12 weeks later. Larger individuals may devour their smaller compatriots. Maturity can be achieved in the second year.

Longevity: Ten to 15 years, sometimes longer.

Mueller's Clawed Frog (*Xenopus muelleri*)

Distribution: Western and central Africa in any still or slow-flowing unpolluted freshwater.

Length: 5.2 to 7.2 cm (2 to 3 in).

Description: Less robust than *Xenopus laevis*. The back is olive-green to light brown. A pair of sensory tentacles is visible just below the eyes (more prominent than in *X. laevis*).

Captive Care: This species is not overly tolerant of low temperatures, with 74 to 84°F (25 to 29°C) being favored. The water

In many pet shops it is easier to purchase a young albino African Clawed Frog, *Xenopus laevis*, than one with regular pigmentation. Albinos are bred in fairly large numbers for the pet trade, often in the same ponds as tropical fishes. Photo: M. Smith.

This interesting African clawed frog, *Xenopus* species, is very unusual in having three hind legs. Extra limbs are not really that unusual in frogs, and often they merely slow the animal down a bit and have little negative impact. Such freaks are of interest to many collectors. Photo: M. Smith.

should be about 8 to 16 inches deep, with plenty of rocks and a good aeration/filtration system. Both young and adults feed avidly on fish, either alive or chopped. Breeding is as for *X. laevis*, although fewer eggs are produced, usually in the region of 200 to 350.

Similar Species: *Xenopus* is a complex genus in which it is hard to distinguish many of the species without doing studies of chromosomes and mating calls. The Platanna, *Xenopus tropicalis*, of slow-moving jungle rivers in western Africa, is some 5 to 7.5 cm (2 to 3 in) long and a bit more slender than typical *X. laevis*. It can tolerate a fairly wide temperature range, but a constant 78°F (26°C) is recommended. Breeding occurs throughout the year.

Banded Clawed Frog (*Xenopus borealis*)

Distribution: Eastern and central southern Africa in slow-moving rivers that dry up in summer to leave isolated ponds.

Length: 6 to 9 cm (2.5 to 3.5 in).

Captive Care: Similar to *Xenopus laevis* in general appearance except for a tendency to have indistinct bands over the back, this species can stand very high water temperatures. It even can stand long periods on dry land, when it searches for water after its pond dries up. The

The species of *Xenopus* look much alike externally, enough that most hobbyists would think they all were the same species. This *Xenopus tropicalis*, for instance, shows no obvious distinctions from *X. laevis*, but internally if differs enough to be placed by some workers in a separate genus, *Silurana*. Photo: Dr. J. P. Bogart.

Banded Clawed Frog enjoys hunting for food in dense vegetation, so the aquarium should be heavily planted (expect it to be in constant disarray, however).

Captive Breeding: Breeding occurs when there is a drop in temperature coupled with an increase of fresh water and food. Up to 1000 eggs only 1.2 mm in diameter are laid and attached to plants and rocks. These hatch in three days at a temperature of 80°F (27°C). Tadpoles develop very long tentacles or feelers, which may persist in the metamorphosed specimens for an extended period.

Dwarf Clawed Frog (*Hymenochirus boettgeri*)

Distribution: Western Africa.

Length: 2.3 to 4.5 cm (1 to 2 in).

Description: A small frog with a flattened, stream-lined body, strong hind limbs, and webbed clawed feet. The back is covered in spiny tubercles and patterned in brown with many dark spots. The eyes tend to be more to the side than in smooth-skinned *Xenopus*.

Availability: Obtainable from most pet shops, especially during spring/summer.

Captive Care: Dwarf Clawed Frogs are maintained in the setup described for *Xenopus*, but because of their smaller size, well-rooted tropical water plants can be grown in the preferred 7 to 10 inches water depth. These frogs are susceptible to cooler temperatures, with 70°F (21°C) being the minimum and 77°F (25°C) preferable. Groups of four to eight individuals can be maintained in a 24-inch aquarium incorporating plenty of rocky hiding places. Prey consists of small water crustaceans, tubifex, bloodworms, and larger fish fry.

Sexual Differences: Females appear plumper than males when ready to lay.

Captive Breeding: Easily accomplished by gradually draining the water level to around 3 inches over a period of two to four weeks before suddenly increasing it with warmer water so that the temperature jumps and remains at 82 to 85°F (28 to 30°C) for several weeks. Once the female is ripe with eggs, the male will clasp her in lumbar amplexus and begin a spawning "dance" similar to that of *Xenopus*. The male rhythmically squeezes her to induce egg laying so that he can synchronize the release of his sperm. As many as 750 eggs are scattered throughout the aquarium. Remove the adults immediately to prevent them from eating the eggs. After hatching two to six days later, the 4–mm tadpoles are immediately carnivorous, feeding on microscopic protozoans and other infusoria, gradually progressing to larger aquatic invertebrates. They metamorphose six weeks later and are only 12 to 14 mm in length.

Other Species: *Hymenochirus curtipes* from the lower Congo

This dwarf clawed frog, *Hymenochirus* species, clearly shows some of the features of the genus, including the eyes set to the side of the head and the obvious webs between the toes. Photo: A. Norman.

A pair of *Hymenochirus* during mating. Like larger clawed frogs, they perform the same somersault leading to eggs being laid at the surface of the water, but their eggs are not adhesive and become spread through the aquarium. Photo: R. Zukal.

Basin of western Africa is virtually identical to *Hymenochirus boettgeri* but has a more finely granulated skin and somewhat shorter hind legs (hard to determine). It can be kept like *H. boettgeri*. Give it a temperature of 68 to 80°F (20 to 27°C). Around 150 eggs are produced. Hatchling tadpoles are carnivores, and by the time they mature they are enjoying tubifex worms and bloodworms.

Surinam Toad *(Pipa pipa)*

Distribution: Slow-moving river systems of northern South America.

Length: 12 to 14 cm (5 to 5.5 in), occasionally 18 cm (7 in).

Description: A curious looking toad with an extremely flattened body and triangular head containing tiny eyes that see so poorly that the frog relies on touch via highly sensitive star-shaped appendages on the fingers

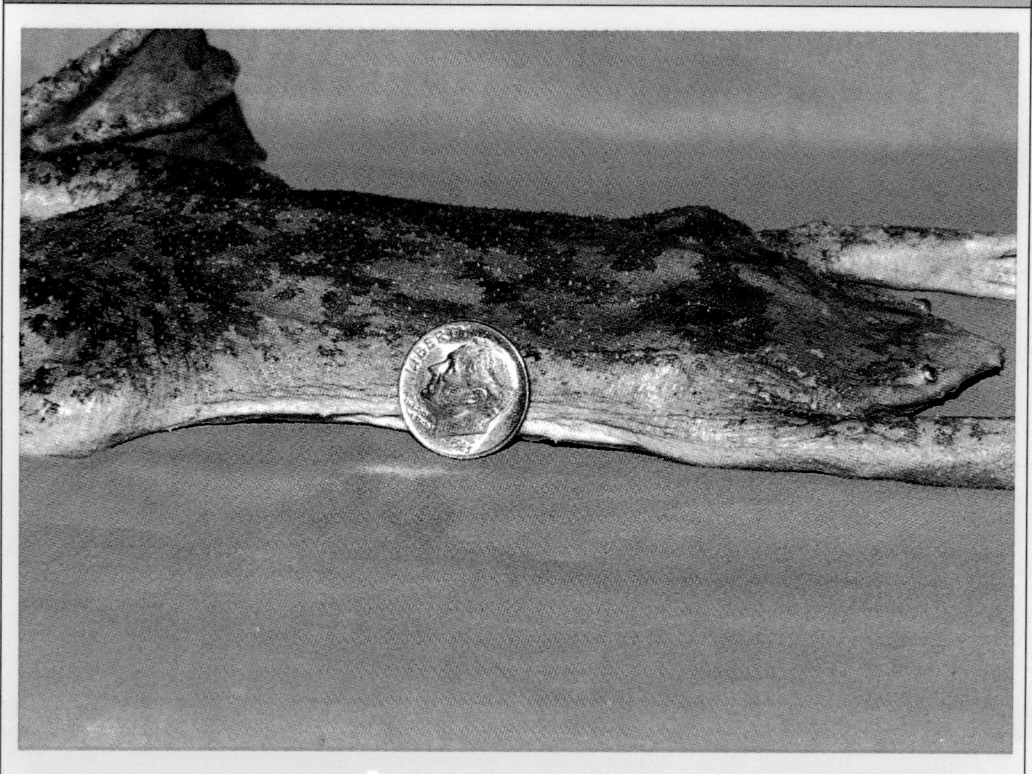

There can be little doubt that *Pipa pipa*, the Surinam Toad, is one of the most bizarre living frogs. The greatly flattened body, odd sensory projections on the head, and split fingertips truly make it unique. Photos: W. P. Mara.

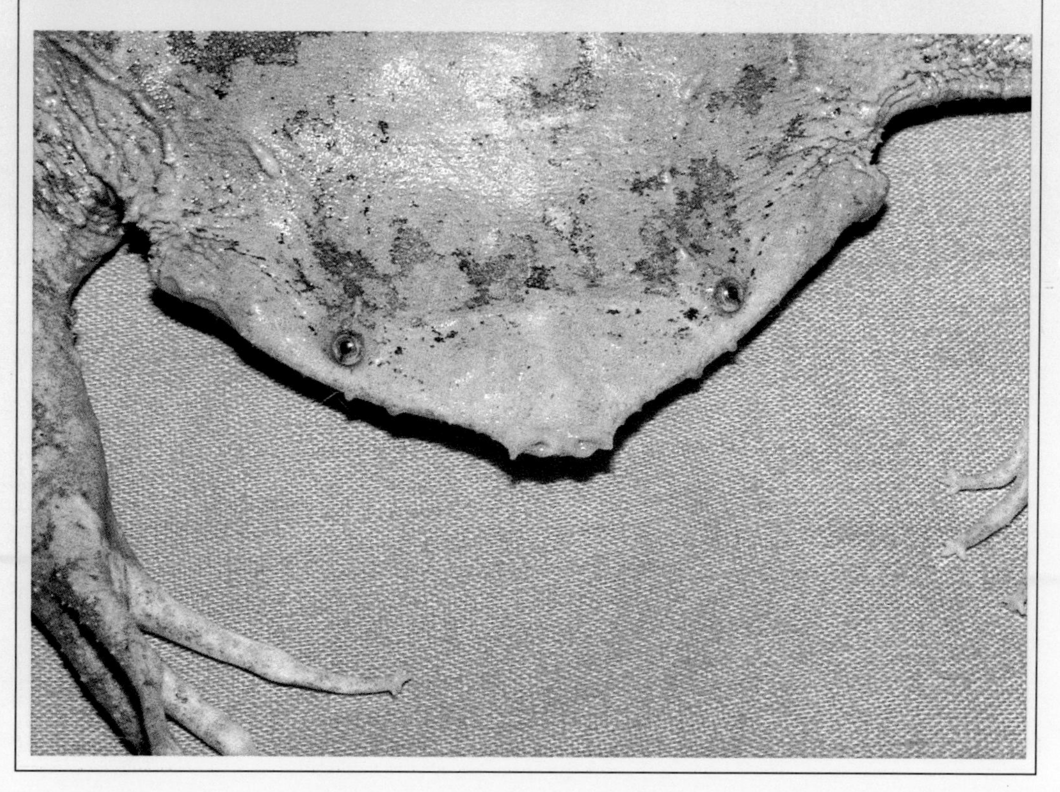

of the front feet. The blue-gray or brown back is covered with many cream or light gray nodules, and the creamy white underside is smooth. The muscular hind limbs have wide webbed feet aiding swift propulsion through water.

Availability: Occasionally offered as wild-caught (few captive-bred) specimens.

Captive Care: A setup in line with that for *Xenopus* is suitable, although a larger aquarium containing around 12 to 20 inches of water and heated to a temperature of 80°F (27°C) is closer to ideal. These creatures inhabit muddy river beds, so lighting should be subdued. Undergravel filtration and aeration are essential. Food ranges from aquatic crustaceans, earthworms, and fishes to small pieces of raw meat.

Sexual Differences: The female has an extensible, tubular ovipositor (an egg-laying organ protruding from the cloaca), while the male may emit a click-like mating call.

Captive Breeding: The bizarre breeding behavior of Surinam Toads occurs less readily than in other pipids but sometimes is stimulated following the cooling of the water by 4 to 8°F (2 to 5°C) for several days before being increased to around 85°F (30°C) along with an increase in crustacean food. Eggs form quickly in the female's ovaries,

Relatively few Surinam Toads, *Pipa pipa*, are imported for the terrarium hobby, and almost all are quickly sold to enthusiasts. It is a real pity that these frogs are so hard to breed. Photo: A. Norman.

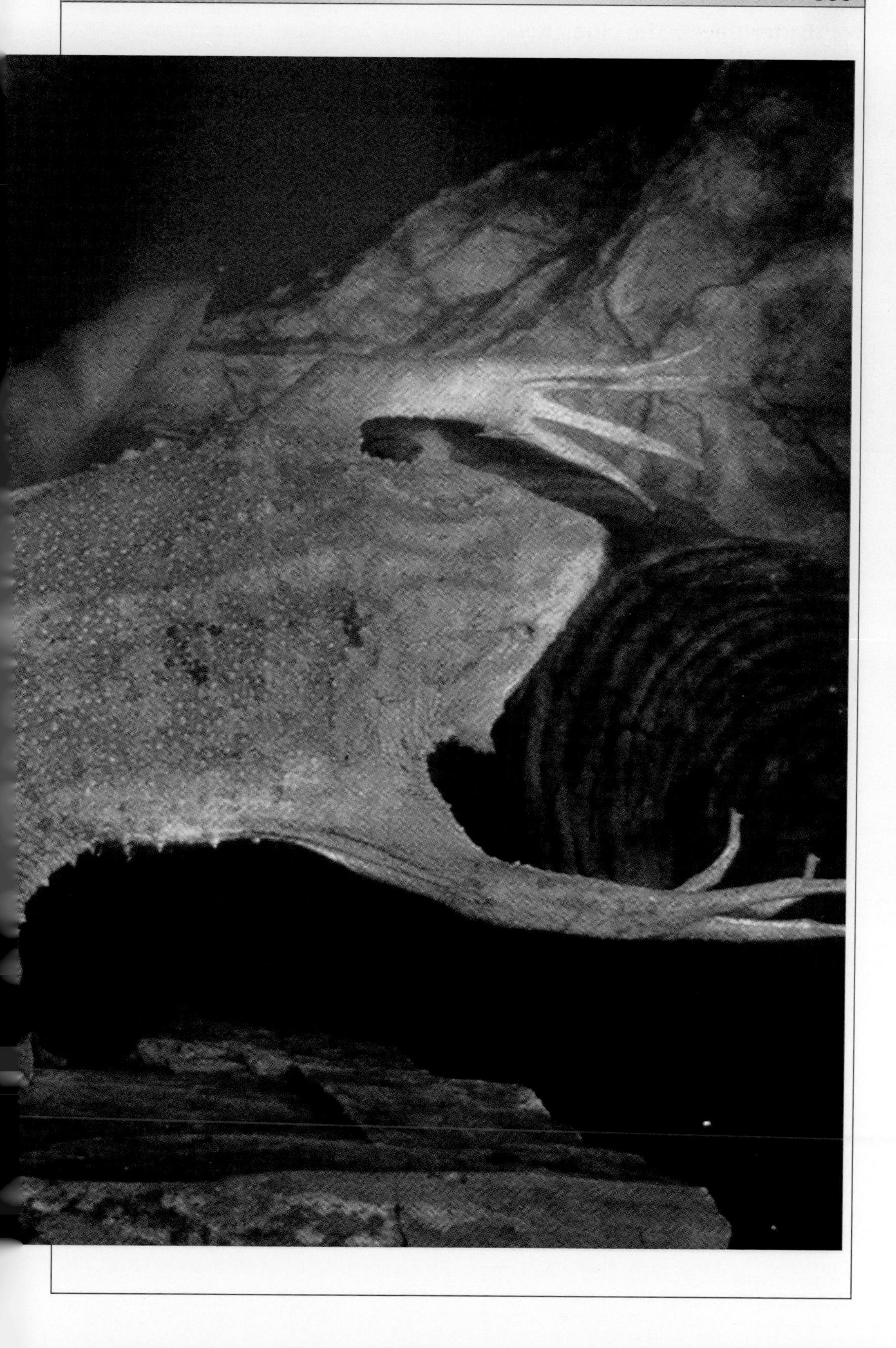

and after the male secures a rather violent clasp around her waist, the pair swims off in somersaults. At this point the female's back is already swelling and she extends her ovipositor so that it is close to the male's cloaca. He squeezes her to encourage egg-laying. On fertilizing each clump of five to ten eggs, the male maneuvers the female into a position so that each egg adheres to her back. After repeating this up to ten times the pair separates, leaving each egg bedded down into chambers located all over her back. Full egg and larval development takes place within these chambers, and after 12 to 18 weeks the 15-mm toadlets appear. Adults will undoubtedly eat them, so they are best removed into a well-oxygenated and filtered aquarium and given plenty of daphnia, aquatic worms, and fish fry.

Like other pipids, *Pipa pipa* lays eggs during a mating swim involving a somersault. Photo: K. Lucas.

Dwarf Surinam Toad (*Pipa parva*)

Distribution: Colombia and Venezuela.

Length: 3.7 to 4.5 cm (1.5 to 2 in).

Description: A tiny, not so flat version of the Surinam Toad with short tubercles at the tips of the fingers.

Captive Care: This occasionally available species (and its almost identical southern relative *P. carvalhoi*) likes a medium-sized aquarium with about 12 to 16 inches of clean, well-aerated water at a neutral pH and a temperature of 74 to 84°F (24 to 29°C). It tends to be very secretive and mainly nocturnal.

Captive Breeding: Breeding follows the basic pattern for the genus, but instead of fully formed toadlets emerging from pockets on the mother's back, well-developed tadpoles instead appear. These must be removed to a separate tank swiftly to prevent cannibalism.

FAMILY DISCOGLOSSIDAE: THE DISC-TONGUED FROGS

The family name Discoglossidae refers to the disc-shaped tongue that is fixed toward the back of the mouth and cannot be extended. Hence, feeding seems to be a clumsy affair with prey stuffed into the mouth using the fore limbs. Genera within this popularly-kept but small family differ greatly in appearance and habits.

Western Midwife Toad (*Alytes obstetricans*)

Distribution: Western Europe.

Length: 2.6 to 4.5 cm (1 to 2 in).

Description: A small, plump toad ranging from green-brown to light gray in color. The short hind legs and back are covered with many rounded tubercles. The eyes are large, with vertically slit pupils, signifying that these toads are nocturnal.

Availability: Only occasionally available because of its secretive nature in the wild. Like many European anurans, it is not bred on a commercial scale.

Captive Care: These odd anurans require a moderately moist woodland terrarium with a shallow water dish and plenty of hiding places. Adult toads dislike heat, with a temperature of 64 to 70°F (18 to 21°C) being preferred; lighting should be subdued. The terrarium can be briefly misted each evening, but the substrate

The Western Midwife Toad, *Alytes obstetricans*, often assumes a delicate silvery tone. Its bizarre breeding habits have made it a popular frog with European hobbyists. Photo: M. Staniszewski.

should not become saturated. Food consists of small crickets, sweepings, and waxworms liberally dusted with a multivitamin powder. Fast prey needs to be cooled down in a refrigerator for several minutes because Western Midwife Toads are fairly sluggish. This species makes an ideal subject for both the outdoor amphibiary and the unheated greenhouse.

Sexual Differences: Adult males are less rounded and slightly smaller than females, and in the breeding season they give a resonant high-pitched "coo coo" call lasting up to 30 seconds. Females also have a broader head.

Captive Breeding: Breeding is possible in the terrarium but is more likely to occur in the outdoor amphibiary. It commences in mid-spring after a hibernation period of four to eight weeks in a cool garage or refrigerator at 40°F (5°C). On warming up they require copious amounts of food for several weeks, during which the male begins calling during the evening. Amplexus is terrestrial and nocturnal, with the male clasping the female just behind her fore limbs. She may carry the male for up to a week before laying 15 to 50 large (3.5 mm) eggs each with a hard, semi-permeable membrane and attached to each other in a long string. The male both fertilizes the eggs as they appear and twines the string around his hind limbs, although

A female Western Midwife Toad, *Alytes obstetricans*. Sexes in this species are difficult to distinguish by structure, so rely on the call of the male to provide accurate sexing. Photo: M. Staniszewski.

The tadpole (above) and metamorphosing toadlet of the Western Midwife Toad, *Alytes obstetricans*. Photos: M. P. & C. Piednoir.

this may not always be the case in captivity, with the clutch sometimes being found loose under moss or a damp rock. If carried, the male frequently enters a shallow water dish to moisten them until 8 to 12 weeks later, when he disposes of them in water. They should be removed to a small aquarium containing 4 inches of unheated, well-planted water. The hard shells take several hours to disintegrate, finally releasing 2.5-cm tadpoles. These slow-growing tads attain a size of 5.5 cm in 12 to 16 weeks. Prior to metamorphosis, the water level should be lowered to around an inch so that the relatively large (2 cm) toadlets do not drown. Transfer those showing only remnants of the tail to a small terrarium containing moss. In their first year they are best overwintered at slightly higher temperatures (70°F, 21°C) than the adults. They reach 3.5 cm after 12 months.

Longevity: Eight to 15 years.

Similar Species: The Iberian Midwife (*A. cisternasii*) is less frequently available, slightly smaller, and more rust or tan colored. It prefers slightly drier and more sandy habitats. The Mallorcan Midwife Toad (*A. muletensis*) was described only in 1977 and is strictly protected.

Yellow-bellied Toad (*Bombina variegata variegata*)

Additional Subspecies: Yugoslavian Yellow-bellied Toad (*B. v. kolombatovici*); Italian (*B. v.*

A pair of Western Midwife Toads, *Alytes obstetricans*. The male is carrying a string of eggs. Photo: H. Heusser.

pachypus); Balkan (*B. v. scabra*).

Distribution: Western, central, and southern mainland Europe except the Iberian Peninsula.

Length: 3 to 4.5 cm (1 to 2 in).

Description: A small, plump, semi–aquatic species with a dark gray or black dorsum that is heavily covered in small, rounded tubercles. Its most striking feature is the yellow and black belly and undersides of the limbs, which it will reveal by concavely arching its back and flipping up its limbs to indicate its poisonous nature or occasionally by completely turning over when molested. A toxic milky secretion is exuded from pores over the whole body. It has a rounded snout and prominent eyes with heart-shaped pupils. The hind feet show well-developed webbing. Subspecies differ in size and amount of yellow coloration: *B. v. kolombatovici* occasionally grows to 5.5 cm, while *B. v. scabra* is the smallest form and has a high proportion of black on its belly. The belly of *B. v. pachypus* may be completely yellow or orange-yellow and have sporadic small white or blue spots.

Availability: The nominate and Italian subspecies frequently are offered by dealers.

Captive Care: This is an easy species to maintain in groups numbering 8 to 12 in a medium-sized, semi–aquatic aquarium setup where their diurnal habits make them interesting captives. Six to 12 inches of water at 72 to 78°F (22 to 26°C) and containing plenty of floating pond plants such as frog-bit and miniature lilies is preferred, therefore good lighting is required. The land part should be kept moist, and during spring and summer a 40W spot lamp can be directed onto one area, creating a "hot spot" beneath which these heliotherms will spend many hours basking. For such a small animal they consume large amounts of food, with most soft-bodied invertebrates being devoured. This species is an excellent subject for the unheated greenhouse amphibiary.

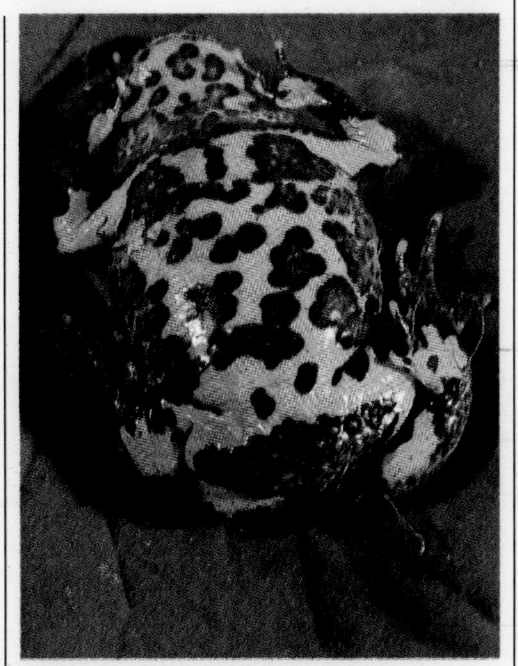

Ventral view of a Yellow-bellied Toad, *Bombina variegata*. When greatly disturbed, these frogs flip over and freeze in a position showing the brightly colored belly. Photo: L. Wischnath.

Sexual Differences: Males are smaller than females, and horny nuptial pads on the toes and underside of each fore limb are present during the breeding season.

Views of *Bombina variegata kolombatovici*, a subspecies of the Yellow-bellied Toad coming from the Balkan area. This form often is considered to be a full species. Photos: M. Staniszewski.

Captive Breeding: Breeding occurs regularly in captivity as long as these toads are given a winter rest at 40°F (5°C) for 8 to 16 weeks. After hibernation they may within weeks breed indoors in heated accommodations, but outdoors they will spend the first few months feeding until temperatures rise, usually during early summer. Males announce the start of courtship with their musical "poo-poo" call, which is quite low due to the absence of external vocal sacs. Heavily spraying the aquarium or enclosure with warm water before dark will induce males to vocally compete with each other and ultimately will result in a successful pairing, with the loudest or strongest male securing a female in lumbar amplexus. Eventually over a period of one to eight hours the female disperses between 25 and 150, 2-mm cream-colored eggs either singly or in small clumps attached to submerged plants near the water surface. Eggs can be left *in situ*, with hatching occurring two to six days later. Tadpoles should be kept at 65 to 75°F (18 to 24°C) and will gradually turn black with a prominent cream spiracle forming on the belly. They feed voraciously on vegetable matter, fish pellets, and raw red meat, and after seven to nine weeks leave the water as 12– to 15-mm toadlets. These are best raised individually in plastic sweater boxes containing half an inch or less of water and a rock and given a diet of aphids, fruitflies, and hatchling crickets. Initially the belly is blotched in gray and cream, but yellow pigment soon becomes evident. Adults may pair several times during the summer.

Longevity: Ten to 18 years.

European Fire-bellied Toad (*Bombina bombina*)

Distribution: Eastern Europe from the Baltic to central Bulgaria.

Length: 3.8 to 5.3 cm (1.5 to 2 in).

Description: Compared to *Bombina variegata*, this species has a more slender build, more pointed head, and smoother skin. The back is light or dark gray with olive to black blotches, while the belly ranges from almost yellow to orange or even vermilion with extensive black or grayish black blotches. In captivity the importance of carotene derivatives in the diet is obvious, ensuring good belly pigmentation.

A European Fire-bellied Toad, *Bombina bombina*, with a bright yellow belly. Color is not always a good character to distinguish these toads. Photo: M. Staniszewski.

Captive Breeding: Although this species makes an easy and very long-lived (14 to 20 years) aqua-terrarium subject, it has proved more difficult to breed than the other *Bombina* species. After extensive research, it has been proved in part that three factors can encourage successful captive breeding: 1) A strict and lengthy hibernation period of two to four months at 38°F (4°C). 2) A tank showing a shallow to deep gradient, containing plenty of water weed, and not too exposed (i.e., surround the aquarium with wood or black card). 3) A water temperature of above 74°F (24°C). Breeding is most likely to commence naturally in the aquarium (or, even better, a greenhouse setup) from June onward, when males start calling in a voice similar to but higher pitched than *B. variegata.* Females become excessively rotund, to the point of appearing obese. With males in close attendance, they attach single eggs or small clumps of light brown, 1.4-mm eggs to weed just below the water surface. About 80 to 140 eggs are laid. Tadpoles hatch in three to seven days and are always smaller and more slender than those of *B. variegata*, but they reach metamorphosis quicker, in six to eight weeks. Emerging toadlets are more agile than other *Bombina* and are able to catch more food and hence attain maturity very quickly. I have bred *Bombina bombina* just eight months after they left the water.

Notice the relatively less warty skin of *Bombina bombina* compared to *Bombina variegata*. This European Fire-bellied Toad has distinct round warts, each with a point. Photo: M. Staniszewski.

Though quite attractive and with strongly contrasting colors, in this Oriental Fire-bellied Toad, *Bombina orientalis*, the back is bright green but the belly is only bright orange. Photo: R. D. Bartlett.

Oriental Fire-bellied Toad (*Bombina orientalis*)

Distribution: Northern China, Korea, and adjacent Russia.

Length: 5 to 7 cm (2 to 3 in).

Description: The grass-green dorsum is the brightest of the genus and has many dark tubercles, while the belly is bright orange to red with black blotches. It is more slender than the Yellow-bellied Toad and has longer hind limbs.

Availability: Commonly offered in the form of captive-bred toadlets.

Captive Care: Prefers somewhat shallower and warmer water than the preceding species, but otherwise care is exactly the same.

Sexual Differences: Females are more rotund than males. Males have nuptial pads in the breeding season.

Captive Breeding: *Bombina orientalis* will not tolerate extended periods of temperatures less than 40°F (5°C), therefore a cool period of 50°F (10°C) should be given rather than full hibernation. Breeding can be encouraged throughout the year, with up to 300 eggs being deposited. Care of the eggs and tadpoles is similar to *Bombina variegata*, with the 2-cm newly metamorphosed toadlets reaching maturity within eight months if properly fed. Another aspect in the feeding of this species as well as *Bombina bombina* is the importance of carotenes in the diet. These give the toad its orange or red belly pigmentation and occur naturally in foods such as aphids, isopods, amphipods, daphnia, and bloodworms, which in turn derive their carotene from plants. Therefore, offering young toads either these foods or supplemented powders that include carotene derivatives is important in ensuring correct belly pigmentation; otherwise the belly may be a cream or yellow color.

Giant Fire-bellied Toad (*Bombina maxima*)

Distribution: Southwestern China and Vietnam in temperate mountain pools and streams.

Length: 6 to 8.3 cm (2.5 to 3.5 in).

Description: A large, handsome, very secretive species with a dark green and black back that is very warty. The belly is predominantly fiery red with only a small amount of black. As usual, males have nuptial pads on the inner thumbs of the front legs.

Captive Breeding: This is the least-known hobby *Bombina* (there are several other species that never reach the hobby), but it makes a vigorous aqua-terrarium subject and will breed regularly under suitable conditions. Breeding occurs mainly in winter to early spring, although under artificial

In *Bombina orientalis* the toe tips mirror the color of the belly and add an extra touch of brilliance to the frog. Photo: W. Mudrack.

This Oriental Fire-bellied Toad displays really nice coloration: bright green above and bright red below. Few specimens like this appear in the hobby today. Photo: B. Kahl.

conditions it can happen at any time of year. A large aqua-terrarium with shallow (3 to 6 inches), well-oxygenated water with much water weed should be used. Temperatures should be in the 65 to 78°F (18 to 26°C) range. As with all *Bombina*, a low-wattage spot lamp should be directed onto a rock for basking. Hibernation is not necessary, although six to eight weeks at 55°F (13°C) during autumn will invigorate courtship. Females produce 200 to 400 whitish eggs in small clumps. Tadpoles reach 6 cm (2.5 in) and develop the fiery red belly long before leaving the water. Adults are especially greedy, even devouring pinkie mice.

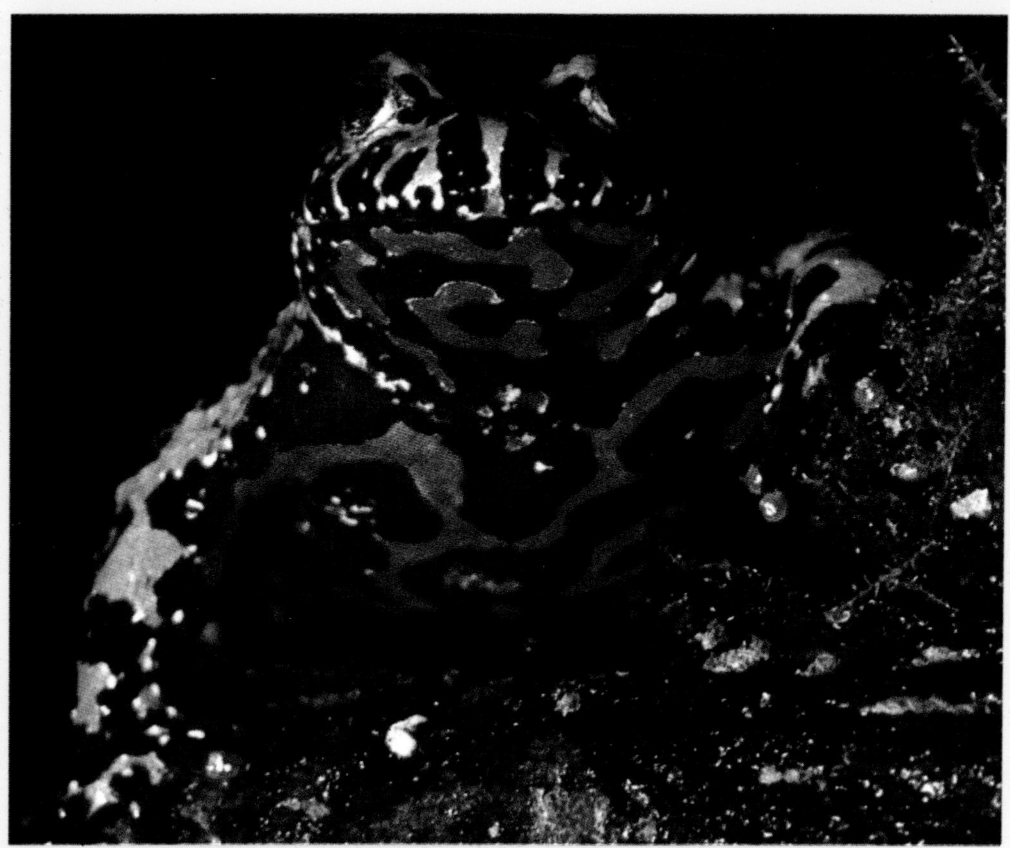

Oriental Fire-bellied Toads, *Bombina orientalis*, are fairly active frogs, though they prefer to spend much of the day loafing at the surface of the water. Photo: W. Mudrack.

European Painted Frog (*Discoglossus pictus*)

Distribution: Iberian Peninsula, southern France, Sicily, Malta, and northwestern Africa.

Length: 5 to 6.5 cm (2 to 2.5 in).

Description: Painted frogs closely resemble true frogs of the genus *Rana* in appearance but differ in the heart-shaped pupils and lack of extensible tongue. Pattern varies considerably, with stripes or blotches of varying shades of brown or gray or a single uniform color and a cream vertebral stripe.

Availability: A popular species in Europe but only occasionally available elsewhere.

Captive Care: A moist woodland/meadow terrarium should be of adequate dimensions to keep this frog from sustaining snout injuries because of its ability to leap long distances. Initially, wild-caught specimens are quite nervous and mainly nocturnal, whereas captive-bred individuals are predominantly diurnal and enjoy short periods of basking. A "shallow to deep" water bowl should be made available because, although not especially aquatic, this species is an excellent swimmer. Provide

Two patterns of the recently described Cadiz Painted Frog, *Discoglossus jeanneae*. The painted frogs occur in many small, isolated populations, several of which recently have been described as species. Photos: Dr. D. Green.

subdued lighting with a maximum temperature of 75°F (24°C) and mist the terrarium regularly to promote high humidity. The appetite is prodigious, and given the chance these frogs will devour other amphibians including smaller individuals of their own species. The normal diet ranges from most invertebrates to pinkie mice, all of which are dealt with aggressively. *Discoglossus* flourish in an unheated greenhouse.

Sexual Differences: Males have nuptial pads on the inner fore arms and webbing of the hind feet.

Captive Breeding: Pairing is spontaneous and most likely in a large aqua-terrarium or greenhouse pool after a hibernation period of six to ten weeks at 40°F (5°C). Mating commences in late spring when the water has warmed sufficiently. Around 400 to 800 eggs are deposited in a globular clump that should be transferred to a large aquarium containing 4 to 8 inches of warm, oxygenated water. Tadpoles hatch out after two to ten days and must be continually divided up to prevent high mortality. Fully grown tadpoles are small compared to other discoglossids, with froglets only 6 to 10 mm long at metamorphosis. Initial feeding can be problematic; many will succumb, but those that survive can attain maturity within 18 to 24 months.

Similar Species: The Tyrrhenian or Sardinian Painted Frog (*D. sardus*) can attain 8 cm (3 in) and is more robust, with fewer dorsal markings. It requires more acidic water with dense vegetation in which to breed.

FAMILY PELOBATIDAE: THE SPADEFOOT TOADS

Malayan Horned Frog (*Megophrys montana*)

Note: Most hobby literature uses the name *M. nasuta* for this species, but currently *nasuta* is considered a synonym or subspecies of *montana* by most herpetologists.

Distribution: Thailand and Malaysia to Indonesia, Borneo, and the Philippines.

Length: 8 to 15 cm (3 to 6 in).

Description: From above, this strange, highly desirable anuran perfectly mimics the dead leaves of the forest floors it inhabits. Its back pattern is composed of dark shades of brown and gray interlaced with vein-like ridges, while the jagged edges of the flanks, fleshy horns above the eyes, and crested appendages around the strong limbs and pointed snout all serve to further disrupt the outline. The vertically slit pupils reveal the mainly nocturnal habits of this fairly large, plump anuran.

Availability: Wild-caught specimens (usually from Malaysia) form the bulk of horned frogs offered by dealers, although several breeders in the U.S.A. are now beginning to commercially produce specimens.

Malayan Horned Frogs, *Megophrys montana*, are very carnivorous ground-dwellers. In many respects their natural history is like that of the South American *Ceratophrys*. Photo: D. Dube.

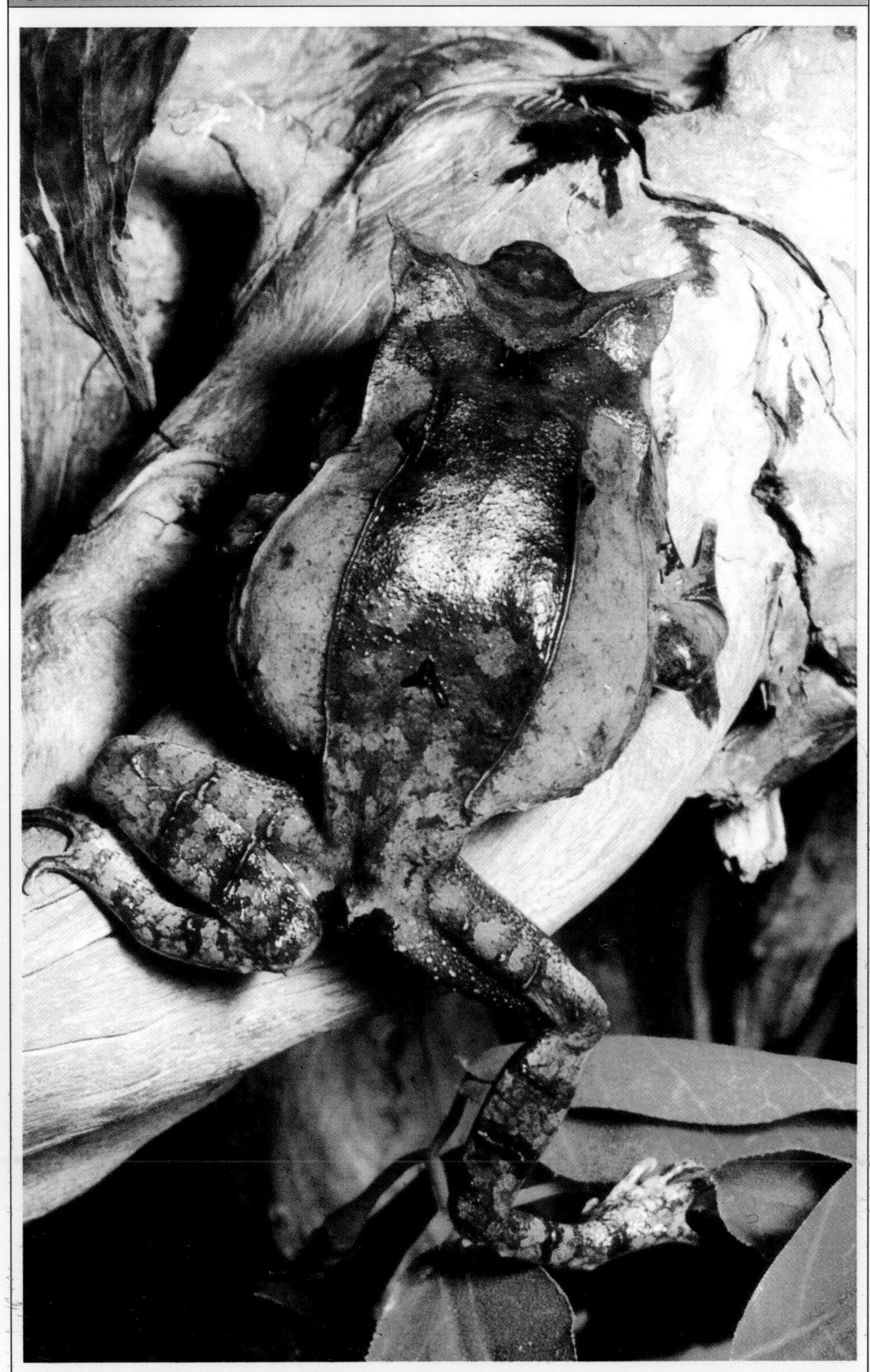

Captive Care: *Megophrys* are frogs that should be maintained in isolation except during breeding because of their cannibalistic tendencies. A 24-inch terrarium will comfortably house a single large specimen and can be furnished in a simple, hygienic manner or as a tropical forest setup including a sphagnum moss base with a layer of dead house plant leaves and a few stronger plants. More important considerations are a temperature of 78°F (26°C) and high humidity accomplished by regular misting. Caves constructed from rocks allow these relatively shy anurans to hide, while a wide, shallow water pan is advantageous in maintaining adequately high humidity. Lighting should be subdued unless live plants are grown; at night the use of a low-wattage red lamp allows the hobbyist to view these frogs's nocturnal behavior. Food includes large crickets, sub-adult locusts, earthworms, pinkie mice, and red raw meat.

Malayan Horned Frogs need high humidity and constantly warm terraria to thrive. Photo: P. Freed.

Sexual Differences: Females are considerably larger than males. Males may emit a mating call reminiscent of a loud mouse squeak.

Captive Breeding: Reproduction can sometimes be stimulated by lowering the terrarium temperature by a maximum of 10°F (about 6°C) and decreasing ambient humidity levels for a period of two to four weeks. Although *Megophrys* will not undergo full dormancy, food is refused and movement is restricted under these conditions. It must be stressed that only healthy specimens that must not have been fed for seven to ten days will tolerate such treatment. On gradually increasing temperature and humidity to slightly above the normal levels, the females may come into condition. Breeding quarters should be a separate large terrarium or warm greenhouse (either heated or used during summer) that is similar to the normal setup but with a third containing a large, shallow (2 to 4 inches) pool initially containing a river sand base and around an

In nature the horns, skin folds, and color pattern allow the Malayan Horned Frog, *Megophrys montana*, to disappear into the leaf litter, becoming virtually invisible. There it sits in wait of prey that passes within reach, a typical ambush predator. Photo: A. Norman.

Compared to a typical Malayan Horned Frog, *Megophrys montana*, below, the seldom-seen species *Megophrys (Brachytarsophrys) carinensis* from Southeast Asia has mere nubbins for horns and has short, divergent skin folds. *Megophrys* is a large and confusing genus. Photos: Top, M. J. Cox; bottom: A. Norman.

inch of boiled rain water. Several large rocks or logs should overhang the water to create niches. Needless to say, specimens should be fed well before a pair is transferred to the breeding setup; a close eye in particular must be kept on the smaller male. Courtship is initiated when the whole terrarium is heavily sprayed and the water bowl is filled with warm water. The male selects a suitable spot on one of the rocks near the water, from which he begins calling at night. If the female responds the male will clasp her in lumbar amplexus and force her into the water, where small clumps of spawn numbering around 700 eggs are attached to the water's edge or in the niches created by rocks. On hatching 12 days later the well-developed 6– to 8-mm tadpoles drop into the water. To avoid these being devoured by the adults, transfer them to an aquarium containing 2 to 5 inches of warm water that is not too vigorously oxygenated. The tadpoles are omnivorous, swimming upside down at the surface sifting detritus, microorganisms, and finely flaked goldfish food through the specialized funnel-like mouthparts. Growth and metamorphosis are completed swiftly, with the 2.5-cm toadlets emerging 25 to 40 days later. They are immediately cannibalistic at this stage and should be separated into individual rearing containers.

A rather different form (subspecies or full species ?) of Malayan Horned Frog is the short-horned *Megophrys montana aceras*, which lacks the projection on the snout. Eye color also seems to differ. Photo: K. H. Switak.

The spadefoots, both of the New World (above, *Scaphiopus holbrooki*, the Eastern American Spadefoot) and the Old World (below, *Pelobates cultripes*, the Western European Spadefoot), are similar in appearance and habits and difficult to keep in the terrarium. Photos: Top: W. P. Mara; bottom: M. Staniszewski.

Spadefoots (Eurasian: ***Pelobates***; American: ***Scaphiopus***)

Members of these two genera, consisting of three and six species respectively, are not regularly kept in captivity due to their highly secretive and fossorial habits. Of the Eurasian species (*Pelobates fuscus, cultripes,* and *syriacus*), the Balkan Spadefoot (*P. syriacus*) has the longest active season and is best maintained in a terrarium containing 4 to 7 inches of river sand incorporating dry and moist zones along with a small, shallow water pan. *Scaphiopus* can either be maintained in a similar manner or by using plaster of Paris tunnel

Though plain in color pattern, the Western American Spadefoot, *Scaphiopus hammondi*, sometimes is collected in numbers from its breeding congresses and thus enters the terrarium market. Since the species normally spends months, perhaps years, buried deep underground awaiting desert rains, it seldom makes a suitable pet. Photo: R. D. Bartlett.

A comparison of the Western European Spadefoot, *Pelobates cultripes* (above), and Couch's Spadefoot, *Scaphiopus couchi* (from western North America, below), emphasizes the resemblance of the two types. Spadefoots are primitive frogs with a long fossil record. Photos: Top, M. Staniszewski; bottom, K. Lucas.

Many spadefoot toads from Southeastern Asia and adjacent China seldom reach the market and are virtual unknowns when it comes to captive maintenance. One of the more attractive is the Red-eyed Litter-frog, *Leptobrachium hasselti*, seen on occasion but seldom kept for very long or bred. Photo: M. Panzella.

casts. *Scaphiopus* tend to be more active than *Pelobates* and often will emerge from their hiding places at night to hunt for invertebrates. All species do well in an unheated greenhouse, especially when breeding is to be attempted. Courtship and egg deposition are brought about by flash floods during warmer months. Constructing shallow concrete pools 1 to 4 inches deep and heavily watering the whole greenhouse with warm water so that the pools fill up may encourage this behavior. Egg and tadpole development are extremely swift.

FAMILY PELODYTIDAE: THE PARSLEY FROGS

Parsley Frog (*Pelodytes punctatus*)

Distribution: France and Iberia.

Length: 3.5 to 5 cm (1.5 to 2 in).

Description: A charming little anuran with a distinctly toad-like appearance because of its warty, sometimes plump, body. The dorsum is colored in brown and gray and garnished in green. The well-developed limbs of this agile anuran make it equally at home in water and on land. The common name is derived from the distinct odor of parsley emitted when this frog is molested.

Availability: Occasionally available as captive-bred specimens.

Captive Care: A cool, humid woodland or meadow terrarium with branches for climbing, a large shallow water bowl, and plenty of hiding places are required. A secure lid is advisable because these frogs are masters at escaping. They also make excellent unheated greenhouse subjects. Food is the normal range of invertebrates.

Sexual Differences: Males have a darker throat, a shorter body, and thicker fore limbs than females. Male nuptial pads

Parsley Frogs, *Pelodytes punctatus*, are unfamiliar to American hobbyists and not even that common on the European market. Though rather plain in appearance, they are hardy and unique frogs. Photo: M. Staniszewski.

Many frogs produce unusual skin secrections that have distinctive smells. The Mink Frog, *Rana septentrionalis*, for instance, smells like musk; Pickerel Frogs, *Rana palustris*, have a distinctive odor; and the Parsley Frog, *Pelodytes punctatus* (above), actually does smell like bruised parsley. Photo: M. Staniszewski.

develop during the breeding season. Females have a broader head.

Captive Breeding: Breeding commences, after a lengthy hibernation period, in a medium to large aquarium containing 2 to 4 inches of tepid water with dense vegetation. Females may not always develop eggs immediately, thus males may be out of synchronization when this happens. This can be avoided by hibernating the males two to four weeks later than the females. Lumbar amplexus and spawning are completed relatively quickly, with 700 to 1,200 eggs being produced singly or in small clumps. A second mating may take place later on in the year. Eggs are reared as for *Bombina variegata.* The tadpoles eventually reach a pre-metamorphosis length of 4 to 6 cm. The 1.5-cm froglets are quite fragile and should be overwintered on a diet of aphids, fruitflies, whiteworms, and small crickets in their first year.

Longevity: Twelve to 18 years.

FAMILY DENDROBATIDAE: THE POISON AND ROCKET FROGS

Dendrobatids are small tropical American frogs that can be broken into two groups. One group, the rocket frogs, centers around the genus *Colostethus* and contains mainly brownish species of little hobby interest. The other group, the poison (or arrow poison or dart poison) frogs, centers around three major genera, *Dendrobates, Phyllobates*, and *Epipedobates*. Rightly called "living jewels of the amphibian world," the poison frogs have developed their own cult following within the hobby. The amazing colors exhibited by these tiny frogs are sometimes beyond comprehension, and as several of the 65 or so species adapt well and breed in captivity, it is easy to see why they are so popular. The brilliant colors of many of the species have one main objective, to warn potential enemies of the frog's extremely toxic nature. All members of the poison frog group can secrete distasteful and mouth-numbing toxins belonging to a great variety of chemical groups. A deadly biotoxin called batrachotoxin is present in members of the genus *Phyllobates*, and in *Phyllobates terribilis* just 5 micrograms of it are sufficient to kill a man. Three species of *Phyllobates* actually were (and still are) used to tip blowgun darts used in hunting and warfare by Amerindian tribes.

A captive-bred example of the Phantasmal Poison Frog, *Epipedobates tricolor*. Photo: W. P. Mara.

Phantasmal Poison Frog (*Epipedobates tricolor*)

Distribution: Southwestern Ecuador and northwestern Peru.

Length: 1.8 to 2.2 cm (0.75 to 1 in).

Description: A highly variable species in terms of coloration. Variable from brown to iridescent red, rose, or dark purple, with narrow white, yellow, or cream stripes stretching along the back and flanks. This ground-dwelling species is fairly plump and has relatively short hind limbs making it less agile than dendrobatids that climb more often.

Availability: In recent years this species has become a firm favorite with hobbyists and now is produced in small commercial quantities.

***Dendrobates tinctorius*, the Dyeing Poison Frog, is perhaps the best poison frog for a hobbyist just starting out in the family. Captive-bred animals are easy to get but rather expensive. Photo: R. D. Bartlett.**

Among the largest poison frogs are the Blue, *Dendrobates azureus* (above) and the Dyeing, *Dendrobates tinctorius* (below). The Blue is rare and difficult to obtain, while the Dyeing is common. The Dyeing Poison Frog comes in both yellow and white patterns. Photos: R. D. Bartlett.

Captive Care: Although poison frogs are generally thought of as arboreal (actually, though many climb and are found in the shrub layer, few live in trees), quite a few species, this one included, may spend most of their time on the humid, leafy forest floor. A good way of assessing their climbing ability is by gauging the toe pad size: smaller pads usually mean a less arboreal species. True *Dendrobates* species have large toe pads and most climb well and often, while *Epipedobates* and *Phyllobates* species are more likely to be found on the ground or at best only a foot or two above it. These frogs thrive in a tropical planted terrarium where they make fascinating, highly active subjects. Use a compost base in which plants and tropical mosses are grown directly. Pieces of bark, dead house plant leaves, and pieces of broken crockery can be spread over the surface for added effect, along with a robust piece of bogwood. Phantasmal Poison Frogs also thrive on a foam base into which holes are cut to hold and partially hide the pots of plants. A shallow water dish that these frogs are able to access and egress safely (a layer of pebbles will help) must be provided—but remember that these frogs are very poor swimmers. The whole setup then should be illuminated with natural daylight fluorescent bulbs suitable for amphibians and must never be allowed to dry out. Temperatures of around 74°F (24°C) for this species (higher for some others) coupled with a relative humidity of over 80% accomplished by frequent misting are important factors in successful maintenance and breeding. If not provided, food is refused and skin sloughing problems will occur. Poison frogs are best kept in groups of between four and ten, territorial males outnumbering females by a factor of 2 to 1. Feeding with ants, termites, aphids, and the like can present problems, especially during colder seasons, so ensuring that a culture of fruitflies or hatchling crickets is at hand is a necessity. (Though these frogs feed largely on ants in nature, they almost never eat them in captivity.) Using a multivitamin powder on their prey can also have a marked effect on captive breeding. Though this species is not especially toxic, when handling them always protect the hands and never touch your eyes, nose, or mouth.

Sexual Differences: Males are a bit smaller and more slender than females and often will call after being misted.

Captive Breeding: If terrarium conditions are favorable, breeding can become a regular occurrence, as often as six times per year not being unheard of. In *Epipedobates tricolor*, increasing daytime temperatures by 4°F (only a couple of °C) for several days can arouse courtship. Males secure a good position on a log, leaf, or rock near the water dish from where they give brief but regular trilling calls and ward off other males that enter their small territory. If a fertile female (easily distinguished by abdominal

Epipedobates tricolor, the Phantasmal Poison Frog, does well in a warm, humid terrarium with adequate cover and a heavy diet of fruitflies or tiny crickets. An easy species to breed, its tadpoles often have stunted front legs. Photo: R. D. Bartlett.

swelling) responds to a dominant male, she will approach and settle beside him. To encourage her to lay her eggs the male may deliver abdominal and cephalic squeezes (there is no amplexus) while the pair slowly move toward the chosen site for egg deposition. When the female lays her ten or so eggs in a damp depression usually near dead leaves, the male crouches over and fertilizes them. The eggs develop and swell by absorbing surrounding moisture (i.e., from fine spraying) and through the instincts of the male, who regularly secretes a watery liquid over them. After 12 to 18 days the 14-mm tadpoles hatch, at which point the male maneuvers them onto his back and transports them to a shallow spot of water such as a hole in a fallen tree, where they will develop. It is wise to transfer these tadpoles to a small aquarium containing about 2 inches of warm (80°F, 27°C) and filtered, neutral water devoid of plants where they will surface–feed on finely ground goldfish flakes, blanched parsley, and microscopic algae. Growth is relatively slow, with hind limbs appearing after five or six weeks and full metamorphosis after a further three to five weeks, during which the water level must be lowered to around an inch maximum and a number of easily accessible platforms provided. Froglets have an average size of 10 mm or so and are best raised individually in humid plastic containers located in a warm, bright position. Such containers must never dry out. Newborn aphids and hatchling crickets are the primary diet. If 50% of the froglets attain maturity eight to ten months later, this must be deemed successful.

Longevity: Around four to ten years.

Lovely Poison Frog (*Phyllobates lugubris*)

Distribution: Atlantic slopes of Costa Rica and Panama.

Length: 1.8 to 2.4 cm (0.75 to 1 in).

Description: This slim species has shiny black skin with two conspicuous yellow dorsal stripes stretching from the snout to the hind limbs. White to silvery, green, or blue stripes and blotches also occur along the mouth, throat, flanks, limbs, and underside; typically the tops of the hind legs are peppered with golden to yellowish spots.

Availability: One of the few *Phyllobates* available to hobbyists on a regular basis.

Captive Care: New acquisitions may take several weeks to acclimate, even those that have been captive-bred. This is mainly a ground-dwelling species and can be maintained in a setup similar to that for *Epipedobates tricolor*. Some individuals seem irritated by a synthetic foam substrate, and for this reason a mossy substrate is recommended. Particularly high humidity is required, along with temperatures near 76°F (25°C); warmer conditions can cause stress. Large numbers of aphids and fruitflies are devoured and should be

Among the more interesting poison frogs bred in captivity on a regular basis is the Lovely, *Phyllobates lugubris*, from Central America. Though small, this is an adaptable animal. Photo: A. v. d. Nieuwenhuizen.

offered twice daily; ants generally are rejected.

Sexual Differences: Males always are smaller than females and are the only ones that call.

Captive Breeding: Courtship and fertilization of the clutch of a dozen or more eggs resemble that of *Epipedobates tricolor*, although eggs usually are laid in a hollow under a damp log or rock that has been cleaned thoroughly by either parent. The eggs are guarded until the tadpoles hatch and either the male or female maneuvers them onto its lower back. Secured by a sticky mucus, they are transported to water no more than an inch deep. Tadpoles are more carnivorous than those of *Epipedobates tricolor*, and if not transferred to an aquarium of sufficient size (minimum 16 x 8 x 8 inches per 12 tadpoles) and containing a dense growth of water weeds they may devour each other. Otherwise tadpoles and froglets can be treated similar to *E. tricolor*. Froglets can prove difficult to raise.

Green and Black Poison Frog (*Dendrobates auratus*)

Distribution: Costa Rica to northwestern Colombia.

Length: 3 to 4 cm (1 to 1.5 in).

Captive Breeding: This semiarboreal species is an ideal poison frog for beginners. It requires the typical tropical planted terrarium with a high humidity and temperatures around 80°F (27°C). Once a small breeding colony has settled down, up to six clutches of eggs each numbering four to six (rarely a dozen) will be produced annually per female. Tadpoles, which the male transfers from the damp terrestrial nest to shallow water, are best removed to an aquarium (12 X 8 X 8 inches for each ten tadpoles) containing 2 to 4 inches of warm (76°F, 25°C or higher), well-oxygenated water with plenty of water weed. They are highly carnivorous and will devour each other if the water is too open or food in short supply. In fact, many

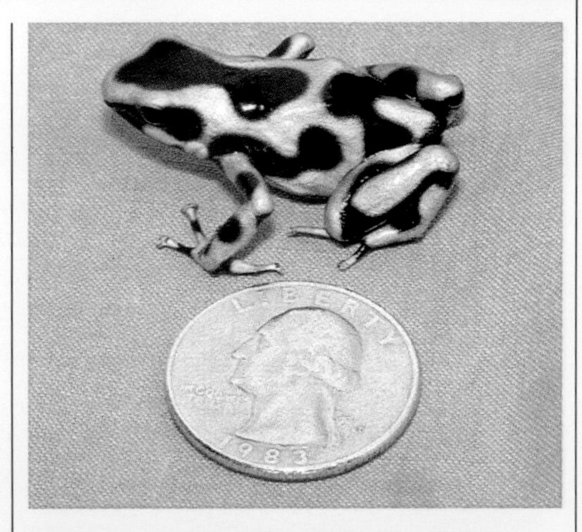

The most commonly kept and usually cheapest captive-bred poison frog is the gorgeous Green and Black Poison Frog, *Dendrobates auratus*. Adults vary greatly in size from less than an inch to almost 2 inches in length and also have numerous colors and patterns. Photos: Top: W. P. Mara; bottom: R. D. Bartlett.

A characteristic glossy green and black *Dendrobates auratus*. Many specimens have more muted colors, but some replace the green with bright blue. Photo: A. Norman.

breeders keep each tadpole in a separate small cup, putting several cups in a larger aquarium. Metamorphosis commences in 9 to 12 weeks, when the water level should be lowered to about an inch and plenty of mossy branches and rock platforms offered.

Yellow-banded Poison Frog (*Dendrobates leucomelas*)

Distribution: Guyana and Venezuela plus adjacent Brazil.

Length: 3.1 to 3.8 cm (1.5 in).

Captive Breeding: A rather robust and easily cared for species that is almost ideal for beginners though a bit expensive. It is a forest floor dweller and can tolerate lower temperatures (best above the low 70's°F, 22°C) and humidity than many other poison frogs. It breeds best, however, at temperatures in the range of 78 to 85 °F (26 to 30°C). The terrarium should be well-planted and possess a fresh, shallow water bowl. Females typically produce small clutches of two to seven large brown eggs laid in damp spots. They are cared for by the male.

The Yellow-banded Poison Frog, *Dendrobates leucomelas*, usually is rather shy. This species seldom climbs. Photo: A. Norman.

Though often imported, Harlequin Poison Frogs, *Dendrobates histrionicus*, are delicate animals that are almost impossible to successfully breed in the terrarium. Photo: W. P. Mara.

Harlequin Poison Frog
(*Dendrobates histrionicus*)

Distribution: Western Colombia and Ecuador.

Length: 2.5 to 3.8 cm (1 to 1.5 in).

Captive Care: A highly variable species with many color variants and several closely related species such as *D. lehmanni.* Most specimens are spotted or banded with yellow or orange on black or brown, no two individuals exactly alike. The breeding behavior of this and several related species makes it almost impossible to breed in captivity, for not only are the eggs cared for by the female, she also feeds the tadpoles on unfertilized food eggs that she lays in the bromeliad funnel or other small water spot where each tadpole develops. The tadpoles feed only on these eggs, not infusoria or worms. They can only be bred (except by specialists) if the mother cares for the young in the terrarium. Adults like warm, humid terraria with lots of vegetation. They are considered delicate and hard to keep alive for long periods. Not recommended for the beginner.

Amazonian Poison Frog
(*Dendrobates ventrimaculatus*)

Distribution: Amazonian region of South America from Peru to the Guianas.

Length: 1.6 to 2 cm (0.75 in).

Harlequin Poison Frogs occur in many different color patterns. This particular specimen is in a "bull's-eye" pattern with a large orange spot on a dark background. Other specimens could have several large spots or have dark spots on a bright background. Photo: A. Norman.

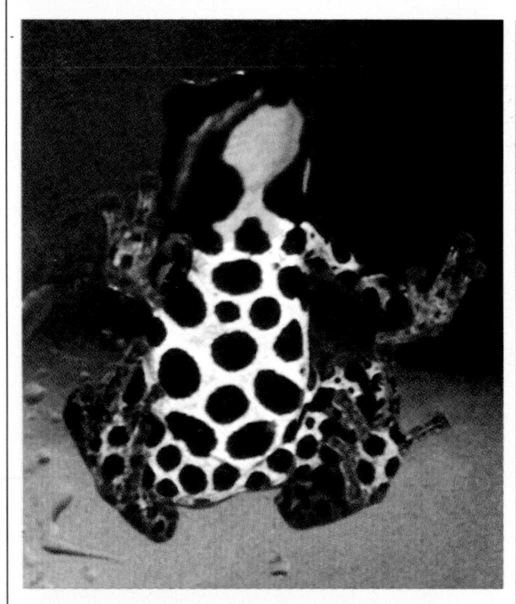

Amazonian Poison Frogs, *Dendrobates ventrimaculatus*, occur over much of northwestern South America and also in the Guianas. The pattern varies quite a bit. Notice the tadpole on the back of the male below. Photos: Top: R. D. Bartlett; bottom: R. Bechter.

Captive Care: A highly variable species or complex of species more commonly known in the hobby as *Dendrobates quinquevittatus*, a different species. Usually it has a stunning arrangement of yellow and black bands (often broken into spots) on the back and silvery blue and black reticulations over the limbs and belly. Related species such as *D. reticulatus* and *D. fantasticus* differ in color pattern. The hind legs are short, so the frog tends to walk more than hop. It needs a tall planted terrarium. Successful breeding is most likely to occur when a single pair is kept in a terrarium. This is because females are very likely to eat the eggs of other females in the terrarium (actually, this is likely to occur in almost all species of poison frogs).

Eggs are laid in the axils of bromeliads and the tadpoles are transported to bromeliad funnels by the male.

Strawberry Poison Frog (*Dendrobates pumilio*)

Distribution: Southern Central America.

Length 1.8 to 2.4 cm (0.75 to 1 in).

Captive Care: Though this is one of the most often imported (wild-caught) poison frogs and one of the most attractive, it is delicate and not recommended for the beginner. In the typical form from Costa Rica (most often sold), the legs are bright blue or blue-black and contrast with a brilliant red back sometimes peppered with tiny black spots. This species need warmth (minimum 75°F, 24°C) and high

Above: **The tiny Red-backed Poison Frog, *Dendrobates reticulatus*. Photo: R. D. Bartlett. *Below:* A brown-spotted variety of the Strawberry Poison Frog, *Dendrobates pumilio*, from Panama. Photo: P. Freed.**

The "normal" Strawberry Poison Frog, *Dendrobates pumilio*, that comes from Costa Rica is brilliant red with contrasting blue-black legs. The brown spots usually are tiny. Strawberry Poison Frogs feed unfertilized eggs to their young, which eat no other food, making them very difficult to raise in captivity. Photo: A. Norman.

humidity at all times. Breeding involves the female feeding food eggs to tadpoles as in the Harlequin Poison Frog, so it cannot be bred by any but specialists. Clutches are small, only two to four eggs on average. This species likes to climb and bathes in shallow elevated pools.

Yellow-striped Poison Frog (*Dendrobates truncatus*)

Distribution: Colombia.

Length: 2.3 to 3.1 cm (1 in).

Captive Care: A species very closely related to the Green and Black but seen less often in the terrarium. The yellow stripes on a nearly black background are fairly distinctive. It needs a humid, planted terrarium with a minimum temperature of 74°F (24°C). A ground-dweller, it feeds on the usual fruitflies and tiny crickets. Females lay five to seven eggs. Care is much as for the Green and Black Poison Frog.

Golfodulcean Poison Frog (*Phyllobates vittatus*)

Distribution: Pacific coast of Costa Rica.

Length: 2.3 to 3.1 cm (1 in).

Captive Care: This fairly robust and smooth-skinned poison frog has a black back with a pair of

Below and Facing page: **Many poison frogs are almost unknown to hobbyists. One of these is the Yellow-striped, *Dendrobates truncatus,* from Colombia. Though attractive, it is small and not really stunning in color, so it probably never will replace its close relative, the Green and Black Poison Frog. Photos: M. Staniszewski.**

The glossy orange to reddish stripes of *Phyllobates vittatus*, the Golfodulcean Poison Frog, are one of its best features. This species is restricted to a very small region of Costa Rica but is captive-bred with regularity. Photo: R. S. Simmons.

broad reddish or golden stripes. It rarely climbs, preferring to hunt around in the leaf litter for ants, which constitute its main prey in nature. In captivity it is one of the few species that will adjust to a simple setup with a foam plastic base. Even so, humidity must be maintained at a high level, temperatures must always be in the 70 to 82°F (21 to 28°C) range, and there must be abundant cover available in the form of logs, bark, rocks, and plants (real or artificial). This is a shy species. The 10 to 20 eggs are deposited on damp litter as usual and the tadpoles are transported by the male to water spots. The tadpoles are best removed from the terrarium and reared in a small aquarium.

Black-legged Poison Frog (*Phyllobates bicolor*)

Distribution: Colombia.

Length: 3.2 to 4.2 cm (1.5 in).

Captive Care: An unusual, highly poisonous (could be deadly—caution is advised), pretty species with a bright yellow to reddish back and black legs and sides. It is best kept in large colonies of eight or more specimens. Males and females go through an elaborate courtship

Phyllobates terribilis, the Golden Poison Frog, is one of three species known to be seriously toxic. There is no doubt that a wild-caught specimen of this species could cause human deaths if mishandled, but captive-bred specimens *appear* to be harmless. Photo: A. Norman.

***Colostethus marchesianus*, one of the rocket frogs, rather undistinguished little dendrobatids that are uncommon in the terrarium. Photo: P. Freed.**

like most other poison frogs. Females can produce a clutch of eggs (usually half a dozen or more) each month.

Trinidad Rocket Frog (*Colostethus trinitatus*)

Distribution: Trinidad, Tobago, and Venezuela.

Length: 2.8 to 3.5 cm (1 to 1.5 in).

Captive Care: Rocket frogs are less colorful than poison frogs, but they make interesting and easily kept captives when available (which is rarely). This species is regularly bred in captivity and requires a waterfall or running water stream created by an air pump. The 8 to 15 eggs per clutch are deposited in close proximity to the water, where the spray will help keep them moist. Males brood over the eggs and transport the tadpoles to a slow-moving part of the stream. Females are very territorial and show bright orange throat spots that they use to warn off other females and even males. Breeding can be stimulated by decreasing and increasing humidity and playing tapes of the male's call. These can be quite noisy, very fast-moving frogs in the terrarium. In captivity this species

Above: Dendrobates granuliferus, **the Granular Poison Frog of Central America. The bright colors hide a delicate personality.** ***Below: Dendrobates variabilis***, **Zimmermann's Poison Frog, is closely related to the Amazonian Poison Frog but differs in a few features of the color pattern. Photos: A. v. d. Nieuwenhuizen.**

***Above: Epipedobates bilinguis*, the Ecuadorean Poison Frog, is a pretty little thing with bright red granules on the back and yellow "flash marks" at the bases of all the legs. Photo: P. Freed. *Below:* Africa is home to many poorly known little frogs that have potential in the terrarium hobby. One of these is the Spiny Reed Frog, *Afrixalus fornasini*, of southern Africa. Photo: K. H. Switak.**

A brightly colored reed frog, *Hyperolius* species, from Malawi. Identifying such frogs is practically impossible for the average hobbyist—and for most herpetologists. Photo: M. Smith.

enjoys climbing over mossy rocks and low plants near the water. It is best kept at 80°F (27°C), though the temperature can safely fall by almost ten degrees.

FAMILY HYPEROLIIDAE: THE REED AND GRASS FROGS

African Reed Frogs (*Hyperolius* species)

This successful genus occurs abundantly throughout moist regions of central and southern Africa. Identification can be highly unreliable because many species are polymorphic (occurring in many different colors and patterns). Most species can be maintained in a similar manner, as can those of the related genus *Afrixalus*, whose members are called clown or spiny reed frogs.

Painted Reed Frog (*Hyperolius marmoratus* complex)

Distribution: Central and southern East Africa.

Length: 2 to 2.8 cm (1 in).

Description: A highly variable and slender, arboreal frog that in its most common color form is beautifully marked with broad black and white stripes and thin yellow lines along the dorsum and limbs. The inner thighs, disc-shaped toe pads, and underside

Not all reed frogs are colorful, though most are at least attractively patterned. This simple brown and cream reed frog has been imported sporadically for several years. The small size does not aid its popularity. Photos: W. P. Mara.

Both the reed frogs on this page have been called *Hyperolius marmoratus*, the Painted Reed Frog, but it really is hard to believe they represent the same species. Notice the bright red toes typical of most reed frogs. Photos: Top: B. Kahl; bottom: K. Lucas.

are red or pink, while the cream throat is speckled in red and black. An indication of the variation within this species is seen in the patterning of other forms, including: uniformly green or golden brown with a pair of pale gray lateral stripes in *H. m. marginatus*; large black spots on a green back in *H. m. nyassae;* and a black back with a broad ivory dorsal stripe in *H. m. albofasciatus*.

Availability: Very abundant throughout much of its range; large numbers are captured for the world pet trade. Also bred in large quantities.

Captive Care: Reed frogs could be at home in anything from a large jar to a tall, planted terrarium and therefore are ideal for the hobbyist who has limited space. In the wild they inhabit the humid vegetation surrounding pools and lakes. In captivity this can be recreated by slotting a shallow tray into the base of the terrarium, which then is filled with around 1 or 2 inches of water. Tall marginal plants and an attractive branch should emerge from the water, which

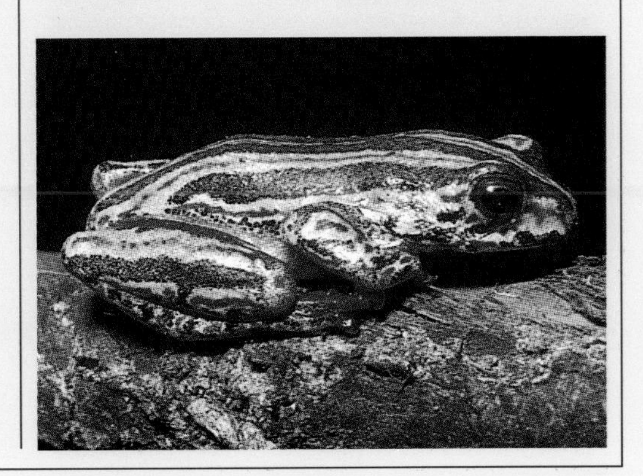

should also contain plenty of submerged vegetation. If space permits, a low-wattage spot lamp can be directed toward one side of the terrarium, and beneath it these frogs frequently will bask. Daytime temperatures should remain a constant 76 to 82°F (25 to 28°C) throughout the year, with a drop to a minimum of 67°F (20°C) at night. Surprisingly large items of food are taken, such as sub-adult crickets. Sweepings collected during summer are particularly nutritious.

Sexual Differences: Adult males have a rounded gular disc covering the throat at the point where the vocal sacs expand. Females have brighter toe pads and cloacal regions than males.

Captive Breeding: Reed frogs are easy tropical anurans to breed in captivity, and success can even be achieved in a glass coffee jar containing a water-filled petri dish. Mating continues throughout the year if the terrarium is misted frequently to give ample humidity. The piercing whistle call of the male is particularly loud for such a small frog because of the amplifying balloon-shaped vocal sacs.

This attractive reed frog appears to belong to the *Hyperolius marmoratus* group of species and subspecies. Notice the resemblance to both the dull frog shown two pages earlier and the brighter one at the bottom of the previous page. Photo: R. D. Bartlett.

Hyperolius marmoratus marmoratus **from Zululand, South Africa. This distinctive pattern is connected by intermediates to striped phases. Photo: Dr. J. Visser.**

Several males may try to vocally better each other, yet this seems to have no bearing on which one will eventually win a prospective mate. Amplexus and egg deposition are, unlike most other hyperoliids, enacted in the water, where small clusters of a dozen or so eggs are either rested on top of water weed or conscientiously attached to submerged rocks or the bases of reeds. Each mating will give rise to 400 or more 1.8-mm black eggs that should be transferred to an aquarium containing 3 to 5 inches of heated (78°F, 26°C), filtered water containing an abundance of oxygenating plants. These hatch after five to eight days, and tadpoles attain 18 mm prior to leaving the water, with the unabsorbed tail still present after four to five weeks. Froglets have a length of 8 mm and are best reared in very moist containers on a diet of tiny invertebrates.

Senegal Running Frog (*Kassina senegalensis*)

Distribution: Savannah regions south of the Sahara.

Length: 3.3 to 5.2 cm (1.5 to 2 in).

Description: An attractive species with a ground color of gray-white to yellow-brown across which spread large black blotches or stripes. Limb coloration varies from population to population,

Kassina maculata, the Red-legged Running Frog of southern Africa. Photo: P. Freed.

Senegal Running Frogs, *Kassina senegalensis*, are found over much of southern and central Africa but are not especially common in the terrarium. They rarely are bred successfully. Photo: M. Staniszewski.

with dark brown and a reddish shade being the most commonly seen. The body is quite long but plump, the hind limbs are short, and the toes are without pads, which gives a clue to the walking/ running (rather than hopping) movements of this frog. The large eyes show vertically slit pupils, unlike hyperoliids where they are horizontal.

Availability: Most specimens are wild-caught rather than captive-bred, with the height of availability typically being December to March.

Captive Care: A planted terrarium with plenty of hiding places and heated to around 79°F (26°C) is most suitable, although lower temperatures of 68°F (20°C) are tolerated at night. The best substrate is sphagnum moss, in which tropical grasses should be grown; a shallow water dish must be provided. Although low humidity levels are tolerated, the whole terrarium should be misted lightly each evening to simulate dew. These frogs emerge at night to hunt for insects, grubs, and caterpillars, at which time air temperatures can drop to 70°F (21°C).

Sexual Differences: Males have a distinctly ovoid gular disc on the throat, which is darker than the throat of the female. In females a series of fleshy papillate projections spread out from below the cloacal opening during the breeding season.

Captive Breeding: In the wild, breeding coincides with warm, heavy rains early in the year that fill wide, dry pans with slightly salty, muddy water. In captivity these frogs seem somewhat reluctant to breed, and success is likely to occur only in a large aquarium or heated greenhouse where a group of frogs is maintained. Males call after rainfall, in response to any repetitive sound, or on sighting a female; the call sounds like the continuous popping of bottle corks. A male may nudge and wrestle a female into water, where he clasps her in lumbar amplexus. Egg deposition is strictly a nocturnal affair, and she lays her total of 70 to 300 (3-mm) eggs singly or in groups of two to ten, attaching them to the underside of submerged plants and rocks. Eggs hatch in six days, and the gold speckled tadpoles grow to about 60 to 80 mm (2.5 to 3 in). In later stages they are highly carnivorous, preying on aquatic crustaceans, mosquito larvae, and each other, so they must, if space permits, be progressively split up into smaller groups. Metamorphosis is completed 10 to 14 weeks after hatching. The 15-mm froglets resemble the adults but are much more brightly colored.

Longevity: Ten years, sometimes longer.

Weal's Running Frog, *Kassina weali*, is another running frog that seldom is imported. It prefers somewhat more moist surroundings than the Senegal Running Frog. Photo: K. Lucas.

Red-legged Running Frogs, *Kassina maculata*, until recently were put in a separate genus, *Hylambates*. Photo: K. H. Switak.

Kassina maculata **is the most commonly seen running frog on the American market, but even it is not especially common. The European market is likely to receive more species because of the better air connections between African exporters and European importers. Photo: R. D. Bartlett.**

Weal's Running Frog (*Kassina weali*)

Distribution: Eastern Africa in slightly moister habitats than *K. senegalensis*.

Length: 2.8 to 4 cm (1 to 1.5 in).

Captive Care: A more attractive and desirable species than the Senegal Running Frog, this species has the back boldly marked in yellow or cream and black bands. The bulging eyes are located near the top of the head. In captivity it requires a relatively small terrarium with a denser growth of tropical grasses, plenty of hiding places, and a small, shallow water dish. It breeds with the advent of heavy rains. Tadpole development and care are as for *K. senegalensis*.

FAMILY MICROHYLIDAE: THE NARROW-MOUTHED TOADS

The narrow-mouths are a large and diverse family so-called because typically the mouth really does have a small gape. Only a few of the many species are available to the amphibian hobbyist, though they often are abundant in any tropical or subtropical setting.

Northern Tomato Frog (*Dyscophus antongili*)

Distribution: Madagascar.

Length: 3.5 to 7 cm (1.5 to 3 in).

Description: An unmistakable toad (not frog as its common name suggests) with a bright red or orange body coloring (brighter in the largest females) and large eyes that have beautiful gold irises and raindrop-shaped pupils. The pearly white underside contrasts sharply to the dorsum. Older individuals grow to be very wide, plump creatures with thickset limbs. Many frogs that hail from Madagascar are bright, conspicuous creatures (see *Mantella*) easily seen on the forest floors they inhabit. This would suggest that before the introduction of "supertramp" species such as rats and pigs they had few natural enemies and therefore camouflage was irrelevant.

Availability: The capture and export of tomato frogs were banned (at least for a while) during late 1991, a warning that it is important that at least some of the specimens already in the hobby must enter captive breeding projects. This species was (and still is) one of the most popular and desirable terrarium amphibians.

The reddest tomato frog is the Northern, *Dyscophus antongili*, but unfortunately that species seems to be disappearing from the hobby market. Photo: A. Norman.

Captive Care: Tomato frogs adapt well to captivity and are equally at home in either a planted terrarium or a simple setup with a pure sphagnum moss or artificial foam base and sparse decoration. Pieces of bark and caves created from sturdy rocks should be provided in both cases. Warmth and high humidity are important considerations, with temperatures consistently around 78°F (26°C) coupled with frequent and heavy misting. A large but shallow water pan that these clumsy anurans can easily enter and egress must be provided, and this also is important for breeding purposes. *Dyscophus* species have wider mouths than most microhylids and prey on most small invertebrates and earthworms.

Sexual Differences: Females are more rotund than males.

Captive Breeding: *Dyscophus* species will breed several times throughout the year when temperatures are favorable. Mating and egg deposition take place in warm, shallow water containing a good growth of vegetation, with males attracting females by using rapid, low-pitched calls. During axillary amplexus females may deposit as many as 2,000 to 3,000 eggs in large clumps. The 1.5-mm eggs are best removed to an aquarium containing 3 to 5 inches of warm (80°F, 27°C), aerated water and hatch out in three days. The tadpoles feed

A newly metamorphosed Southern Tomato Frog, *Dyscophus guineti*, lacks the colors of the adult and looks much like a typical microhylid. Photo: P. Freed.

A tomato among tomatoes, *Dyscophus antongili.* Photo: K. H. Switak.

mainly on algae and fish pellets. Tadpoles should be split into small groups of 50 or so, but even if well-treated many tadpoles will succumb. After 50 days the 3-cm tadpoles transform into 10– to 12-mm froglets. These grow quickly to attain maturity within 12 to 16 months if individually housed and given plenty of multivitamin-fortified invertebrates.

Other Species: The Southern Tomato Frog, *Dyscophus guineti*, is very similar but paler in color, often an orange-yellow over the back. There are many tiny brown spots on the back and usually a large inverted V near the middle of the back. Because of reduced importations of Northern Tomato Frogs, this species has in some places largely replaced *D. antongili* as the available tomato frog. It can be kept and bred

This juvenile *Dyscophus guineti* has assumed most of the adult color pattern but still has not fully colored-up. Adults usually are a bright orange tan or orange yellow. Notice the inverted V on the back, a feature found in most specimens of the Southern Tomato Frog. Photo: R. D. Bartlett.

much like the Northern Tomato Frog; its tadpoles are a bit hardier, a bonus to compensate for the reduced color. It is a nocturnal and secretive semi-burrowing species that spends most of its time concealed in the moss, leaf litter, or soft soil. Such conditions must be provided accordingly in captivity, otherwise it may stubbornly refuse food and eventually starve. A large, shallow water bowl should also be provided, combined with temperatures of 74 to 80°F (24 to 27°C). Its prey consists of crickets, worms, and spiders, which are pursued at night. Dust all food with vitamin/ mineral powder to aid breeding potential. Breeding can become a regular biennial event under proper conditions, with around 1,000 to 1,500 eggs being deposited in small clumps attached to submerged water weed. The water should be no more than 2 inches deep, with a temperature of 74°F (24°C) to encourage egg-laying.

Malaysian Painted Toad or Malaysian Bullfrog (*Kaloula pulchra*)

Distribution: Around human settlements throughout Southeast Asia.

Length: 6 to 10 cm (2.5 to 4 in).

Description: A stout, sometimes obese species with a slightly warty, chocolate-colored back bordered by a pair of wide, uneven mustard or pink bands running down the flanks. Juvenile coloration is much brighter. The small head has a short snout, and the bulbous eyes are almost in line with the nostrils. The short front limbs end in well-developed disc-shaped toe pads (although this species rarely climbs), and the hind limbs each have a horny spade for occasional burrowing activities. As with many microhylids, a milky, toxic fluid is secreted when they are molested.

Availability: This species is very popular with hobbyists and is collected in large numbers from the villages and towns of Southeast Asia, particularly Malaysia.

Captive Care: Malaysian Painted Toads are highly active anurans and interesting and easily maintained captives. Like most frogs hailing from the tropics, new wild-caught acquisitions should be treated with a mild anti-parasitic drug course to eradicate internal parasites and to prevent infection of other amphibians even where

Malaysian Painted Toads, *Kaloula pulchra*, are common pet animals and do quite well. However, be cautious when handling them because their skin toxins can be quite dangerous even to humans. Photo: B. Ka hl.

Though they are relatively small frogs, Malaysian Painted Toads, *Kaloula pulchra*, have loud voices, perhaps a reason they sometimes are called Malaysian Bullfrogs. Photo: A. Norman.

Several species of *Kaloula* have a pattern similar to *K. pulchra* and might be exported on occasion from southern China or Thailand. All can be treated in much the same way, however. Photo: Dr. J. P. Bogart.

they are kept separate. The terrarium can be set up in a simple fashion, with a moisture-retaining substrate such as moss or synthetic foam rubber being recommended. A fairly large, shallow water pan must be made available along with adequate hiding places. Temperatures near 76°F (25°C) will suffice, although a smaller form originating from the cool Annam Highlands prefers lower temperatures near 68°F (20°C). The terrarium must be misted at least twice daily. Food in the wild consists of ants, termites, and other small invertebrates. This can be supplemented with freshly sloughed mealworms, crickets, and waxworms in captivity, all liberally dusted in multivitamin powder.

Sexual Differences: Adult males are considerably smaller and slimmer than females.

Captive Breeding: Breeding sometimes takes place in captivity without any artificial inducement, although noticeable sexual activity may result during periods of high temperatures and increased humidity, with males calling vociferously during the evening. If the female responds, the male clambers onto her back. Like other microhylids such as *Breviceps*, *Gastrophryne*, and *Microhyla*, his short front limbs cannot gain a good grasp so special glands on the belly secrete a sticky mucus that eventually hardens to bond the pair together. He remains in this position until the female decides to spawn, which can be four weeks or

Although the microhylids form a rather large family of frogs, few have ever been of interest to hobbyists because they are too small and tend to be brownish burrowers. *Probreviceps macrodactylus* (above) from Tanzania does not look remarkably different (to a hobbyist) from the common eastern North American *Gastrophryne carolinensis*, the Eastern Narrowmouthed Toad (below). Photos: Top: Dr. J. P. Bogart; bottom: R. D. Bartlett.

Two of the more unusual and colorful microhylids are the tropical American *Dermatonotus muelleri* (top) and *Otophryne robusta* (below). Oddball frogs like these sometimes are imported as unknowns and make interesting projects for more advanced hobbyists. Photos: Top: Dr. R. S. Simmons; bottom: Dr. J. P. Bogart.

longer. She enters shallow water containing dense vegetation and deposits up to 30 clutches of 10 to 15 eggs about 2 mm in diameter. Any attempt to forcefully remove the male can cause lethal injury; after spawning, the sticky substance breaks down or the female sloughs, releasing the male. Tadpoles hatch after four days and remain stationary for around a week until the yolk sac is absorbed. They eventually gather en masse to feed on trout pellets and raw meat (in the aquarium), and just before metamorphosis are quite plump with short, fat tails. Newly metamorphosed 2-cm Malaysian Painted Toads should be kept in containers with a 5-mm depth of water or sodden absorbent tissue for several months as they are liable to dehydrate very easily. Very small food must be provided; many succumb very easily.

FAMILY PHRYNOMERIDAE: THE RUBBER FROGS

This small family formerly was included in the family Microhylidae but has been separated because of an extra cartilage section in each toe. Recently the name *Phrynomerus* has been replaced by an older name, *Phrynomantis.*

Red-backed Crevice Creeper (*Phrynomerus microps*)

Distribution: Southeastern Africa.

Length: 3.8 to 4.4 cm (1.5 to 2 in).

Description: The common name of the family refers to the plump body and large fat storage gland located on the lower back, giving the frog an unusual texture. The small head has a narrow mouth, and behind the eyes are a pair of small parotoid glands. The short limbs end in disc-shaped digits reminiscent of arboreal anurans, although *Phrynomerus* rarely climb. The normal color consists of a brick red back, black flanks, and stippled red limbs, although depending on the light intensity these frogs have the ability to change color: in bright sunlight they turn pale brown with salmon, pink, or cream stripes.

The Red-backed Crevice Creeper, *Phrynomerus microps*, is a fascinating little frog closely related to the microhylids. The skin secretions are quite toxic, however, making it a dangerous addition to the community terrarium. Photo: M. Staniszewski.

Availability: *Phrynomerus microps* is one of two species likely to be encountered in captivity (*P. bifasciata* is the other), and like many other unusual anurans hailing from southern Africa, it is becoming increasingly popular.

Captive Care: *Phrynomerus* must not be kept with other frogs because of their highly poisonous nature. A moist, planted terrarium heated to around 79°F (26°C) and with subdued lighting

Seen even more often in the American terrarium hobby is the Red-banded Crevice Creeper or Rubber Frog, *Phrynomerus bifasciatus*. Photo: Dr. J. P. Bogart.

is required. A substrate consisting of a chopped sphagnum moss/ river sand mix will enable these nocturnal and secretive, semi-fossorial frogs to excavate burrows. Several rocks and hollow logs will provide extra refuge. The terrarium should be misted lightly each evening to create humidity. In captivity small crickets and waxworms are avidly devoured, although ants and termites are the favorite food.

Sexual Differences: Males have black throats.

Captive Breeding: Breeding is opportunistic, coinciding with heavy rains, and recreating such conditions in captivity may prove successful. Initially temperatures are reduced slightly to 74°F (24°C) and the terrarium is kept quite dry for four to six weeks, but still ensuring that the substrate is kept uniformly moist. The frogs are then transferred to a larger aquarium containing 2 inches of damp, washed river sand over an undergravel filtration system, several pieces of hollow bark beneath which to hide, and several rocks. After a further two weeks, the aquarium suddenly is flooded with warm, dechlorinated water so that the sand lies submerged under an inch of warm water. A few bunches of water weed are added and with

Breeding crevice creepers and many other frogs works best in a small tank with an undergravel filter servicing a deep bed of washed sand. Photo courtesy of Hagen.

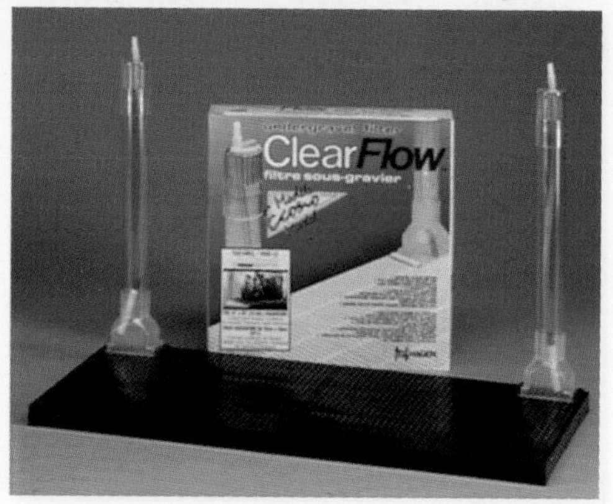

In captivity, bright lights tend to wash out the red colors of *Phrynomerus microps*, resulting in a frog with a uniformly bright coppery or bronzy back. Photo: M. Staniszewski.

any luck the male will start calling with his high-pitched trill from a rock he has chosen. Amplexus occurs in the water. A sprawling mass of 400 to 650 eggs each 1.2 mm in diameter is deposited entangled in the weed. Adults are then returned to their terrarium, leaving eggs to hatch four days later. Increase the water depth to 3 inches. On a diet of liquid fish fry food and dried, powdered algae the strange, diamond-shaped tadpoles will quickly reach a length of 40 mm. The fragile-looking 1-cm froglets that emerge a month after hatching develop the banded pattern soon after metamorphosis. They are best raised in plastic containers on a damp moss or kitchen tissue base for the first year.

The taxonomy of the rubber frogs is uncertain. Most herpetologists now feel that the group is just a member of the Microhylidae, not a full family. Additionally, the genus *Phrynomerus* recently has been changed to *Phrynomantis*, a name long used for frogs from New Guinea. Confusion reigns. Facing page: *Phrynomerus microps*, M. Panzella; below: *Phrynomerus annectens*, juvenile and adult, P. Freed.

FAMILY RANIDAE: THE TRUE OR TYPICAL FROGS

Golden Mantella (*Mantella aurantiaca*)

Note: The family position of the mantellas is uncertain at the moment. They often are placed in their own family, Mantellidae, and also may be placed in the Rhacophoridae by some authorities.

Distribution: Madagascar.

Length: 2 to 3 cm (1 in).

Description: One of the most beautiful terrarium subjects, this frog is progressively gaining in popularity and rightly so. In terms of shape it looks like a miniature typical frog (*Rana*), but its streamlined body is strikingly colored in orange (more rarely red) and its large black eyes are highly conspicuous. The hind limbs are well developed, enabling it to leap considerable distances.

Availability: Commonly the Golden Mantella is offered by pet shops in the form of wild-collected adults, although an increasing number are captive-bred. Collecting *Mantella aurantiaca* and other species from their native Madagascar may be prohibited in the near future, though currently the species are imported in large numbers at low prices.

Captive Care: Although Golden Mantellas are fairly tolerant of unnaturally low temperatures and adapt well to captive conditions, they may take several weeks to fully

An obviously gravid female Golden Mantella, *Mantella aurantiaca*. Photo: M. Staniszewski.

A slender male Golden Mantella, *Mantella aurantiaca*. Photo: M. Staniszewski.

acclimate. The preferred temperature range is around 76°F (25°C), and nighttime temperatures can fall to 65°F (18°C) without harm. A natural setup similar to that for tomato frogs is perfectly acceptable, although I have found that a sphagnum moss substrate or, in the case of an artificial setup, a foam that holds moisture extremely well is to be preferred. Mantellas enjoy bathing, therefore the terrarium should accommodate a shallow water bowl. They are largely diurnal and spend much of their time hunting for food, which in the terrarium consists of fruitflies, spiders, small waxworms, and small crickets. Wild-caught individuals may refuse to eat earthworms, while captive-bred specimens are readily coaxed into taking such prey.

Sexual Differences: Externally sexes can be difficult to determine, with males sometimes being smaller. A more reliable method is to view a specimen from the underside where, barely visible in the male's abdomen, are the unbroken opaque lines of the ureters. In the female these are partially hidden by the oviduct.

Captive Breeding: Breeding can be a regular event in

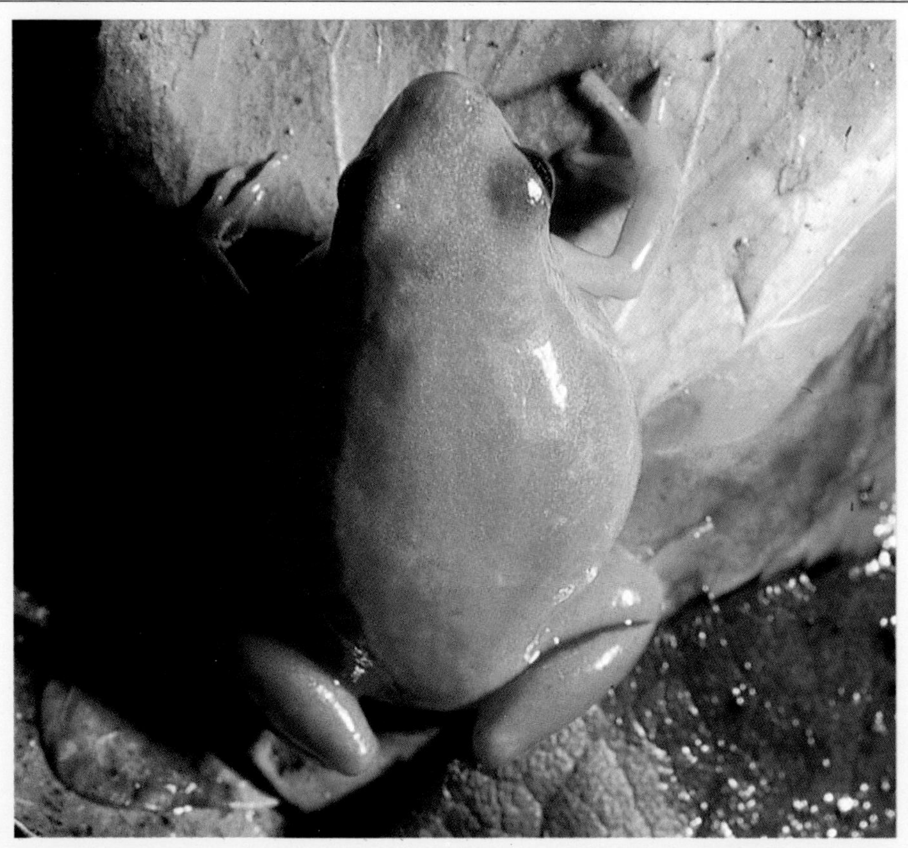

Though few hobbyists have been able to breed Golden Mantellas consistently in captivity, it is not impossible. In many ways *Mantella aurantiaca* breeds like poison frogs, Dendrobatidae. Females (above) are even more obviously egg-laden because they lay relatively large clutches (below) in a hidden depression in the ground cover. Photos: M. Staniszewski.

captivity once Mantellas have settled down. They are best maintained in small breeding colonies of four to eight, with males outnumbering females by 3 to 1. Both courtship behavior and egg deposition are not dependent on a body of water. Females can be encouraged to develop eggs and males stimulated into courtship activity by lowering daytime temperatures to 72°F (22°C) for around 15 to 20 days, during which they become less active and consequently eat less food. After this cool period, temperatures should be increased to 78 to 80°F (26 to 27°C), 74°F (24°C) at night, and the terrarium sprayed heavily each evening. The female soon will become gravid and males will begin calling from their hiding places during the day. A male will grasp and squeeze the female's abdomen in an attempt to induce spawning. After a gestation of 18 to 30 days, females deposit beneath damp wood or in sphagnum moss around 45 to 80 cream/white eggs (1.2 mm) that one or more males then fertilize. Both sexes regularly secrete moisture over the eggs as the tadpoles develop inside. Eggs reach a diameter of 12 mm prior to hatching 58 to 90 days later, the orange-brown froglet still showing some of the tail when it breaks free. These 8– to 10-mm froglets are best raised individually as described for *Dendrobates*. Females may produce up to ten clutches each year.

Brown Mantella (*Mantella betselio*)

Distribution: Madagascar, in open but mossy rocky regions usually in close proximity to waterfalls where there are plenty of crevices.

Length: 2.4 to 3.5 cm (1 to 1.5 in).

Captive Care: This species is larger and more robust than the Golden Mantella. Its back is an attractive pale brown or creamy yellow color. (Identification of this frog as *M. betselio* may be in error, most specimens in the hobby representing *M. crocea*. Mantella identification is loaded with problems.) It does equally well in a damp, rocky tropical terrarium carpeted with moss and in a simple, hygienic setup. It needs a temperature of about 75°F (24°C) with a drop to about 65°F (18°C) at night. Too high a temperature may cause stress in any mantella, so be sure that lights, heating pads, and even room temperature do not become too high. Breeding occurs throughout the year, but especially when humidity is higher than normal.

Captive Breeding: The 35 to 50 eggs are slightly larger (1.6 mm) and browner than those of the Golden Mantella. They are laid in damp depressions or under rocks, where development takes place entirely within the gelatinous egg casing, or near water that the 7-mm tadpole slides into on hatching after four to six days. In both cases the froglets form within four weeks, but those from water tend to be around 9 mm, 3 to 4 mm longer than those that hatch directly from the egg.

***Mantella crocea*, one of the more recently imported species of mantella. Photo: P. Freed.**

Variegated Mantella (*Mantella cowani*)

Distribution: Madagascar and Reunion Island.

Length: 2 to 2.6 cm (1 in).

Captive Care: An extremely attractive and desirable species (which may be more correctly known as *M. madagascariensis*), its finely granulated back is a patchwork of black, green, orange, and yellow, sometimes finished off with a yellow or cream stripe running along each flank. This species settles down well in captivity and can be kept in a setup virtually identical to that for the Golden Mantella, though it will not tolerate temperatures below 65°F (18°C) and requires high humidity throughout the year.

The mantella shown above and below often is called *Mantella cowani* by hobbyists, but it probably is either a form of *M. madagascariensis* or a poorly known species called *M. pulcher*. Photos: Top: P. Freed; bottom: W. P. Mara.

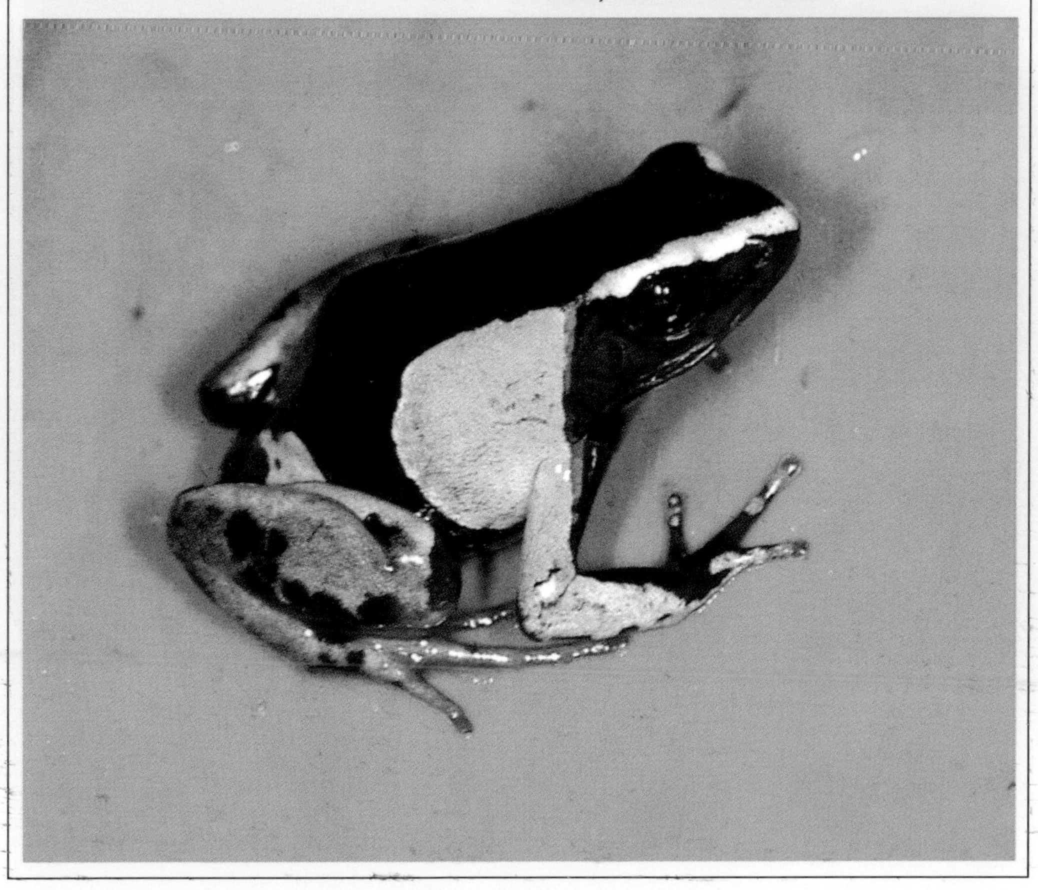

Captive Breeding: Males are noticeable smaller than females and have bluish gray throats. During courtship it is important to ensure that there is interaction between males, which will wrestle and nudge each other as well as chirp endlessly to secure a female. A breeding group of three to five males per female therefore is a prerequisite for successful breeding. Females deposit their 18 to 50 large, pale brown eggs close to or actually within a shallow water source over which males keep a close watch. The care of the tadpole is exactly the same as for Golden Mantellas.

American Bullfrog *(Rana catesbeiana)*

Distribution: Central and eastern North America, introduced elsewhere including western U.S.A. and northern Italy.

Length: 15 to 21 cm (6 to 8 in).

Description: An impressive, powerfully built frog that varies in patterning and coloration. Southern populations tend to be an attractive marbled brown and green color, while northern forms range from dark brown-green to gray. The belly is cream with gray mottling. The skin of older individuals is granulated with large numbers of small tubercles.

Most specimens of *Mantella viridis* have a distinctly greenish or mustard tinge to the color of the back. Photo: P. Freed.

Mantella colors are as varied as those of the poison frogs. Some species are relatively plain, like the *Mantella expectata* above, while others have brilliant colors both exposed and hidden in the joints of the limbs (*Mantella madagascariensis*). Photos: Top: W. P. Mara; bottom: P. Freed.

The American Bullfrog, *Rana catesbeiana*, is more familiar served in restaurants than sold in pet shops, but given enough room they make satisfactory pets. Photo: A. Norman.

An albino variety of the American Bullfrog, *Rana catesbeiana*, is bred and marketed commercially. These attractive albinos often appear in pet shops while still small and make interesting pets for several months or a few years. Photo: K. H. Switak.

As with most ranids, the hind limbs are very muscular, enabling these frogs to jump considerable distances.

Availability: Extremely common in many pet shops in the form of large tadpoles. Wild-caught sub-adults and adults are occasionally offered.

Captive Care: A hardy, largely aquatic frog that requires a large terrarium (36 inches minimum) with access to a substantial, clean water reservoir. Too small a terrarium may result in injury and bruising to the snout. A hygienic setup with a synthetic moisture-retaining base such as foam is the easiest way of keeping American Bullfrogs because they are liable to crush or uproot the strongest plants and generally create a mess. The most attractive method for housing Bullfrogs is either the unheated greenhouse or the outdoor amphibiary covered with chicken wire to prevent escapes; either should have deep hibernation quarters and an expansive, shallow pool. Whatever setup is chosen, where Bullfrogs are to be grouped their relative sizes should not vary too much or cannibalism may occur. Indoors, provide basking facilities with a 40W to 60W spot lamp directed onto a large flat rock and away from the water. Temperatures need to be in the 68 to 80°F (20 to 27°C) range, falling to 60°F (16°C) at night. Feeding presents few problems, with anything remotely edible being attacked. Limiting feeding to once or twice weekly and varying the diet with adult locusts, earthworms, strips of unfilleted fish, raw meat, and frozen mice will ensure healthy, long-lived specimens.

Sexual Differences: In females the tympanum (ear drum) has a diameter equal to or smaller than the eye and the throat is white or cream colored. In males the tympanum is greater than the eye and the throat is bright yellow.

Captive Breeding: Breeding is unlikely unless very spacious quarters or an unheated greenhouse is used. A long period of hibernation is essential in stimulating breeding activity, although southern forms are less hardy and require some form of supplementary heating in outdoor setups during harsh conditions. They do not emerge from hibernation and breed until water temperatures exceed 67°F (20°C), usually from late spring onward. The male announces his presence with a bellowing "jug-o-rum" call during the entire day from within reed-filled shallows. Females swell substantially after hibernation. During an amplexus lasting 15 to 22 hours, a female deposits a mass of floating spawn containing 12,000 to 25,000 eggs, each 1.3 mm in diameter. It is best to remove only part of the spawn, say 500 eggs, into a large aquarium containing deep, cool, oxygenated water. Transferring all the spawn may result in huge egg losses through fungal infection or tadpoles (which take 6 to 12 days to hatch) may succumb to poor water quality, overcrowding, and starvation. Tadpoles feed greedily on algae, trout pellets, and raw meat but can take 20 months to metamorphose, when they measure 8 cm (3 inches). The 3-cm American Bullfrogs that emerge grow quickly, attaining 8 cm in their first year. Maturity is achieved in the second or third year.

Longevity: Fourteen to 25 years.

Leopard Frog (*Rana pipiens* and relatives)

Note: The Leopard Frog of the basic biology books now is known to be a complex of a dozen or more very similar but often easily distinguished species replacing each other over much of North America. Species from drier or warmer habitats should have allowances made for their natural ecology.

Distribution: Northeastern United States (in the typical species) west to the Rocky Mountains and south into Central America (in various related species).

Length: 5 to 11 cm (2 to 4.5 in).

Captive Care: This is the North American equivalent of the European Brown Frog (*Rana temporaria*), although its attractive greenish to olive dorsal coloration and boldly marked spots have made it a far more popular terrarium subject. It requires a moist woodland terrarium that incorporates both a small dry area and a shallow water bowl. Where a soft substrate is present, it often will excavate itself a wide burrow where it will spend most of its time waiting for large earthworms, woodlice, and crickets to pass by. Leopard Frogs should not be housed with smaller amphibians or even smaller individuals of their own species, which are likely to be devoured. Leopard Frogs are good subjects for unheated greenhouses but seem less resilient to open outdoor enclosures in cold climates, especially if hibernacula are not deep enough.

Captive Breeding: Breeding takes place from March to May when temperatures rise to about 50°F (10°C). An expansive shallow pond is preferred. Females deposit 2,000 to 7,000 eggs, depending on their size and age. Eggs take 14 to 20 days to hatch at this temperature and after about 15 weeks transform into surprisingly large (2.6 cm) froglets. These take a further three or four years to reach maturity and live up to 12 years in captivity.

Other Species: As mentioned, the Leopard Frog is a complex of many similar species. One other species, the Pickerel Frog, *Rana palustris*, of eastern North America, also is very similar but has the dorsal spots square and arranged in two regular rows; the back of the thigh is bright yellow or orange. Pickerel Frogs should not be housed with other amphibians (or reptiles) because they secrete a lethal skin toxin when disturbed or stressed.

The North American leopard frogs form a complex group of a dozen or more species that superficially are very similar. The one most commonly seen in the terrarium is the Southern Leopard Frog, *Rana sphenocephala* (sometimes called *R. utricularia*), recognized by the pointed, spotless snout plus a white spot at the center of the tympanum. Photo: R. D. Bartlett.

The large spot on the rounded snout plus a plain tympanum indicate this probably is the true Northern Leopard Frog, *Rana pipiens*. Photo: A. Norman.

Green Frog ***(Rana clamitans)***

Distribution: Southeastern Canada and eastern U.S.A. near water, especially streams and small rivers.

Length: 7 to 10 cm (3 to 4 in).

Captive Care: This common species varies considerably in color from bronzy brown in southern populations to bright green in northern areas. Males have a bright yellow throat. They are good leapers and need a high terrarium but soon calm down. Somewhat more aquatic than typical Leopard Frogs, they prefer a large outdoor pond or a greenhouse with a large water area.

Marsh Frog ***(Rana ridibunda)***

Distribution: Eastern Europe and western Asia.

Length: 9 to 15 cm (3.5 to 6 in).

Description: The largest native European frog is similar in shape to other members of the family although the dorsum often has large elongated warts and a pair of pronounced dorsolateral folds. The ground color varies from dark brown or green to a light or yellowish green with black spotting or mottling. A conspicuous light green or yellow vertebral stripe also is present.

Availability: Regularly bred by hobbyists in Europe, but with

The Green Frog, *Rana clamitans melanota*, is the northern subspecies of a frog that in the southern United States becomes virtually all brown. This is one of the most common ranids over the eastern United States and makes a decent pet if given a tank large enough to allow it to jump. Photo: A. Norman.

only a limited availability elsewhere.

Captive Care: The Marsh Frog can be maintained in a similar setup to the American Bullfrog but is rather shy and often remains hidden during the day. The best way to maintain this species is in small colonies numbering six to ten individuals in an outdoor terrarium or unheated greenhouse (male to female ratio 3 to 1). Water should be warm and shallow, with dense vegetation. Long periods are spent basking in hot sun or beneath a spot lamp. Large food items often are tackled aggressively, and these agile frogs will leap good distances to catch winged insects in flight.

Sexual Differences: Males have nuptial pads on the inner digits of the front limbs and are 2 to 3 cm smaller than the female.

Captive Breeding: Requirements are the same as those detailed for breeding the American Bullfrog. Marsh Frogs breed after a long dormancy in late spring when water temperatures rise to 65°F (19°C). Males congregate in the water, where they croak raucously day and night, their calls amplified by a pair of external vocal sacs

The Eurasian Marsh Frog, *Rana ridibunda*, is large by European standards, reaching about 6 inches in body length. This is one of those oddball frogs that like to bask in direct sunlight. Photo: M. Staniszewski.

located behind the mouth. Some 10,000 eggs are deposited in a mass of cream–colored spawn. In warm water the eggs hatch within five days. Tadpoles grow quickly to 3 cm, although the froglets that emerge 30 to 45 days later are barely 1 cm in length and can be quite troublesome to rear. It may prove better to concentrate on rearing a small number of froglets rather than the whole lot. Aphids and fruitflies are the primary food. Maturity is reached in their third year.

Longevity: Eight to 12 years.

European Brown Frog *(Rana temporaria*)

Distribution: Throughout central and southern Europe, the northern Iberian Peninsula, and the northern Balkans, eastward to the Urals. Found in most cool, moist habitats, tending to be a mountain-dweller in the southern part of its range.

Length: 6 to 9.7 cm (2.5 to 4 in).

Captive Care: This rather plain species is the most robust of the brown ranids and is an ideal beginner's frog that should be maintained in a cool, moist (not waterlogged) terrarium containing an ample water bowl. It does not like temperatures above 75°F (24°C) and needs hibernation for four or five months during autumn and winter.

Captive Breeding: Breeding is likely to occur only in very early spring either in a large aquarium containing cold, shallow, weed-filled water, in an outdoor enclosure, or in a garden pond. Males are distinguished by their yellow throats and nuptial pads

***Rana temporaria*, the European Brown Frog, makes an ideal beginner's frog for European enthusiasts. Photo: Dr. D. Green.**

Several species of *Rana* from around the Northern Hemisphere are "masked" frogs, easily recognized by the dark bar running along the upper lip to the tympanum and shoulder. *Rana dalmatina*, the European Agile Frog, is one of these attractive species. Photo: M. Staniszewski.

during courtship and should outnumber females in the realm of 3 to 1. Females deposit in excess of 3,000 eggs in huge gelatinous masses. Tadpoles are reared as for the Marsh Frog.

Agile Frog (*Rana dalmatina*)

Distribution: Northwestern and central Europe in moist lowland meadows and fairly open woodlands.

Length: 5.6 to 9 cm (2 to 3.5 in).

Captive Care & Breeding: A slender species with very long hind limbs enabling it to leap considerable distances. Therefore, its housing must be fairly roomy to prevent snout injuries. Its coloration is more variable than that of *Rana temporaria*, ranging from sandy or pinkish brown to an off-yellow. The Agile Frog always breeds later than the European Brown Frog, usually in April. The smaller males must outnumber the females by 3 to 1. In captivity it will breed only rarely unless given access to a large open pool where females can lay clumps of jelly-like spawn consisting of 2,000 to 4,000 grayish 1.6-mm eggs.

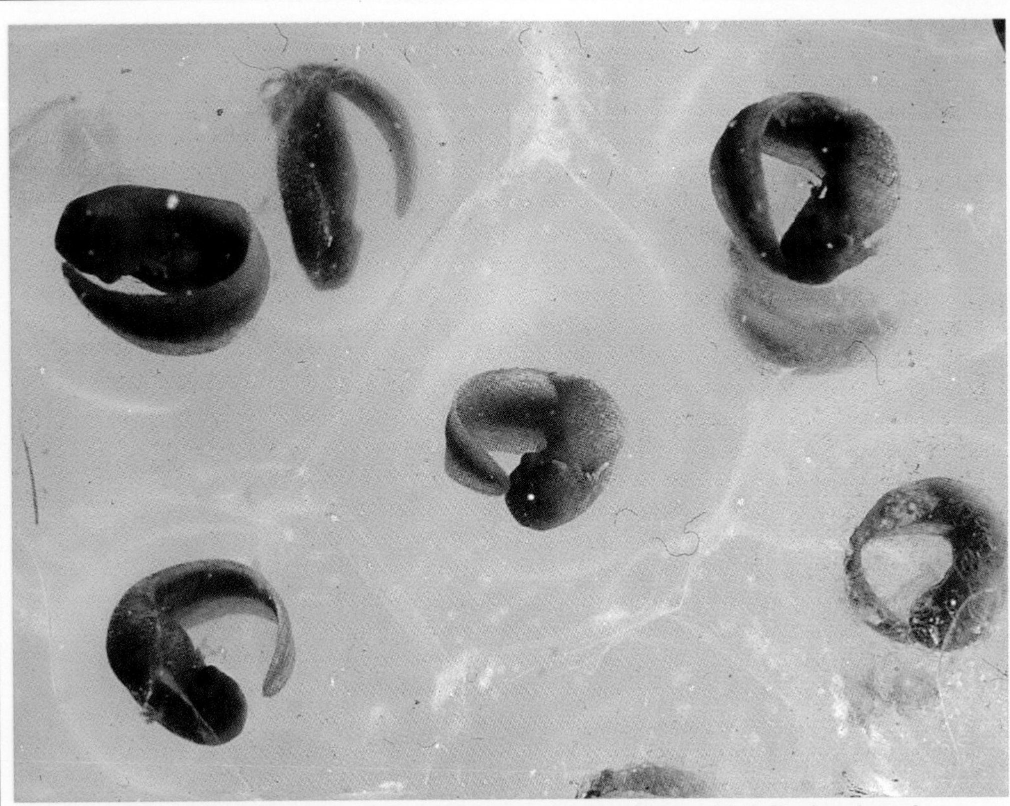

Development of the Agile Frog, *Rana dalmatina*. Above: Eggs with fully developed embryos. Below: Early tadpoles. Photos: M. P. & C. Piednoir.

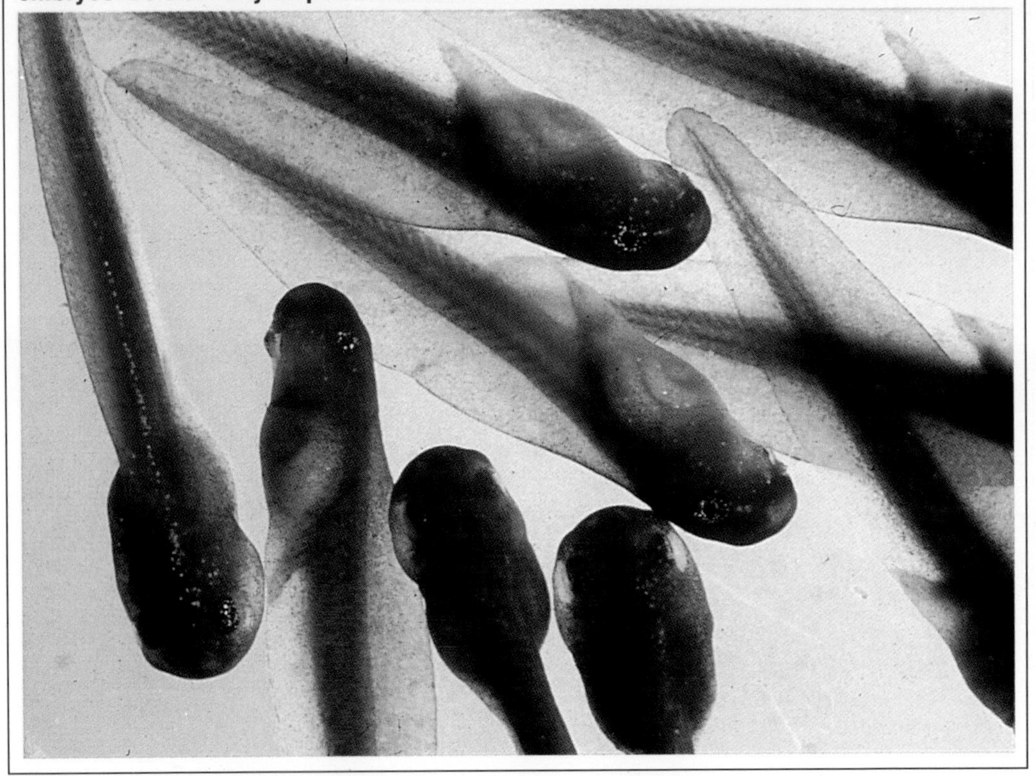

Rana iberica, the Spanish Frog, is one of several European true frogs with relatively small ranges. Photo: M. Staniszewski.

Spanish Frog *(Rana iberica)*

Distribution: Portugal to central Spain, usually in close proximity to cold streams and ponds in montane areas.

Length: 4.5 to 6.4 cm (2 to 2.5 in).

Captive Care & Breeding: Probably one of the most desirable ranids, this small plump species is beautifully colored in a salmon pink or brick red with black and white marbling on the flanks. In captivity it does equally well in a cool, damp meadow terrarium or an unheated greenhouse, where it becomes bold and even basks during the day. Breeding does not commence until June, when the male calls with what sounds like a resonant mouse squeak. Amplexus takes place on land and in water. The female deposits golf-ball sized clumps of whitish eggs totaling 1,000 to 1,600. The resultant tadpoles grow quickly to around 3 cm if split into groups of 40 and fed regularly on fish pellets and blanched parsley. Water temperatures must not be

The Indian Bullfrog, *Rana tigrina* (here the subspecies or related species *rugulosa*), is one of the largest Asian true frogs and, like other bullfrogs, faces tremendous losses at the hands of man. Photo: R. D. Bartlett.

The North American masked frog is the Wood Frog, *Rana sylvatica*. This beautiful small species often is bright reddish brown over the entire back and always has a contrasting mask. It breeds during the cold spring rains. Photo: A. Norman.

allowed to exceed 70°F (21°C), and good aeration and filtration are essential. Newly metamorphosed froglets measure only 7 mm and can be difficult to rear for the first few months. The Italian Frog (*R. latastei*) and the Greek Frog (*R. graeca*) occasionally are offered and require similar care.

Indian Bullfrog *(Rana tigrina*)

Distribution: Widespread from Pakistan through India and southern China over much of Southeast Asia in marshes, woodland swamps, and paddy fields.

Length: 13 to 17 cm (5 to 7 in).

Captive Care: This shy, attractive frog adapts well to captivity, where it requires a spacious aqua-terrarium (minimum 36 X 12 X 12 inches per pair) with a warm, shallow water section. The preferred substrate of gritty river sand enables it to partially bury itself and leap out on unsuspecting foods such as locusts, small rodents, and strips of raw meat dangled from the end of long forceps. The normal temperature should be between 77 and 84°F (25 and 29°C), but for part of the year the terrarium should be allowed to dry out and cool down

It is not typical for true frogs to have brilliant colors, but the Malayan Painted Frog, *Rana signata*, is an exception. This small and colorful species is occasionally available to hobbyists but seems to be delicate. Photo: P. Freed.

True frogs (*Rana* and close allies) are abundant in Eurasia, Africa, and North and Central America but scarce in South America and absent from Australia. The Dusky-throated Frog, *Rana angolensis*, and its tadpole (below) are common sights throughout central Africa. Photos: M. Smith.

so these frogs can "cocoon" themselves to estivate. This is especially true where breeding is to be attempted.

Captive Breeding: Given spacious conditions, Indian Bullfrogs will immediately start courting after the onset of warm (imitation monsoon) rains. Males have a raucous croak that is liable to drive the hobbyist up the wall, but the prize at the end is a successful pairing producing in the region of 6,000 eggs. Tadpoles hatch after two weeks and are voracious predators that eventually reach 12 cm. Newly metamorphosed bullfroglets that appear eight weeks later are 3.5 cm long and highly carnivorous and cannibalistic. They are best reared individually in small, humid margarine tubs on a diet of waxworms, crickets, and small fishes or strips of fish. Indian Bullfrogs are in danger of extinction over much of their range due to excessive collecting for their legs, a prized delicacy.

The Pool Frog, *Rana lessonae*, is a pretty Eurasian true frog of interest to herpetologists because it is one of the parents of a hybrid species, the Edible Frog, *Rana esculenta*. It is thought that *R. lessonae* and *R. ridibunda* (the Marsh Frog) hybridized to produce a frog intermediate between the parents but able to reproduce itself, *R. esculenta*. Such stable hybrids are found in several groups of amphibians. Photo: M. Staniszewski.

Sand or Rice Paddy Frog (*Occidozyga lima*)

Distribution: Southeastern Asia.

Length: 2 to 3.2 cm (1 in).

Captive Care: This tiny, interesting, and easily kept species requires a shallow aqua-terrarium with very warm water (it can tolerate as high as 95°F, 35°C, but of course should be kept cooler) and dense water weed growth. It is highly aquatic and seldom strays far from shallow streams, ponds, and flooded fields. The eyes are positioned on top of the head, enabling it to survey the sky for flying insects and predators. It takes large amounts of aquatic invertebrates, which in captivity should consist of bloodworms, tubifex, amphipods, and isopods. During the cool period when temperatures fall below 60°F (16°C), usually during March and April, it hibernates in the muddy bottom for three to six weeks.

Captive Breeding: On emerging from hibernation, breeding is almost instantaneous. During lumbar amplexus females expel about 1,000 small yellow eggs. The eggs hatch and the tadpoles develop rapidly, with froglets emerging from the water after just four weeks. Because of their small (6 mm) size, they are best housed

Rice Paddy Frogs, *Occidozyga lima*, are very rough-skinned aquatic true frogs that often are abundant in Southeast Asian fields and ditches. The eyes are located toward the top of the head as in the African Clawed Frog, *Xenopus laevis*, making it easier to spot prey and predators while floating at the surface. Photo: R. D. Bartlett.

Though Rice Paddy Frogs are available on a sporadic basis and often are said to be hardy aquarium inhabitants, many hobbyists keep them at too low a temperature, leading to short lives in captivity. Photo: R. D. Bartlett.

in groups of ten and fed on clumps of tubifex worms and bloodworms.

African Bullfrog (*Pyxicephalus adspersus*)

Note: Also called Grooved Frog, Giant Burrowing Bullfrog, Numbskull, and Pac-Man Frog.

Distribution: Central and southern Africa.

Length: 13 to 23 cm (5 to 9 in).

Description: Older specimens are huge, obese, and somewhat grotesque-looking with their shiny, dark green dorsum along which run many high dorsolateral ridges. As they grow more prominent, bony scapular plates at the back of the head lend the frog armor-like protection. The mouth is extremely wide and contains a formidable set of three bony, canine-like projections on the lower jaw, while the jaw itself is operated by well-developed muscles enabling this frog to gain a bulldog-like grip and inflict a nasty bite. Layers of loose skin develop naturally at the flanks and throat on the short, muscular limbs and should not be mistaken for obesity. Hard metatarsal growths develop on the hind feet as a burrowing tool. African Bullfrogs from different regions vary considerably in overall size; those from Malawi are considerably smaller and more brightly colored than the more typical form hailing from South Africa.

A five-year-old African Bullfrog, *Pyxicephalus adspersus*. The bony nature of the warts and ridges shows well in this photo. Heavy jowls are not developed until the frog matures, perhaps another three years. Photo: M. Staniszewski.

Availability: Availability fluctuates from year to year depending on the success rate of breeders and to a lesser extent the collecting of wild individuals. Presently captive-bred babies are quite common in the U.S.A.

Captive Care: This is an easy species to maintain individually in a simple and relatively small terrarium, where most of its time is spent inactively "squatting" in a corner. For normal housing arrangements synthetic foam, layers of loose leaves, or sphagnum moss is recommended as the substrate rather than a compost layer in which these fossorial frogs would burrow out of sight. A deep water bowl also should be present in which the frog will regularly bathe, slough, and defecate. The terrarium should be heated to 75 to 82°F (24 to 28°C) and have a 60W spot lamp present, although lower temperatures are tolerated without ill effects. *Pyxicephalus* enjoys an occasional misting but can easily survive extended periods of xerophytic conditions by cloaking itself in a watertight skin cocoon composed of several layers of dead epidermis. Feeding can cause problems in that these frogs often will leap out on sighting potential prey and may accidentally grasp a hobbyist's hand. They eventually learn to recognize their owner and can become quite tame, although for safety purposes long forceps should be used for feeding chunks of lean raw red meat, unfilleted fish, and thawed pre-frozen mice along with the normal complement of large earthworms and invertebrates such as locusts. Being an instinctively cannibalistic species, it should be housed in isolation apart from during breeding.

Sexual Differences: Males are several inches longer than females and have a bright yellow throat tinged with red. Females are more patterned above and have a cream throat.

Captive Breeding: Unless there is access to a greenhouse that is either heated or utilized during warm weather, breeding in captivity is unlikely. In this setup there must be a shallow and fairly expansive pool that initially is empty. Adult African Bullfrogs are primed for breeding by estivating them in a container filled with 10 inches of a dry but loose river sand/chopped sphagnum moss substrate for around three to five months at a temperature of 75°F (24°C). To stir them into activity the substrate is moistened to the point of being uniformly damp but not waterlogged, and when they

An adult female *Pyxicephalus adspersus*. This species has one of the most unique appearances (leading to the common name African Ridged Frog) among the true frogs, and one of the most unusual natural histories. Photo: K. H. Switak.

emerge they must be offered as much food as possible (to avoid cannibalism during mating) before being transferred to the greenhouse. Actual courtship is induced by flooding the whole greenhouse with warm (80 to 90°F, 27 to 32°C) water, filling the pool in the process. Males may enter the water and begin calling with a low growling sound, and they also jostle and nudge each other in contention for the smaller female. This behavior may continue for three to four weeks until she is fully gravid. Then she allows the dominant male to clasp her just in front of the hind limbs. Amplexus lasts for two to eight hours, during which she deposits a mass of cream-colored eggs numbering 3,000 to 12,000. Males remain with the eggs and resultant tadpoles, both vigorously defending and devouring them. If possible, it is better to remove a clump or two of around 1,000 eggs into rearing quarters where they are maintained in a similar manner to the American Bullfrog except shallower water at a temperature of 82°F (28°C) is necessary. Tadpoles are gregarious and carnivorous, swimming around in black swarms. They will attack and feed on fish or other amphibians if given the chance, and unless sufficient food is provided they will eat each other. Metamorphosis starts after just 30 days, when the 2.5-cm froglets emerge and immediately begin feasting on each other. Juvenile African Bullfrogs tend to be cream-colored with green or brown mottling and a conspicuous yellow vertebral stripe that fades with age. Their bulbous eyes have horizontal pupils, while the mouth is characteristically wide. They are best reared individually in small plastic containers with a moistened kitchen paper tissue substrate. Bullfrogs may take up to eight years to reach maturity. Many captive African Bullfrogs seen today are a result of specialist breeders inducing their frogs to reproduce by the injection of a pituitary stimulating hormone.

Longevity: A life span in excess of 35 years is not unusual.

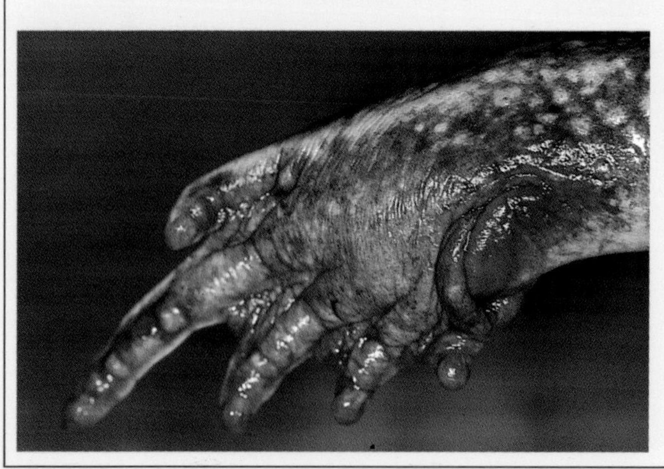

The digging spade of the African Bullfrog. Photo: K. H. Switak.

Dorsal view of a young (not fully adult) *Pyxicephalus adspersus*. Notice the rows of bony ridges are still forming. The light stripe over the backbone often disappears with age. Photo: M. Staniszewski.

Above: African Bullfrogs, *Pyxicephalus adspersus*, are excellent burrowers, a fact to be remembered when designing a terrarium for these animals. Photo: K. H. Switak. *Below:* Sometimes called the Mouse-eating Frog, *P. adspersus* is one of the most vicious anuran carnivores, making it unsafe to cage two specimens together at any time—even during breeding. Photo: J. Merli.

FAMILY RHACOPHORIDAE: THE OLD WORLD OR FOAM-NEST TREEFROGS

This large family is distributed throughout southern Asia, Madagascar, and Africa, occupying habitats similar to the family Hylidae in the American tropics. Rhacophorids generally are similar in shape and habits, with some being famous for their gliding ability aided by huge webbed feet.

Asian Foam-nest Treefrog (*Polypedates leucomystax*)

Note: Often seen in the hobby literature as *Rhacophorus leucomystax* and called the Asian Flying Frog (though it seldom flies or glides).

Distribution: India to Southeast Asia.

Length: 4 to 7.8 cm (1.5 to 3 in).

Description: A slender treefrog with a large head, prominent eyes, and pointed snout. Although its long hind limbs are slender, this frog is very agile and the digits end in specialized discs for its climbing habits. Coloration ranges from light brown to dark gray, although a form exists that shows attractive yellow or orange mottling on the dorsum.

Availability: One of the more popular frog species in captivity because it is easy to maintain, breed, and makes an ideal beginner's frog.

Captive Care: A medium-sized, tall terrarium comprising natural or artificial features will comfortably accommodate three pairs. In a natural arrangement, sturdy plants such as *Aspidistra*, *Ficus*, and *Scindapsus* should be used and therefore natural lighting is required. Temperatures between 74 and 80°F (24 to 27°C) will suffice, and humidity should be high. The terrarium substrate for rhacophorids and other arboreal anurans is not critical, although a material that holds moisture should always be preferred. A large water vessel containing 3 inches of water (pH 6 to 7) should be situated centrally and a sturdy piece of bogwood or rock should be placed across it. Like many treefrogs this species is nocturnal, spending the daytime resting. Food mainly consists of crickets, small locusts, mealworms, and waxworms and regularly should be supplemented with sweepings and multivitamin powder.

Sexual Differences: Females are considerably larger than males.

Captive Breeding: Breeding can become a regular and fascinating event if conditions are suitable, and courtship may occur throughout the year. To attract a mate, males call incessantly at night with a rapid "cheek-cheek" sound. When successful, the female is clasped in axillary amplexus. She then begins to search for a suitable nesting site, usually selecting vegetation or a branch directly overhanging water, hence the need to provide for this in the terrarium. Here she adheres 20 to 60 sticky eggs, then both sexes secrete a sticky mucus (the male also secretes sperm)

A pair of Asian Foam-nest Treefrogs, *Polypedates leucomystax*. Because the scientific species name translates literally to "white moustached, " some authors have used the common name White-bearded Flying Frog for the species, even though it usually does not glide. Photo: M. Panzella.

Some *Polypedates leucomystax* are very pale, often almost yellowish or orangish. Notice the lack of wide webs between the fingers; gliding species have large webs here. Photo: A. Norman.

that is lathered by their hind limbs to eventually cloak the eggs in a ball of foam. Construction may take anything up to 12 hours. The outside of the 5– to 8-cm nest hardens to form a protective coating around the eggs developing within. Upon hatching, the movement of the tadpoles causes the nest to dissipate, allowing them to fall into the water below. *Polypedates* tadpoles are easy to rear in clean, well oxygenated water but are highly susceptible to disease when poor water quality is evident. Average development time is 45 days at 75°F (24°C), with tadpoles growing to 2.5 cm then transforming into 12-mm froglets. These are reared in large glass jars or small terraria in groups of 10 to 20. Adequate amounts of aphids, fruitflies, and small crickets must be available.

Longevity: Eight years or more.

African Gray Treefrog (*Chiromantis xerampelina*)

Distribution: Southern and eastern Africa in arid areas such as savannahs, scrubland, and urban areas.

The African Red Treefrog, *Chiromantis rufescens*, of western Africa is similar in most ways to the more common African Gray Treefrog. Photo: Dr. J. P. Bogart.

Length: 6.2 to 8.5 cm (2.5 to 3.5 in).

Captive Care: This and other species of the genus are well-suited to a tall terrarium with a few robust logs, plants, and a relatively dry atmosphere. They even enjoy basking under a 60W spot light. A small water bowl and a light misting with a hand sprayer during the evening should be sufficient moisture, though these frogs secrete and lather themselves in a waxy mucus to prevent water loss.

Captive Breeding: They breed several times a year after heavy rainfall, when as many as ten individuals congregate and wrestle each other. Those that achieve amplexus attach their 100 or more sticky eggs (1.7 mm) in one clump to a log, rock, or plant overhanging temporary shallow water at a height of 36 inches or more. The eggs then are enclosed in a fluffy mass of foam composed of mucus and sperm. Several pairs may choose the same nesting site, so a football-sized nest can develop. In captivity, if a sufficiently tall terrarium can be acquired, this fascinating breeding display is accomplished regularly even under artificial conditions. The small (1 cm) tadpoles that fall from the nest into the water four to six days later are best removed to an aquarium containing 2 inches of good quality water at 78°F (26°C). They feed avidly on fish pellets and flake foods and reach metamorphosis into 1.2-cm frogs within eight to ten weeks.

African Gray Treefrogs, *Chiromantis xerampelina*, are well adapted to dry conditions, secreting a waxy mucus to prevent evaporation of surface water. Their large foam nests are quite a sight when successful breeding occurs in the terrarium. Photo: P. Freed.

Rhacophorus nigropalmatus **is one of several flying (actually gliding) frogs found in China and Southeast Asia. Notice the enlargement of the front feet and the extensive webbing that helps the frog parachute from trees. Photo: R. D. Bartlett.**

Malayan Flying Frog
(Rhacophorus reinwardti)

Distribution: Southeast Asia.

Length: 4 to 7 cm (1.5 to 3 in).

Captive Care: This is an exclusively arboreal species living in the upper reaches of humid forests. Unless a tall terrarium at least 4 feet high by 3 feet wide or a heated greenhouse is available, it is pointless attempting to keep these frogs, which will injure themselves and die when trying to glide down from the branches. Dense plant growth, temperatures around 80°F (27°C), and regular misting to ensure high humidities are fundamental requirements for such frogs, especially when breeding is considered. Their breeding behavior is in line with that of other species of the family.

FAMILY BUFONIDAE: THE TRUE TOADS AND HARLEQUIN TOADS

Superb Harlequin Toad (*Atelopus varius*)

Note: The harlequin toads (*Atelopus* and several allied genera) often have been considered a full family, but there is much recent work to indicate that they merely are one of several groups closely related to the true toads and best treated as a subfamily or perhaps just a tribe of Bufonidae. Though harlequin toads are highly sought after by advanced amphibian hobbyists, they should only be attempted by those with considerable experience. Many subspecies of the Superb Harlequin Toad have been described, but none are considered here; the Golden Harlequin Toad, *A. varius zeteki*, of Panama often is considered a full species on very weak grounds.

The Superb Harlequin Toad, *Atelopus varius*, one of the most colorful animals on Earth—and now unfortunately disappearing from many areas where it once was common. Photo: A. v. d. Nieuwenhuizen.

The hardy *Atelopus flavescens* from the Guianas (above and below) has a pink to violet belly that in some individuals is quite striking. Photos: A. v. d. Nieuwenhuizen

At the other extreme is the very toad-like *Atelopus ignescens*, a harlequin toad with few bright colors and enough warts to make it look like a common toad at first glance. Photos: A. v. d. Nieuwenhuizen.

Some of the many faces of the Superb Harlequin Toad, *Atelopus varius.* This frog exhibits complex variation between and within populations, leading to many different names having been applied to it in the past, most without proper foundation. Photos: A. v. d. Nieuwenhuizen.

Recently *Atelopus varius* has begun to disappear from parks and other locations in Costa Rica where only a decade ago it was very common. As with other frogs around the world, it appears to be succumbing to some combination of human interference and (probably unnatural) changes in global climate. Photo: K. Lucas.

Distribution: Central America into northwestern South America, confined to moist tropical forests.

Length: 2.4 to 3.8 cm (1 to 1.5 in).

Description: A highly variable species often showing bizarre and beautiful mosaic-like coloration, with the most common form being black with red or orange interlaced blotches. The most beautiful subspecies (at least in the opinion of some) is the black–spotted, golden yellow *A. v. zeteki.* The function of this coloration is to warn would-be predators of the frog's highly poisonous nature. *Atelopus* are oddly shaped toads with long, flattened bodies and thin, gangly limbs, while the head is triangular or square, often with an overhanging snout. A pronounced vertebral groove is present, as are heavy webs on the hind feet of many species.

Availability: This species and several other harlequin toads are commercially available in North America but only occasionally offered elsewhere. *A. v. zeteki* is strictly protected in the wild and is uncharacteristically shy and nocturnal.

Captive Care: *Atelopus varius* can be maintained in a similar manner to *Epipedobates tricolor* except for providing constantly high temperatures of 82°F (28°C) and humidity levels of above 85%. Like other lowland harlequin toads, these excellent swimmers require running water and therefore the necessary power filter and stream construction that can be accommodated only in a fairly large terrarium. Food consists of very small items such as ants, termites, aphids, fruitflies, and hatchling crickets, which should be offered in small quantities two or three times daily. Maintaining *Atelopus* can be almost impossible for hobbyists who cannot consistently maintain such a feeding regimen.

Sexual Differences: Males have smooth skin on the flanks, while in females it is rough and bristly.

Captive Breeding: Moving water and a good deal of patience are the main requirements. Wild-caught *Atelopus* may take quite a while to settle down before they show small signs of courtship behavior. Breeding can be triggered by heavy spraying or an increase in food. The male has no vocal sacs and attracts the female by performing unusual movements such as leg and head twitching, ground stamping, and hopping on the spot. Amplexus normally occurs at the edge of running water, where the female attaches her 30 to 75 eggs (1.2 mm) in strings just below the water surface. The specialized tadpoles that hatch out just 36 hours later have a flat body, specialized mouthparts, and an abdominal sucker enabling them to move around without being swept away by the current. Even so, it is preferable to transfer the tadpoles after a week to an aquarium containing warm, vigorously aerated water. Metamorphosis is completed in four weeks. Their pre-metamorphosis care and care of the minuscule toadlets are as described for *Epipedobates tricolor.*

Marine (Giant or Cane) Toad (*Bufo marinus*)

Distribution: A native of tropical America, but due to introductions into the Caribbean Islands, Florida, Hawaii, New Guinea, and Australia in unsuccessful attempts to control the cane beetle, it is now one of the most widespread amphibians.

Length: To 24 cm (10 in), usually much less.

Description: Quite a variable species in terms of patterning and coloration, the skin normally is a uniform dull to rusty brown above, with some individuals being mottled in dark and light gray or showing light speckling. The underside is light gray to creamy yellow. The Marine Toad is heavily built and has extremely warty skin with a pair of huge parotoid glands at the back of the head. When roughly handled a noxious substance called bufotoxin is secreted that causes itching on exposed skin and respiratory problems if swallowed; a large toad mouthed by a persistent small dog may kill the dog.

Availability: Huge numbers are taken from the wild for the pet trade, although in some parts of the world keeping this

A nice adult Marine Toad, *Bufo marinus*, showing the gigantic triangular parotoid gland that has made this species infamous. Photo: M. Staniszewski.

When young, many Marine Toads have a rather contrasting dark and creamy pattern. The parotoid gland may not develop fully until the toad becomes mature, but it always is long and at least somewhat triangular. Photo: A. Norman.

species is prohibited.

Captive Care: This toad makes an excellent pet and is quite at home in a large terrarium with sparse decoration, a soft basal substrate, shallow water bowl, and a hide. Dry conditions are favored, and the terrarium should never be allowed to become too moist for long periods as skin problems may occur. The terrarium should be heated to around 78°F (26°C) and a basking spot via a spot lamp should be provided. Food includes most invertebrates, fish, raw meat, and small mice, and it will even learn to accept tinned cat/dog food from a dish.

Sexual Differences: Females are generally larger than males.

Captive Breeding: Breeding is likely only within the heated greenhouse under the same conditions described for the African Bullfrog. Females have a high fecundity, producing in excess of 30,000 eggs in long gelatinous strings. Tadpoles hatch, grow, and metamorphose in 18 to 30 days, with the toadlets measuring 2 cm.

Longevity: Twenty years or more.

Marine Toads, *Bufo marinus*, vary greatly in color shade, from almost uniformly tan to nearly black, with or without paler marbling. The extent of wartiness also varies. Notice the white toxic secretions exuding from the parotoid of one of the toads above. Photos: Top: K. H. Switak; bottom: A. Norman.

An Arabian Green Toad, *Bufo viridis arabicus*. Only isolated green tones are present in this southern individual, much of the green being obscured by sandy brown areas. Photo: M. Staniszewski.

Eurasian Green Toad (*Bufo viridis*)

Distribution: Eastern Europe and northwestern Africa, spreading through central and southern Asia to the Himalayas. Often occurs in and around man's dwellings, especially street lamps at night.

Length: 6 to 10 cm (2.5 to 4 in).

Description: A highly variable species, with conspicuous green and light gray marbling seen in Balkan and Asia Minor specimens making this one of the most attractive bufonids. In northern African and eastern Asian forms the light areas are replaced by a sandy or dark brown, sometimes obscuring the green patterning. The body is plump and heavily warty, and as with many typical toads the hind legs are quite short, often prompting a walking rather than hopping motion.

Availability: Although this species is quite rare and protected throughout much of its range, substantial numbers are now being produced in captivity, so obtaining these delightful toads should present no difficulties.

A truly green Green Toad, *Bufo viridis*. Bright specimens of this species are among the most colorful toads and make excellent terrarium animals. Photo: M. Staniszewski.

Captive Care: In the wild both damp and dry areas are inhabited, and this should be reflected in the terrarium layout. Use a sandy substrate for the base, in which can be grown a number of succulent plants to give the terrarium more appeal. Hides constructed from rocks or cork bark and a shallow water bowl also should be included. The Green Toad is primarily nocturnal, but during cool periods it often will bask under a low wattage spot lamp. Temperatures between 68 and 74°F (20 and 24°C) are required, with a drop to as low as 55°F (13°C) at night. The terrarium should be lightly misted each evening. Alternatively, Green Toads do equally as well in a simple terrarium. Himalayan and more northerly European Green Toads can be maintained in the unheated greenhouse, but more southerly types may need supplementary heating during winter.

Sexual Differences: Females are larger than males, and the throat skin of the male is loose because of an external vocal sac.

Captive Breeding: A strict hibernation period at 40°F (4°C) is necessary, 50°F (10°C) for southern forms, as is a fairly large aqua-terrarium or greenhouse with a pool containing warm, shallow water with dense vegetation. Green Toads and their tadpoles are amazingly tolerant of waters that are badly polluted or high in alkalinity such as brackish pools and estuaries. Breeding commences in July or August in cooler climates. Twelve thousand to 18,000 black eggs are produced in long strings. Due to the high water temperature, the 8-mm toadlets emerge from the water 24 to 50 days later. Expect a high mortality rate in tadpoles and toadlets, the latter because finding suitably small foods in sufficiently high quantities can be very difficult.

Longevity: Eighteen to 30 years.

Other Species: The North American Green Toad (*Bufo debilis*) shows similar coloration but is an overall smaller species rarely attaining 5 cm (2 in). It is far more secretive in its habits and rarely appears even at night. Otherwise its care is exactly the samc.

Eurasian Common Toad (*Bufo bufo*)

Distribution: Throughout mainland Europe and northwestern Africa, west across Asia to Japan and Korea. This species is found in a wide variety of lowland and mountain habitats from dry scrubland to moist woodlands and exists in a multitude of described subspecies and varieties, many of which probably are good species but are almost unrecognizable externally.

Length: 8 to 13 cm (3 to 5 in).

Captive Care & Breeding: The Common Toad is a placid, robust frog that has been known to live 35 years in captivity. It requires either a medium to large woodland terrarium with temperatures in the 50 to 74°F (10 to 24°C) range or an outdoor

A young Eurasian Common Toad, *Bufo bufo*. The bright golden eye led to many stories and myths about this animal, and we won't even mention the strange beliefs about warts. Photo: M. P. & C. Piednoir.

enclosure. In both cases it should have access to dry areas and a shallow pond. Breeding occurs after a two– to four-month hibernation, usually in March or April when these toads congregate in large number. The smaller males outnumber females by five or ten to one. Endless double strings of spawn composed of 10,000 or more 2-mm black eggs are entwined around surface water weed. In cold water the tadpoles may not hatch out for 10 to 15 days. Many eggs and tadpoles succumb to various infections and predation, and only a small percentage may survive to metamorphose into 1.3-cm toadlets some 12 to 16 weeks later.

Other Species: The subspecies from southern Europe, *Bufo bufo spinosus*, can attain 16 cm (6 in) and, unlike the smooth warty skin of the typical subspecies, its skin is covered with sharp, spiny tubercles. It also requires somewhat higher temperatures and estivates rather than hibernates. The Natterjack Toad, *Bufo calamita*, is becoming increasingly scarce across most of its European and western Asian range due to its preference for scrubland dunes with warm, shallow water. It needs to be bred on a wider scale in captivity to ensure its survival, but only by experienced hobbyists. It responds well to captive care and may live for many years.

Above: A mating pair of Eurasian Common Toads, *Bufo bufo*. Photo: B. Kahl. *Below:* An unusual red phase individual of the American Toad, *Bufo americanus*. Toads often adapt to local soil coloration over a period of several days to weeks. Photo: R. T. Zappalorti.

American Toad (*Bufo americanus*)

Distribution: Southern Canada south over much of the central and eastern U.S.A., usually at moderate to high elevations. Found in a variety of habitats, including gardens, woodlands, and fields.

Length: 5 to 8.8 cm (2 to 3.5 in).

Description: The head of this brown to brick-red toad shows very prominent cranial crests and large parotoid glands; there usually is only one wart, sometimes two, in each dark spot on the back.

Captive Care: The basic care is very similar to that for *Bufo bufo*, but it is shy and likes lots of hiding places. Food includes most small insects, especially crickets, slugs, and earthworms.

Other Species: The very similar Southern Toad (*Bufo terrestris*) of the southeastern U.S.A. needs a bit higher temperatures and is at home in drier conditions. The crests between the eyes in this species are greatly developed into tall knobs. Woodhouse's Toad (*Bufo woodhousi*, including the very common *Bufo fowleri* as a synonym) is found over most of the U.S.A. east of the Rocky Mountains and may be very

The American Toad, *Bufo americanus* (below and facing page) occupies a large area in eastern North America, including frigid areas of Canada. The brightly colored northern Canadian form (below) once was considered a distinct subspecies, *copei*. Calling male American Toads are familiar sights in much of the northeastern United States. Photos: Below: Dr. D. Green; facing page: M. Panzella.

Not all toads are dull brown animals. The Canadian Toad, *Bufo hemiophrys*, above has an attractive pattern and also an interesting head structure with a large boss between the eyes. The American Toad, *Bufo americanus*, below also possesses a nicely variegated pattern. Photos: Top: W. P. Mara; bottom: A. Norman.

The common Western Toad, *Bufo boreas*, is unfortunately not longer common in many areas of northwestern North America where it was abundant just a few years ago. Its eggs and tadpoles seem to be reacting unfavorably to increased radiation penetrating an ozone-poor atmosphere at higher elevations. The future looks bleak for this once-familiar species. Photo: J. Coborn.

common. It is very variable but usually has three or four warts in each spot on the back. Check a field guide to proper identification of North American toads—there are many species and they often are confusingly alike.

Western Toad (*Bufo boreas*)

Distribution: Western North America, from the southwestern tip of Alaska to northern Baja California.

Length: 7 to 13 cm (3 to 5 in).

Captive Care: This very plump toad has a pale yellow or white vertebral stripe, sparsely warty skin, low cranial crests, and somewhat rounded parotoid glands. It makes an interesting captive because of its mainly diurnal habits. A relatively large, dry terrarium is required, although a shallow water bowl should be present. Like most bufonids, it enjoys basking under spot lamps that are not too hot. Breeding is likely only in an unheated greenhouse.

***Bufo boreas haplophilus*, the California Toad, is a southern subspecies of the Western Toad. *Bufo boreas* lacks an external vocal sac, so its breeding congresses are relatively quiet. Photo: P. A. Vargas.**

Though it is small, the Oak Toad, *Bufo quercicus*, of the southeastern United States has a large sausage-shaped vocal sac and is exceedingly loud. Its breeding congresses can be heard from considerable distances. Photo: R. T. Zappalorti.

Oak Toad (*Bufo quercicus*)

Distribution: Southeastern U.S.A. in relatively dry pinelands and grasslands.

Length: 2 to 3.5 cm (1 to 1.5 in).

Captive Care & Breeding: A tiny, very plump, and colorful toad with a narrow white line down the back and multicolored warts. It makes an excellent subject for a small terrarium, preferring temperatures in the range of 60 to 76°F (16 to 25°C). Like many toads that inhabit drier areas, it is an opportunistic breeder making use of water troughs, rain puddles, leaking water pipes, and other such areas, but usually breeds in small and temporary ponds (where it may be preyed upon by the Marine Toad). In captivity, keeping the terrarium dry for most of the year and then suddenly flooding it to a depth of 3 inches may sometimes encourage egg-laying. Females produce as many as 800 small grayish eggs in dozens of 5-cm gelatinous strands containing around ten eggs each. Newly emerged toadlets measure just 8 mm and need plenty of fruitflies, aphids, and bloodworms.

Colorado River Toad (*Bufo alvarius*)

Distribution: Extreme southwestern U.S.A. and northwestern Mexico in dry, rocky habitats with many crevices and burrows.

Length: 11 to 17 cm (4.5 to 7 in).

Care and Breeding: This is the largest native North American toad (excluding the Marine Toad, of course). It settles down well in captivity, where it will accept strips of raw meat and dog food as well as more normal toad foods. The parotoid glands are particularly large, and the secretions (from the glands on the head and also those on the hind legs) have a mild narcotic effect. A medium to large terrarium setup in the savannah or desert style will house two to four individuals, though a large shallow water bowl must be present. It hides during the day, when temperatures should be in the area of 74°F (24°C). At night a drop to 55 to 65°F (13 to 18°C) and a good

Close-up of the head of the Colorado River Toad, *Bufo alvarius*, one of the most popular pet toads (unfortunately almost all wild-caught). Photo: A. Norman.

The large body size and large parotoid glands (notice the one on the hind leg) of the Colorado River Toad have led to the unusual behavior of "toad licking" by certain odd people who have gotten high by licking or smoking the secretions of the parotoids. This illegal practice has led to excessive collecting of *Bufo alvarius* in the wild and more restrictive laws against its possession. Photo: A. Norman.

misting will encourage the toads to leave their burrows and hunt. Breeding is only likely in the greenhouse with supplementary heating—these toads will not stand temperatures below 45°F (8°C). Give them long periods of hot, dry weather to stimulate estivation and then heavy spraying to produce temporary pools. Up to 15,000 eggs are deposited in thick gelatinous strands attached to submerged rocks. In warm water they hatch very quickly and the tadpoles feed on microscopic algae and each other. They tend to metamorphose quickly, producing surprisingly small (1.4 cm) toadlets that are more brightly colored and less warty than the parents.

African Red Toad *(Bufo carens)*

Note: Often placed in the genus *Schismaderma.*

Distribution: The Congo delta east to Kenya and south into central South Africa in woodlands and sometimes open savannah.

Length: 5.4 to 10 cm (2 to 4 in).

Description: This species shows quite a variety of colors, with South African specimens being the most beautiful, orange-red on the back separated by a black stripe from the grayish flanks. The body is very plump, the legs short, the head wide, and there are no external parotoid glands.

Captive Care & Breeding: It requires a savannah or moist woodland terrarium with a

A nicely colored African Red Toad, *Bufo carens*. When the genus *Bufo* is split or partitioned (as is happening currently), this species is placed in the distinct genus *Schismaderma*. Notice that there is no external parotoid gland behind the eye. Photo: G. Dibley.

shallow water bowl and plenty of hiding places. Breeding commences in November or December after heavy rainfall, with as many as 11,000 eggs being deposited in 5-mm diameter single strings or 12-mm double strings. Their care is as for other bufonids apart from the necessity of well-oxygenated water at 72 to 78 °F (22 to 26°C) and a depth of 4 inches to promote healthy growth. Emerging toadlets are 2 cm at metamorphosis and require a moist rearing container until they are 4 cm long.

Moroccan Toad *(Bufo mauretanicus)*

Distribution: Northwestern Africa in pine woodlands and dry plateaus.

Length: 10 to 18 cm (4 to 7 in).

Captivc Care: This huge bicolored toad has a criss-cross pattern of sandy brown and chocolate spots. In captivity it becomes extremely tame and will even follow its keeper around in the hopes of acquiring food. Its appetite seems endless, and most foods are accepted. A terrarium similar to that for *Bufo alvarius* but larger is required. Breeding occurs during autumn or winter after the onset of heavy rains. Unfortunately, this species is not offered as regularly as many other

Above: **Not all Red Toads, *Bufo carens*, are brightly colored, but all have a rather streamlined appearance (for a toad) that makes them interesting pets. Photo: K. Lucas. *Below:* A Moroccan Toad, *Bufo mauretanicus*. This is an uncommon species in the terrarium. Photo: M. Staniszewski.**

Moroccan Toads, *Bufo mauretanicus*, are large and have large appetites. Notice that the parotoid gland is rounded, not triangular as in *Bufo marinus*. Trade in this species sometimes is restricted by various conservation laws. Photo: M. Staniszewski.

species and breeding successes are rare. Its delightful disposition, intelligence, and attractive appearance deserve to lend it greater popularity.

Colombian Giant Toad (Blomberg's Toad) *(Bufo blombergi)*

Distribution: Northwestern South America in humid forests and cultivated meadows.

Length: 15 to 25 cm (6 to 10 in).

Captive Care & Breeding: As large as or even larger than the Marine Toad, Colombian Giant Toads are desirable animals that seldom are available to hobbyists. The back is an attractive bronze or golden brown, contrasting sharply with the dark chocolate brown or black flanks. In captivity it is quite content with a small terrarium (28 X 16 X 16 inches for an adult pair). It is mainly nocturnal, but soon settles down and appears during the day, spending its hours sitting in shallow water or urging the keeper to feed it. Its appetite is enormous, with anything from locusts to mice being devoured. Breeding can be achieved given high humidity, constantly high temperatures, and heavy daily spraying, but it is much more likely in a tropical greenhouse than a terrarium. Up to 20,000

The striking Colombian Giant Toad, *Bufo blombergi*, wasn't described until 1951 and has never been common in the terrarium hobby. Today it is a highly desirable but seldom available species. Photo: W. B. Allen, Jr.

A juvenile Rococo Toad, *Bufo paracnemis*. This little toad has the potential to grow into an 8-inch adult. Like many other interesting toads, it seldom is available to hobbyists. Photo: R. D. Bartlett.

eggs are laid in shallow pools with dense weed growth. These hatch in eight days. The tadpoles take about five to eight weeks to metamorphose into light gray and blue-stippled toadlets 2 cm long. The toadlets should be given individual care.

Rococo Toad (*Bufo paracnemis*)

Distribution: Brazil and Argentina in rainforest and moist grasslands.

Length: 14 to 21 cm (5.5 to 8.5 in).

Captive Care & Breeding: Only occasionally seen in captivity due to rules banning export from its home countries, this impressive toad requires care like that for *Bufo blombergi* but it can tolerate lower temperatures, to the 65°F (18°C) mark, but prefers 76°F (25°C). It tends to estivate over some of its range, which may be a pointer to successfully breeding it in captivity. There are few records of terrarium or greenhouse breeding. Apparently the toadlets are among the largest known newly metamorphosed anurans, which may be due to the highly voracious appetite, the 8– to 11-cm black tadpoles swarming over anything that moves.

Asian Black Toads, *Bufo melanostictus*, always look like they have worn or eroded crests on the head. An abundant species over much of tropical Asia, its lack of bright colors has always kept it from appealing to more hobbyists. Photos: Top: R. D. Bartlett; bottom: W. Wuster.

Asian Black Toad *(Bufo melanostictus)*

Distribution: Southern China and India over most of Southeast Asia in all lowland habitats.

Length: 5 to 10 cm (2 to 4 in).

Description: A highly variable species, usually recognizable by the brown body and the black crests on the head. One form from Malaysia is light orange, the black crests, parotoids, warts, and dorsolateral ridges being especially prominent. Its care is as for *Bufo bufo*, apart from a higher temperature requirement of around 76°F (25°C).

Above: Africa has many toads, most related to a species called *Bufo regularis*. The one shown here, the Raucous Toad, *Bufo rangeri*, is restricted to Lesotho and parts of South Africa. Identification of African toads is complex to the extreme. Photo: K. H. Switak. *Below:* The Asian Rough Toad, *Bufo asper*, is common over much of Thailand and Indonesia but seldom imported. Photo: A. Norman.

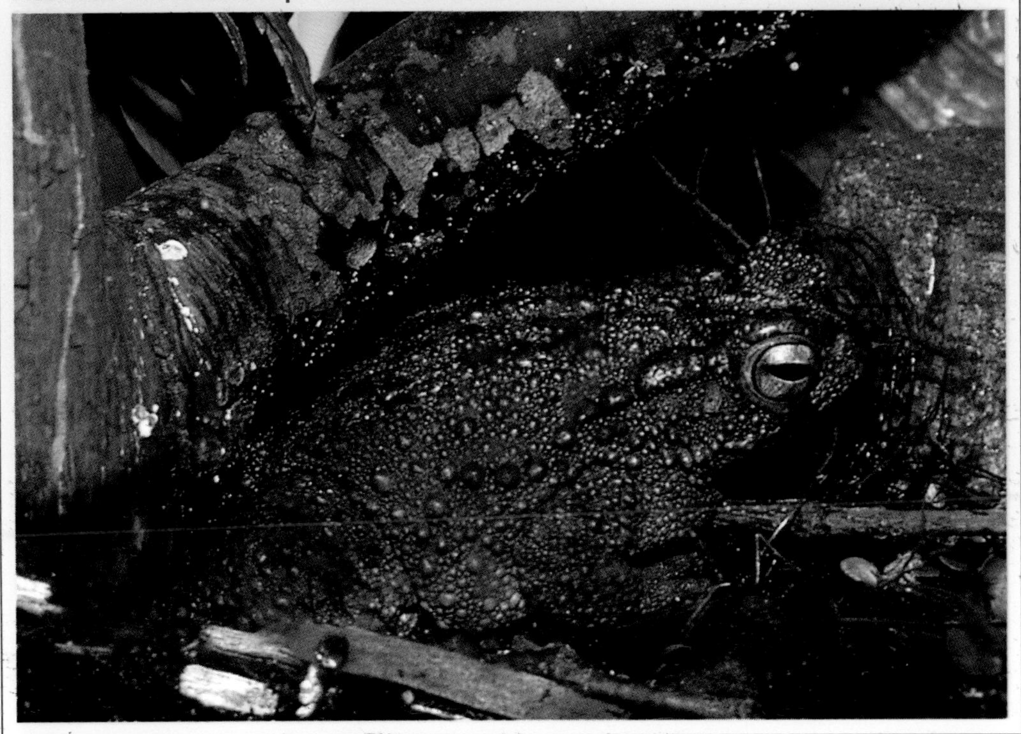

Natterjack or Running Toads, *Bufo calamita*, are popular pets in Europe and sometimes appear on the American market as well. They are attractive, personable animals that exhibit many unusual behaviors in the terrarium and can be bred with persistence. Unfortunately, their habitat is disappearing, and the species often is covered by restrictive conservation laws. Photos: M. Staniszewski.

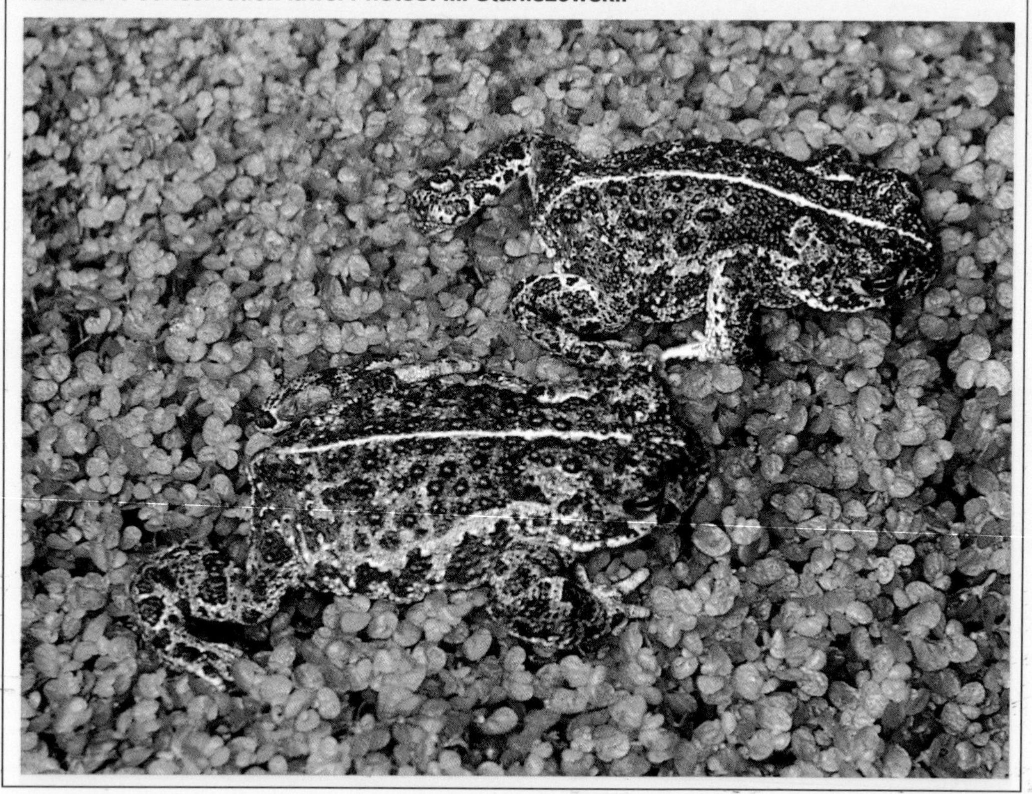

Spotted Tree Toad (*Pedostibes hosi*)

Distribution: Southeast Asia in humid forests.

Length: 6 to 9 cm (2.5 to 3.5 in).

Description: An unusual, somewhat fragile-looking toad with a gray-blue dorsum covered with yellow spots. The long legs have webbed feet and disc-shaped toepads, though the toad is by no means an accomplished climber.

Captive Care: It needs a fairly large tropical woodland terrarium containing sturdy branches for its limited arboreal behavior and a large water bowl in which it can bathe. Temperatures should be between 74 and 84°F (24 to 29°C); if given a low wattage spot lamp this toad will bask.

Captive Breeding: Breeding occurs throughout the year whenever there is a noticeable increase in rainfall. Males are about 2 cm shorter than females and have a dark gray vocal sac that they use to emit a rapid squeaking call. Eggs are deposited in curious short strings and total 2,000 to 3,000. Tadpoles take six weeks to metamorphose, and the newly metamorphosed toadlets appear extremely odd because of their pencil-thin, wiry legs. They are best raised in groups of 10 to 20 and fed on small crickets and waxworms.

FAMILY HYLIDAE: THE TREEFROGS

This very popular family contains some of the most attractive and interesting amphibians available to hobbyists. The majority are expert tree-dwellers with specialized toe pads and streamlined bodies.

American Green Treefrog (*Hyla cinerea*)

Distribution: Central and southern U.S.A.

Length: 3.5 to 6 cm (1.5 to 2 in).

Description: The normal dorsal coloration is bright grass green with a distinct broad cream or pearl stripe edged with black running along the upper lip and each flank, although in some populations the stripe is absent on the side. Like many hylids, it can alter its color to dark brown, gray, or yellow to match its mood, the surroundings, or the air temperature. The build of this species is more slender than many other popular hylids, while the specialized disc-shaped toe pads are somewhat larger.

Availability: Collected in large quantities from the wild during its breeding season from early spring to late summer. In some parts of its range it is becoming increasingly scarce. Sometimes confused with other American treefrogs by dealers.

Captive Care: American treefrogs and other arboreal hylids may suffer from stress and refuse food if they are not given access to plenty of green plants in a tall terrarium. They also enjoy bathing in a fairly deep water vessel from time to time, and a 40W spot lamp directed onto an exposed branch will enable them to bask frequently. Temperatures of 68 to 74°F (20 to 24°C) are

A Spotted Tree Toad, *Pedostibes hosi.* This tropical Asian climbing toad shows great variation in colors and patterns from locality to locality and also individually. Often the yellow or orange spots are found only on the female, the male having a brown and green back or various types of mottling. Several species of the genus could in theory be imported sporadically. Photo: A. Norman.

Two of the more interesting toads. *Above:* The Red-spotted Toad, *Bufo punctatus*, of the southwestern United States and Mexico often is one of the most colorful toads—but not all specimens show so much contrast. Photo: Dr. D. Green. *Below:* South American Crested Toads, *Bufo typhonius*, are variable, and the name probably includes several distinct species. This is one of the odder variants, with high crests and a row of erect warts down the center of the back; most Crested Toads are not nearly so distinctive. Photo: J. Visser.

American Green Treefrogs, *Hyla cinerea*, are collected in large numbers in the southern United States and are among the most available and inexpensive of the treefrogs. They make good pets but unfortunately seldom are bred in captivity. Photo: R. D. Bartlett.

preferred, and the terrarium should be sprayed regularly to maintain high humidity.

Sexual Differences: The throat of the male tends to be grayer and wrinkled, caused by the single vocal sac. In females the throat is cream or white.

Captive Breeding: Although this species is not as hardy as some other temperate treefrogs, it must have a cool period at around 50°F (10°C) for several months. Males voice their presence in harmony throughout the year but especially during the breeding season and immediately following heavy spraying. Amplexus and spawning take place at night in shallow water usually containing dense vegetation. The female deposits up to 700 dark brown eggs in several globular clumps. Transfer these to a large aquarium containing around 8 inches of well-oxygenated water at a temperature of 68°F (20°C). After hatching six days later, the tadpoles grow quickly on a diet of blanched parsley and trout pellets (or equivalents). They metamorphose into 9-mm froglets 38 to 60 days later and are best housed in small groups on a diet of aphids, fruitflies, and small crickets.

Eurasian Green Treefrogs, *Hyla arborea*, represent a variable group of subspecies and varieties that probably really are several distinct species. Taxonomy of treefrogs often necessitates knowledge of their calls, breeding behavior, and tadpoles. Photo: M. Gilroy.

Eurasian Green Treefrog (*Hyla arborea*)

Note: This wide-ranging frog is a complex of subspecies and varieties, many of which are now considered full species though not identifiable with certainty from external appearance.

Distribution: Throughout Europe and western Asia.

Length: 4 to 5 cm (1.5 to 2 in).

Description: Somewhat similar in coloration to the preceding species, the Eurasian Green Treefrog is a bit more robust and has a broad pinkish brown stripe

The treefrog of southern Europe and North Africa is very similar to *Hyla arborea* but is considered a full species, *Hyla meridionalis*, the Stripeless Treefrog. It requires warmer temperatures than other European species. Photo: M. P. & C. Piednoir.

along the flanks and tympanum over the eye to the nostril.

Availability: Now protected through much of its range but commercially produced in Europe and to a lesser extent in the U.S.A.

Captive Care: Similar to *Hyla cinerea*, although this species is hardy and will tolerate unheated greenhouse conditions.

Sexual Differences: Males have a darker throat and are less robust than females.

Captive Breeding: Successful breeding is likely only in a larger terrarium where a substantial water source is present. Hibernation at 40°F (4°C) for a period of four months is essential. After feeding for several months, breeding commences from late May onward. Females deposit up to 1,000 whitish eggs. The relatively large (1.5 cm) froglets emerge after 8 to 12 weeks and are maintained as for *Hyla cinerea*.

Longevity: Twelve years or more.

Other Species: The Tyrrhenian Treefrog (*Hyla sarda*) from Corsica and Sardinia and the Stripeless Treefrog (*H. meridionalis*) from southwestern Europe and North Africa are very similar to *Hyla arborea* although in captivity they will not tolerate low temperatures.

Barking Treefrog (*Hyla gratiosa*)

Distribution: Southeastern U.S.A.

Length: 4.4 to 6.5 cm (1.5 to 2.5 in).

Captive Care: This species, the largest native U.S.A. treefrog, also

Barking Treefrogs, *Hyla gratiosa* (above and facing page), are large southern United States frogs with very granular skin, an interesting spotted pattern that changes with mood, and a loud voice. They are active feeders on crickets in the terrarium and will eat incredible numbers of these insects unless put on a diet. Photos: facing page: W. P. Mara; above: R. D. Bartlett.

has one of the loudest calls, a factor that should be taken into consideration before buying a specimen. It is extremely hardy, making it ideal for unheated greenhouses where it can hibernate deep underground during cold weather. Although habitually nocturnal, it also benefits from a low wattage spot light beneath which it will spend most of the day basking while asleep. In captivity a medium-sized tall temperate planted terrarium will house around four to six specimens that will need large numbers of waxmoths, crickets, and other insects.

Captive Breeding: Breeding commences in April or May, when males entice females to the breeding pool with their "dog bark" call. During amplexus the female lays small clumps of large (4 mm) green to yellow eggs numbering 2,000–plus over the submerged vegetation. Tadpoles hatch quickly under the influence of the warming sun, and seven or eight weeks later they measure nearly 5 cm long and are an extremely attractive bright green. At metamorphosis the froglets (2.5 cm) are an attractive bright or mottled green like the adult. They reach maturity in the second year.

The other commonly seen United States treefrog is the Gray Treefrog, *Hyla versicolor*. This species is easy to recognize by the large cream spot below the eye and the dark (often greenish) pattern on the back. The backs of the thighs usually are bright orange. This type of frog occurs as two externally indistinguishable species (the other is *Hyla chrysocelis*) told apart only by calls, size of blood cells, and chromosomes. Photos: Below: R. D. Bartlett; facing page: M. Gilroy.

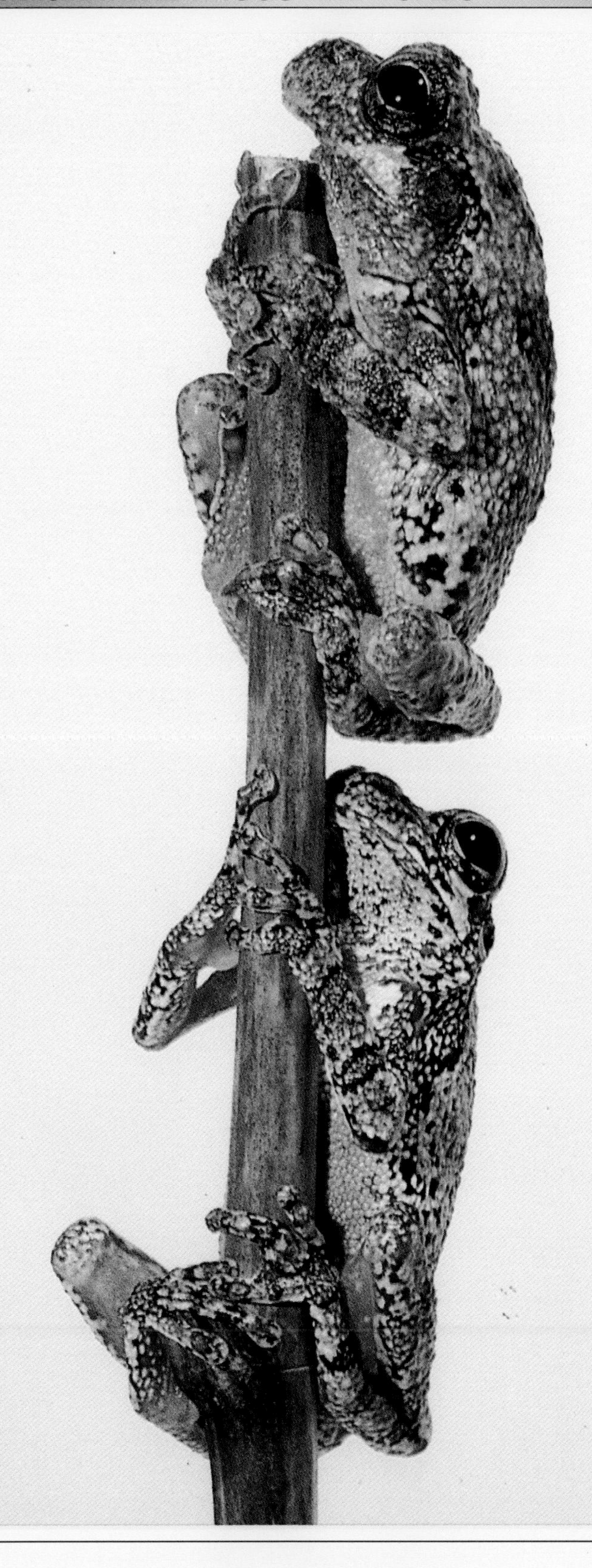

Gray Treefrog (*Hyla versicolor*)

Distribution: Central and eastern U.S.A. in a multitude of habitats.

Length: 3 to 5.2 cm (1 to 2 in).

Description: Unlike most North American treefrogs, the skin of the Gray is quite warty. It can alter its colors somewhat depending on surroundings and mood, varying from a mottled green or light gray to almost chocolate brown, varied with irregular whitish areas. The overall pattern often resembles a lichenose piece of tree bark, providing excellent camouflage. There is a large white spot under the eye, a trademark of the species. Two other very similar species (*Hyla avivoca* and *H. chrysocelis*) also have the eye spot, *H. chrysocelis* differing only in chromosome number and size of blood cells as well as mating call.

Captive Care & Breeding: Gray Treefrogs need a fairly large planted tall terrarium with plenty of logs and other cover. They enjoy extended periods of basking under a spot light. The terrarium should be about 75°F (24°C) during the day, dropped to around 55°F (13°C) at night. Breeding occurs from November to April, with up to 2,000 eggs being laid.

The Spring Peeper, *Pseudacris crucifer*, is a small ground-dwelling treefrog found over the eastern United States. The dark X on the back is fairly distinctive. Photo: R. D. Bartlett.

The Spring Peeper often is the first frog heard in the early spring in the northeastern United States and has garnered quite a bit of its popularity from that fact. Its small size may make it hard to feed in the terrarium. Photo: R. D. Bartlett.

Spring Peeper (*Pseudacris crucifer*)

Distribution: Southeastern Canada and over all the eastern U.S.A.

Length: 2.7 to 3.4 cm (1 in).

Captive Care: This attractive, very agile little hylid (formerly in the genus *Hyla*) is distinguished by the dark X over the center of its back. Its small size makes it ideal for smaller planted terraria, though it can be kept in unheated greenhouses during the summer months. When the temperature drops below 44°F (6°C) it tends to retreat into burrows and becomes dormant.

Captive Breeding: Breeding occurs in the early spring (it often is the first frog to be heard calling in the spring, thus the common name) after snowmelt or heavy spring rains. About 200 to 300 whitish eggs are deposited in ditches, temporary puddles, and the edges of small ponds. Tadpoles reach 3.5 cm in length, the 1.3-cm froglets emerging after 11 to 14 weeks.

Giant Treefrog (*Hyla vasta*)

Distribution: Hispaniola in the Caribbean.

Length: 8 to 14.2 cm (3 to 5.5 in).

The Spring Peeper, *Pseudacris crucifer*. Photo: A. Norman.

Hyla vasta, a very large treefrog from the Caribbean island of Hispaniola, makes an interesting terrarium animal. Because of deforestation in Haiti and to a lesser extent in the Dominican Republic, natural populations must be greatly reduced in numbers. Photo: G. Dibley.

South and Central America are home to dozens of treefrogs, many with bizarre color patterns, shapes, and habits. Above is a stunning male Spotted Treefrog, *Hyla punctata*, and below is the Nesting Treefrog, *Hyla boans*. Both species are found throughout northern South America, and the latter is unusual in digging large bowl nests in which to lay the eggs. Photos: P. Freed.

There are not many treefrogs in the western United States. The most common, and only one occasionally sold, is the Canyon Treefrog, *Hyla arenicolor*, a very variable species most notable for the bright yellow hidden in the groin. Photo: R. D. Bartlett.

***Hyla ebraccata*, the Golden Palm Frog of Central America, is a spectacular little treefrog that often is imported but seldom is bred. Photo: M. Panzella.**

Captive Care & Breeding: The largest species of treefrog, *Hyla vasta* makes an impressive subject for the tall tropical terrarium, although only small numbers are exported from the West Indies due to its limited range. It rarely has been bred in captivity, mainly because it requires a very spacious terrarium heated to around 82°F (28°C) and containing plenty of vegetation and hiding spots. A heated greenhouse with a shallow, vegetated pool might work very well. This is a shy species, but it should be maintained only with amphibians of similar size to prevent it from overpowering and eating any smaller animals. With age this species tends to become extremely rotund, living life at a slow pace and preferring to squat in one position for days on end. It has been known to live 15 years in captivity.

White's (Dumpy) Treefrog (*Litoria caerulea*)

Distribution: New Guinea and northeastern Australia.

Length: 7 to 11.5 cm (3 to 4.5 in).

Description: The body of this large, rotund frog ranges from a light or emerald green to a brown or blue color depending on its surroundings. The rubbery skin is waxy in appearance, which reduces water loss and enables this frog to tolerate fairly arid conditions. In older specimens fleshy folds begin to develop over the eyes and throat and along the flanks so that the tympanum and bases of the upper limbs are

The White's or Dumpy Treefrog, *Litoria caerulea*, has become perhaps the most commonly sold frog. Photo: D. Dube.

The newly metamorphosed White's Treefrog, *Litoria caerulea*, shown below has a long way to grow before it can match the large adult shown above. The color changes and heavy folds develop behind the eyes along with growth. Photos: Top: M. Staniszewski; bottom: W. P. Mara.

A natural, wild-collected piebald (mottled) adult White's or Dumpy Treefrog. *Litoria caerulea* has the potential to throw many different color varieties. Photo: A. Box.

completely hidden. The limbs are muscular and end in large feet with huge globular toe pads needed to support this frog's bulk during its climbing activities.

Availability: Widespread breeding success, an unusual appearance, placid disposition, and ease of maintenance have resulted in this treefrog being a favorite with hobbyists throughout the world.

Captive Care: An easier anuran species to maintain in captivity would be difficult to imagine. They are best maintained in groups of four to eight, with at least two males present, and seem perfectly content with a large, tall terrarium furnished with a couple of sturdy branches and house plants, a wide but shallow (1 to 3 inches deep) water bowl, and a spot lamp to bask under. The terrarium should be lightly misted each evening, often prompting the males to burst into song, and temperatures should be between 74 and 79°F (24 and 26°C) during the day with a drop to 65°F (18°C) at night. They are mainly nocturnal creatures but often will awaken when offered food or when the terrarium is misted. Although their appetites are prodigious, feeding should be limited to either one large or several smaller meals per week, with a whole range of invertebrates, fishes, raw red

The more slender Indonesian White's Treefrog, *Litoria caerulea*, often is imported, but most hobbyists agree it is not quite as hardy or interesting as the captive-bred Australian form. Photo: W. P. Mara.

The piebald mutation of the Dumpy or White's Treefrog (top) may prove to be the source of new color varieties for the terrarium. Golden spotted individuals (below) occur naturally and are considered quite desirable by hobbyists. Recently *Litoria caerulea* has been placed in the old genus *Pelodryas*, and it and it relatives in *Litoria* have been placed in the subfamily or family Pelodryadidae. So far few herpetologists have followed these changes, however. Photos: J. Coborn.

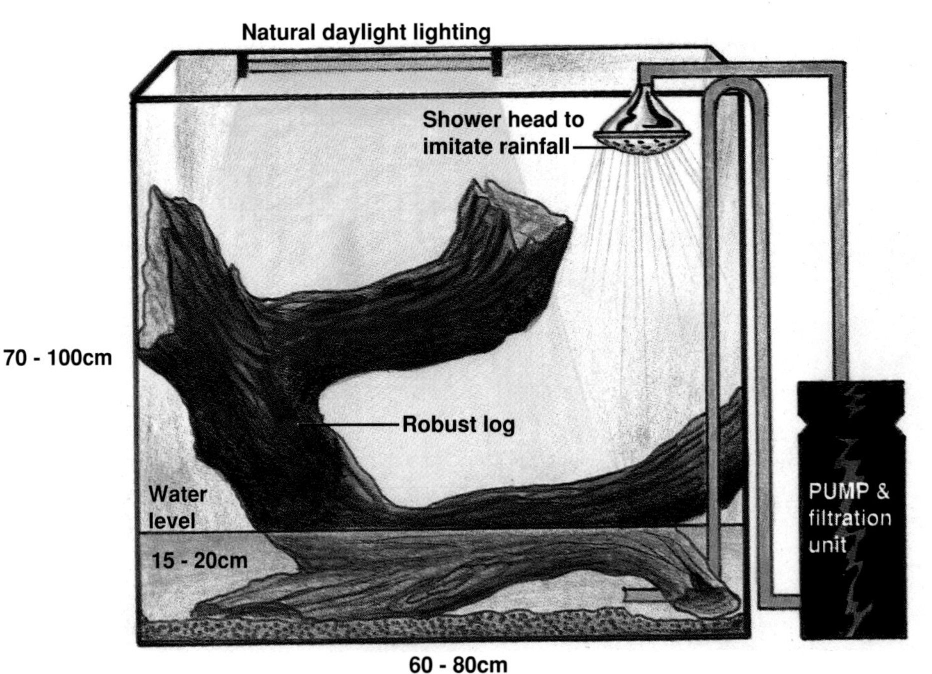

A suitable breeding setup for *Litoria caerulea*.

meat, and small mammals being devoured. Larger specimens can even tackle a fully grown mouse, although this is not an essential nutritional requirement.

Sexual Differences: Females are larger and more rotund than males, while males have grayer, more wrinkled throats.

Captive Breeding: Breeding behavior is only likely when the treefrogs are transferred to an estivation/breeding chamber. Frogs are initially subjected to dry conditions for four weeks, which prompts them to enter estivation by cloaking their body in a watertight cocoon consisting of several layers of sloughed epidermis. To rouse them, the chamber is sprayed heavily with warm water for an hour, during which a large water bowl containing dense vegetation is put at the base of the chamber. Some or all of the treefrogs may eventually awaken and move down to the water bowl, where males call until they have secured a receptive female. Amplexus lasts up to 24 hours, during which the female lays several golf ball-sized clumps of spawn totaling 150 or so eggs. Breeding may occur up to four times per year. Spawn must be removed to a warm, shallow aquarium, where tadpoles hatch out in one to three days, although in the early stages many tadpoles will succumb, especially if overcrowded. Full development is completed in as little as 18 days if sufficient fish pellets, raw meat, and chopped earthworm are offered. Newly metamorphosed 2-cm froglets are slender in comparison to their parents but have a similar appetite and grow swiftly to attain maturity within two years.

Longevity: Fifteen years or more.

White-lipped Treefrog *(Litoria infrafrenata*)

Distribution: New Guinea and northern Australia.

Length: 10 to 13.5 cm (4 to 5.5 in).

Captive Care & Breeding: This large treefrog is a more slender, agile version of the Dumpy Treefrog. It cannot tolerate dry conditions, therefore a spacious, tall, planted tropical terrarium with a large water bowl and a basking light is necessary. The terrarium must be misted frequently and the temperature kept in the 75 to 86°F (24 to 30°C) range. Breeding can take place at any time of the year. Females are brought into condition by both heavy feeding and the raucous croaking of several smaller males. The successful male grasps the female and drags her to the water, where she deposits 200 to 400 whitish eggs about 3 mm in diameter. Their care is the same as that of *Litoria caerulea*. Many hobbyists feel that the White-lipped Treefrog is more delicate than the Dumpy and more of a problem; many specimens seen for sale are wild-caught.

The White-lipped Treefrog, *Litoria infrafrenata*, though a large species, seems to be less hardy than White's Treefrog when in the terrarium. It seldom is bred. Photo: A. Norman.

Cuban Treefrog (*Osteopilus septentrionalis*)

Distribution: Native to Cuba and other Caribbean islands, but now introduced into southern Florida and abundant.

Length: 8 to 14 cm (3 to 5.5 in).

Description: A large, impressive species with uniform coloration varying from silvery gray to brownish green or sandy brown. Some individuals show a dark mottling or bright green flashes on the legs and flanks. The feet are equipped with huge toe pads. The large head has the skin fused to the skull and has a prominent ridge running over each eye and tympanum. The golden eyes are huge, with horizontal pupils.

Availability: Frequently offered by dealers as wild-caught specimens and a very popular terrarium subject.

Captive Care: *Osteopilus* can be kept in a tall terrarium setup similar to that for the Dumpy Treefrog but prefers moist surroundings. It cannot tolerate too cool a temperature, with 74 to 88°F (24 to 31°C) being most suitable. Food requirements are similar to the *Litoria* species, and it will not hesitate to devour smaller amphibians including its own species.

Sexual Differences: Males are much smaller than females and have a pair of external vocal sacs.

Captive Breeding: Like the Dumpy Treefrog, this species will

Though not especially colorful, the Cuban Treefrog, *Osteopilus septentrionalis*, definitely is a frog with a personality. It is hardy, inexpensive, and fairly noisy. Photo: K. Lucas.

The gem of any treefrog collection probably would be a nice Red-eyed Treefrog, *Agalychnis callidryas*, or two. However, be aware that this is a strongly nocturnal, usually slow-moving species that does not compete well with other treefrogs. Photo: D. Dube.

opportunistically breed in temporary pools created by flash floods, but it differs by being active throughout the year, tending to inhabit moist microhabitats that rarely dry out. Success has been achieved by maintaining these treefrogs in a humid terrarium without a water vessel for most of the year. Prior to attempting breeding, the terrarium is cooled slightly to 70°F (21°C) for several months. Then an empty water bowl is added, the temperature is increased, and the terrarium is heavily sprayed for a extended period, gradually filling up the bowl. Should this induce courtship, 80 to 130 eggs are deposited. Eggs and tadpoles are cared for like the *Litoria* species, although shallow, slightly alkaline water is preferred.

Red-eyed Treefrog (*Agalychnis callidryas*)

Distribution: Central America in humid forests.

Length: 5.5 to 7.4 cm (2 to 3 in).

Captive Care: A slender bright green tropical treefrog with striking red eyes, red feet, and barred blue and white sides, this is a very popular and highly prized terrarium subject, but it is not recommended for the inexperienced hobbyist because of its strict housing requirements.

The tall terrarium must be spacious, densely planted, preferably incorporate a waterfall to ensure high humidity, and be kept at a temperature between 78 and 84°F (26 and 29°C). Although temperatures can and should fall to around 72°F (22°C) during the night, imported specimens are best kept warmer until they have put on sufficient weight. Studying its slow, stalking movements as it creeps up on its prey is a highly fascinating aspect of its care.

Captive Breeding: Breeding rarely occurs more than twice per year and there is no specific stimulus. During amplexus within the plants, a female attaches a clump averaging 75 sticky jelly-covered yellowish eggs to a leaf directly above the water. As the 1-cm tadpoles hatch out, they fall into the water and then are best transferred to a large aquarium containing 6 to 8 inches of warm, oxygenated water. They are gregarious by nature and feed voraciously on fish pellets, blanched parsley, and raw meat. Within 45 days they metamorphose into 1.5-cm treefroglets. At this stage plenty of branches and mat-forming surface vegetation should be offered to allow them a safe passage onto dry land. They reach maturity in two years if fed on blowflies and small crickets dusted with supplements.

Other Species: The Yellow-eyed Treefrog, *Agalychnis annae,* is a slightly smaller species with sky-blue flanks and large yellow eyes. It comes from northern Colombia and southern Panama and requires similar conditions to the Red-eye though it is more tolerant of less suitable terrarium conditions.

One of the heaviest-bodied treefrogs is *Phyllomedusa bicolor*, a striking green and white animal that secretes a skin toxin that causes considerable pain and even convulsions if it enters through a cut. Photo: A. Norman.

Few leptodactylid frogs are popular with hobbyists (other than the horned frogs, of course), though many are colorful and not difficult to keep. The large *Leptodactylus fallax* is one of the heavy-limbed species often called South American bullfrogs. Photo: R. D. Bartlett.

Lemur Treefrog (*Phyllomedusa lemur*)

Distribution: Central America.

Length: 4 to 6.5 cm (1.5 to 2.5 in).

Captive Care & Breeding: A slender, very long-limbed species with well-developed toe pads and amazingly large, golden eyes like a lemur, hence its name. It requires a setup similar to the *Agalychnis* species, and breeding also occurs in a similar manner. Eggs are fewer in number (25 to 40) but are larger. The tadpoles grow to 6 cm (3 cm more than the Red-eye) and are ready to transform in four to six weeks. At this point it is wise to lower the water level to around an inch and add plenty of rocks and sticks that connect the water with an area of dry land, for the 2-cm froglets are poor swimmers. They grow extremely quickly if fed well and are capable of breeding just eight months later.

FAMILY LEPTODACTYLIDAE: THE RAINFROGS

This is the largest and most diverse anuran family, but few of its members are available to hobbyists and there is a disappointing shortage of information concerning their behavior and husbandry. However, a few of the species encountered in captivity presently are among the most popular terrarium frogs.

Ornate (Argentine) Horned Frog (*Ceratophrys ornata*)

Note: The common name "horned frog" is derived from the pointed, fleshy skin projections that develop above the eyes. These serve not only to cryptically

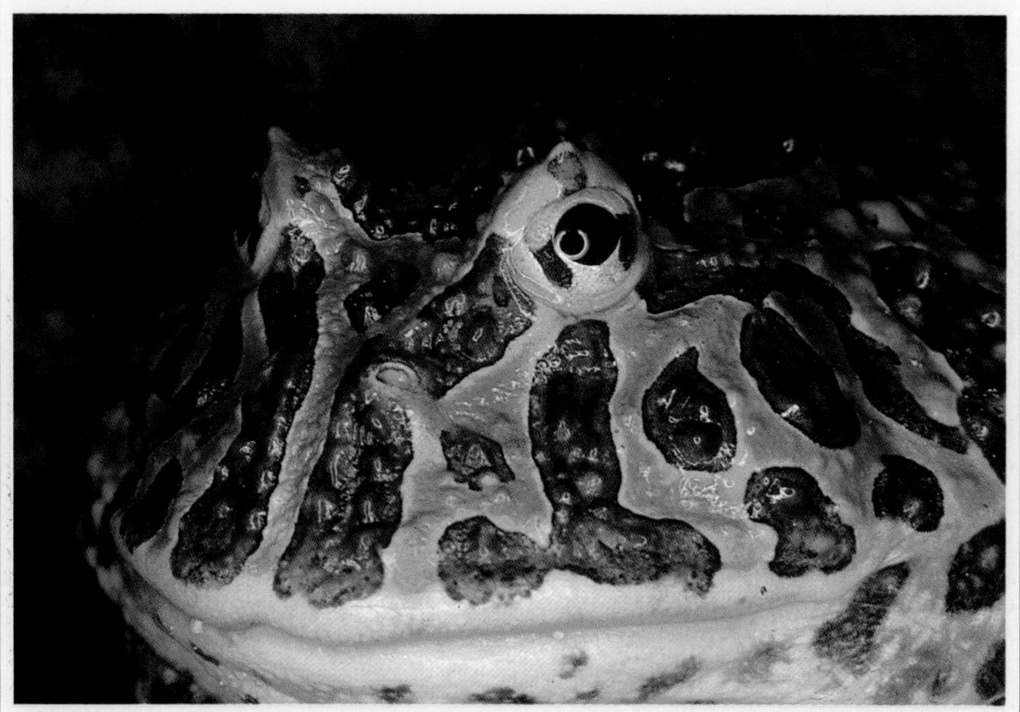

Close-up of a colorful adult Ornate Horned Frog, *Ceratophrys ornata*. Recently these bright green horned frogs have been somewhat supplanted by hybrids of various sorts. Photo: M. Staniszewski.

conceal the frog's presence when ambushing prey, but also add to its foreboding appearance when in confrontation with its few predators. In the most common hobby species, however, the horns are virtually absent. All species are highly cannibalistic, and this is one of the means by which they control their numbers in the wild.

Distribution: Argentina to Uruguay and southern Brazil.

Length: 10 to 14 cm (4 to 5.5 in).

Description: A very stocky frog garishly adorned in bright grass green, bright red, yellow, and brown spots, blotches, and stripes. The underside ranges from pink to yellow and the throat is mottled in gray. The powerful limbs are short, the digits are blunt, and an enlarged metatarsal tubercle or spade is present on each hind leg. From the subadult stage onward folds of rubbery, warty skin develop along the limbs, flanks, and throat. Often a specimen will have a width greater than its length. The Ornate Horned Frog's most striking attribute is its huge, dorsoventrally depressed head and wide mouth with yellow rubbery lips. The powerful jaws are lined with pin-like teeth as well as three bony projections growing from the lower jaw bone, so this extremely pugnacious frog can inflict a nasty bite. The eyes are set as much as three times higher from the lower jaw than in most anurans, enabling this frog to completely burrow into a loose substrate with just its eyes exposed to maintain a lookout for unsuspecting prey. The horns are not as pronounced as in other species.

Availability: Argentine Horned Frogs currently are being produced in huge numbers and shipped worldwide by breeders in the U.S.A., who typically are using the hormone-inducing technique. The resultant frogs represent healthy creatures with good coloration.

Captive Care: An Ornate is a tolerant frog that will live many years if maintained in solitary confinement and given a correct diet and clean living quarters. A specimen can live in a relatively small terrarium with the basic furnishing consisting of a sphagnum moss/leaf litter mixture into which it can conceal itself and a shallow (1 inch) bathing dish. Lighting should be subdued and temperatures kept in the 75 to 80°F (24 to 27°C) range, although much cooler conditions are endured. Humidity is not too important, but a regular misting will keep the substrate damp. The diet is similar to that of the African Bullfrog, although very large food items should be avoided as these may cause blockages. Using long forceps when feeding and a container to scoop the frog up when cleaning is advisable because they may launch into a screaming fit and bite repeatedly.

Sexual Differences: Females are 2 to 4 cm longer than males. Males have a blue-gray tinted throat with loose skin caused by an external vocal sac, and black, horny nuptial pads are present on the inner toes of the front feet.

Captive Breeding: Breeding sometimes is induced naturally in a large aqua-terrarium or the heated greenhouse. Initial priming of these frogs prior to breeding and subsequent conditions thereafter are as described for the African Bullfrog except that they are poor swimmers and may drown in water that comes above their nostrils. It is essential to keep an eye on horned frogs when they are introduced to each other because most would rather eat each other than mate. Lumbar amplexus lasts one to four hours, with the female depositing a tennis ball-sized clump of 200 to 1,000 1.3-mm eggs. On removing these to a large aquarium (36-inch minimum) containing 8 to 12 inches of filtered and oxygenated water at a minimum temperature of 77°F (25°C), the eggs hatch within 18 hours. Too low a temperature may cause deformities and high mortality rates. The tadpoles grow quickly and are carnivorous from the onset, moving in swarms to overwhelm other aquatic creatures. A fresh strip of raw red meat should be dangled into the water daily. After 20 to 32 days the first 2-cm froglets begin to emerge, often with large remnants of their tail and little sign of the horns. These are best reared individually in small plastic containers with a shallow (5 mm) water reservoir at the base. Froglets are fed on chopped, unfilleted fish, earthworms, and

The large, deep head of an Ornate Horned Frog, *Ceratophrys ornata*, is an adaptation to make it easier to stuff large struggling prey into the mouth, where tooth-like jaw projections and fangs on the roof of the mouth help dispatch the food. Photo: A. Norman.

waxworms, with a temperature of 80°F (27°C) recommended for proper digestion and metabolism. Water must be changed each day because horned froglets expel large amounts of ammonia in their waste that can build up to be resorbed. As they grow they should progressively be moved into larger and drier housing to prevent what is known as water retention syndrome, where fluid accumulates under the skin and the frog eventually dies.

Longevity: Sixteen to 25 years.

Surinam Horned Frog
(Ceratophrys cornuta)

Distribution: Northeastern South America.

Length: 7 to 15 cm (3 to 6 in).

Description: The Surinam Horned Frog is the gem of the genus with its subtle gray, light brown, or green dorsum and the most pronounced horns of all *Ceratophrys*. The warts are smaller and more spiny than in the preceding species and a dorsolateral ridge edged with a dark triangular pattern runs on either side of a vertebral groove. The underside is gray, with the throat being dark purple or black, and the lips of the extremely wide mouth are white. The limbs are short and the toes end in globular pads.

Availability: Not offered as frequently as *Ceratophrys ornata* because it does not respond well to hormone-induced breeding techniques. The majority of specimens originate from Guyana and Surinam.

Captive Care: Wild-caught specimens are very sensitive to low temperature and humidity levels and often refuse food, so they are not recommended for the beginner. Captive-bred individuals fare much better and can be maintained like *Ceratophrys ornata*. Temperatures in the 80 to 86°F (27 to 30°C) range and regular misting to encourage humidity are critical. Although juveniles are more placid in disposition than other horned frogs, adults can be aggressive. This species can be quite finicky, with earthworms and fish being favored rather than small mice, although they can eventually be coaxed into accepting the latter.

A simple small terrarium for rearing *Ceratophrys cornuta* and similar amphibians. Photo: M. Staniszewski.

Sexual Differences: Males are smaller than females and have dark nuptial pads on the inner toes of the front limbs.

Though not as colorful as the Ornate Horned Frog, the Surinam Horned Frog, *Ceratophrys cornuta*, has large horns over the eyes that add to its appeal. Recently it has been commercially bred in some numbers and also has been hybridized with Cranwell's Horned Frog. Photo: M. Staniszewski.

Captive Breeding: See *Ceratophrys ornata*, which is very similar in behavior. Smaller numbers of eggs are deposited, higher water temperatures of around 84°F (29°C) are needed, and good water quality is critical in hatching and rearing tadpoles. Tadpoles take up to 90 days to metamorphose and the froglets measure 1 to 1.3 cm. For the first six to eight months they can be raised in groups of ten and fed on waxworms, strips of whitebait, and chopped pinkie mice. I have found that juveniles will drown easily in the slightest amount of water and are best reared on uniformly damp kitchen towels or synthetic foam. By the time they are a year old they measure 3 cm and should be feeding on whole pinkie mice. Maturity is not attained until they are three to four years old.

Longevity: I have had a specimen in my care for 15 years now and it is still growing!

Cranwell's Horned Frog (*Ceratophrys cranwelli*)

Distribution: Central and northern Argentina and adjacent Bolivia, Brazil, and Paraguay in arid grasslands.

Length: 8.8 to 14 cm (3.5 to 5.5 in).

Description: Previously thought to be a variety of *C. ornata*, it has subtle differences in

This little horned frog illustrates the problem of massive hybridization currently going on in the commercial production of *Ceratophrys*. This could be a hybrid of *C. ornata* and *C. cranwelli* or it could be a pure but odd *C. ornata*. Today's horned frogs are coming to look like barnyard mallards—an unpredictable mixture of colors and shapes. Photo: M. Staniszewski.

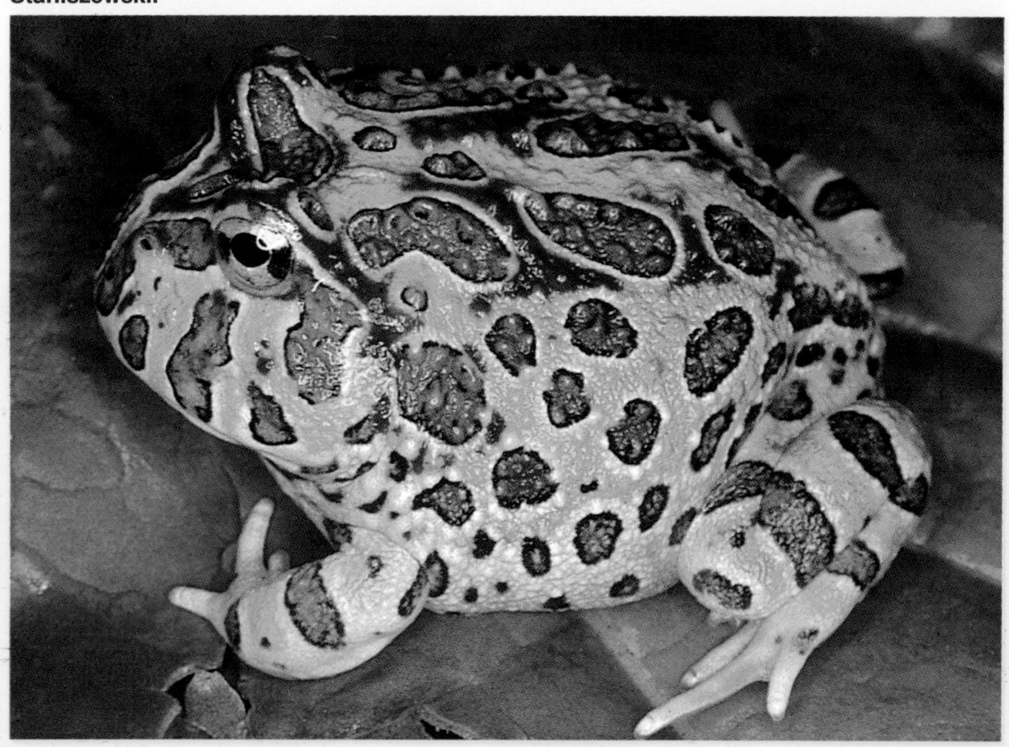

The true Cranwell's or Chacoan Horned Frog, *Ceratophrys cranwelli*, lacks bright colors but is very hardy. Photo: A. Norman.

snout and head shape (longer, more sloping snout) and coloration. It also differs greatly in chromosomes.

Captive Care: Its requirements are very similar to the Ornate Horned Frog, though it prefers somewhat drier conditions when adult and can tolerate surprisingly low temperatures. For safety reasons it is best maintained at around 75°F (24°C), especially when young. Overall it tends to be one of the more active horned frogs, especially at night when it will actually search for prey ranging from large crickets, earthworms, and locusts to small mice.

Captive Breeding: Breeding commences after a lengthy dry, cool period when the frogs will estivate in a cocoon of dry dead skin and mucus. A shallow or deep pool with plenty of grasses or water weeds will prompt the male to entice the female with his quacking calls and then grasp her just behind the armpits. The female tends to swim out to a deeper part of the water with the male still clasping her. She dives down and releases a small gelatinous mass containing 12 to 35 gray and white 2-mm eggs that float and adhere to weeds on the surface. The male synchronizes his sperm release with egg release, as usual. This routine is repeated until some 2,000 to 4,000 eggs are laid. Further development is exactly the same as for *C. ornata*.

Brazilian Horned Frog (*Ceratophrys aurita*)

Distribution: Central and southern Brazil and northern Argentina in humid forests.

Length: 14 to 23 cm (5.5 to 9 in).

Captive Care: The giant of the genus, this huge, multicolored frog is a desirable but rarely kept terrarium subject (Brazil forbids export). In captivity it is a squatter, rarely moving from a moist, leafy depression it has excavated for itself, so its terrarium requirements are simple: a relatively small cage to house each specimen in isolation, a mossy or leafy substrate, and a shallow water bowl. A temperature range of 72 to 85°F (22 to 30°C) is necessary, and it dislikes low temperatures. Hobbyists lucky enough to obtain this species must be wary of its aggressive disposition, as it has a particularly unpleasant bite and hangs on like a bulldog. Unlike most other horned frogs, it does not estivate, breeding being stimulated by heavy rainfall and food availability. Normal food in captivity includes most edible things, including raw meat and dog food, as well as mice.

Other Species: The 10-cm (4-inch) Colombian Horned Frog (*Ceratophrys calcarata*) once was commonly seen but proved difficult to maintain because most

The Brazilian Horned Frog, *Ceratophrys aurita*, is a true giant frog, but it seldom is available to hobbyists because of its restricted range in southeastern Brazil, where it is protected from export. Photo: Dr. I. Sazima.

Budgett's Frog, *Lepidobatrachus laevis*, is one of the odder frogs and has been said to resemble a hand puppet more than a living animal. Photo: M. Panzella.

were imported specimens with heavy infestations of internal parasites and arrived in an emaciated condition. In captivity it has strict temperature requirements (78 to 86°F, 26 to 30°C) and is very choosy about food, apparently preying exclusively on fishes and other amphibians, although it eventually learns to accept strips of raw meat and pinkie mice.

Budgett's Frog (*Lepidobatrachus laevis*)

Distribution: Argentina and Paraguay in arid grasslands.

Length: 10 to 15 cm (4 to 6 in).

Captive Care: This species ranks as one of the most unusual frogs in appearance because of the fleshy body, extremely wide mouth, and eyes located so high on the head that they point upward. Only in recent years has it been distributed among the world's amphibian fraternity as a result of successful captive breeding projects. In captivity it requires a relatively simple setup based on a shallow tray fitted into the bottom of a terrarium that holds about 2 inches of warm water over a substrate of an inch of fine washed river sand. It enjoys partially burying itself in the wet sand, though a dry land area in the form of a flat mossy rock also should be present. Live plants are unlikely to withstand this frog's burrowing habits, and specimens should be maintained in isolation or cannibalism may occur. Average temperatures around the 75°F (24°C) mark with a drop to 65°F (18°C) at night will suffice.

Captive Breeding: For five to ten weeks of the year, depending on the frog's health, it should be permitted to estivate by allowing the water pool to dry up and then adding another 2 inches of damp sand into which the frog will burrow and cocoon. When the frogs are awakened by saturating the sand with water, breeding may follow. Females lay about 2,000 grayish white 2-mm eggs in stringy clumps attached to weeds and debris in shallow water. These must be removed to a large aquarium containing 8 to 12 inches of warm, densely planted water. Tadpoles hatch within five days at 80°F (27°C) and are voracious from the start, swallowing small aquatic invertebrates whole with their tube-like mouth. They attain a large size, 9 to 12 cm. Metamorphosis commences about 25 days after hatching, at which point the water level should be lowered to around 2 to 3 inches and plenty of land platforms made available. Remove the 4-cm froglets to individual plastic tubs containing an inch or so of warm water (replaced daily). With proper feeding (these are very greedy animals) and regular cleaning, plus regular transfer to larger containers, the frogs will mature in 8 to 12 months.

Other Species: The Chacoan Burrowing Frog, *Chacophrys pierotti*, of salt flats in northern Argentina is a nicely colored and quite active frog that is just beginning to gain recognition as a suitable terrarium subject. It requires a setup similar to that for the Ornate Horned Frog and temperatures around 75°F (24°C). This fairly large species (5.5 to 9 cm, 2 to 3.5 inches) is very tolerant of dry conditions and can estivate for up to two years if necessary. It takes smaller prey than other horned frogs (actually, it has no horns), mainly in the form of waxworms, earthworms, small fishes, and sometimes strips of raw meat. Breeding occurs after heavy rainfall, with about 500 eggs being deposited in shallow, muddy temporary pools. Their care is much as for Budgett's Frog.

Greenhouse Frog
(*Eleutherodactylus planirostris*)

Distribution: Cuba. Also introduced into Florida, where it survives the lower winter temperatures by inhabiting greenhouses and conservatories.

Length: 1.8 to 3.7 cm (0.75 to 1.5 in).

Description: An attractive and slender little frog with a mottled gray, bronze brown, and green back heavily covered in small tubercles. The pointed snout is made conspicuous by its pink coloring, and the flanks are light gray or light blue.

Availability: A popular terrarium subject throughout the world even if only because it hides in cargoes of fruit and vegetables. Greengrocers often are a good source for this species!

Captive Care: Like so many of the 500 or so *Eleutherodactylus*

Although they are common in Florida and the Caribbean, Greenhouse Frogs, *Eleutherodactylus planirostris*, find little popularity with hobbyists because of their small size and dull colors. Like many other frogs, they are of interest mostly to specialists. Photo: R. T. Zappalorti.

species, this is an ideal amphibian for hobbyists with limited space. It easily can be accommodated in a plastic sweater box or small terrarium, where its semi-diurnal habits make it an interesting subject. It is able to tolerate both dry and wet habitats, but a compromise between the two is recommended, with the temperature maintained at 78°F (26°C). A base of live sphagnum moss, a shallow water bowl, a piece of bark, and a few climbing branches are the basic requirements. Food consists of aphids, fruitflies, whiteworms, and small crickets.

Sexual Differences: Sexes are difficult to determine, but males are somewhat smaller.

Captive Breeding: This species is totally independent of water, with a small clump of 10 to 28 eggs being deposited beneath a damp log or in sphagnum moss. The mother may guard and moisten the 2-mm eggs until the fully developed froglets (6 to 8 mm long) hatch out 12 to 20 days later. The froglets still have a tail that can take several weeks to disappear. Raising the froglets can be very difficult due to the tiny size of the food they eat, with chopped tubifex or whiteworms being given initially. They are also liable to desiccate and are therefore best raised on moistened kitchen paper towels.

Glossary

Amplexus: The mating clasp of many frogs and certain salamanders (i.e., *Euproctus*).

Annuli: Shallow but prominent concentric body grooves found in caecilians.

Anuran: Frog.

Autotomy: The phenomenon seen in certain salamanders that enables them to rapidly shed their tail by constricting a line of weakness across the blood vessels, muscles, and vertebra of the tail at a specific point, resulting in separation at that point. As the tail comes loose it continues wriggling under the action of the contracting muscles, deterring or confusing the predator in the process. A new tail often is regenerated in place of the old one but is composed of a bony cartilage, not vertebrae.

Caudate: Salamander.

Cloaca: The single chamber into which the alimentary canal, kidneys, and genital ducts discharge their contents.

Costal Grooves: Vertical indentations on the flanks of some salamanders that are caused by the positional stress exerted by the ribs on the muscles and skin.

Crepuscular: Active during twilight or just prior to dawn.

Crest: A soft and often highly colorful cutaneous formation that develops along the back, tail, legs, and sometimes digits of male (and to a lesser extent female) newts.

Digit: A finger or toe.

Diurnal: Active during daylight hours.

Dorsal: Relating to the upper part of the body; the back (dorsum).

Estivation: A period of dormancy during which the surrounding temperature becomes too high or the habitat too dry for an amphibian to remain active. It goes into hiding and becomes inactive until the temperature drops or rains come. Often it is sheathed in a protective layer of dead skin and mucus that allows it to retain sufficient moisture to survive.

Flanks: Sides of the body.

Heliothermy: An interaction between the sun and an amphibian basking in its rays; attraction to the sun or a basking light.

Herpetology: The study of reptiles and amphibians.

Hibernation: A resting period when the surrounding temperatures become too low for an amphibian to remain active and it seeks a frost-free but cool refuge where it enters a state of dormancy.

Lateral: To the side.

Metamorphosis: The process that occurs when an amphibian larva or tadpole transforms into a form resembling its parent. In most cases this involves the loss of oxygen–extracting gills, heavy body crests, and tail (in frogs), and the development of conventional respiratory apparatus, legs, a proper mouth, and primary sexual organs.

Metatarsal Tubercle: An enlarged hardened tubercle located on each hind foot of mainly fossorial (burrowing) frogs.

Montane: Inhabiting high altitude or mountainous regions.

Nasolabial Groove: A narrow channel that extends from just below each nostril to the upper lip of plethodontid salamanders.

Nocturnal: Active mainly during the nighttime hours.

Nuptial Pads: Small rough or horny cutaneous growths found on the thumbs, inside or top of the front or hind limbs, and underside of the tail (in some salamanders) mainly of males that have entered breeding condition. These pads enable a male to gain a better purchase on the female and are particularly useful in slimy-skinned species.

Oviparity: The production by the female of undeveloped eggs that are self–contained in terms of nourishment (from a yolk sac) and develop independently of the parent's body; reproduction by laying eggs.

Ovoviviparity: The condition in which eggs develop within the mother's body, gaining nutrition from a yolk sac, and often are born either partially or well-developed and therefore only remain inside the mother for protection; reproduction by giving live birth from eggs that develop in the mother's body but without being fed by the mother.

Parotoid Gland: A swollen gland (usually behind the eye) that is prominent in many bufonids, *Salamandra*, and some ambystomatids, and barely visible but present in many other amphibians. It acts as a storage region for watery toxins used as a defensive mechanism.

Pole: The point of an amphibian egg from which the embryo develops as a result of progressive cell division. It usually is cloaked in several gelatinous layers that act as a protective and heat retaining medium.

Premaxillary Teeth: Teeth on the upper center pair of bones of the upper jaw; they perforate the upper lip of certain male salamanders and can be used in determining the sex of such species.

Seminal Receptacle: A specialized storage chamber in the female's reproductive system that allows her to store indefinitely the male's spermatophores.

Setup: A terrarium along with its furnishings and appliances.

Spermatophore: The tiny gelatinous sac released by many male salamanders and some frogs that houses the sperm. These sacs often are sticky or barbed so that they attach themselves to the female's cloacal opening.

Thigmothermy: The interaction of an object that retains heat from the sun during non-sunny hours and an amphibian that rests on the object to utilize this heat; attraction to warm surfaces.

Ventral: Relating to the underside of the body or any other organ; the belly.

Vertebral: Relating to the narrow line running along the spine.

Viviparity: The condition in which the embryo develops within the mother's body and results in the birth of live-born, sometimes fully-developed young; reproduction by giving birth to young that have been fed at least in part by the mother's body during development.

Warts: Swollen tubercles often occurring in large numbers about the back and sides of many bufonids, some other frogs, and a few salamanders.

Photo Index

FROGS & TOADS
. . . as a hobby
RAY HUNZIKER

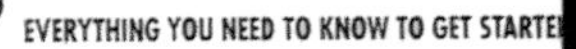

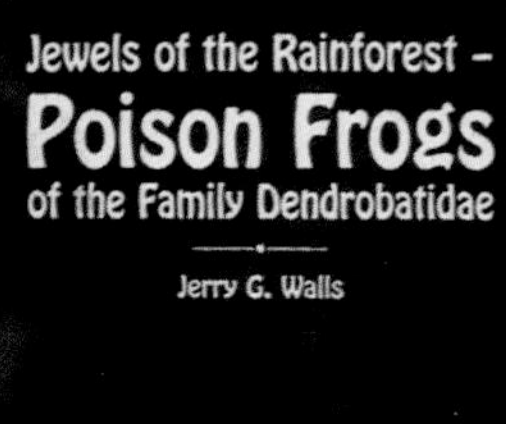

WHITE'S
TREE FROGS
JOHN COBORN

These and thousands of other animal books have been published by TFH. TFH is the world's largest publisher of animal books. You can find our titles at the same place you bought this one, or write to us for a free catalog.